BOMBER BOYS ON SCREEN

BOMBER BOYS ON SCREEN

RAF Bomber Command in Film and Television Drama

S. P. MacKenzie

BLOOMSBURY ACADEMIC
LONDON • NEW YORK • OXFORD • NEW DELHI • SYDNEY

BLOOMSBURY ACADEMIC
Bloomsbury Publishing Plc
50 Bedford Square, London, WC1B 3DP, UK
1385 Broadway, New York, NY 10018, USA
29 Earlsfort Terrace, Dublin 2, Ireland

BLOOMSBURY, BLOOMSBURY ACADEMIC and the Diana logo are trademarks of
Bloomsbury Publishing Plc

First published in Great Britain 2019
Paperback edition published 2021

Copyright © S. P. MacKenzie, 2019

S. P. MacKenzie has asserted his right under the Copyright, Designs and Patents Act, 1988, to be identified as Author of this work.

For legal purposes the Acknowledgements on p. vii constitute an extension of this copyright page.

Cover Image: VeRA, a Mark X - KB726 Lancaster. Squadron Mark VR-A, in honour of Pilot Officer Andrew Mynarski VC. Used in *Death by Moonlight* (1992) and *Map of the Human Heart* (1993). (© Chas Stoddard)

All rights reserved. No part of this publication may be reproduced or transmitted in any form or by any means, electronic or mechanical, including photocopying, recording, or any information storage or retrieval system, without prior permission in writing from the publishers.

Bloomsbury Publishing Plc does not have any control over, or responsibility for, any third-party websites referred to or in this book. All internet addresses given in this book were correct at the time of going to press. The author and publisher regret any inconvenience caused if addresses have changed or sites have ceased to exist, but can accept no responsibility for any such changes.

A catalogue record for this book is available from the British Library.

A catalog record for this book is available from the Library of Congress.

ISBN: HB: 978-1-3500-2484-7
PB: 978-1-3500-2485-4
ePDF: 978-1-3500-2487-8
eBook: 978-1-3500-2486-1

Typeset by Newgen KnowledgeWorks Pvt. Ltd., Chennai, India

To find out more about our authors and books visit www.bloomsbury.com and sign up for our newsletters.

CONTENTS

List of Illustrations	vi
Acknowledgements	vii
List of Abbreviations	viii
INTRODUCTION	1
Chapter 1 TEAMS: THE 1940s	5
Chapter 2 LEADERS: THE 1950s	43
Chapter 3 FIGHTERS: THE 1960s	69
Chapter 4 PATHFINDING: THE 1970s	89
Chapter 5 CHIEFS: THE 1980s	107
Chapter 6 MARTYRS: THE 1990s	123
Chapter 7 VETERANS: THE 2000s	143
CONCLUSION	159
Bibliography	169
Index	189

ILLUSTRATIONS

1.1	Richard Attenborough towards the end of *Journey Together*	4
2.1	Richard Todd in *The Dam Busters*	42
3.1	Poster for *633 Squadron*	68
4.1	Cast members contemplate one of the radio-controlled Lancaster models used in *Pathfinders*	88
5.1	John Thaw and Robert Hardy in *Bomber Harris*	106
6.1	Avik, played by Jason Scott Lee, lands amidst the Dresden firestorm in *Map of the Human Heart*	122
7.1	Edward Woodward and Christopher Plummer in *Night Flight*	142

ACKNOWLEDGEMENTS

I would like to express my thanks to the staff of the following archives and libraries, without whose assistance this book would not have been possible: the BBC Written Archives Centre, Caversham; the British Film Institute Library; the British Library; the CBC Archives, Toronto; Concordia University, Records Management and Archives; the Imperial War Museum, Lambeth; Special Collections, Brigham Young University; the Mass-Observation Archive, University of Sussex; the National Archives, Kew; the Research Centre, Science Museum; Robarts Library, University of Toronto; the Royal Canadian Military Institute; Special Collections, University of Victoria; the Surrey History Centre; and Thomas Cooper Library, University of South Carolina. Thanks go also to James Chapman for passing along information on Film Finances, Inc, and to my colleague Joe November for enlightening me as to the provenance of the computer game *Bomber Crew!* I also wish to express my appreciation to the readers of the initial proposal, selected by the publisher, who thought it worth pursuing, and to the various figures at Bloomsbury who shepherded the volume through from conception to completion.

ABBREVIATIONS

ABC	Australian Broadcasting Corporation
ABPC	Associated British Picture Corporation
ACM	Air Chief Marshal
AHB	Air Historical Branch
BAFTA	British Academy of Film and Television Arts
BBC	British Broadcasting Corporation
BBCWA	BBC Written Archives Centre
BFI	British Film Institute
BOAC	British Overseas Airways Corporation
BYU	Brigham Young University
CAC	Churchill Archives Centre
CBC	Canadian Broadcasting Corporation
CBS	Columbia Broadcasting System
CFU	Crown Film Unit
CND	Campaign for Nuclear Disarmament
CRTC	Canadian Radio-television and Telecommunications Commission
CUA	Concordia University Archives
GFD	General Film Distributors
GPO	General Post Office
HBO	Home Box Office
HMSO	Her/His Majesty's Stationary Office
IBCC	International Bomber Command Centre
ITV	Independent Television
JICTAR	Joint Industry Committee for Television Advertising Research
LMF	Lack of Moral Fibre
LWT	London Weekend Television
MEW	Ministry of Economic Warfare
MGM	Metro-Goldwyn-Mayer
MoD	Ministry of Defence
MoI	Ministry of Information
MOMI	Museum of the Moving Image
NFB	National Film Board of Canada
OCLC	Online Computer Library Center
PBS	Public Broadcasting System
PFF	Pathfinder Force
RAAF	Royal Australian Air Force
RAF	Royal Air Force
RAFFPU	Royal Air Force Film Production Unit

RAFM	Royal Air Force Museum, Hendon
RCAF	Royal Canadian Air Force
RNZAF	Royal New Zealand Air Force
TMP	The Memory Project
TNA	The National Archives, Kew
UCL	University College London
USAAF	United States Army Air Forces
UVic	University of Victoria, Special Collections
WAAF	Women's Auxiliary Air Force
ZDF	*Zweites Deutsches Fernsehen* [Second German Television]

INTRODUCTION

Despite a steadily expanding body of scholarly literature devoted to British war films, it is striking how little has been written about big- and small-screen representations of Bomber Command. Entire books have been devoted to 'The Few' in the Battle of Britain, while analysis of how 'The Many' who subsequently flew in the central offensive campaign mounted by the Royal Air Force (RAF) at night over Germany has been confined to passing references and one or two isolated studies of particular titles.[1]

Lack of attention may be in part due to the fact that while pieces featuring RAF bomber crews have appeared on both the big and small screen, film and television subjects have tended to be studied separately.[2] There is also a widespread belief that, once the war was over, questions concerning the morality of inflicting mass civilian casualties meant Bomber Command screen dramas became *rarae avis*.[3]

This assumption, however, turns out to be based on superficial accounting. Though the targeting by night of entire German cities became a significant ethical issue in Britain and elsewhere in the post-war decades that producers, writers and directors had to confront – along with the growing challenge of assembling a sufficient number of airworthy period bombers – they were less deterred than sometimes imagined. Just as technical problems could be dealt with using a certain amount of ingenuity, so too could the question marks surrounding area bombing in relation to stories and scripts. If television productions as well as cinema releases in formats ranging from single picture to docudrama and episodes from series are included, it turns out that Bomber Command has in fact received dramatic exposure rivalling that of the American Eighth Air Force and its purportedly precise and thus acceptable daylight strikes against war industries.[4]

Studying the screen projections of the bomber boys that have appeared both during and since the war, a span of eight decades now, as part of a set rather than strictly as individual productions, appears worthwhile in a number of ways beyond the existence of an overlooked screen subgenre. Elements of both change and continuity can be discerned over the course of time with respect to everything from developing plots and solving technical problems to representing class structures and national identities within Bomber Command. With or without various types of support from government ministries, vintage aircraft organizations and veterans groups, each dramatization aimed to reflect or inform contemporary conceptions of 'The Many' and those who led them. Most centrally, perhaps, these screen dramas mark the ways in which filmmakers have chosen over time to confront or avoid questions of efficacy and ethics with respect to the RAF bombing campaign directed against Germany. Some of these big- and small-screen dramas have been more popular or more controversial that others, varying reception indicating the ways in which particular audiences and the general public have been willing or unwilling to accept the version of Bomber Command currently on offer.[5]

Whether projected, broadcast, played or streamed, these productions cannot be understood in isolation. Trends in other forms of representation, including published histories and novels, war comics, television documentaries, commemorative statues, campaign memorials and pertinent stage or radio plays will also be examined in order to provide context necessary for understanding what was being done in terms of screen drama and why at particular junctures. It is also important to take into account how films developed in the UK were received overseas in dominions which had themselves made a significant numerical contribution to Bomber Command – and, in certain instances, how their own home-grown efforts were interpreted both on their home turf and back in the British Isles. The view from America is confined for the most part to a few Hollywood productions and what British and Commonwealth audiences thought of them. As for the German perspective on Bomber Command, this has already been the subject of extensive critical scrutiny by other scholars and so will not be discussed in these pages except in connection with a *sui generis* occasion when a major small-screen drama developed in Germany that centred on a particular firestorm raid was also eventually broadcast in Britain.[6]

Notes

1 For fine analyses of specific Bomber Command films see Mark Connelly, '*Bomber Harris*: Raking through the Ashes of the Strategic Air Campaign', in *Repicturing the Second World War: Representations in Film and Television*, ed. Michael Paris (Basingstoke: Palgrave, 2007), 162–76; and John Ramsden, *The Dam Busters* (London: I.B. Tauris, 2003). For books on the Battle of Britain on screen, see e.g. Garry Campion, *The Battle of Britain, 1945–1965: The Air Ministry and the Few* (Basingstoke: Palgrave, 2015); *The Good Fight: Battle of Britain Propaganda and the Few* (Basingstoke: Palgrave, 2009). Passing mention of particular Bomber Command films can also be found in, e.g., Martin Francis, *The Flyer* (Oxford: Oxford University Press, 2008); and Robert Wohl, *The Spectacle of Flight* (New Haven, CT: Yale University Press, 2005). Brief references can also be found in surveys ranging from Jeremy Havardi's *Projecting Britain at War: The National Character in British World War II Films* (Jefferson, NC: McFarland, 2014) to Robert Murphy's *British Cinema and the Second World War* (London: Continuum, 2000). It should be noted, however, that a good deal of attention has been devoted to films of all sorts, including those involving Bomber Command, made during the war years: see e.g. Anthony Aldgate and Jeffrey Richards, *Britain Can Take It: British Cinema in the Second World War*, new edition (London: I.B. Tauris, 2007); James Chapman, *The British at War: Cinema, State and*

Propaganda, 1939–1945 (London: I.B. Tauris, 1998); Jo Fox, *Film Propaganda in Britain and Nazi Germany: World War II Cinema* (Oxford: Berg, 2007); Neil Rattigan, *This Is England: British Film and the People's War, 1939–1945* (Madison, NJ: Fairleigh Dickinson University Press, 2001).

2 What combined studies there are often tend to be in the form of edited collections in which different authors tackle either a particular film or a television title – see e.g. Paris, *Repicturing the Second World War* – or are largely filmographic in nature: see e.g. Jonathan Falconer, *RAF Bomber Command in Fact, Film and Fiction* (Stroud: Sutton, 1996).

3 See e.g. Patrick Bishop, *Bomber Boys: Fighting Back, 1940–1945* (London: HarperPress, 2007), 383; Angus Calder, *Disasters and Heroes: On War, Memory and Representation* (Cardiff: University of Wales, 2004), 136; Rupert Matthews, *RAF Bomber Command at War* (London: Hale, 2009), 220. To be fair, the idea that the bomber boys were treated as an embarrassing legacy to be swept under the carpet, if not criticized outright, was one that both former senior commanders and ordinary ex-aircrew themselves might strongly adhere to down the decades. See e.g. Arthur Harris, *Bomber Offensive* (London: Collins, 1947), 268; Dudley Saward, *'Bomber' Harris* (London: Buchan and Enright, 1984), xi, 326–9; Arthur White, *Bread and Butter Bomber Boys* (Upton on Severn: Square One, 1995), 2; Royan Yule, *On a Wing and a Prayer* (Derby: Derby Books, 2012), 161; see also Frances Houghton, 'The "Missing Chapter": Bomber Command Aircrew Memoirs in the 1990s and 2000s', in *British Cultural Memory and the Second Word War*, ed. Lucy Noakes and Juliette Pattinson (London: Bloomsbury, 2014), 155–74. To add insult to injury, when the bomber boys did appear on screen, those on whom they were based might criticize the results for lacking realism: see e.g. Russell Margarison, *Boys at War* (Bolton: Ross Anderson, 1986), iii; Tom Wingham, *Halifax Down! On the Run from the Gestapo, 1944* (London: Grub Street, 2009), 42.

4 At the time of writing, six full-length films, several television plays, a dramatic series (plus another, *Bomber Command* [Spectrum Multimedia Hollywood] in development) and a docudrama have appeared since the war's aftermath in which Bomber Command is a central feature. This compares well to the seven full-length dramas and the single dramatic series (plus miniseries, *The Mighty Eighth*, apparently in pre-production limbo) involving the Eighth Air Force.

5 The most controversial of all, at least thus far, has been the *Death by Moonlight: Bomber Command* segment of the Canadian docudrama trilogy *The Valour and the Horror*, which – as Chapter 6 indicates – generated a huge amount of very heated debate on both sides of the Atlantic.

6 For work on German screen and other representational perspectives on bombing, see e.g. Alex Bangert, *The Nazi Past in Contemporary German Film: Viewing Experiences of Intimacy and Immersion* (Rochester, NY: Camden, 2014); *Screening War: Perspectives on German Suffering*, ed. Paul Cooke and Marc Silberman (Rochester, NY: Camden, 2010); David F. Crew, *Bodies and Ruins: Imagining the Bombing of Germany, 1945 to the Present* (Ann Arbor: University of Michigan Press, 2017); *A Nation of Victims? Representations of German Wartime Suffering from 1945 to the Present*, ed. Helmut Schmitz (Amsterdam: Rodopi, 2008); *Bombs Away! Representing the Air War over Europe and Japan*, ed. Wilfried Wilms and William Rasch (Amsterdam: Rodopi, 2006); see also Dietmar Süss, 'The Air War, the Public, and Cycles of Memory', in *Experience and Memory: The Second World War in Europe*, ed. Jörge Echternkamp and Stefan Martens (Oxford: Berghahn, 2010), 181–96.

Figure 1.1 Richard Attenborough towards the end of *Journey Together* (RAF Film Production Unit, 1945).

Chapter 1

TEAMS: THE 1940s

The ways in which the bomber offensive was portrayed in cinemas during and in the immediate aftermath of the conflict were heavily shaped by the publicity and propaganda needs of the wartime state. Working in concert with various other government agencies – notably the Ministry of Information (MoI) – as well as the film industry, the Air Ministry facilitated the development and completion of more than half a dozen feature films depicting Royal Air Force (RAF) Bomber Command at work. While plot lines, emphasis and audience reception varied a good deal, the pictures released in this period all had two interrelated themes in common: that the bombing war was a success and that its achievements were due to teamwork rather than individual heroics.

The first cinematic dramatization of the RAF as a striking force came to be developed in the first days and weeks of the Second World War in Europe. Even before hostilities began, the Air Ministry had been in negotiations with London Films to produce a documentary chronicling the recent expansion of the RAF.[1] By the time an agreement was formalized at the end of August 1939 it was clear that war with Germany was about to break out, and in the context of widespread public fear of a subsequent aerial Armageddon and at the urging of his friend Winston Churchill, movie mogul Alexander Korda committed himself 'to make a film to reassure the public of the power of the Royal Air Force'.[2] According to Ian Dalrymple, associate producer for Korda on the project, the central aim would be to show the British public 'that they weren't going to be blown to pieces in five minutes: that the Royal Air Force would prevent it'.[3] At the same time, Dalrymple was instructed 'that the Royal Air Force's striking power must be shown in the film'.[4]

How the latter aim was achieved was the result of fortuitous circumstances on the second day of the war. The officer assigned to the project by the Air Ministry, Squadron Leader H. M. S. Wright, that morning flew director Michael Powell, responsible for the aerial sequences of what was dubbed *The Lion Has Wings*, to RAF Mildenhall in order for the latter to be able to shoot some footage using a handheld camera of the bombers based there. As it happened, and unbeknownst to either man, when they arrived, eight Wellingtons of 149 Squadron were being fuelled and armed to launch an attack on German warships at the western mouth of the Kiel Canal. Despite his urgent pleas, Powell was not allowed to participate in the raid as a camera-armed observer; but he nonetheless got some good shots of the bombers being prepared, taking off, landing and disgorging their crews.[5]

Very little was actually achieved on this operation, a lot went wrong and of twenty-nine planes dispatched seven did not return.[6] But the day after, the Air Ministry issued a communiqué indicating a 'successful attack' by the RAF on various naval targets.[7] The press immediately made this into a famous victory – 'German Fleet Bombed', 'First R.A.F. Attack of the War', 'Successful Raids at Kiel Canal Entrance' and 'Heavy Damage to Two Battleships' were among the front-page headlines in the *Telegraph* – the strictly military nature of which contrasted with the drowning of over a hundred civilian passengers a day earlier when a U-boat sank the liner *Athenia*.[8] When the prime minister, Neville Chamberlain, offered a personal 'tribute to the very gallant attack which was made by units of the Royal Air Force' in the House of Commons towards the end of the week, MPs cheered.[9] In its coverage of the 'Brilliant R.A.F. Raid', the *Illustrated London News* depicted an exploding bomb causing massive damage amidships to a German pocket battleship.[10]

Powell thus seemed to have been filming history in the making. 'Here was the theme of the film's bombing sequence ready-made', as publicist John Ware explained, 'and more real than fiction could have made it'.[11] Footage of Wellingtons flying at height could be obtained through the Air Ministry; but there would still have to be a fictive element to the story given that the director had not been allowed to fly and film aboard one of the planes engaged in the raid. Thus various London Films regulars, notably Anthony Bushell and Derrick De Marney, were engaged to play aircrew in scenes shot amidst briefing-room scenery hastily built on a soundstage at Denham Studios and inside the fuselage of an unserviceable Wellington Mk I helpfully provided by the Air Ministry and lodged in an adjoining car park.[12] Powell was fully occupied shooting scenes for the Fighter Command segment of the film, so Dalrymple had Desmond Hurst serve as director for the reconstructed Kiel Raid segment.[13]

Though comprising only fifteen minutes of a film that alternated documentary and drama over the course of seventy-six minutes, the Bomber Command portion of *The Lion Has Wings* served several important functions. It reconstructed through docudrama an actual clash of arms that had already taken place, as opposed to projecting dramatically the outcome of a future German bomber assault on England; it reminded people that the RAF wielded a sword as well as a shield; and, last but not least, it showed that – in marked contrast to the enemy – Britain was striking at military objectives rather than innocent civilians.

The segment begins with shots of actual aircrew relaxing by their Wellingtons, each of whom, the film's commentator, E. V. H. Emmett, explains, are 'waiting for orders to avenge the outrage of the *Athenia*', each plane a 'battleship of the sky' standing ready for war: 'massive, forbidding, deadly, the symbol of modern power'.[14] There follows a staged sequence in which orders are conveyed by telephone from the chief of air staff, played by Robert Rendel, down via Bomber Command and Group HQs to aerodromes, including 'Hanbury', where the station commander and his subordinates prepare to brief the crews on their mission. Footage shot by Powell is then shown of Wellingtons being fuelled and bombed up, Emmett commenting on how the planes' defensive machineguns can 'spit out a double stream of bullets swifter than thought itself' and how a 'complicated apparatus for bomb aiming' makes hitting the target 'exact and mathematical'.[15]

The segment then switches to a briefing room where an intelligence officer (IO), played by Robert Douglas, goes over mission details with the assigned bomber crews, led by a squadron leader played by Anthony Bushell dressed in distinctive white flying overalls.[16] The task is to 'secure direct hits' on German heavy units: 'you must get those battleships', Douglas firmly stresses at the end of his remarks. Meanwhile a written weather forecast is distributed, and route details and enemy defences outlined. 'About ten miles from your target is a hospital', the IO adds: 'It's a large white building; you can't miss it.' The import of this last line – that the RAF is serious about not breaching the laws of war concerning what are considered illegitimate targets for bombardment – was such that it was considered unnecessary for Douglas to go on to stress in the final film, as the shooting script indicates he was supposed to, that the hospital was to be avoided 'at all cost'.[17] Bomber Command is aiming for precision both figuratively and literally, Bushell reiterating this by telling his aircraft captains in a follow-on exterior scene that 'you heard what was said. We've got to get direct hits.'

The next scenes show 149 Squadron crews boarding their aircraft, various take-offs, a bit of staged operations-room reporting and then three Wellingtons photographed in flight from another plane, accompanied by periodic voiceover commentary from Emmett.[18] The film now focuses in on the bomber flown by Bushell. On the way to the target over the North Sea, the five men aboard – pilot, navigator, bomb aimer, bow gunner, tail gunner – are depicted as a relaxed bunch, the navigator and pilot lightly bantering with the wireless operator and each other. Especially when action looms, though, the commentator makes sure in voiceover that viewers understand that these aircrew members are professionals, each knowing his individual job while acting in concert.[19]

It is noteworthy, however, that there are no regional accents to be heard. Though probably merely the result of which players London Films had ready to hand along with the non-music-hall Received Pronunciation elocutionary mores of actors who performed as regularly on the theatrical stage as on the cinema screen, this absence perhaps reinforces the idea of the crew as a band of brothers but is nonetheless exclusionary.[20] Furthermore, there are discernible auditory and visual distinctions between officers and other ranks. The aircraft captain played by Bushell, for instance, calls the rear gunner by his second name, 'Saunders'.[21] The latter, along with the wireless operator and bomb aimer, the other airmen, always address the pilot as 'sir'. This was, to be sure, fairly true to life in relation to the RAF in the late 1930s, when air gunners, for example, were other-ranks armourer tradesmen and commissioned bomber pilots were an elite.[22] But, coupled with the pilot being the only crew member distinctively dressed and speaking in a differentiating upper-middle-class accent – Bushell was cast throughout his film career as an officer and gentleman because he both looked and sounded the part to perfection – this sort of thing does not seem to have gone over well in certain circles hostile to the existing social order in Britain.[23]

As the trio of Wellingtons head towards what is shown on the navigator's map as the entrance to the Kiel Canal, Bushell announces that he is going down to a hundred feet for the approach, very much in accordance with his pre-take-off statement to the effect that 'I'm pretty certain it will be low-level bombing'. The navigator indicates that this will make it difficult for the enemy to depress their anti-aircraft guns sufficiently. 'There she is!' Bushell then exclaims as he glimpses his target – as does the audience through a few inserted seconds of frames showing British warships and old footage of a German pocket battleship – and orders his Wellingtons into a line-ahead attack formation. In a manner replicated in Bomber Command films for years to come, the bomb aimer is shown face-on while staring down through his bombsight, giving slight course corrections to the pilot ('right, right, steady') and pressing the release button while announcing 'bombs gone, sir'. Through a mixture of stock footage and model work in the Denham tank, bombs are shown leaving the bomb bay and whistling down in salvo, producing huge waterspouts and, for a second, what appears to be a direct hit. 'Get him?' Bushell asks De Marney in the cockpit. The latter looks down the fuselage to see the rear gunner giving a thumbs up, which he repeats for the pilot's benefit.

As the plane turns for home, it is attacked by enemy fighters. Doubtless because there were no suitable shots of *Luftwaffe* machines to hand, the aircraft shown in the subsequent short engagement were in fact single-engine planes of the RAF. Rapid cross-cutting with shots of the two Wellington gunners firing their twin machine guns, though, likely made it difficult for all but the cognoscenti among audiences at the time to notice this.[24] 'The German pursuit planes were shaken off', Emmett intones, and the flight of Wellingtons are shown returning home right to left on the screen, rather than the left to right of the outward journey.

Once more, the moral legitimacy of British bombing is emphasized, the commentator stressing that the crews had dropped their bombs 'not upon unfortified towns [as the *Luftwaffe* had done in Spain and Poland] but upon a heavily protected naval base; a legitimate target of modern warfare'. To be sure, 'not all came back'; but 'they achieved what they set out to do'. That this message was authentic was reinforced by the 4 September footage of 149 Squadron Wellingtons landing and crews disembarking: 'although you have been watching a reconstruction of that raid upon the Kiel Canal', Emmett confirms, 'the men you now see stepping out of these bombers are the officers and men of the RAF who actually carried out that heroic raid'.[25] As a jauntily upbeat martial tune written by Richard Addinsell and conducted by Muir Matheson swells to a climax on the soundtrack, Emmett concludes: 'These are the men who flew the planes and dropped the bombs on Hitler's battleships'. Such commentary, combined with the stated mission objective and glimpses of hits staged in the Denham tank, reinforces the perception that at least one German capital ship has been sunk or at least very badly damaged. This was not stated outright, however, perhaps because the RAF's own intelligence assessments, in contrast to the optimistic tone of its press releases, indicated that the Wellington attack, 'the centerpiece of *The Lion Has Wings*', was, as one historian succinctly put it, 'a failure'.[26]

This was not widely known at the time, though; and it remained to be seen how the press and public would respond to the Kiel Raid along with the various other segments of the film once it was ready.[27] The work of multiple scriptwriters, directors, editors and sundry others exhorted to work at great speed by Korda, *The Lion Has Wings* was shot over the course of twelve days and assembled in the space of five weeks in order to preserve its topicality.[28] The haste with which it was made, coupled with how soon its assurances concerning everything from the effectiveness of barrage balloons over Britain to the efficacy of daylight bombing over Germany would be exposed by the realities of the air war, led some of those who had worked on it to express retrospective embarrassment and various writers and filmmakers to later claim that *The Lion Has Wings* had been an inept failure.[29] Yet there is plenty of contemporaneous evidence that, whatever people may have felt later on, *The Lion Has Wings* was quite a success from its premiere at the end of October 1939 – the vast majority of press reviews were very positive and it was the top-grossing film on general release across the UK by the end of the following month – to January 1940 when the book of the film was published.[30]

Moreover, the Bomber Command segment was one of the most praised sections of *The Lion Has Wings* among press critics and cinema audiences alike. In the *News Chronicle* it was described as 'outstanding', in the *Guardian* as 'tremendous' and in the *Telegraph* as 'a marvel of realism'.[31] Echoing opinion elsewhere, the reviewer for the *Yorkshire Post* stated that 'one of the most effective parts of the film is a graphic reconstruction of the famous Kiel raid'.[32] Periodicals were often equally effusive. The BBC review in *The Listener*, for instance, indicated that 'the reconstruction of the Kiel raid' was 'brilliantly done', while the *New Statesman* critic found it 'both inspiring and touching'.[33] Observers in various cinemas noted that the footage of the Wellington crews disembarking prompted audience members to clap for several seconds.[34]

There were, to be sure, some dissenters. Graham Greene, writing for the *Spectator*, found that the 'fake elocutionist voices of trained actors' – implying, among others, Anthony Bushell – undermined the authenticity of this and other parts of *The Lion Has Wings*, while his counterpart at the *New Statesman* took a swipe at the presence of '*Journey's End* officers', likely an allusion to Bushell's first screen role in the 1930 film version of the stage play.[35] Among ordinary filmgoers, there were also those who found they had trouble suspending disbelief during the Kiel Raid segment due to the absence of anti-aircraft fire, the limited model work or Spitfires standing in for Messerschmitts.[36] Yet the *New Statesman* concluded that the Kiel Raid was 'both inspiring and touching', while one of those audience members who prided himself on knowing one aircraft silhouette from another conceded that this was still 'the best part of the film'.[37] *The Lion Has Wings*, which was widely distributed overseas as well as at home, would go on to generate over £50,000 in profits.[38]

Its messages concerning the effectiveness of the RAF, however, were soon overtaken by events. Though ultimately victorious by day in the Battle of Britain in the summer and autumn of 1940, Fighter Command could not, despite what had been confidently predicted in the film, effectively shield London from German bombers during the subsequent Blitz lasting into the spring of 1941 any more than the balloon barrage. As for Bomber Command, heavy losses due to enemy fighters coupled with poor results in terms of damage inflicted had led to the abandonment by the end of 1939 of the type of daylight attack shown on screen. From the spring of 1940 onward, RAF efforts to strike at Germany would take place almost exclusively during the hours of darkness when it was harder for the *Luftwaffe* to locate and shoot down British aircraft. The kind of air war depicted in *The Lion Has Wings*, in short, was all-too-obviously obsolete in the eyes of the general public within a year of its release.[39]

Within the documentary film movement, meanwhile, and specifically in the pioneering film production unit transferred from the Post Office into the new MoI at the start of hostilities which, starting in 1941, would bear the title Crown Film Unit, there were those who thought *The Lion Has Wings* had lacked authentic realism because it had mixed in elements of the commercial cinema, notably professional actors and well-known stars, with narration and footage of real people and places.[40] From the start of the war through much of 1940, the unit's own work had largely dealt with documenting, sometimes through recreations using the ordinary folk actually involved rather than commercial thespians, how Britain was coping with the Nazi assault.[41] With the Blitz in full swing towards the end of 1940, Harry Watt, who had been involved in the making of several such short pieces, including the famous *London Can Take It!*, wondered if it was not time to start thinking about a 'hitting back film'.[42]

At this point in the war, with the British Army having been driven off the Continent at Dunkirk and the Royal Navy engaged in defending the vital sea lanes, the only arm actually taking the war directly to Germany was the RAF through night bombing. To be sure, an RAF attack had been reconstructed in *The Lion Has Wings*; but the war context was now entirely different – and in any event, Watt thought the effort 'ghastly'.[43] He pitched the idea of a new film about Bomber Command to the head of the MoI films division, Jack Beddington, and his advisor, Sidney Bernstein, in the second week of November and was given a green light to approach the Air Ministry.[44]

As it happened, the latter were at this juncture themselves 'keen to have more films of R.A.F. activities presented on the Screen'.[45] Two months before Watt made his pitch, the Air Ministry had produced a script written by one of its air marshals, Philip Joubert, dealing with the development, training and current activities of Bomber Command, and had approached the MoI about turning it into a one-reel documentary using mostly stock footage.[46] Harry Watt, however, had something more ambitious in mind: 'the dramatizing of reality'.[47] He wanted to focus on a single aircraft on a typical raid, using a dramatic script of his own devising that would be based on actual bomber crew experiences, choosing players from among real RAF personnel, with shooting to take place on both soundstages and airfields. 'I am sure we can get a film both worthy of the Bomber Command and excellent propaganda', he wrote to Wing Commander Bill Williams of the Air Ministry directorate of public relations.[48]

Though it seems to have taken some time to arrange, Watt, shepherded around by an official minder, Flight Lieutenant Derek Twist, was allowed to visit Bomber Command headquarters and, at greater length, an operational Wellington unit – 149 Squadron at Mildenhall, as it happened, last seen in *The Lion Has Wings* – in order to gather material by talking to personnel, attending briefings and reading reports.[49] The story he developed was simple, 'just the choice of a new small target, the selection of a squadron to bomb it, and the adventures of one bomber, "F for Freddie", during the raid'.[50] By late February 1941, Watt had completed a script which, after some hesitation over its dramatic elements, was approved by Air Vice-Marshal Richard Peck at the Air Ministry and Air Marshal Richard Pierse, head of Bomber Command.[51] In late April, Jack Beddington opined that 'though large and expensive', the project was 'fully justified' as the Air Ministry 'were anxious for the film to be made'.[52]

By this point Watt had chosen his principal cast from among those he had already interacted with at Mildenhall and was back filming exterior sequences with a small camera team. The commissioned skipper of F-for-Freddie, 'Dickson', would be played by Squadron Leader P. C. 'Pick' Pickard, an easy-going blond daredevil Englishman who commanded a bomber squadron at a nearby aerodrome. Watt was careful, however, to give his crew a much more varied regional and class flavour than had been the case in *The Lion Has Wings*.[53] The commissioned co-pilot, played by Gordon Woolatt, was also English, as was the wireless operator, Warrant Officer 'Lee'; but 'McPherson', the sergeant navigator/bomb aimer, was played by a Scot, Alexander More, and the two air-gunner sergeants represented the dominions in the form of a Canadian front gunner and a rear gunner played by Jack Harris from New Zealand.[54] Barring a degree of swearing that would have been blocked by the British Board of Film Censors – 'cluck', for instance, had to substitute for 'fuck' in one instance – his script also reflected the colloquial speech and attitudes Watt had overheard during his initial research at Mildenhall.[55] The dialogue aboard the aircraft is also somewhat more egalitarian than in *The Lion Has Wings*, the pilot being addressed as 'skipper' or 'skip' as often as 'sir' by the non-commissioned crewmembers.[56]

Though rarely afforded even a stage name in the script or identified in the credits, air force officers would play the kind of executive or supporting roles they performed in real life in both exterior and interior scenes shot in various studio locations and inside a Wellington Mk Ic fuselage produced by the Air Ministry. Squadron Leader Peter Riddell, for example, really was a photographic interpreter, while Group Captain F. J. Fogerty and Wing Commander J. A. 'Speedy' Powell were, respectively, station commander Mildenhall ('Millerton' in the film) and an experienced bomber pilot seconded from 311 Squadron. Watt was able to convince even more exalted figures to participate briefly as themselves, including Air Vice-Marshal J. A. Baldwin, commanding 3 Group ('33 Group' in the film), and to populate one day in the third week of June a larger-than-life set of the Bomber Command HQ operations room built at Denham, the C-in-C Bomber Command himself, Air Marshal Sir Richard Pierse, as well as his senior staff officer,

Air Vice-Marshal Sir Robert Saundby, and various other figures.[57] At the other end of the hierarchy of RAF rank and privilege, the ground-crew servicing personnel were real 'erks', and even extras wore air force blue. The responsible Air Ministry figure having failed to produce on time a promised gaggle of airmen for a scene on a set of a crew room built at Elstree, Watt instead went to the recruiting deport at Uxbridge and convinced a bunch of mostly Canadian aircrew to volunteer instead.[58]

The result was a linguistic and class mélange on the ground at 'Millerton' as well as aboard F-for-Freddie in the air that suited Watt's desire to show 'a democratic service at war, without regimentation or pomposities'.[59] Among those seen and heard are a Canadian sergeant navigator and a Canadian officer in charge of the bomb dump, an IO with a distinctly Celtic lilt to his speech and both non-commissioned officers and 'erks' whose accents range between cockney and BBC English. And while the English wing commander enunciates in unadulterated South-of-England upper-class tones, his superior, the group captain, has a discernible Northern accent.

The scenario that Watt devised and then directed for what was variously called *Bomber Command, Night Bomber, A Target Is Bombed,* and finally, of course, *Target for Tonight,* was straightforward.[60] The film begins with the delivery of recent aerial reconnaissance pictures to a photographic interpretation unit which reveal a newly constructed German oil storage and transport terminal in the vicinity of 'Freihausen' on the Rhine. The scene then shifts to Bomber Command HQ, where the decision is taken to divert one squadron from the main planned raid on naval docks and barracks at Kiel to attack at low level what has been earlier described by one officer as 'a peach of a target'.

The directive is passed down through Group HQ to the station commander at RAF 'Millerton' where, amidst flying personnel and ground crews going about their normal business, careful planning for the raid involving the IO and wing commander occurs. The bombing up and arming of the planes is then traced, followed by a detailed briefing of the aircraft crews by the wing commander and others, the wing commander emphasizing that this is 'an extremely important target' that they must first locate and then destroy. The bomber crews are then shown chatting and joking as they don their flying clothing, including the six men of F-for-Freddie. On the airfield, 'Dickson' starts up the engines of F-for-Freddie and, located in the flare-path caravan, the wing commander orchestrates several individual take-offs and finally that of F-for-Freddie itself.

On their way to the target, 'Dickson' and his crew engage in some banter but are clearly all competent at their jobs. 'Freihausen' is located, and the bomb run begins, the face of the bomb aimer highlighted as he instructs the pilot – 'left, left, steady, right, steady, steady' – before pressing the bomb-release button and scoring, in his words, 'a bull's eye'. This time, however, the Wellington does not emerge unscathed, German anti-aircraft fire scoring a hit that damages the port engine, knocks out the radio and wounds its operator.[61] The crew of F-for-Freddie keep calm and carry on regardless, despite steadily losing height on the return journey. Back at 'Millerton' there is growing stiff-upper-lip concern about the fate of F-for-Freddie, what with its last wireless signal abruptly ceasing, the amount of time that passes after it is expected return time and the appearance of fog over the airfield.

Once back over England, the skipper canvasses the others as to whether they want to take to their parachutes or try a landing despite the poor visibility. They collectively opt for the latter and, with help from flares ordered lit by the wing commander, land safely. In the subsequent debriefing scene, the gunners and second pilot back up the bomb aimer's opinion that he scored a direct hit with his last bomb, having observed a massive eruption and copious amounts of flame and smoke. The film ends with an IO reporting by telephone to Group HQ on that night's operations: 'the objective was reached and heavily bombed. Large fires and explosions were seen. All our aircraft returned.' The apparently routine, all-in-a-night's-work nature of what has been depicted is underlined by the last words of dialogue as the IO puts down the phone and asks one of his colleagues: 'Well, old boy, how about some bacon and eggs?'[62]

Target for Tonight, fifty minutes in length and costing roughly £8,000, was finished in some haste to meet the July 1941 deadline set by the MoI, complete with a musical score written by Leighton Lucas and played by the RAF Central Band and an agreement with Associated British Film Distributors to show the film in cinemas as a commercial venture.[63] It remained to be seen what the press, public and air force would make of what Watt later claimed to have thought of at the time as 'just as ordinary account of a minor operation'.[64]

The response to *Target for Tonight* was all that its sponsors and maker could have wished for. At the press showing, the *Express* representative pronounced it 'a damn good picture' and asked that it be run again.[65] In the upmarket broadsheets, the response was highly positive: the film was described as 'inspiring' in *The Times* and in both the *Telegraph* and *Guardian* as 'exciting'.[66] Enthusiasm was also the order of the day elsewhere among the dailies. 'It is a grand film', argued the reviewer for the *Herald*, echoing the 'superb' verdict given in the pages of the *Express*.[67] The upmarket weeklies, both left and right, were equally enthusiastic. Writing for the *New Statesman*, William Whitebait called *Target for Tonight* 'a model of pictorial brevity' that 'without sensationalism provides thrills that can hardly be measured'. In the *Spectator*, Edgar Anstey confessed to have found it 'deeply moving'. Even the wing commander's 'la-de-da' accent, in the context of this film, came across as 'just the voice of a real man talking competently about his job'.[68] RAF officers asked to review the picture were unstinting in their praise.[69] The film periodicals also liked it and, perhaps more significantly in terms of generating publicity, so too did the trade and cinemagoer magazines. 'Take my advice', the editor of *Picturegoer* announced to film fans: 'Go and see it.'[70]

They did, and in large numbers. After only a couple of weeks in cinemas, *Target for Tonight* was being pronounced an 'outstanding success' in the trade paper *Kine Weekly*: 'It has proved a far more powerful magnet to the public than even the most enthusiastic could have hoped.'[71] The scenario was serialized by Paul Holt in the *Daily Express* and then published as a sixpenny pamphlet ('the book of the famous film') by Hutchinson.[72] When a print of *Target for Tonight* was run for the prime minister at Chequers, 'Churchill was as tense as any movie fan when things looked bad for the bomber that was over Germany', an observer remembered, adding: 'He chuckled when its bombs hit their target.'[73] It was routinely shown to RAF aircrew recruits, and within Bomber Command the principal players were celebrated as much for their roles in *Target for Tonight* as for their accomplishments as aircrew.[74] The film, which did very well overseas as well as at home, earned over £73,000 for the Treasury.[75]

The fact that *Target for Tonight* made what industry analyst Josh Billings described as 'box-office history' was in large part a matter of timing.[76] It was the first of the official wartime narrative or story documentaries in which instead of a commentator a group of actual participants speak scripted but true-to-life dialogue.[77] This not only gave it novelty value but also – announced as it was in the titles sequence – an air of realism and authenticity not present in commercial features. Thus the plot was accepted as fact rather than fiction or, at worst, lightly dramatized reality.[78] Allied to this was the topicality of *Target for Tonight*. In the wake of the Blitz and other calamities, it struck a responsive chord because it showed Britain 'hitting back' rather than just 'taking it', more specifically the RAF striking directly and effectively at Germany itself. 'It was a glimmer of hope', Watt recalled, 'and the public rose to it'.[79]

Target for Tonight was not in fact particularly accurate about the ability of the RAF to find and hit precise locations at night. At the start of the year, in response to an Air Ministry request for post-raid photographs that could be given out to the press, Bomber Command headquarters had proven reluctant to comply. 'As you know', one official minuted another, 'some of our most heavily attacked targets have not shown any discernible damage'.[80] An analysis of over six hundred photographs taken by bombing aircraft at night revealed that only one in five aircraft had come within 5 miles of the intended target in the fifty-four days before the premiere of the film. During the period in which *Target for Tonight* was reaping accolades, the newly established operational research section of Bomber Command was concluding that only 15 per cent of RAF bombers were dropping their bombs within 5 miles of the aiming point.[81]

In the corridors of power this led to a protracted debate about the future of the strategic bombing offensive, ultimately resolved in early 1942 with a decision to expand the force and concentrate on area bombing aimed at destroying entire built-up urban areas using high explosive and incendiary bombs. None of this secret information was passed along to the general population, the Air Ministry continuing to assert or imply to the public that RAF bombers were quite capable of navigating their way at night over the Continent and depositing their loads with great accuracy and effectiveness on distant industrial or military targets.[82]

Maintaining what was described in an internal Air Ministry narrative as 'the cloak of complacent publicity which kept the British people happy' involved among other things deciding whether or not to support a number of commercial projects dealing with the RAF strategic bombing campaign.[83] A full colour film with a projected budget of £150,000 which was meant 'to show the real pictures of the R.A.F.'s nightly smashings of German industrial towns' was rejected in November

1941 mainly due to a melodramatic script but doubtless also because generating such footage under current navigational conditions would be difficult.[84] There were, however, several other prospective features that were given the green light by the Air Ministry and screened in cinemas in 1942.

The first dated back many months to an idea circulating within the MoI for a film dealing with the ways in which Britain was undermining the German war economy. This was to be a commercial venture more akin in form to *The Lion Has Wings* than *Target for Tonight* but took much longer to complete. Michael Balcon, head of production at Ealing Films, having taken on the project, got into a spat with both the MoI and the Air Ministry in late 1940. The former, he stated in the press, did not give enough credence to his instincts as to what would and would not resonate with audiences, while the latter was obstructionist or lackadaisical in granting facilities.[85] The Ministry of Economic Warfare, to whom Balcon turned next, was keen for the project to come to fruition.[86] Obstacles, primarily financial in nature, remained into early 1941. Balcon wanted £25,000 of public money to cover production costs since Ealing, according to a Board of Trade official, 'do not feel justified in undertaking it as a private venture'.[87] Under fire from parliament for having subsidized another commercial project, *49th Parallel*, to the tune of just under £60,000, the MoI, using a certain amount of subterfuge, was only willing to go as high as £12,500.[88] A bargain was struck in April, whereby Ealing undertook to do without a subsidy in return for full support from the MoI in obtaining necessary cooperation from the Admiralty and Air Ministry.[89]

In the second week of June 1941, production began on what was given at one point the title *Siege* but emerged as *The Big Blockade*.[90] The Air Ministry did its part by allowing director Charles Frend to film exterior footage of Hampden bombers of 50 Squadron at Skellingthorpe, assigning an RAF bomber-pilot advisor, John Wooldridge, familiar with the Hampden, and providing an actual aircraft for interior filming at Ealing Studios where models and sets were being constructed.[91] The entry of the Soviet Union into the war shortly after production started caused some delay as a new sympathetic character, a Russian played by Michael Redgrave, had to be written into the film by scriptwriter Angus McPhail.[92] Later on, differences of opinion between Frend and the editor, Charles Crichton, may also have contributed to post-production continuing well into the autumn. By the turn of the year, however, *The Big Blockade* was complete.[93]

Almost a quarter of *The Big Blockade*, designed to showcase the war-winning work of the Ministry of Economic Warfare through a mixture of staged scenes – using mostly actors this time – and straight documentary with journalist Frank Owen narrating throughout, dealt with Bomber Command.[94] Early on the narrator introduces the Hampden bombers of '1020' Squadron, 'one of scores to fly to Germany, in raid upon raid', striking this particular night at specific industrial targets in the Hannover region ranging from an oil refinery to a steel foundry. Owen then focuses in on 'T-for-Tommy', crewed by 'George' the pilot (Michael Rennie), 'Tom' the navigator/bomb aimer (John Mills), rear gunner 'Percy' (Peter De Greeff) and radio operator/air gunner 'David' (David Evans).[95] Their particular objective, the commentator explains, is an industrial power plant.[96]

Over the course of the next hour, as various plotlines unfold, it becomes apparent that this group of flyers, with 'Tom' more to the fore than the others, is a close-knit team whose members are relaxed and confident enough to make wry comments even when under pressure.[97] They are also united in other ways, insofar as all four are clearly English and speak with a received pronunciation (RP) accent.[98] That this was a deliberate choice, at least as far as 'Tom' was concerned, seems likely given that John Mills was quite capable of adopting a working-class accent when the role called for one.[99] The Bomber Command of *The Big Blockade* was thus a much more exclusively middle-class English organization than that of *Target for Tonight*, though perhaps less hierarchical than that of *The Lion Has Wings*.[100]

It is to this Hampden crew that the film eventually returns during an extended climax when, after driving off a night fighter, they go in to strike their designated target amid searchlights and flak. The bombing sequence includes the now familiar close-up shots of the face of the bomb aimer as he looks through the bombsight and presses the bomb-release button and scores a 'direct hit'; but *The Big Blockade* goes further than its predecessors in showing T-for-Tommy engage in a total of three consecutive and successful bomb runs over the target. The film also goes beyond shots of the subsequent explosions by depicting for the first time the reactions of those at the receiving end. Portrayed in bombastically comedic fashion throughout, the managerial and other personnel in the air raid shelters are clearly rattled; though nobody is actually shown being killed or seriously wounded. The raids by Bomber Command, it seems, are undermining enemy morale as well as, to quote the earlier words of the commentator, 'destroying the mechanism of war itself'. The featured Hampden, though, does not get away totally unscathed. An anti-aircraft shell burst starts a fire amidships, and in an unusually graphic scene we see that the radio operator has badly burned one of his hands and is clearly in great pain. The blaze is eventually extinguished and the message of a successful strike radioed home. T-for-Tommy and its crew land safely, having demonstrated once more the kind of pinpoint accuracy that Bomber Command was in reality quite incapable of achieving.[101]

The exhibitors campaign book issued by the studio for *The Big Blockade* showed bombs raining down in a searchlight-crossed night sky and bursting among buildings, emphasizing the centrality of the T-for-Tommy storyline in *The Big Blockade*.[102] It was doubtless hoped that a more overtly commercial picture than *Target for Tonight* showing Britain 'dishing it out' would strike a chord.[103] It remained to be seen how the newspapers and public would react to this and other aspects of what one film enthusiast described as 'an all-star semi-documentary' after it finally premiered in mid-January 1942.[104]

The press was ambivalent. On the one hand, J. E. Sewell of the *Telegraph* praised 'an excellent presentation of a bombing raid' in a film that was overall 'dramatic and amusing'. William Whitebait of the *New Statesman* wrote that *The Big Blockade* was both instructive and at times funny and singled out the bombing raid as 'brilliant'.[105] On the other hand *The Times* critic, while conceding that 'some of the flying sequences are remarkably good', damned the film as a whole for being 'woefully unconvincing'. Edgar Anstey, writing for the *Spectator*, found the RAF attack was 'exciting enough' but unreal in comparison to the one shown in *Target for Tonight* and set within a film which he thought 'a shapeless series of fragmentary episodes'.[106] The public evidently agreed with the more negative view, the picture making little impression at the box office: both the studio and the Ministry of Economic Warfare eventually conceded that *The Big Blockade* had been a failure.[107]

Luckily for the Air Ministry, a more promising commercial picture featuring Bomber Command was already in the works. Back in November 1940, director Michael Powell had fallen into the habit of listening to the Nine O'Clock News, which included bulletins on RAF bomber raids. 'I had become fascinated by a phrase that occurred only too often: "One of our aircraft failed to return."'[108] From this germ of an idea his screenwriter-collaborator, Emeric Pressburger, developed a plotline in which 'we tell the story of a typical British bomber crew' who are forced to bail out over German-occupied Holland and must rely on their wits and help from the Dutch resistance to make it back across the Channel. The MoI liked the idea and gave the pair a positive introduction to the Air Ministry and the Dutch government-in-exile, which also proved enthusiastic. Having conceded that *One of Our Aircraft Failed to Return* sounded a little too pessimistic, Powell and Pressburger changed the name of the project to *One of Our Aircraft Is Missing* and obtained the backing of British National Films.[109]

By the late summer of 1941 and on into the autumn, interior shooting was underway at Denham Studios on sets as well as in and around a Wellington fuselage provided by the Air Ministry, while exterior footage was being shot in East Anglia for the sequences set in Holland and at an RAF station at Marham for Bomber Command material.[110] The latter was home to the Wellington Mk III crews of 115 Squadron, practically all of whom were enlisted in the creation of ground and aerial scenes.[111]

In the end, about a third of the total screen time in *One of Our Aircraft Is Missing* would be devoted to the crew of 'B-for-Bertie' preparing for, and engaging in, a bombing raid of a Stuttgart engine plant: as the director told one of the principal actors, this was a film about the RAF as much as anything else.[112] Particular sequences and dialogue within the script closely mirrored those of *Target for Tonight*. In both films, for instance, a Canadian air gunner is informed by an officer that he has been taken off operations that particular night, the conversation ending with the officer saying 'bad luck' to the unhappy sergeant.[113] During the squadron take-off sequence, moreover, Michael Powell – here taking on the role of actor as well as director – repeats the dialogue and manner of his namesake, 'Speedy' Powell, from the earlier film.[114] The course of the night bombing raid in which 'B-for-Bertie' and its crew participate also follows the pattern of *Target for Tonight*; so much so that at least one later observer concluded that aerial footage from the earlier film had been inserted into *One of Our Aircraft Is Missing*.[115] As before, the air gunners spray the searchlights, there are close-ups of the bomb aimer's face as he issues course corrections to the pilot on the bomb run, and despite searchlights and flak, all the bombs explode spectacularly in the targeted factory. Like F-for-Freddie, B-for-Bertie is hit by flak immediately afterward. Only then do the plots diverge, the crew of the former making it home while the crew of the latter are forced to bail out.[116] By the end of the film, though, having made it back to England, the crew are back in business as they stand in front of a big new four-engine Stirling bomber. 'Right', an officer in the operations room announces: 'The target's Berlin!'[117]

The crew of B-for-Bertie, like that of F-for-Freddie, is both regionally and socially diverse but here given much more depth than in earlier bomber films. The skipper, Flying Officer John Glyn Haggard (Hugh Burden), is a youthful upper-middle-class Englishman from the Home Counties as his accent, plus a reference to a professional army officer father and childhood nurse, indicates. Observer – i.e. navigator/bomb aimer – Flying Officer Frank Shelly (Hugh Williams), whose accent is also refined, was a stage actor before the war. The second pilot, Flying Officer Tom Earnshaw (Eric Portman), comes from a prosperous Northern sheep-farming family, with strong Yorkshire accent to match. The radio operator is Sergeant Bob Ashley (Emrys Jones), a pre-war professional football player from Wales, and the front gunner Sergeant Geoff Hickman (played by Bernard Miles with his characteristic Hertfordshire/Buckinghamshire rural yeoman accent). Replacing the crew's Canadian sergeant rear gunner for the night in question is Flying Officer Sir George Corbett (Godfrey Tearle), a character whom Pressburger had based on Sir Arnold Wilson, a Tory MP with an adventurous past who, despite being in his mid-fifties, had volunteered for aircrew and served as an air gunner aboard Wellingtons before being killed in action.[118]

Though Sir George is a late addition to the flying roster and a bit of a grim old man, the crew of B-for-Bertie are shown working as a team in the air, the younger men relaxed enough to banter about Stuttgart and its inhabitants but professionals all the same, everyone communicating vital information succinctly, navigator working at plotting table, pilot and second pilot flying the plane and both gunners constantly scanning the skies for enemy fighters. They are also a bit more egalitarian than their screen predecessors, the officers on a first-name basis with each other and when addressing the sergeants, the sergeants referring to the aircraft captain as 'skipper' and replying to all without reference to rank: the honorific 'sir' is uttered only once and in passing.[119] There is, however, still a hierarchy of function at work in the air in *One of Our Aircraft Is Missing*, with the pilot clearly in charge.[120]

The picture was completed on time by early 1942 at a cost of £70,000. Though not completely satisfied with the result despite the fine cinematography of Ronald Neame and excellent editing by David Lean, Powell thought 'we had a hit'.[121] He was soon to be proven correct. In the wake of the trade showing *One of Our Aircraft Is Missing* was immediately booked to go into the Odeon Leicester Square for a four-week run before going out on general release.[122] 'Spectacular, up-to-the-minute war time aerial epic', enthused the trade paper *Kine Weekly*.[123] Amidst the official premiere the following month, the daily press were equally enthusiastic about the picture. 'The film is, of course, fiction', noted the *Manchester Guardian*: 'But it is so well done, and so directly related to current nightly happenings, that its appeal to be seen is enormous and immediate.' It was 'an important film', according to *The*

Times, in which the personalities of the bomber crew were properly fleshed out. The mass-circulation dailies were less restrained in their praise. 'A great piece of film craft and one of the most realistic and exciting of modern adventure stories', was the verdict of the *Daily Mirror*: it was also a picture containing 'some superb flying sequences, notably a most spectacular raid on Stuttgart'. To readers of the *News Chronicle* it was billed as a terrific war drama which had 'the conviction of fact'.[124] Those writing for the weeklies and monthlies were also impressed. 'Exemplary in taste and verisimilitude', wrote Roger Manville for the *New Statesman*, adding 'this film is also intensely gripping'.[125] Ordinary filmgoers evidently agreed: on general release in the summer of 1942, *One of Our Aircraft Is Missing* did well and was considered one of the best British films of the year at the box office.[126]

It certainly overshadowed the last of the quartet of features in this period dealing with Bomber Command. This was one of a series of Hollywood-backed pictures in which a maverick hero crosses the Atlantic to fly with the RAF, successfully engages with the opposite sex and learns the importance of service teamwork.[127] Unlike the others, however, *Flying Fortress*, directed by Walter Forde, was a production based in England with sets built at Teddington Studios owned by Warner Brothers.[128] The title, of course, referred to the famous Boeing B-17 bomber, made in the United States and introduced with much fanfare into the RAF in the spring of 1941. By the autumn, footage was being shot of the Fortress Is of 90 Squadron based at Polebrooke in Northamptonshire.[129]

The plot, designed by British screenwriter Brock Williams, adhered closely to the standard Yank-in-the-RAF storyline. It climaxes in a high-level daylight raid on Berlin during which the American protagonist Jim Spence (Richard Greene), aided by fellow American Sky Kelly (Donald Stewart), heroically extinguishes an engine fire manually while Lord Ottershaw (Sydney King), despite his wounds, maintains a stiff upper lip in keeping the plane level.[130] 'The Flying Fortress lands safely', the press flyer for the film explains: 'Bomber Command has made its target.'[131]

For the American studio, a film made in the UK costing well over £100,000 would soak up the profits from its Hollywood films that exchange controls prevented it from repatriating to the United States. Yank-in-the-RAF features thus far had made money for Hollywood at home and abroad, and Warners doubtless hoped that with a title recognizable to Americans – 'Flying Fortress' was, after all, a description of the big bomber coined in the United States – the film could make money on both sides of the Atlantic.[132] When the film was released in mid-June 1942, the aerial sequences aroused critical interest, notably in the *Daily Telegraph*: 'The subject is one to grip the imagination of the public on both sides of the Atlantic; the shots of the great plane's interior and of the raid on Germany have considerable interest; and the climax – the hero's climbing out on a wing to put out a fire – is hair-raising enough for anybody.'[133] Yet even in the *Telegraph* the by now overly familiar Yank-in-the-RAF plot elements and caricature dialogue were criticized; and the British press as a whole did not take kindly to *Flying Fortress*.[134] It fared even worse on the other side of the Atlantic, the *New York Times* dismissing it as a 'sloppy, ramshackle job'.[135] It was not among the year's box-office winners.[136]

Though the Air Ministry had backed the film in 1941, the failure of *Flying Fortress* in 1942 was perhaps not such a bad thing from a public relations perspective. The Yank-in-the-RAF trope was no longer a useful publicity angle for Britain now that the United States was in the war, and the Fortress I had proven both costly and ineffective as a day bomber. It had in fact been quietly withdrawn from RAF service five months before the release of the film.[137] As for Warner Brothers, work was already well underway back in the United States that would replicate elements from earlier British features yet employ the box-office appeal of established Hollywood stars.[138]

The plot for what was originally called *Forced Landing* was the work of screenwriter Arthur Horman. Almost two years earlier he had worked in Montreal on the script of *49th Parallel*, then being shot in Canada under the direction of Michael Powell. The plot of that film involved the attempt by a handful of U-boat survivors stranded in North America to evade capture and make their way home, and it occurred to both men that this scenario could be reworked for an RAF bomber crew shot down over Germany.[139] The result was two pictures with the same basic plot: one a British drama with a wartime pseudo-documentary feel, the other a standard American action-adventure yarn of the period.

The Hollywood version of *One of Our Aircraft Is Missing*, shot in the spring of 1942, was released under the title *Desperate Journey* in September, two months before the former appeared in the United States. Directed by Raoul Walsh, it starred Errol Flynn as the daring Australian co-pilot Flight Lieutenant Terrence Forbes and co-starred Ronald Raegan as Flying Officer Johnny Hammond, the Yank-in-the-RAF bombardier of RAF Fortress I 'D-for-Danny' of 282 Squadron, assigned to strike a rail junction at 'Shmeidemühl' in north-eastern Germany. The target is bombed with destructive precision after a pursuing fighter is shot down, but there are casualties and D-for-Danny is hit by flak and forced to crash-land. The story then becomes an escape-and-evasion adventure across Germany to Holland, crewmen falling by the wayside at various stages despite help from the underground until only Forbes and Hammond remain to steal a captured RAF plane and fly it home to England. The Air Ministry was not involved in the making of this feature, which relied on model work and, for ground scenes, a rather poor fuselage mock-up reputedly rented from Paramount Studios.[140]

Desperate Journey drew mixed reviews from the critics but was a hit with the public on both sides of the Atlantic as typical Hollywood entertainment with no pretensions to reflect reality.[141] In the United States, it grossed over $2 million for Warner Brothers.[142] In the UK, it shared second place in terms of ticket sales during the first month of its general release.[143]

Bomber Command, meanwhile, had been growing in size and starting to engage in the mass saturation raids of German cities that would become its hallmark under the direction of Air Marshal Sir Arthur Harris. The first thousand-bomber raid had taken place in May of 1942 over Cologne, and in late July of 1943, over forty thousand inhabitants of Hamburg were killed when incendiaries ignited a firestorm. This was not the kind of bombing depicted in the feature films discussed above, but it should not be thought that ordinary people was entirely unaware of the kind of huge and indiscriminate devastation being wrought by Bomber Command at night. In the second half of 1942 the Air Ministry was still suggesting to the public that specific industrial targets were being hit but admitting, with reference to Cologne, that 'casualties among the population were certainly heavy' and that as expected enemy morale was being undermined.[144] Stories of raids with headlines such as 'Kassel Ruins – 300 Out of 315 Acres Devastated' or 'Another Town Smashed – Mulheim Left in Flames by RAF Bombers' which appeared in the press meant readers understood implicitly what was being done by Bomber Command.[145]

So too did audiences who saw a popular made-in-Hollywood Twentieth Century-Fox extravaganza entitled *Thunder Birds: Soldiers of the Air*, released in the United States in October 1942 and in the UK in late 1943. Shot in full Technicolor by William A. Wellman at Falcon Field in Arizona, where the Air Corps was undertaking the training of foreign as well as home-grown pilots for the war effort, *Thunder Birds* centred on the conflicts between veteran American civilian flying instructor Steve Britt, played by Preston Foster, RAF trainee pilot Peter Stackhouse, played by John Sutton, and their common romantic interest, Kay Saunders, played by Gene Tierney. Though the film has a training rather than a combat setting, what kind of operational flying the RAF trainees are destined for is made abundantly clear through Stackhouse explaining that he wanted to be a pilot in order to seek retribution for the death of a brother killed while serving in Bomber Command, and through the words of narrator John Gunther who notes at the start of the film that the enemy engaged in 'wanton destruction of life and property' during the Blitz and states at the end that 'these young Englishmen are going to bomb Berlin, just as they bombed Essen, Cologne, and Dusseldorf'.[146] There was also a short MoI propaganda film, *The Biter Bit*, made by Alexander Korda at the instigation of the prime minister in 1943, in which the destruction being wrought by Bomber Command is framed in terms of retributive justice for the devastation of Coventry and other cities by the *Luftwaffe* earlier in the war.[147]

At the same time, however, the indiscriminate nature of area bombing was not made fully explicit out of fear of a public backlash on moral grounds. Harris himself thought that it was a misrepresentation of the facts to tell the public 'that Bomber Command is concerned, not with the obliteration of German cities and their inhabitants as such, but with the bombing of specific factory premises'.[148] That was intentional on the part of the Air Ministry, however. Harris was informed in no uncertain terms by the Air Council that it was 'desirable to present the bomber offensive in such a light as to provoke the minimum of public controversy and so as far as possible to avoid conflict with religious and humanitarian opinion'.[149]

Nonetheless, given what was essentially understood by the public about the nature of the RAF's strategic bombing campaign, another feature film suggesting precise industrial targeting by Bomber Command was likely to lack credibility and one on area bombing unlikely to meet with official approval. In any event, with no less than five of the former type of picture having appeared in England between July 1941 and December 1942, official and commercial filmmakers likely thought the subject matter had exhausted its possibilities.[150] Bomber Command did nonetheless occasionally figure, albeit often somewhat tangentially, in both shorter and full-length dramatic features dealing with other aspects of the conflict released in the latter war years or soon after. These were films which focused more on the individual and those to whom he was attached outside the crew than on the crew-as-team, and for the first time suggested that RAF bombing operations could exact a serious toll on flyers and those closest to them.

Millions Like Us, directed by Frank Launder and Sidney Gilliat, and released by Gainsborough Pictures in November 1943, was about a group of women of varying background and temperament who have been conscripted to work in an aircraft factory, and it was to their stories that audiences responded positively.[151] One of the several plot threads involved the courtship and marriage of factory girl Celia Crowson, played by Patricia Roc, and a Glaswegian RAF sergeant, Fred Blake, played by Gordon Jackson. A newly minted wireless operator/air gunner posted to heavy bombers, Blake clearly lacks the level of self-assurance seen among flying personnel in earlier features. Perhaps even more significant is the fact that he gets killed one night over Germany, the first time an aircrew character from Bomber Command disappears as a result of enemy action, and an initial hint at what would by war's end be a horrendously high casualty rate.[152]

Individual uncertainty and the likelihood of death among bomber aircrews was at the heart of a twenty-minute drama from Strand Films released a month later. Directed by Leslie Fenton, *There's a Future in It* was based on a short story by H. E. Bates.[153] Employed in uniform by the Air Ministry to write up RAF crew life in fictionalized form under the pseudonym 'Flying Officer X', Bates had spent a good deal of time in 1942 with 7 Squadron, which flew Stirling bombers from Oakington.[154] Johnny O'Connor, a pilot played by Barry Morse, returns from an op with his Stirling, Q-for-Queenie, shot up and with a wounded man aboard. Outside a pub his girlfriend, Kitty, played by Ann Dvorak, helps him open up a bit about how dangerous and frightening his job is, and how much he dislikes it while thinking it necessary to carry on despite the risks. Her parents, played by John Turnbull and Beatrice Varley, think he is taking advantage of their daughter at their expense, but Kitty knows otherwise. Morse was perhaps too smooth an actor for the part of a bomber pilot suffering from what might be termed combat fatigue; but critical reception at the time was quite positive, and as one observer later commented, 'it was refreshing to see a bomber pilot admitting that operations were not some sort of boy scout jamboree.'[155]

Then there was *The Way to the Stars*, a Two Cities film directed by Anthony Asquith, which appeared in June 1945, a month after the war in Europe had ended. A major focus in this picture was relations between American servicemen and their British hosts; but the first thirty minutes of the film covered RAF light bomber operations from 'Halfpenny Field' in 1940 and then 1942.[156] There is little attempt here to depict bomber crews as cross-class teams. Reflecting the sensibilities of the author of the screenplay, Terence Rattigan, and perhaps the start of a shift away from the 'we're-all-in-it-together' theme of films made in earlier years, the major RAF characters are all officers who wear pilot's wings. As in his earlier stage play *Flare Path*, the sole working-class character among the aircrew, Clark, played by

Bill Owen, is a sergeant air gunner seen only infrequently who always addresses his pilot as 'sir' while the latter addresses him by his rank or by nickname, 'Nobby'.[157] Nonetheless, *The Way to the Stars* does remind audiences that bombing operations, in this case by daylight over France rather than by night over Germany, came at a price, and that not all aircrew were completely confident or, indeed, competent. Every operation seems to produce losses, including early on the commanding officer, Carter, played by Trevor Howard, and eventually his successor, David Archdale, played by Michael Redgrave. The latter sometimes displays signs of the psychological stress he is under as a leader, while another major character, Peter Penrose, played by John Mills, is initially a poor pilot who by the end of his first tour of duty is finding it increasingly difficult to cope emotionally. The tone is one of understatement, but expressions and body language as much as words convey the kind of inner fear that Rattigan himself had experienced as an air gunner with Coastal Command and inserted into *Flare Path*. Back in 1942, the C-in-C Bomber Command had been outraged by the play when he saw it – 'Bloody disgraceful', he told the leading actor, 'showing cowardice in the face of the enemy' – but by the time the film was complete in 1945, Harris was on his way out; and *The Way to the Stars*, at least in Britain, turned out to be a critical and box-office success.[158]

Meanwhile, Bomber Command was playing a more central and familiar part in in a number of shorter-length documentary films produced at the behest of various agencies in the latter war years. They provide extra evidence of the teamwork theme and project an ability to square the circle concerning the question of what was being struck.

Target, Berlin was a fifteen-minute docudrama released at the start of 1944 by the National Film Board of Canada for its 'Canada Carries On' newsreels. Written by Leslie McFarlane, it followed the first Lancaster bomber built in Canada from the drawing board to its initial raid as Q-Queenie, dubbed 'Ruhr Express'. Though there is narration by Lorne Greene, both Victory Aircraft managers and workers and a Royal Canadian Air Force crew led by Squadron Leader Reg Lane are given dialogue in the fashion of *Target for Tonight*. True to this pattern, the crew speak and perform as an egalitarian team. The film follows the crew from assuming ownership of the plane through to the climax, a raid on Berlin in which footage of extensive fires down below is used while the bomb aimer calls 'Bullseye!' after the bomb release. Though neither the aircraft production process nor the actual bombing went anywhere near as smoothly as depicted, *Target Berlin* was of 'considerable local interest' when shown in Toronto.[159]

Aimed at audiences in New Zealand at the behest of the MoI and lasting about twenty minutes, *Maximum Effort* followed a typical night raid by a Lancaster crew dominated by New Zealanders.[160] Directed by Michael Hankinson for Merlin Films based on a story by Arnot Robertson, this was largely shot on location at the station in Cambridgeshire where 75 (New Zealand) Squadron was based in the spring of 1944. It follows the crew of O-Oboe, identified only by their first names, positions, nationalities – one Englishman, one Canadian, four Kiwis – and, as the film unfolds, focuses of their inner lives.[161] With the skipper serving as occasional narrator, *Maximum Effort* depicts the crew bantering on the ground regardless of rank yet entirely professional once in the air, addressing each other by position. After a night fighter is beaten off and the oxygen system damaged, the crew-as-team motif is emphasized when the pilot polls the crew about how to proceed, and they explicitly or tacitly agree to continue on to the target at a height that does not require oxygen. Over the target, identified only as 'the Ruhr again' earlier in the film, flak and big fires on the ground – combat footage rather than model work – are shown, followed by the standard shots of the face of the bomb aimer over his bombsight giving the skipper course corrections ('left, left, steady', etc.). After 'bombs gone!', a fairly concentrated pattern of explosions is shown far below. The aircrew involved in the making of *Maximum Effort* seem to have enjoyed themselves, but the film only reached its intended audience after the war in Europe had ended.[162]

The same was true of an RAF Film Production Unit title of similar length, *RAAF Over Europe*, which dealt in part with Australians in Bomber Command and featured a raid on Berlin – one of what the narrator terms now-routine 'massed bomber raids' – that included a staged crew briefing, kitting out, starting up and take-off rolls by the men and aircraft 463 Squadron RAAF as well as combat footage of blazing streets far below. The critic for the Australian Associated Press praised it for containing 'some excellent flying shots, especially of Lancasters bombing'.[163]

For British and foreign audiences there was the MoI-sponsored *Target Germany*, a retrospective summary from Phoenix Films of the latter stages of the strategic bombing campaign waged by Bomber Command against the Third Reich. The narrator makes clear early on what was being sought: 'the smashing of the German war industries'. A map of Germany with various cities and regions filled with sketched-in factories and chimneys visually supports more detailed explanations of why urban centres were targeted – e.g. 'Hamburg and Bremen: U-boats, oil, and aircraft'. Using newsreel footage and earlier documentaries, including *Target for Tonight*, the film then recreates a typical area bombing night raid. 'In the target area', the narrator explains, 'lay the largest chemical works in Europe, I. G. Farben. Vital marshalling yards and a large dock area. Mannheim was [note the use of the past tense] one of the busiest ports on the Rhine. Engineering plants and factories making diesel engines.' The way the raid unfolds suggests a certain amount of discrimination in what is being aimed at and hit, and enemy casualty figures are not cited. *Target Germany*, nonetheless, goes on to make the level of physical destruction being caused fully evident through extensive use towards the end of low-level footage of gutted cityscapes – 'the death roll of German cities' – taken in daylight immediately after the surrender. 'The German people believed Hitler when he told them that Britain was weak and helpless', the narrator explains, 'and now, Germany lies in ruins'.[164]

A final feature film which in many ways summed up how the Air Ministry wished Bomber Command to be thought of both in terms of men and mission was *Journey Together*, work on which had begun in January 1944 but that was complete only in September of 1945.[165] This too had a screenplay with input from Terence Rattigan and included one of the secondary players seen in *The Way to the Stars*, David Tomlinson.[166] The two films, however, were otherwise very different. *Journey Together* was developed by the RAF Film Production Unit based at Pinewood

Studios, which took combat footage and later on made short documentary films chronicling everything from the work of balloon crews to night navigation, but which by the latter wars years contained a wealth of industry talent.[167] Commissioned to highlight the work of Flying Training Command in the war effort, *Journey Together* turned out to be a much bigger and more ambitious affair than other unit films – 'not a technical documentary', as a publicity handout for the film explained, but a full-length feature 'that has all the polish and finish of Hollywood's best'.[168]

With Flight Lieutenant George Brown as associate producer and under the overall direction of Flight Lieutenant John Boulting, *Journey Together*, dedicated to 'The Few Who Trained the Many', drew almost exclusively on the large pool of technical and acting talent already wearing air force blue, including Rattigan, with whom Boulting co-wrote the screenplay. Behind the camera there were people such as Flight Sergeant Harry Waxman, the director of photography, and Flight Lieutenant John Howell, in charge of special effects.[169] In front of the lens, in addition to Flying Officer Tomlinson, there were promising or experienced actors such as Aircraftsman Richard Attenborough, Aircraftsman Jack Watling and Flight Lieutenant John Justin, among others.[170] This saved a great deal on salary costs while adding to the film's authenticity; yet it also lengthened the filming process because of the actors' regular service commitments; as did, for the sake of realism, the shooting of exterior footage not only in England – everywhere from Cambridge and Manchester to RAF airfields at Denham, Friston, Methwold, Pembrey and Waterbeach – but also in Canada and the United States.[171]

The title of the film referred to the experiences of two aircrew recruits, David Wilton, played by Richard Attenborough, and John Aynesworth, played by Jack Watling, who become friends while moving through the flying training system in England, North America, then England again from initial acceptance to operational status. Wilton, however, is the true protagonist of *Journey Together*, a 19-year-old from a lower-middle-class background with limited schooling who works on his educational qualifications while serving as an RAF electrical fitter and gets the chance to become aircrew. In the classroom he does much better than public school- and ancient university-educated Aynesworth. In the air, however, it eventually becomes clear that Wilton does not have what it takes to be a pilot. Despite the best efforts of a sympathetic American instructor – Dean McWilliams, played by Edward G. Robinson, one of only three civilians in the film[172] – he crashes an aircraft during landing and is diverted to train as a navigator while Aynesworth gets his pilot's wings. Denied the prospect of becoming a pilot himself, Wilton does not take his training in Canada seriously until a problem in the air impels him to grasp that the safety of the crew of a multi-engine plane depends on accurate navigation. Wilton is posted back in England to the operational squadron '522', where Aynesworth is already piloting a Lancaster. Treated as an inexperienced outsider, Wilton gets his chance to prove himself when, while substituting for Aynesworth's regular navigator, his Lancaster is badly shot up after bombing Berlin and eventually forced to ditch in the North Sea. It is due to Wilton's accurate navigational fix transmitted over the radio that search-and-rescue aircraft find the crew's dinghy and they are all saved.[173]

It is striking that the preparations for and the actual bombing operation, which take up the last third or so of the film, do not specify or even indirectly suggest that industrial targets are being struck. A montage sequence of Wilton waiting for his first combat sortie shows newspaper headlines indicating cities being hit and the heavy damage being caused; the briefing officer for the raid simply says of Berlin, 'prang it, and prang it hard'; and combat footage of entire districts on fire below amid explosions is used during the bomb-run sequence.

The same tacit acknowledgement of area bombing appears in a later feature film to which the Air Ministry also lent technical support. Premiering thirteen months after *Journey Together*, Powell and Pressburger's *A Matter of Life and Death* follows the trials and tribulations of Squadron Leader Peter Carter, played by David Niven, a Pathfinder skipper who has had to jump from a burning Lancaster and should perhaps be dead. Though this Technicolor picture can be classed as a fantasy-romance rather than a war drama, it opens as the camera moves in towards Europe on a spinning globe, with a narrator, John Longden, explaining, 'It's night over Europe; the night of the Second of May, 1945; that point of light [Berlin] is a burning city. It had a thousand-bomber raid an hour ago.'[174] A title suggested for the memoirs of Air Marshal Harris, *War against Cities*, a book which appeared the same year as *A Matter of Life and Death*, made it clear what Bomber Command had been doing, as did some of the contents of what ended up being called *Bomber Offensive*.[175]

Returning to *Journey Together*, it is also noteworthy that, as in many of the earlier dramas featuring Bomber Command, the crew of a particular aircraft, in this case the Lancaster piloted by Aynesworth, are depicted as a group of people from different geographic and social backgrounds united in a common cause. There is a Canadian, a Scot and a pair of Australians. Among the English crewmembers, those with refined accents are balanced by two cockneys: as well as Wilton there is Curly the air bomber, played by George Cole. In contrast to previous films, though, the entire crew, including Aynesworth, are NCOs; the only commissioned officer aboard being a flying instructor, played by John Justin, sent along for the ride who defers to Aynesworth as the aircraft captain. Almost invariably everyone addresses everyone else over the intercom by their crew position. The banter among the crew is perhaps a bit more sardonic than in, say, *Target for Tonight*, but when things get rough – a fighter attack over the target which leaves Curly wounded and the Lancaster crippled to the point of eventual ditching – everyone behaves with the utmost professionalism. It has been suggested by one historian that the fact that it is very upper-middle-class Aynesworth, whom Wilton fervently admires, rather than distinctly lower-middle-class Wilton himself, who gets his pilot's wings and becomes an aircraft commander, rather undermines the levelling, technocratic vision of the filmmakers in which they both become, through the training process, non-commissioned officers with vital roles to play as part of a bomber team regardless of background.[176] Perhaps so; but it is still significant that Aynesworth is not given the natural rank befitting his social station – i.e. a commission – and that a third character on the journey towards operations, another middle-class type, A. T. Smith, played by David Tomlinson, fails to become a pilot and ends up as an air bomber.

Most critics thought *Journey Together*, released in the autumn of 1945, accomplished what its makers had hoped for and liked what they saw in terms of authentic atmosphere and acting. It was a 'worthy tribute' (*Daily Mirror*), 'first-rate cinema and excellent entertainment' (*Reynolds News*), 'very exciting' (*Spectator*), 'realistic and brilliant' (*News Chronicle*) and a 'study in teamwork' that was 'moving and exciting' (*Sunday Times*).[177] The trouble was, even according to many of those who liked the picture, that it had taken so long to reach the screen and, with the war over, had much less topicality. 'What a pity it is that this film', commented the reviewer for the *Sunday Express*, 'was not shown when the war was on'. It was 'a year late' (*Daily Herald*) and 'could have scored a direct hit two years ago' (*Daily Sketch*). The critic C. A. Lejeune, who liked *Journey Together* very much – 'a grand film' – worried on the radio: 'I doubt if many people are frantically interested today in the training of R.A.F. crews and their first operational bombing flight.'[178] This proved to be the case: distributed through RKO-Radio Pictures, *Journey Together*, despite high production values and excellent acting, made no notable impression at the box office.[179]

It did, though, have a more successful semi-sequel. With production on *Journey Together* underway, in 1944 the RAF Film Production Unit had undertaken preliminary work on a film about the development of radar. This was one subject that *Journey Together* had not touched on at all for security reasons, but with the war coming to an end such considerations came to seem moot. The unit, however, was wound up at the end of hostilities, and with the support of the Air Ministry the project passed into the hands of Filippo Del Giudice as head of the commercial film company Two Cities, part of the Rank Organization. George Brown stayed on in a civilian capacity as co-producer with the man Del Giudice chose to write and direct, the young Peter Ustinov.[180]

The original plan seems to have been to make the radar film a semi-documentary in which real scientists such as Robert Watson-Watt and Henry Tizard would appear.[181] In the hands of Ustinov, however, what was at first called *The Boffins Went to War*, then *Top Secret* and finally *School for Secrets* became a somewhat whimsical story written, as one senior official put it, 'mainly with an eye to the Box Office', in which the scientists were fictional eccentrics played by professional actors such as Ralph Richardson and Raymond Huntley.[182] A hint of continuity with *Journey Together* nonetheless remains, both through the full cooperation proffered by the RAF in terms of aircraft and equipment and also via the presence of cast members from the previous film. David Tomlinson returns as one of the boffins; Patrick Waddington, last seen as the squadron leader in charge of navigation training at 522 Squadron, gets a promotion to group captain as a liaison officer with the team of scientists; and Richard Attenborough receives both pilot's wings and a commission for the role of an RAF test pilot.[183]

The place of Bomber Command in *School for Secrets* is linked to the development of radar as a navigational and blind-bombing aid. With the war over, the Air Ministry seems to have decided that the kind of eyeball accuracy portrayed in *Target for Tonight* and other films in the 1941–2 period finally could be admitted publicly to have been mythical. An air vice-marshal from Bomber

Command, played by Douglas Bradley-Smith, admits in the film to a group of assembled scientists and RAF types *circa* 1941, 'The results at present being achieved by Bomber Command in no way justify the losses we are incurring. Quite apart from the fact that our bombing is not nearly accurate enough once we have found the target. We have on too many occasions not found the target at all.' When some aircrew present at the meeting speak of having seen their bombs cause destruction, the air vice-marshal mentions that the Germans have become adept at lighting decoy fires. This leads in to a segment of *School for Secrets* dealing with the development of new devices, including a downward-looking airborne radar set which, according to Mr. Watlington, the character played by Tomlinson, will mean that 'very soon we'll be able to bomb blind, through cloud, with pinpoint accuracy'. The latter assertion suggests the Air Ministry, while admitting to problems earlier in the war, was making a case that aiming improved dramatically later on. A subsequent montage sequence merges the reality of area bombing with at least residual reference to specific targets: at one briefing assembled aircrew are told that 'your target for tonight is this marshalling yard north of Hamburg', while in another it is stated simply that 'the target for tonight is Berlin'.

School for Secrets premiered thirteen months after *Journey Together*, in early November 1946. A mostly light-hearted look at a complex subject it was, in the words of its writer-director, 'a great success'.[184] A month later *A Matter of Life and Death* also turned out to be a big hit with the public, if not some of the critics.[185] With that, the cycle of feature films dealing directly or more tangentially with Bomber Command which had been initiated during the war came to a close. The absence of further pictures on the subject in the latter part of the decade – beyond perhaps the slightest of suggestions in a pair of films starring David Farrar that former RAF bomber pilots were having difficulty settling down[186] – was likely due to so many such films having been produced in the recent past rather than any developing squeamishness about the ethics of bombing.[187]

It is interesting to note, though, that in his war memoirs, published within months of the feature films mentioned above, former C-in-C Arthur Harris, while asserting that 'Germany would have been defeated outright by bombing' if resources had not been diverted from his command in the middle war years, stated that attacking civilian morale was something that the Air Ministry, rather than he himself, had promoted.[188] In any event, film trade representatives had long argued that the market for war films was becoming saturated, and it would take until the next decade for such pictures to witness a hugely successful revival. By then, a lot had changed.[189]

Notes

1 John Ware, *The Lion Has Wings* (London: Collins, 1940), 168; see K. R. M. Short, *Screening the Propaganda of British Air Power: From R.A.F. (1935) to* The Lion Has Wings *(1939)* (Trowbridge: Flicks, 1997), 7–8.

2   Ian Dalrymple, 'The Crown Film Unit, 1940-1943', in *Propaganda, Politics and Film, 1918-45*, ed. Nicholas Pronay and D. W. Spring (London: Macmillan, 1982), 209. On the involvement of Churchill see Michael Powell, *A Life in Movies: An Autobiography* (London: Heinemann, 1986), 329. On fears of an aerial Armageddon see Uri Bailer, *The Shadow of the Bomber: The Fear of Air Attack and British Politics, 1932-1939* (London: Royal Historical Society, 1980); Michele Haapamaki, *The Coming of the Aerial War: Culture and the Fear of Airborne Attack in Inter-War Britain* (London: I.B. Tauris, 2014); Brett Holman, *The Next War in the Air: Britain's Fear of the Bomber, 1908-1941* (Farnham: Ashgate, 2014).
3   Ian Dalrymple in Elizabeth Sussex, *The Rise and Fall of British Documentary: The Story of the Film Movement Founded by John Grierson* (Berkeley: University of California Press, 1975), 124.
4   Ware, *Lion Has Wings*, 169.
5   Powell, *Life in Movies*, 333-4.
6   John Terraine, *The Right of the Line: The Royal Air Force in the European War, 1939-1945* (London: Sceptre, 1988), 99-100.
7   See *The Times*, 5 September 1939.
8   *Daily Telegraph*, 5 September 1939; see also, e.g., *Daily Express*, 5 September 1939; *The Times*, 5 September 1939; *The Times*, 8 September 1939.
9   *House of Commons Parliamentary Debates*, 5th Series, vol. 351, col. 581. On the cheering see *Daily Telegraph*, 8 September 1939.
10 *Illustrated London News*, 23 September 1939.
11 Ware, *Lion Has Wings*, 171; see also John Mitchell, *Flickering Shadows: A Lifetime in Movies* (Malvern Wells: Martin and Redman, 1997), 64.
12 Ware, *Lion Has Wings*, 171-2.
13 Ian Dalrymple in *Powell, Pressburger and Others*, ed. Ian Christie (London: BFI, 1978), 26.
14 RAF intent to launch a strike at the Germany navy in fact predated the sinking of the *Athenia*. See Terraine, *Right of the Line*, 98.
15 The course setting bombsight shown in *The Lion Has Wings* and used by the RAF at this time had worked well in training but proved to be far from accurate under combat conditions. See Henry Black, 'Major Bomb Sights Used in WW2 by RAF Bomber Command', Lancaster Archive, accessed 13 January 2017, lancaster-archive.com/majorbombsights.htm.
16 Harry Watt, director of *Target for Tonight*, misremembered Ralph Richardson – also in *The Lion Has Wings* but in other segments – as the actor in white decades later; but likely was correct in recalling how 'ghastly' he felt at the time it was to have a lead player – in fact Anthony Bushell – 'in beautiful clean overalls, white, and everyone else in black overalls, so that the star would stand out, you know'. Watt in Sussex, *Rise and Fall of British Documentary*, 120; see also Harry Watt, *Don't Look at the Camera!* (London: Paul Elek, 1974), 143. In fact, as a very class-conscious Australian film scholar has rightly pointed out, white overalls were standard pre-war flying dress. Neil Rattigan, *This Is England: British Film and the People's War, 1939-1945* (Madison, NJ: Fairleigh Dickinson University Press, 2001), 259. Moreover, some of the footage shot by Powell was of aircrew in such overalls climbing out of aircraft in the wake of the actual Kiel Raid, including a blond officer (see Short, *Screening the Propaganda of British Air Power*, 39), so Bushell's costume may well have been provided for continuity purposes.

17 Short, *Screening the Propaganda of British Air Power*, 79, n. 26. The sentence was retained for the print adaptation. See Ware, *Lion Has Wings*, 78. Though international rules concerning aerial bombardment drawn up in the early 1920s that forbade, among other things, the bombing of hospitals were never ratified by the British or other governments, the 1907 Hague rules concerning war on land had been widely adopted, and these did indeed make it a breach of international law to bombard any well-marked hospital. On the problems of air warfare and international law, see e.g. Tami Davis Biddle, 'Air Power', in *The Laws of War: Constraints on Warfare in the Western World*, ed. Michael Howard, George J. Andreopoulos and Mark R. Schulman (New Haven, CT: Yale University Press, 1994), 140–59.
18 The aerial shots of the Wellingtons apparently came from official footage taken during exercises in the summer of 1939. See *The Aeroplane*, 9 November 1939, 563.
19 See Short, *Screening the Propaganda of British Air Power*, 66–7.
20 On the aircrew accents and class in *The Lion Has Wings* see Rattigan, *This Is England*, 259.
21 Short, *Screening the Propaganda of British Air Power*, 67, 85.
22 Johnathan Falconer, *The Bomber Command Handbook, 1939–1945* (Stroud: Sutton, 1998), 41, 43.
23 See e.g. *Daily Worker*, 6 November 1939. Though Tom Harrisson, co-founder of Mass-Observation (M-O), was not an egalitarian (see Judith M. Heinemann, *The Most Offending Soul Alive: Tom Harrisson and his Remarkable Life* [Honolulu: University of Hawai'i Press, 1998], 125), those involved often thought of M-O as a social research project that could be used to spur social change and improvement (Penny Summerfield, 'Mass-Observation: Social Research or Social Movement?', *Journal of Contemporary History* 20 [1985], 439–52). Harrisson himself directed Leonard England to do an M-O survey of *The Lion Has Wings* (England in Heinemann, *Most Offending Soul*, 159), and both disliked it so much that they asserted – contrary to the M-O evidence gathered – that *The Lion Has Wings*, including its portrayal of the RAF, did not click with ordinary people. See Mass-Observation, File Report 57, Len England, Film Report, 17 March 1940, 11; Tom Harrisson, 'Public Reaction: The Lion Has Wings', *Documentary News Letter*, February 1940, 5. Anthony Bushell, who had played screen officers since 1930, spent the bulk of the war as a real officer in the army before reverting to acting, where his screen officer parts generally rose in rank as he got older. His only other RAF role was as a group captain in *The Purple Plain* (Two Cities, 1954). The uniformity of the other crew members in their sheepskin flying clothing is illustrated by the way in which two girls watching the film found it difficult to pick out Derrick De Marney. M-O, FR 15, Len England, overheard remarks.
24 What were described as 'Messerschmitts' by the navigator were in fact RAF Spitfires and Battles.
25 Dalrymple had wanted the narrator to give names and personal details of the crewmen Powell had taken footage of, but the Air Ministry forbade this on the grounds that the raid had been an RAF 'team effort' and that connecting specific service flyers with a particular operation could put them at risk if captured. Ware, *Lion Has Wings*, 140.
26 Short, *Screening the Propaganda of British Air Power*, 40. The Germans were not slow to point out the factual and other inaccuracies in what was shown in this sequence. See Jo Fox, *Film Propaganda in Britain and Nazi Germany: World War II Cinema* (Oxford: Berg, 2007), 41–2, 76.

27 Michael Paris, *From the Wright Brothers to Top Gun: Aviation, Nationalism and Popular Cinema* (Manchester: Manchester University Press, 1995), 142.
28 Paul Tabori, *Alexander Korda* (London: Oldbourne, 1959), 216. According to one of the film's directors, Korda revealed that he had promised his friend Churchill in late August 1939 that the film would be ready within a month. Powell, *Life in Movies*, 329.
29 See Roy Armes, *A Critical History of the British Cinema* (London: Secker and Warburg, 1978), 147; Adrian Brunel, *Nice Work: The Story of Thirty Years in British Film Production* (London: Forbes Robertson, 1949), 186; Tom Harrisson, 'Films and the Home Front – The Evaluation of Their Effectiveness by "Mass Observation"', in Pronay and Spring, *Propaganda, Politics and Film*, 237; C. A. Oakley, *Where We Came In: Seventy Years of the British Film Industry* (London: Allen and Unwin, 1964), 155; Powell, *Life in Movies*, 335.
30 See *Kinematograph Weekly*, 11 January 1940, 7; Ware, *Lion Has Wings*, 2. Mass-Observation found that that over two-thirds of those who saw the film reacted positively. See Mass-Observation, FR 15. See also *Kinematograph Weekly*, 4 January 1940, 18, 11 January 1940, 26, 25 January 1940, 22; Julian Poole, 'British Cinema Attendance in Wartime: Audience Preference at the Majestic, Macclesfield, 1939–1946', *Historical Journal of Film, Radio and Television* 7 (1987), 20; Guy Morgan, *Red Roses Every Night: An Account of London Cinemas Under Fire* (London: Quality, 1948), 26; Rosalie Moore in *Picturegoer*, 16 December 1939, 14. On the preponderance of positive film reviews see Jeffrey Richards and Dorothy Sheridan, *Mass-Observation at the Movies* (London: Routledge and Kegan Paul, 1987), 154; see also, for the positive reaction in the Dominions, *Globe and Mail*, 23 November 1939; *Toronto Star*, 22 November 1939; *Sydney Morning Herald*, 4 December 1939; *The Age*, 1 January 1940; *Daily News*, 2 March 1940; *Northern Champion*, 11 May 1940.
31 *Daily Telegraph*, 31 October 1939; *Manchester Guardian* [London edition], 31 October 1939; *News Chronicle*, 31 October 1939.
32 *Yorkshire Post*, 28 November 1939; see also e.g. *Daily Express*, 31 October 1939.
33 *New Statesman*, 4 November 1939, 644; *The Listener*, 23 November 1939, 1023; see also *Monthly Film Bulletin*, 6 (1939), 201.
34 Short, *Screening the Propaganda of British Air Power*, 143, 146.
35 *New Statesman*, 4 November 1939, 644; *Spectator*, 3 November 1939, 619.
36 See P. G. M. in *The Aeroplane*, 9 November 1939, 563; M-O, FR 15.
37 P. G. M. in *The Aeroplane*, 9 November 1939, 563; *New Statesman*, 4 November 1939, 644.
38 By the spring of 1944, the government – with whom Korda split the profits 50/50 (see *Today's Cinema*, 31 October 1939, 2) – had received £25,140 from showings of *The Lion Has Wings*. TNA, INF 1/199, Receipts from Commercial Distribution of Films: Summary of statement 18 prepared for evidence to the Public Accounts Committee in May 1944). On the overseas distribution see James Chapman, *The British at War: Cinema, State and Propaganda, 1939–1945* (London: I.B. Tauris, 1998), 64–5; Nicholas John Cull, *Selling War: The British Propaganda Campaign against American 'Neutrality' in World War II* (New York: Oxford University Press, 1995), 49, 137. On success in Australia see Richard Farmer, '"The Dominions Will Love It": *The Lion Has Wings* (1939) and British Film Propaganda in Wartime Australia', *Studies in Australasian Cinema* 7, 1 (2013), 35–47.
39 Tom Harrisson of Mass-Observation, admittedly never a fan of *The Lion Had Wings*, damned it as 'a powerful contribution towards Chamberlainish complacency' in the

latter part of 1940. Tom Harrisson, 'Social Research and the Film', *Documentary News Letter*, November 1940, 10.
40 See e.g. Arthur Elton in Sussex, *Rise and Fall of British Documentary*, 119–20. On the documentary film movement see James Chapman, *A New History of British Documentary* (Basingstoke: Palgrave, 2015), 41–122.
41 On the work of the Crown Film Unit see also Chapman, *British at War*, 114–37.
42 Watt, *Don't Look at the Camera*, 145–6.
43 Harry Watt in Sussex, *Rise and Fall of British Documentary*, 120.
44 IWM, Raymond Egerton 'Harry' Watt interview, 5367/3; TNA, INF 5/78, Watt to Williams, 12 November 1941; see also INF 1/249, Home Planning Committee minutes, 20 November 1940.
45 TNA, AIR 14/1451, minute 2, Lawrence to Bootham, 21 November 1941.
46 TNA, INF 1/249, Planning Committee minutes, 9 September 1940, paragraph 65; INF 1/210, undated Bomber Command Film outline. Joubert was presumably chosen to write the script based on his commentaries on the RAF then being broadcast by the BBC. See Philip Joubert de la Ferté, *The Fated Sky: An Autobiography* (London: Hutchinson, 1952), 193–8.
47 BFI Library, Harry Watt in National Film Theatre interview, 1974.
48 INF 5/78, Watt to Williams, 12 November 1940.
49 Watt, *Don't Look at the Camera*, 146–7; IWM, 5367/3, Raymond Egerton 'Harry' Watt interview. As one film historian remarked: 'One gets the impression that RAF Mildenhall and No. 149 Squadron was something of a darling of the Air Ministry.' K. R. M. Short, 'RAF Bomber Command's "Target for Tonight" (1941)', *Historical Journal of Film, Radio and Television* 17 (1997), 203, n. 17.
50 Watt, *Don't Look at the Camera*, 147.
51 TNA, INF 5/78, Lawrence to Williams, 29 January 1941, Watt to Williams, 7 February, 1 March 1941.
52 TNA, INF 1/249, Home Planning Committee minutes, 24 April 1941.
53 IWM, 5367/4, Raymond Egerton 'Harry' Watt interview.
54 Royal Air Force Commands, Forum, Target for Tonight cast list thread, accessed 21 January 2017, http://www.rafcommands.com/forum.
55 IWM, 5367/4, Raymond Egerton 'Harry' Watt interview. On the authenticity of the dialogue in *Target for Tonight* see Cecil Beaton, *Winged Squadrons* (London: Hutchinson, 1942), 33; Bruce Sanders, *Bombers Fly East* (London: Herbert Jenkins, 1943), 169.
56 See Short, 'RAF Bomber Command's "Target for Tonight" (1941)', Dialogue Appendix.
57 See Charles Carrington, *Solder at Bomber Command* (London: Leo Cooper, 1987), 50–1; Jonathan Falconer, *RAF Bomber Command in Fact, Film and Fiction* (Stroud: Sutton, 1996), 83; John Johnston and Nick Carter, *Strong by Night 'Fortis Nocte': History and Memories of No. 149 (East India) Squadron, 1918/19–1937/56* (Tunbridge Wells: Air-Britain, 2002), 36, 46; Watt, *Don't Look at the Camera*, 149–50.
58 See Howard Hewer, *In for a Penny, In for a Pound: The Adventures and Misadventures of a Wireless Operator in Bomber Command* (Toronto: Stoddart, 2000), 31; Watt, *Don't Look at the Camera*, 148–9; IWM, 5367/4, Raymond Egerton 'Harry' Watt interview.
59 Quoted in Short, *Screening the Propaganda of British Air Power*, 186.
60 This was the writer/director's intention. Watt, *Don't Look at the Camera*, 147; see also BFI Library, *Target for Tonight* pressbooks. On the changing title see INF 1/210, INF 6/335, *passim*.

61 On the methods used to simulate flak and explosions in *Target for Tonight* see IWM, 5367/11, Raymond Egerton 'Harry' Watt interview.
62 See Short, 'RAF Bomber Command's "Target for Tonight"', Appendix – *Target for Tonight* dialogue.
63 *Kinematograph Weekly*, 3 July 1941, 21; Short, 'RAF Bomber Command's "Target for Tonight"', 199.
64 Watt, *Don't Look at the Camera*, 151.
65 Ibid.
66 *Guardian*, 25 July 1941; *Daily Telegraph*, 24 July 1941; *The Times*, 23 July 1941.
67 *Daily Express*, 24 July 1941; *Daily Herald*, 24 July 1941.
68 *Spectator*, 1 August 1941, 106; *New Statesman*, 2 August 1941, 111; see also e.g. *The Listener*, 14 August 1941, 241. Not everyone agreed with Anstey on this with regard to the wing commander. P. L. Mannock argued that such 'ultra-British accents' were 'grounds for criticism' not only in America and the Commonwealth but also in 'countless areas north of Birmingham'. *Kinematograph Weekly*, 20 November 1941, 34.
69 See *Documentary News Letter*, August 1941, 147; *The Listener*, 7 August 1941, 187.
70 *Picturegoer*, 16 August 1941, 3; see also *Kinematograph Weekly*, 31 July 1941, 13; *Monthly Film Bulletin*, 31 August 1941, 98; *Sight and Sound*, autumn 1941, 48.
71 *Kinematograph Weekly*, 14 August 1941, 4; see also Graham Greene on the success of *Target for Tonight* in *The Graham Greene Film Reader*, ed. David Parkinson (Manchester: Carcanet, 1993), 521.
72 Paul Holt, *Target for To-Night: The Book of the Famous Film: The Record in Text and Pictures of a Bombing Raid on Germany* (London: Hutchinson, 1941).
73 Quentin Reynolds, *By Quentin Reynolds* (London: McGraw-Hill, 1963), 228.
74 See e.g. Jack Currie, *Lancaster Target: The Story of a Crew Who Flew from Wickenby* (London: Goodhall, 1981), 91; Grace 'Archie' Hall, *We, Also, Were There: A Collection of Recollections of Wartime Women of Bomber Command* (Braunton: Merlin, 1985), 25; Bill Jackson, *Three Stripes and Four Brownings* (North Battleford, SK: Turner-Warwick, 1990), 136; Murray Peden, *A Thousand Shall Fall: A Pilot for 214* (Stittsville, ON: Canada's Wings, 1979), 280; Humphrey Phillips with Sean Feast, *A Thousand and One: A Flight Engineer Leader's War from the Thousand Bomber Raids to the Battle of Berlin* (Leeds: Bomber Command Books, 2017), 46; Eric Simms, *Birds of the Air: An Autobiography of a Naturalist and Broadcaster* (London: Hutchinson, 1976), 71; Brian Stoker, *If the Flak Doesn't Get You the Fighters Will* (Hailsham: J&KH, 1995), 20. On the showing of *Target for Tonight* to RAF aircrew recruits, see e.g. Victor Hewes in Will Largent, *RAF Wings over Florida: Memories of World War II British Air Cadets* (West Lafayette, IN: Purdue University Press, 2000), 36.
75 TNA, INF 1/199, Receipts from Commercial Distribution of Films, May 1944. On *Target for Tonight* in the United States, see Cull, *Selling War*, 137; Short, 'RAF Bomber Command's "Target for Tonight"', 198–9. On positive reviews in e.g. Australia see *Evening Post*, 3 December 1941; *Western Mail*, 26 February 1942; *The Age*, 20 December 1941; *Sydney Morning Herald*, 13 October 1941.
76 *Kinematograph Weekly*, 8 January 1942, 40.
77 Chapman, *British at War*, 129, 286–7.
78 'It dramatizes reality' (*Monthly Film Bulletin*, 31 August 1941); 'You're going to be able to see for yourself exactly what happens when a bomber squadron raids Germany' (*Daily Herald*, 24 July 1941); 'It is proof of the power of truth that the result is more exciting than the most lavish Hollywood spectacular' (*Daily Telegraph*, 24 July 1941); 'the screen's best piece of factual reporting' (*Spectator*, 1 August 1941).

79 Watt, *Don't Look at the Camera*, 152. Chapman, *New History of British Documentary*, 108; Morgan, *Red Roses Every Night*, 70; see also TNA, CAB 102/848, A People at War: Thoughts on Mood on the Home Front, f. 5.
80 TNA, AIR 14/1451, Minute 14, 23 January 1941; Guy Hodgson, 'All in This Together? Manchester and its Newspapers in the Aftermath of the Christmas Blitz 1940', in *World War II & the Media: A Collection of Essays*, ed. Christopher Hart, Guy Hodgson and Simon Gwyn Roberts (Chester: University of Chester, 2014), 112.
81 TNA, AIR 41/40, The R.A.F. Bombing Offensive against Germany, Volume III, Area Bombing and the Makeshift Force, June 1941–February 1942, ff. 41–2; see also Charles K. Webster and Noble Frankland, *The Strategic Air Offensive against Germany, 1939–1945*, vol. 4 (London: HMSO, 1961), 205–13.
82 See e.g. the Air Ministry's pamphlet, *Bomber Command: The Air Ministry Account of the Bomber Command's Offensive against the Axis* (London: HMSO, 1941), which sold 1,360,000 copies. TNA, AIR 41/9, Propaganda and Publicity, f. 456
83 TNA, AIR 41/40, The R.A.F. Bombing Offensive against Germany, Volume III, Area Bombing and the Makeshift Force, June 1941–February 1942, f. 65.
84 *Daily Express*, 14 November 1941.
85 On Balcon and the Air Ministry, see *Kinematograph Weekly*, 7 November 1940, 7. On Balcon and the MoI, see *Evening News*, 11 December 1940. The films division of the MoI, for its part, was unhappy with a clumsy attempt by Balcon to take the GPO Film Unit out of MoI hands. See Chapman, *British at War*, 75–6; Chapman, *New History of British Documentary*, 100.
86 On Balcon turning to the MEW, see TNA, INF 1/249, Home Planning committee minutes, 16 December 1940. On the MEW being keen on the project see TNA, T 162/1002, Minister of Economic Warfare to Chancellor of the Exchequer, 19 March 1941.
87 TNA, T 162/1002, M3186/41, Somervell to Barlow, 26 February 1941.
88 Ibid., Bamford to Barlow, 7 April 1941. On the controversy surrounding the MoI and *49th Parallel* (Ortus/GFD, 1941) see Chapman, *British at War*, 72.
89 TNA, T 162/1002, Bamford to Barlow, 9 April 1941.
90 *Kinematograph Weekly*, 12 June 1941, 36. On *Siege* as the working title of *The Big Blockade* see *Kinematograph Weekly*, 31 July 1941, 17.
91 TNA, AIR 2/6354, Encl. 21A, PR1 Air Ministry, Documentary and Feature Film Position, 20 September 1941, f. 2; *Kinematograph Weekly*, 31 July 1941, 17; Chaz Bowyer, *Bomber Barons* (London: Kimber, 1983), 96; Robert Sellers, *The Secret Life of Ealing Studios: Britain's Favourite Studio* (London: Aurum, 2015), 179.
92 *Kinematograph Weekly*, 3 July 1941, 21.
93 On the friction between Frend and Crichton on *The Lion Has Wings* see Crichton in *An Autobiography of British Cinema: By the Actors and Filmmakers Who Made It*, ed. Brian McFarlane (London: Methuen, 1997), 152. On shooting taking place in the autumn see *Picturegoer*, 20 September 1941.
94 In the course of a seventy-four-minute film, over seventeen minutes were devoted to the RAF. *The Big Blockade* as a whole, the biographer of its associate producer rightly suggests, is 'a complex and sometimes awkward combination of documentary, comedy and didactic discourse'. Ian Aitken, *Alberto Cavalcanti: Realism, Surrealism and National Cinemas* (Trowbridge: Flicks, 2000), 106.
95 The commentator does not give last names to these four characters, who – rather implausibly – never address each other by name, rank or position over the intercom. The cast list in studio publicity for *The Lion Has Wings* gives the four actors' names

under the heading 'Royal Air Force' with no character names attached, last or first. BFI Library, *The Big Blockade* pressbook.
96 There are some continuity problems in *The Big Blockade*, including '1052 Squadron' on the operations board at base instead of – as the commentator has stated is the case – '1020 Squadron' – and indications that T-for-Tommy actually attacks an ersatz rubber factory rather than a powerhouse. See Mark Ashley, *Flying Film Stars: The Directory of Aircraft in British World War Two Films* (Walton-on-Thames: Red Kite, 2014), 47.
97 On how the British are portrayed in *The Big Blockade* see Charles Barr, *Ealing Studios: A Movie Book*, 3rd edn. (Berkeley: University of California Press, 1998), 27.
98 The only concession to the geographical reach of Bomber Command comes during a briefing scene in which a Canadian NCO asks a question.
99 See John Mills, *Up in the Clouds, Gentlemen Please* (New Haven, CT: Ticknor and Fields, 1981), 123.
100 In one scene in which Leslie Banks briefs RAF personnel on their part in the waging of economic warfare, however, an RAF officer speaks in a refined tones somewhat reminiscent of 'Speedy' Powell in *Target for Tonight* or even Anthony Bushell in *The Lion Has Wings*.
101 As one film scholar rightly observed, the action sequences in *The Big Blockade* 'pay little regard to authenticity'. Indeed, 'the protracted treatment of a bombing raid on Hannover is as frivolous as *The Lion Has Wings*'. Robert Murphy, *British Cinema and the Second World War* (London: Continuum, 2000), 129.
102 BFI Library, *The Big Blockade*, exhibitor's campaign book, cover.
103 Jeremy Havardi, *Projecting Britain at War: The National Character in British World War II Films* (Jefferson, NC: McFarland, 2014), 85.
104 Leslie Halliwell, *Seats in All Parts: Half a Lifetime at the Movies* (London: Granada, 1985), 105.
105 *New Statesman*, 17 January 1942, 40; *Daily Telegraph*, 19 January 1942; see also *Daily Herald*, 17 January 1942; *The Age*, 7 December 1942; *Sydney Morning Herald*, 21 December 1942; *Picturegoer*, 21 March 1942.
106 *Spectator*, 16 January 1942, 58; *The Times*, 14 January 1942; see also e.g. *The Listener*, 22 January 1942, 109; *Monthly Film Bulletin*, 28 February 1942, 13; *Documentary News Letter*, May 1942, 67.
107 See Michael Balcon, *Michael Balcon Presents ... A Lifetime in Films* (London: Hutchinson, 1969), 136; William Norton Mendlicott, *The Economic Blockade*, vol. 2 (London: HMSO, 1959), 52. On the lack of impact at the box office of *The Big Blockade* see its absence from the list of successes in *Kinematograph Weekly*, 14 January 1943, 47.
108 Powell, *Life in Movies*, 384.
109 Ibid., 388. On the original title see also *Kinematograph Weekly*, 3 July 1941, 5.
110 See TNA, AIR 2/6354, Encl. 21A, PR1 Air Ministry, Documentary and Feature Film Position, 20 September 1941, f. 1; *Kinematograph Weekly*, 4 September 1941, 15; Powell, *Life in Movies*, 388–91.
111 On help from 115 Squadron see RAFM, X006-254/001, John Alfred Chamberlain diary, 22–23 September 1941; Ralph Edwards, *In the Thick of It: Autobiography of a Bomber Pilot* (Upton: Images, 1994), 61.
112 Jill Bennett, *Godfrey: A Special Time Remembered* (London: Hodder and Stoughton, 1983), 72.

113 'Bad luck, Catford' (*Target for Tonight*), 'Bad luck, old man' (*One of Our Aircraft Is Missing*).
114 This may not have been intentional, given the necessary technical language in play and Michael Powell's own rather refined accent. Powell himself stated that he played the role simply because it was cheaper. He also claimed that *One of Our Aircraft Is Missing* was the first film to deal with a bombing raid, which suggests that he had not in fact seen *Target for Tonight*. Kevin Gough-Yates, *Michael Powell in Collaboration with Emeric Pressburger* (London: Faber and Faber, 1971), 7, 9.
115 Falconer, *RAF Bomber Command in Fact, Film and Fiction*, 86. (This was not in fact the case.)
116 It was decided that the sputtering engine aboard B-for-Bertie would pick up again, allowing the empty plane – as shown in the opening minutes of the film before an extended flashback begins – to go on flying on autopilot until it crashes into an electrical pylon. See Powell, *Life in Movies*, 396.
117 On the conclusion of the film see Andrew Moor, *Powell & Pressburger: A Cinema of Magic Spaces* (London: I.B. Tauris, 2005), 51. The background footage at this juncture is of Stirlings from 7 Squadron based at RAF Oakington (see Tom Docherty, *No. 7 Bomber Squadron RAF in World War II* [Barnsley: Pen and Sword Aviation, 2007]), but the tight shot of the crew in front of an example of the bomber and of a take-off may have been filmed once more courtesy of 149 Squadron, which starting in September 1941 was reequipped with Stirlings (see Johnston and Carter, *Strong by Night*, 40).
118 Powell, *Life in Movies*, 392. Wilson was killed in action at the end of May 1940. See John Marlowe, *Late Victorian: The Life of Sir Arnold Talbot Wilson* (London: Cressett, 1967). On Tearle and the role see *Picturegoer*, 27 December 1941, 4.
119 As a major film critic recalled shortly after the war: 'the democratic feeling of community, of men with equal rights and responsibilities, is present.' Dilys Powell, *Films since 1939* (London: Longmans Green, 1947), 22.
120 Once on the ground in Holland as evaders, the hierarchy changes as Sir George takes charge. See Rattigan, *This Is England*, 133–4. The 'book of the film', written by Powell, is a narrative from the perspective of Corbett. Michael Powell, *One of Our Aircraft Is Missing* (London: HMSO, 1942); see also *Picturegoer*, 25 July 1942, 14.
121 Powell, *Life in Movies*, 39.
122 Ibid.
123 *Kinematograph Weekly*, 26 March 1942, 15.
124 *News Chronicle*, 22 April 1942; *Daily Mirror*, 22 April 1942; *The Times*, 22 April 1942; *Manchester Guardian*, 28 April 1942; see also e.g. *Daily Express*, 25 April 1942.
125 *New Statesman*, 2 May 1942, 288. See also e.g. *Picturegoer*, 25 July 1943; *Observer*, 26 April 1942; *Sunday Pictorial*, 26 April 1942; *Monthly Film Bulletin*, 30 April 1942; *Sight and Sound*, Summer 1942, 18. The film also went down very well in Australia (see *Sydney Morning Herald*, 2 August 1943), Canada (see *Globe and Mail*, 9 December 1942; *Toronto Star*, 18 December 1942) and New Zealand (see *Bay of Plenty Beacon*, 22 October 1943). The *New York Times* critic also responded positively (*New York Times*, 8 November 1942); see also Charles Drazin, 'The Distribution of Powell and Pressburger's Films in the United States', *Historical Journal of Film, Radio and Television* 33 (2013), 60. It was also shown to the prime minister, though his reaction in not recorded. Charles Barr, '"Much Pleasure and Relaxation in These Hard Times": Churchill and Cinema in the Second World War', *Historical Journal of Film, Radio and Television* 31 (2011), 577.

126 *Monthly Film Bulletin*, 14 January 1943, 46–7; see also Poole, 'Wartime Cinema Attendance', 22.
127 Mostly dealing with fighter pilots rather than bomber pilots, these Hollywood pictures included *A Yank in the R.A.F.* (Twentieth Century-Fox, 1941), *International Squadron* (Warner Brothers, 1941) and *Eagle Squadron* (Universal, 1942). See Mark Glancy, *When Hollywood Loved Britain: The Hollywood 'British' Film, 1939–45* (Manchester: Manchester University Press, 1999), 117–27.
128 See BFI Library, *Flying Fortress* press material, 'Building Bombers for New Warner Film', 17 October 1941.
129 TNA, AIR 28/625, Polebrook ORB, 26 September 1941, 11 October 1941; AIR 2/6354, Encl. 21A, PR1 Air Ministry, Documentary and Feature Film Position, 20 September 1941, f. 3.
130 The episode in which Richard Greene is shown crawling along the wing to put out the fire was doubtless based on an actual event in July 1941 when a New Zealand sergeant pilot, James Allen Ward, performed this heroic feat on a Wellington.
131 See BFI Library, *Flying Fortress* press release.
132 Warner Brothers' own *International Squadron* (1941) had generated over $1.5 million in revenue. Glancy, *When Hollywood Loved Britain*, 121. On the cost of *Flying Fortress* see *Daily Telegraph*, 15 June 1942.
133 *Daily Telegraph*, 15 June 1942; see also e.g. *Daily Express*, 13 June 1942; *Monthly Film Bulletin*, 30 June 1942, 69.
134 *Daily Telegraph*, 15 June 1942; see e.g. *The Times*, 15 June 1942; *Sunday Times*, 14 June 1942; *Observer*, 14 June 1942.
135 *New York Times*, 19 December 1942.
136 See *Kinematograph Weekly*, 14 January 1943, 47; *Variety*, 6 January 1943, 13.
137 Ashley, *Flying Film Stars*, 56.
138 Leading film critic Bosley Crowther thought that *Desperate Journey* lifted elements directly from *Target for Tonight*. See *New York Times*, 8 November 1942.
139 *Los Angeles Times*, 4 April 1942; Powell, *Life in Movies*, 385.
140 James H. Farmer, *Celluloid Wings: The Impact of the Movies on Aviation* (Blue Ridge Summit, PA: Tab, 1984), 170. Though the Air Ministry in London was not involved, the picture did have a technical advisor from the RCAF, Squadron Leader O. Cathcart-Jones. Though the B-17 was a mockup, the RAF aircraft liberated at the end of the film was a real Lockheed Hudson. Simon D. Beck, *Aircraft-Spotter's Film and Television Companion* (Jefferson, NC: McFarland), 74.
141 On the importance of Hollywood escapism to British wartime audiences see Mark Glancy, *Hollywood and the Americanization of Britain: From the 1920s to the Present* (London: I.B. Tauris, 2014), 144–5. For a positive review of *Desperate Journey* as exciting entertainment, see e.g. *Globe and Mail*, 29 October 1942. Bosley Crowther (*New York Times*, 26 September 1942), though, was not the only film critic to argue that *Desperate Journey* was greatly inferior to *One of Our Aircraft Is Missing*: see Roly Young in *Globe and Mail*, 9 December 1942.
142 *Variety*, 6 January 1943, 58.
143 *Kinematograph Weekly*, 13 January 1943, 532; see also Poole, 'Wartime Cinema Attendance', 24.
144 See Air Ministry, *Bomber Command Continues: The Air Ministry Account of the Rising Offensive against Germany, July 1941–June 1942* (London: HMSO, 1942), 51–2. Over half a million copies were sold. TNA, AIR 41/9, Propaganda and Publicity, f. 46.

145 *The Times*, 9 November 1943, 24 June 1944; see also e.g. headlines repeated in TNA, AIR 2/7852, AUS(G) to ACAS(G), 29 October 1943. On implicit public understanding of what was being done by Bomber Command see Mark Connelly, 'The British People, the Press and the Strategic Air Campaign against Germany, 1939–45', *Contemporary British History* 16, 2 (2002), 39–58; Andrew Knapp, 'The Allied Bombing Offensive in the British Media, 1942–45', in *Liberal Democracies at War: Conflict and Representation*, ed. Andrew Knapp and Hilary Footitt (London: Bloomsbury, 2013), 39–66. The same held true in the Dominions: see e.g. Laurie Peloquin, 'A Conspiracy of Silence? The Popular Press and the Strategic Bombing Campaign in Europe', *Canadian Military History* 3, 2 (1994), 22–30.

146 On the popularity of *Thunder Birds* (Twentieth Century-Fox, 1942) on both sides of the Atlantic see *Variety*, 6 January 1943, 58; *Kinematograph Weekly*, 13 January 1944, 53. On RAF trainee extras used in *Thunder Birds* see Campbell Muirhead, *Diary of a Bomber Aimer: Training in America and Flying with 12 Squadron in WWII*, ed. Philip Swan (Barnsley: Pen and Sword Aviation, 2009), 8, 125 and Sean Feast, *Thunder Bird in Bomber Command: The Wartime Letters and Story of Lionel Anderson, the Man Who Inspired a Legend* (Hitchin: Fighting High, 2015), 35–6. Another Hollywood film about aircrew training released some months earlier, *Captains of the Clouds* (Warners, 1942), filmed at air bases in Canada with the support of the RCAF (see Ted Barris, *Behind the Glory* [Toronto: Macmillan, 1992], 141–58) and starring Jimmy Cagney, had also been popular (see *Kinematograph Weekly*, 14 January 1943, 47) but did not explicitly stress that the young airmen being trained were destined for Bomber Command.

147 TNA, INF 6/546, script, 'The Biter Bit'; see Chapman, *British at War*, 111; Clive Coultass, *Images for Battle: British Film and the Second World War, 1939–1945* (Newark, NJ: University of Delaware Press, 1989), 144–5. See also *The Times*, 29 May 1943, 22 September 1943; IWM, 27255/8, Douglas Fry.

148 TNA, AIR 2/7852, C-in-C Bomber Command to Air Ministry, 25 October 1943. Harris, it should be stressed, was quite keen on publicity for what Bomber Command was doing, including through film. See e.g. RAFM, Harris Papers, H27, Balfour to Harris, 9 October 1942; Harris to Jones, 15 October 1945.

149 TNA, AIR 2/7852, Street to Harris, 15 December 1943.

150 *Desperate Journey* appeared in British cinemas in December 1942.

151 See *Kinematograph Weekly*, 13 January 1944, 52.

152 The overall fatality rate for bomber aircrew was 44 per cent. See Denis Richards, *The Hardest Victory: RAF Bomber Command in the Second World War* (New York: Norton, 1995), 305. On *Millions Like Us* see Bruce Babington, *Launder and Gilliat* (Manchester: Manchester University Press, 2002), 50–65.

153 TNA, INF 6/611, script, 'There's A Future in It'. Bates adapted the script from his short story. The title was changed for the film from the original 'There's No Future in It', presumably because it was feared that audiences would not grasp the sardonic way in which aircrew used the original to describe their job. Two years later, with the war all but won, Terence Rattigan was able to insert the phrase into *The Way to the Stars* through the character Peter Penrose.

154 H. E. Bates, *The World in Ripeness: An Autobiography, Volume Three* (London: Michael Joseph, 1972), 14–24.

155 Paris, *From the Wright Brothers to Top Gun*, 149; see *Monthly Film Bulletin*, 1 January 1944, 138; Coultass, *Images for Battle*, 145–6; see also, on *There's A Future in It*, Barry Morse with Robert E. Wood and Anthony Wynn, *Pulling Faces, Making Noise: A Life*

on Stage, Screen, & Radio (Bloomington, IN: iUniverse, 2004), 104; Christina Rice, *Ann Dvorak: Hollywood's Forgotten Rebel* (Lexington: University Press of Kentucky, 2013), 21. For positive critical reaction, see e.g. *Spectator*, 20 January 1944, 11.

156 The RAF aircraft in *The Way to the Stars*, photographed on the ground, taking off and landing, and in the sky only from a ground-based perspective, were mainly Bristol Blenheims (1940) and Douglas Bostons (1942). In *Millions Like Us* there are only model shots of four-engine bombers overhead at night and – despite Blake supposedly being on Stirlings and being shown at once point boarding one – the take-off of a Lancaster. See Ashley, *Flying Film Stars*, 77–8, 85–8. In view of the absence of aerial photography and the two films' major themes, there is no depiction or obvious discussion of targets; though a comment early in *The Way to the Stars* hints at problems in sinking enemy invasion barges in 1940 and one in *Millions Like Us* indirectly indicates that Bomber Command is hitting enemy aircraft factories in 1943.

157 See Martin Francis, *The Flyer: British Culture and the Royal Air Force, 1939–1945* (Oxford: Oxford University Press, 2008), 48; Rattigan, *This Is England*, 117–27. Bill Owen was quite aware that he was the token lower-class type among the flyers in *The Way to the Stars*. See Owen in McFarlane, *Autobiography of British Film*, 447. See also the 'Dusty' Miller part in Terence Rattigan, *Flare Path* (London: Nick Hern, 2011).

158 Geoffrey Wansell, *Terence Rattigan* (London: Fourth Estate, 1995), 125; see Rattigan, *Flare Path*, 74. On *The Way to the Stars* see Anthony Aldgate and Jeffrey Richards, *Britain Can Take It: The British Cinema in the Second World War* (London: I.B. Tauris, 2007), chapter 12; see also Mills, *Up in the Clouds*, 193; Michael Redgrave, *In My Mind's Eye: An Autobiography* (London: Weidenfeld and Nicolson, 1983), 171–2.

159 *Toronto Daily Star*, 5 February 1944; see also Linda Greene Bennett, *My Father's Voice: The Biography of Lorne Greene* (New York: iUniverse, 2004), 26–8.

160 See *Auckland Star*, 21 November 1945.

161 'Eric' Francis Witting (RNZAF pilot); William Edwin 'Ted' Anderson (RNZAF navigator); Glen Osmond Marshall (RNZAF wireless operator); Reg Gunn (RAF flight engineer); William Bryce 'Jerry' Campbell (RCAF mid-upper gunner); Joseph William Collins (RNZAF rear gunner). Maximum Effort – The Witting Crew, accessed 4 February 2017, https://75squadron.wordpress.com/tag/maximum-effort/.

162 See *Press* [Christchurch], 16 June 1945; *Auckland Star*, 24 August 1945; *New Zealand Herald*, 24 August 1945. On 75 Squadron participation in *Maximum Effort* see Ron Mayhill, *Bombs on Target: A Compelling Eye-Witness Account of Bomber Command Operations* (Sparkford: Patrick Stephens, 1991), 68.

163 *Argus* [Melbourne], 23 May 1945. See Australian War Memorial, FO1372, RAAF over Europe, accessed 27 January 2018, https://www.awm.gov.au/collection/C188909.

164 TNA, INF 6/783, script, 'Target Germany'. For one of the few scholarly references to *Target Germany* see Paris, *From the Wright Brothers to* Top Gun, 149.

165 On the production timeline of *Journey Together* (Production 26) see TNA, AIR 29/481, ORB, RAF Film Production Unit, 1944–5.

166 See David Tomlinson in *High Flyers: Reminiscences to Celebrate the 75th Anniversary of the Royal Air Force*, ed. Michael Fopp (London: Greenhill/RAFM, 1993), 213; David Tomlinson, *Luckier Than Most* (London: John Curtis, 1990), 81–2.

167 On the RAFFPU see IWM, File B6/1, History of the Royal Air Force Film Production Unit, [1945]; Keith Buckman, 'The Royal Air Force Film Production Unit, 1941–45', *Historical Journal of Film, Radio and Television* 17 (1997), 219–44.

168 BFI Library, *Journey Together* publicity material, 'The Technical Talent Is Hero', 1.
169 Ibid.
170 BFI Library, *Journey Together* publicity material, "JOURNEY TOGETHER": THE PRINCIPAL PLAYERS; see also George Cole with Brian Hawkins, *The World Was My Lobster: My Autobiography* (London: Blake, 2013), 37–8; Tomlinson, *Luckier Than Most*, 86; Fletcher Markle in *Five Directors: The Golden Years of Radio*, ed. Ira Skutch (Lanham, MD: Scarecrow, 1998), 91.
171 On the length of the production see TNA, AIR 29, RAF Film Production Unit ORB, January 1944 through October 1945. A sense of the time that had passed can be gleaned from the fact that Attenborough held the rank of aircraftsman while filming but was a sergeant by the time of the film's release. See Richard Attenborough and Diana Hawkins, *Entirely Up to You, Darling* (London: Hutchinson, 2008), 88–9, 93; BFI Library, *Journey Together* publicity material, 'JOURNEY TOGETHER', 2. On the desire for authenticity see Toby Haggith, 'Journey Together', in *The Family Way: The Boulting Brothers and British Film*, ed. Alan Burton, Tim O'Sullivan and Paul Wells (Trowbridge: Flicks, 2000), 109. On locations see Falconer, *RAF Bomber Command in Fact, Film and Fiction*, 90; B. W. Martin, *War Memories of an Engineer Officer in Bomber Command* (Hailsham: J&KH, 1998), 58; BFI Library, *Journey Together* publicity material, 'JOURNEY TOGETHER': REAL-CO-OPERATION, 1. On service commitments slowing production, see ibid., 2; IWM, 9252/2, George Hambley Brown.
172 On Edward G. Robinson in *Journey Together* see *Jewish Chronicle*, 27 July 1944. Besides Robinson, the only civilians in the film were Bessie Love, who played his wife, and Ronald Squire, who played a senior RAF officer at Wilton's aircrew interview board.
173 The essential plot of *Journey Together* was recycled in Commando comic 2286, *Master Bomb-Aimer*, published in June 1989.
174 See also Eric Warman (adaptor), *A Matter of Life and Death: The Book of the Film* (London: World Film, 1946), 7. On this film see Ian Christie, *A Matter of Life and Death* (London: BFI, 2000); see also, on this scene, Patrick Dear, *Culture in Camouflage: War, Empire, and Modern British Literature* (Oxford: Oxford University Press, 2009), 83. At least one veteran thought the recreation of a stricken Lancaster was very well handled in this film. See UVic, Robert L. Masters oral history interview.
175 Arthur Harris, *Bomber Offensive* (London: Collins, 1947), 261; Henry Probert, *Bomber Harris: His Life and Times* (Toronto: Stoddart, 2001), 360. Harris, of course, vigorously defended what Bomber Command had been doing: but it is worth noting that some reviewers disagreed (see e.g. J. M. Spaight in *Spectator*, 17 January 1947, 81). Shortly afterward the first book-length critique appeared, in which it was argued that area bombing dangerously diverted resources from other needs and was morally questionable. See Gerald Dickens, *Bombing and Strategy: The Fallacy of Total War* (London: Samson Low, Marston, 1947).
176 Rattigan, *This Is England*, 173–81.
177 *Sunday Times*, 7 October 1945; *News Chronicle*, 21 September 1945; *Spectator*, 19 October 1945, 359; *Reynolds News*, 7 October 1945; *Daily Mirror*, 5 October 1945; see also e.g. *Guardian*, 8 October 1945; *New Statesman*, 20 October 1945, 228; *Auckland Star*, 9 October 1945.
178 *The Listener*, 11 October 1945, 411; *Daily Sketch*, 5 October 1945; *Daily Herald*, 2 October 1945; *Sunday Express*, 7 October 1945; see also *Kinematograph Weekly*, 4 October 1945, 26; Haggith, 'Journey Together', 120–1.

179 See *Kinematograph Weekly*, 20 December 1945, 50–1. *Journey Together* may also have suffered from lack of a conventional love interest: though Wilton has a fiancée, only a photograph is shown. The actress Shelia Sim, who married Richard Attenborough in January 1945, was due to play the role; but along with parts designated for Alistair Sim, Rex Harrison (who was in the RAF) and Miles Malleson, hers was cut. Coultass, *Images for Battle*, 191.

180 Peter Ustinov, *Dear Me* (Boston, MA: Little Brown, 1977), 203; TNA, AIR 2/5667, encl. 44A, DPR to MoI, 7 June 1945, encl. 82A, PR1 to AOC-in-C Maintenance Command, 4 December 1945.

181 See TNA, AIR 2/5667, encl. 70B.

182 Ibid., encl. 80A, Renwick to Robertson, 30 November 1945.

183 See Tomlinson, *Luckier Than Most*, 86; see also Patrick S. Waddington, *Patrick – Or, That Awful Warning* (York: Waddington, 1986), 120–30. Interestingly, in a small but significant role in *A Matter of Life and Death*, which premiered a month earlier, Attenborough had played a deceased Bomber Command sergeant-pilot.

184 Ustinov, *Dear Me*, 215; see *Kinematograph Weekly*, 18 December 1947, 13; see also e.g. *The Times*, 8 November 1946; *The Age* [Melbourne], 26 April 1948; *Sun* [Sydney], 20 October 1947.

185 See *Kinematograph Weekly*, 18 December 1947, 14; Christie, *Matter of Life and Death*, 59–62.

186 The films were *Cage of Gold* (Ealing, 1950), in which Farrar is seen briefly wearing the Pathfinder badge on his RAF tunic, though also identifying himself as a former fighter pilot, and *Frieda* (Ealing, 1947), in which the post-Dunkirk period in which Farrar's character indicates he was shot down suggests he is a bomber rather than a fighter pilot like his top-button-undone brother. The play on which the film was based is less clear on this point (see Ronald Millar, *Frieda: A New Play in Three Acts* [London: English Theatre Guild, 1947], 27). There was also *Landfall* (ABPC, 1949), based on the novel of the same name – Nevil Shute, *Landfall: A Channel Story* (London: Heinemann, 1940) – in which a patrolling RAF bomber appears to accidentally sink a British submarine rather than a U-boat. In the novel, the aircraft belongs to Bomber Command but in the film it hails from Coastal Command. On the subject matter of the films dealing with the Second World War that appeared in the latter part of the 1940s see Stephen Guy, 'After Victory: Projections of the Second World War and Its Aftermath in British Films, 1946–1950' (PhD diss., University of London, 2002).

187 During the war itself, beyond one or two voices in parliament, organized criticism of bombing on moral grounds had been tiny in scale: see Richard Overy, 'Constructing Space for Dissent in War: The Bombing Restriction Committee 1941–1945', *English Historical Review* 131 (2016), 596–622. Post-war, for indications that on the left at least, there was a growing sense that area bombing had been a matter of overkill, see e.g. Ritchie Calder review of *Bomber Offensive* in *New Statesman*, 18 January 1947, 46; Victor Gollancz, *In Darkest Germany* (London: Gollancz, 1947). Harris himself seems to have thought that what he and his men had accomplished was now being swept under the carpet. See Harris, *Bomber Offensive*, 268.

188 Harris, *Bomber Offensive*, 26. On targeting morale see ibid., 74–9.

189 On the war-film boom of the 1950s, see e.g. Havardi, *Projecting Britain at War*, 128–57. On claims of war-film saturation of the British market in the course of the war, see e.g. Aubrey Flannigan, 'British Showmen Protest Too Many War Films', *Motion Picture Herald*, 3 July 1943.

Figure 2.1 Richard Todd in *The Dam Busters* (ABPC, 1955).

Chapter 2

LEADERS: THE 1950s

After the cessation of hostilities both the Ministry of Information and its films division, along with the Royal Air Force (RAF) film production unit, were wound up – and with them official efforts to promote the idea of a people's war.[1] Though the Air Ministry continued to be interested in cultivating a positive screen image for prestige or recruiting purposes, and indeed decided on terms concerning assistance if requested, it was now entirely up to the film executives of Wardour Street to decide if a feature film that would require such help possessed commercial potential.[2]

At the beginning of the new decade there certainly seemed no reason to hesitate on the grounds of significance, what with Churchill himself asserting in print that Bomber Command had 'made a decisive contribution to victory'.[3] Within the film industry, moreover, with the backlog of war pictures produced late in the conflict or reissued during the second half of the 1940s having run their course, the auspices were increasingly positive.[4] The Associated British Picture Corporation (ABPC) film *Landfall*, which chronicled the trials and tribulations of a Coastal Command pilot using period aircraft and locations provided by the RAF and was based on a wartime novel by Nevil Shute, had in the last months of 1949 done reasonably well at the British box office; and, amid other signs that films about the exploits of the wartime services would likely generate a good return on investment in the course of 1950-1, by the following year no less than three features involving the RAF at war were under development, with a further quartet appearing in the mid-1950s.[5]

The idea for the first Bomber Command feature of the new decade came from a man best known in the post-war film world for his musical composition skills. John Wooldridge had written the scores for over half a dozen features by the early Fifties; but during the war he had flown a large number of bombing sorties and ended up leading his own squadron.[6] Between composing scores, he had written a fictional story based on his experiences with 106 Squadron in the middle war years. Maxwell Setton and Aubrey Baring, co-producers for Mayflower Films, were on the lookout for plots that could be transformed into adventure features and thought the story could be refashioned into a screenplay with the help of their regular script doctor, Robert Westerly, with Wooldridge providing the score.[7] It was clear to all involved, though, that within a projected budget of £136,244 a film about the bomber boys would require a lot of technical support from the RAF.[8] In the course of 1951 the Air Ministry had reached an agreement to provide what was needed, and by the spring of the following year four Lancasters had been taken out of storage and flown to a bomber station, RAF Upwood, for exterior filming purposes, while most interior shooting took place at Shepperton Studios under the overall direction of documentarist Philip Leacock in the summer of 1952.[9]

The resulting film, *Appointment in London*, follows the individual fortunes of a number of bomber pilots in the fictional '188 Squadron' over the course of a month in the summer of 1943. The main focus is on the character played by Dirk Bogarde, Wing Commander Tim Mason, introduced on his return from a special three-plane night bombing mission to a target at 'Meltzheim'. Having flown the equivalent of almost three tours of duty, Mason is approaching both his physical and emotional limits; but, as he tells the concerned group medical officer played by Walter Fitzgerald, he is determined to complete his ninetieth raid before going off operations. He is able to continue leading the squadron in the face of mounting aerial adversity in part due to a sympathetic Women's Royal Naval Service intelligence officer, Eve Canyon, played by Dinah Sheridan, with whom he develops a romantic relationship despite the competing attentions of a suave American liaison officer, Major 'Mac' Baker, played by William Sylvester.[10]

The story also involves the two squadron pilots who had accompanied Mason on the special mission, Australian flight lieutenant Bill Brown, played by Bill Kerr, and English pilot officer Peter 'The Brat' Greeno, played by Bryan Forbes. The former is interested only in doing his job, tracking down English ancestors while on leave, and raising sheep back home after the war. The latter, however, appears distracted between operations and is eventually killed. Mason learns that the young pilot has been sending telegrams in code to a girlfriend and orders him to stop; but he only discovers that Greeno was in fact married to this young woman when he meets the grieving and somewhat accusatory widow, Pam, played by Anne Leon. This only adds to his psychological burdens, but Mason presses on in attempting to convince the squadron it is not jinxed after heavy losses through intensive training and a riotous mess party.[11]

The last quarter of the film follows preparations for, and the execution of, a mass raid on a new unnamed factory town where enemy secret weapons are being manufactured. At the last moment the station commander, played by Ian Hunter, pulls Mason from the order of battle at the insistence of Bomber Command HQ because of the recent loss of another veteran wingco. However, as Brown admits to being shaken after his rear gunner is crushed to death by a 4,000-pound bomb falling out of the bomb bay in an accident just before take-off, Mason decides to disobey orders and fly with him as moral support on what will be his ninetieth and final operation, with Mac sitting in for the rear gunner despite a ban on the American flying further combat missions with the RAF. After the bomb run amid flak, flares and an abortive fighter attack, Mason takes on an active role when the officer orchestrating the attack over the radio is shot down along with his deputy, causing the wingco to assume the role of master bomber and offer targeting instructions to the rest of the force. The raid is a success, with Mason returning home safely to be reunited with Eve and paying for his transgression merely with a posting to the Far East. The film ends with the event referred to in the title as Tim Mason, Bill Brown and Pam Greeno take a taxi together to Buckingham Palace where they will receive the medals awarded for the special mission featured at the start of the picture.

While it mirrored in certain respects *Twelve O'Clock High*, the Hollywood feature released a few years earlier which dealt with the trials and tribulations of a B-17 bomb group commander in the Eighth Air Force, *Appointment in London* marked an important milestone in the cinematic representation of Bomber Command through its focus on the psychological stresses of operational command, the distressing effect on loved ones and the high probability of a violent end on active service.[12] The audience not only sees the damage caused to the wing commander's aircraft in the initial special mission but also later witnesses, along with him, a catastrophic crash-landing by a crippled Lancaster, and at the climax of the film hear the death throes of the master bomber. In the interim, the number of times Mason has to rub out chalked-in names, including that of Peter Greeno, from the squadron operations board shows that the group medical officer was not wrong in warning him early on that 'only four crews in ten' were completing their tours across Bomber Command.[13]

Appointment in London also broke ground in other ways. In the climactic raid, an enemy operations room is depicted, with actors Carl Jaffe, Carl Duering and Wolf Frees all speaking German rather than accented English.[14] Commonwealth aircrew had been shown in earlier Bomber Command films, but the Wooldridge script was unique in depicting, albeit only briefly, a black commissioned pilot from the West Indies. This was also the first film in which someone from the Dominions, in this case Bill Kerr of Australia, played a major rather than supporting-cast role.[15] As might be expected given who was behind it, the screenplay contained plenty of authentic touches, ranging from the footprints-on-the-ceiling escapade during a mess party to the tendency of aircrew to become superstitious.[16]

It is important to note that, in class terms, *Appointment in London*, in line with most other British war films of this decade, is more akin to *The Way to the Stars* than to *Journey Together*.[17] There are occasional hints that The Brat is lower middle class in origin, but none of the major characters, all commissioned officers, sports a Celtic or English regional accent.[18] On the bomber station there are only a trio of working-class speaking parts, none of them commissioned officers, all tertiary in nature, and two out of three groundlings rather than aircrew.[19] The social gulf is illustrated when Tim Mason – perfectly at ease in Eve Canyon's large and well-appointed Hampstead flat in another scene – finds himself chatting in a hanger with Greeno's aircraftsman fitter from Sheffield, played by Sam Kydd, a conversation in which both men, widely separated by both rank and class, are clearly uncomfortable.[20]

As to the purpose and nature of strategic bombing, *Appointment in London* is ambiguous. On the one hand, the three-plane special raid with which the film opens is clearly a precision attack on a special target, while the climactic mass attack towards the end of the film is directed at a secret weapons manufacturing complex.[21] A good deal of effort is put into striking at the aiming point, with bombs briefly shown exploding in a railyard in the manner of *Target for Tonight*.²² On the other hand, Mason says of the first raid that 'we wrecked the place', which suggests a certain lack of discrimination, and of the second that it is 'a straightforward saturation attack' by over six hundred bombers aiming to wipe out an entire new industrial town. The extensively used wartime footage shot from around eighteen thousand feet of street after street on fire below also suggests area bombing.²³

Reviewing the completed film for exhibitors in February 1953, Josh Billings argued that *Appointment in London*, distributed by British Lion, with its aerial sequences, fine acting and human-interest elements, was 'bound to make a firm impression on all classes'.²⁴ Not everyone agreed, some in the press finding it boring and too much akin to the Bomber Command films of the previous decade.²⁵ There were, however, many enthusiastic verdicts – 'magnificent' (*Daily Mail*), 'beautiful' (*Daily Sketch*), 'excellent' (*Evening News*), 'a war-picture which cannot fail to move and enthrall you' (*Sunday Graphic*) – and *Appointment in London* was a winner at the British box office against some pretty stiff competition.²⁶ Reviews overseas tended to be more respectful than enthusiastic, however; and, retitled *Raiders in the Sky*, the film did not, despite the producers' hopes, do well in the United States.²⁷ Nonetheless, *Appointment in London* eventually enjoyed a significant afterlife on television.²⁸

By this point, a major effort by the Air Ministry to explain the wartime role of the RAF to the general public was about to appear in print. A couple of years after the war Denis Richards and Hilary St. George Saunders had been commissioned to write a three-volume chronological account of RAF wartime operations to be published under official auspices. Richards had already composed a number of in-house narratives for the Air Historical Branch, and Saunders – who died before the work was complete – had written an account of the rise of pre-war British air power.²⁹ First published in 1953–4 and then reprinted several times in the latter 1950s and on into the 1960s, the *Royal Air Force, 1939–1945* met with a generally positive critical response.³⁰

Since the work was comprehensive in nature, chapters on the activities of Bomber Command appeared in all three volumes. In the first, *The Fight at Odds*, the problems of the early war years were admitted to but justified in terms of lessons learned and indirect positive effects. Thus the bombing of Germany in 1940–1 did not achieve what it was supposed to but remained the only means of striking directly at Germany and 'had tied down more than a million Germans to civil and anti-aircraft defence'.³¹ As to the undermining of enemy morale and the beginnings of area bombing in the summer of 1941, this was inevitable because experience had demonstrated the futility of attacks on more specific targets given the state of night navigation and bomb aiming at the time. In any event, the focus on enemy morale did not mean 'the deliberate slaughter of civilian populations' but rather 'the destruction of homes, factories, and all the amenities of life in the great industrial cities'.³² It was evidence of the latter, rather more than civilian casualty figures, which was most often highlighted in the second volume, *The Fight Avails*, now that area bombing under the direction of Arthur Harris had become 'the standard basis of our policy'.³³

Conversely, in the final volume, *The Fight Is Won*, which among other things covered the firestorm raids on Hamburg and Dresden, the effects on the people below were rendered more graphically, and the inability of Bomber Command to break German morale despite the massive destruction caused by area bombing accepted.[34] The concluding chapter, however, directly defended Bomber Command against charges (apparently in general public circulation by this point) that the resources devoted to the strategic bombing campaign had been in no way commensurate with the results achieved. Context was everything, since the heavy bombers 'were for a long time then only means we possessed of striking directly at the enemy and that for an equally long time the main weight of attack was of necessity confined to night operations against industrial areas'.[35] The offensive had tied down over two million enemy personnel on anti-aircraft duties, degraded German production increases through physical destruction on a massive scale and, admittedly in a way impossible to quantify, generated 'the decrease in each individual workman's capacity brought about by the lowering of his standards of life and the heightening of his nervous tension'.[36] Beyond that, the *Luftwaffe* had been forced to concentrate its efforts on home defence, the introduction of German secret weapons had been delayed and, 'most importantly of all', once circumstances allowed oil production facilities and transportation nodes to be restored to the target list in 1944–5, 'bombing destroyed the German oil industry and paralysed all forms of transport'.[37]

The Air Ministry also had been working through the comparatively new medium of television in the first half of the decade on publicizing wartime RAF achievements, including those of Bomber Command. Negotiations with the British Broadcasting Corporation (BBC) went smoothly, with both sides keen to see produced a British answer to the influential American multipart television documentary, *Victory at Sea*. The result was *War in the Air*, the fifteen episodes of which, once completed, appeared each week on televisions across the UK between 8 November 1954 and 14 February 1955, with between 16 and 21 per cent of the adult population with a TV set tuning in each week.[38]

Like the three-volume history, the fifteen-part BBC documentary, directed by Philip Dorté and written by John Elliot, sought to be as comprehensive as possible. Of necessity, therefore, several episodes of *War in the Air* dealt at some length with both the tribulations and triumphs of Bomber Command.

The fourth instalment, *Maximum Effort*, began with footage from *Target for Tonight*; but in place of the upbeat original script there was narration explaining the multiple problems faced by bomber crews in the early war years: 'even if they find the target, who knows if they'll hit it.' By the spring of 1942, though, the situation has changed, with Bomber Command gaining accuracy and strength through the development of a navigation aid (Gee) and the deployment of four-engine heavy bombers. With Harris in command, the plan is 'to saturate' the 'industrial centres' of western Germany. The first thousand-bomber raid on Cologne is recreated through the use of wartime footage and a rather stiff re-enactment set at Bomber Command headquarters in which Robert Saundby reprises his role as senior staff officer to the C-in-C.[39] That the effect of this and other such raids was psychological – 'war has come home to the Germans' – as well as physical – 'the ruin of their cities' – is suggested by the concluding footage of homeless refugees, collapsed buildings and rubble-strewn streets.

The eighth episode, *Round the Clock*, opened with a quote from the general directive Harris had been given in early 1943: 'Your primary object will be the progressive destruction and dislocation of the German military and economic system.'[40] That meant – the editor switching to the filmed wartime remarks Harris had made on the subject of bombing – that the Reich was now going to 'reap the whirlwind'. There were elements in the episode that suggested what was being done even in 1943–4 was not entirely indiscriminate in nature, the introduction of airborne ground-search radar (H2S) meaning that an aircraft 'can see a town anywhere in Europe' and that another, more precise radio navigational device (Oboe) meant that bombs could be 'plotted onto smaller targets' by Pathfinder aircraft.[41] Nevertheless, the overall emphasis on general ruination is underlined by references to the devastating Hamburg raids of August 1943, in which both a decline in factory production and the death of forty thousand inhabitants are said to be undermining the German war effort. The famous dams raid is recreated, but the precision involved is shown only as a means to call forth a rolling tide of destruction. The narrator, echoing the biblical language used by Harris, concluded that 'flood has been added to fire'. The battle in the skies over Germany, though, continues for Bomber Command.[42]

The twelfth film, titled *The Cold Dawn*, brought the story down to the last months of the war in Europe. 'Our bombardment goes on', the narrator intones, 'deeper and deeper into Germany, until the enemy can hardly work, or move [thanks to attacks on oil and transportation], or fight'. It had been a long, hard slog for the crews involved, many of whom had lost their lives; but the strategic bombing campaign in the end produced decisive results. 'For the past five years the wreckage of our planes has littered the broad fields of the Reich; but the airmen who have died have destroyed the enemy's last hope. From Kiel to Stuttgart, from Aachen to Berlin, no part of Germany has escaped our onslaught. The war machine that was built to conquer the world has been bombed to ruins.' Bomber Command, in short, had proved itself a key component of victory over Nazi Germany.

As yet, though, less than a third of households in Britain possessed television sets, while over a billion cinema tickets were being sold annually in the mid-1950s.[43] This was also a decade in which British war films were almost always a success at the box office and thus made in large numbers.[44] Even as Maxwell Setton and Aubrey Baring were putting together *Appointment in London* for Mayflower, Robert Clark was preparing to option the screen rights of a bestselling account of the Dam Busters raid for ABPC.[45]

A feature film about this particular Bomber Command operation had a lot to recommend it. The raid had been one of the few truly precision attacks carried out by the heavy bombers of the RAF in the middle war years and unlike some of the other efforts had been a great success. A special Lancaster unit, 617 Squadron, had been formed in order to attack the main water supply of the war industries of the Ruhr Valley using a new type of depth charge that, when spun at high speed and released at low level, would skip over the water, thereby avoiding booms and torpedo nets, hit the inner wall of a dam, then roll down before exploding with tremendous force at a preset point and finally, it was hoped, cause the dam wall to rupture and collapse. Operation Chastise, launched on the night of 16/17 May 1943 under the command of Wing Commander Guy Gibson, had breached both the Möhne and the Edersee dams to spectacular effect. Aerial reconnaissance photographs and the basic outlines of the raid were immediately released to the press, providing Bomber Command with something of a publicity coup.[46]

The cinematic possibilities were obvious, and while Gibson was on a public-relations tour of North America later that year American director Howard Hawks sought to develop a Hollywood movie. Roald Dahl, the assistant air attaché at the British embassy in Washington, was persuaded to write a script which the Air Ministry, after some deliberation and suggestions for revision, decided to accept as the basis for a film towards the end of 1943.[47] By this point, however, Hawks was committed to making *To Have and Have Not* with Warner Brothers, followed by *The Big Sleep*, and the project was not pursued. The posthumous publication three years later of Guy Gibson's memoir, *Enemy Coast Ahead*, rekindled interest in the raid. A short radio adaptation written by Alexander McKee based on the book was broadcast on the British Forces Network in Germany to mark the seventh anniversary, and in the summer of the same year Ealing Studios explored the possibility of a feature-film version before giving up. There is also speculation that John Wooldridge, who served under him in 106 Squadron, used Gibson as a model for aspects of Tim Mason in plotting *Appointment in London*.[48]

However, it was the runaway success of a popular history of 617 Squadron written by ex-RAAF fighter pilot and former prisoner of war Paul Brickhill that really got things moving. First published by Evans in the latter part of 1951, *The Dam Busters* quickly became a bestseller, allowing the author to sell the rights the following year for a multipart radio adaptation broadcast in Australia during 1954 which featured a young Rod Taylor and also to entertain offers from film companies. Among those interested was Robert Clark in his capacity as head of production at ABPC.[49] Before buying the film rights, Clark requested a screen treatment from Brickhill, who recognized that the plot would have to focus exclusively on the dams raid and forgo the subsequent operations which he had chronicled in the book. Satisfied with the result, the ABPC production chief paid Brickhill for his work and brought R. C. Sherriff on board to produce a full-scale screenplay by the summer of 1952. Though there would be subsequent script changes, the company production team liked the result, with filming scheduled to begin the following year.[50]

The projected expenses, however, soon began to mount. The Air Ministry was happy to lend all possible assistance, including four de-mothballed Lancasters and the men to operate them from Hemswell and other stations, apparently leaving Clark under the impression that the RAF was giving him everything he needed for next to nothing.[51] ABPC would have to pay, however, for the Lancs to be modified to make them resemble more closely the special versions used in the actual raid, chiefly through the removal of bomb bay doors, H2S blisters and mid-upper turrets, plus the manufacture of fake bouncing bombs. Moreover the crews would cost £130 each hour, while the company would be charged £100 per engine-hour from start-up to shutdown. Mayflower films had kept costs down by virtually abstaining from aerial photography for *Appointment in London*, but this was simply not possible for Associated British given the nature of *The Dam Busters*. Since the Lancs each had four engines, and each of the two camera planes also lent by the RAF a pair of their own, aerial photography would involve up to five aircraft at a total cost of over £1,600 per hour.[52]

Then there was the size of the cast to consider. Clark eventually settled on Michael Redgrave to play engineer-inventor Barnes Wallis, one of the two leading roles, and from the start had Richard Todd in mind to impersonate the other, Wing Commander Guy Gibson.[53] Beyond the two principals, though, the screenplay involved well over two dozen other speaking parts, not including the extras. Given the film was supposed to be a dramatic reconstruction rather than a fictional drama it was important to include as many of those involved in the events portrayed as possible, both for the sake of authenticity and because people left out might take offence.[54] There were no less than fifteen parts for members of 617 Squadron besides Gibson, as well as roles for Gibson's superiors, ranging from Group Captain John Whitworth, station commander at Scampton (the airfield from which the raid was launched), through Air Vice-Marshal Ralph Cochrane, Air Officer Commanding 5 Group, all the way up to Arthur Harris himself. On the civilian side there was David Pye, director of scientific research at the Air Ministry; William Glanville, director of the road research laboratory where tests on scale-model dams were conducted; and Vickers test pilot Joseph 'Mutt' Summers. Even then it was deemed necessary to insert a couple of fictional characters for expository purposes and have Wallis's wife, Molly, help flesh out the character and tribulations of her husband. Given the numbers involved, the combined salaries for the secondary parts might eat up as much as £18,000 over four weeks of shooting.[55]

Adding yet more to the prospective bill were the wide range of anticipated location and studio scenes, plus necessary model work and special effects. It soon became apparent that the budget would far exceed the £150,000 limit that ABPC set for its productions. In the context of declining box office receipts, Clark worried in early 1953 that the production was 'becoming a financially dangerous proposition'.[56]

The projected costs, though, might have been higher. ABPC had a reputation for frugality with salaries, but Richard Todd was a contract player and Michael Redgrave desperately needed money to restore his finances.[57] The director chosen for the project, Michael Anderson, seeking a semi-documentary feel, planned to use monochrome film stock. As well as avoiding the glamour associated with colour, black-and-white film was less expensive and allowed for the insertion of wartime footage of bouncing-bomb tests.[58] It also meant that the Lancasters would not have to be repainted, since monochrome obscured the fact that the upper surfaces were not fully sprayed in wartime camouflage tones.[59] The bill could also be kept within bounds through keeping a tight rein on the filming schedule and the amount of film exposed.[60]

Despite his concerns, Clark eventually decided to gamble that the film would be a big success and committed at least £200,000 to the production. The many secondary and tertiary parts were cast, a process which drew in a pair of faces seen previously in *Appointment in London* – Harold Siddons, reprising his role as an operations-room officer at the end of a telephone, and Bill Kerr, once more an Aussie Lanc pilot, in the role of Flight Lieutenant H. B. 'Micky' Martin – as well as relative unknowns who would later make their names in film or television such as George Baker, John Fraser, Patrick McGoohan, Robert Shaw and Nigel Stock. Following a good deal of further deliberation and preparation, including consultations over the script with veterans of the raid and cast members meeting their real-life counterparts, location shooting on *The Dam Busters* finally got underway in the spring of 1954, with studio filming at Elstree, including elaborate model work and complicated special effects, finished by the middle of July and editing complete by the autumn, including the insertion of a rousing score from Eric Coates.[61]

The first fifth of *The Dam Busters* concerns the dogged efforts of a somewhat otherworldly Barnes Wallis to convince Whitehall to back the development of his bouncing bomb idea. The first five minutes or so introduce the concept to the audience through Wallis explaining to a doctor making a house call the nature of the experiments with a slingshot, marbles and tin bathtub he is shown conducting with the help of his children. Members of the relevant committee are sceptical at various stages, but he is allowed to conduct scientific tests at official facilities to prove the efficacy of his theories, the first set demonstrating the power of an underwater explosion next to a model dam wall, the second showing in precise terms how an object can be made to skip across water and then roll down the side of the obstacle it hits. Despite further obstruction, Wallis then obtains the use of a Wellington bomber to see if a dummy bomb dropped at a precise height and speed can indeed skip across the sea. It does, but more bureaucratic roadblocks emerge concerning allocation of scarce material resources for further development and testing, and no less a figure than Air Marshal Harris himself, played by Basil Sydney, appears irascibly suspicious about the practicality of the idea. Friction between the persistent advocate and those in charge reach the point where Wallis is reprimanded by his aviation-firm employer and resigns ... only for all to be forgiven after it emerges that the prime minister wants to see the weapon developed and a green light is given.[62]

It is only at this point that, almost half an hour into the story, Bomber Command comes fully into the picture. Harris is still rather dubious but allows one of his group commanders, the rather less sceptical Ralph Cochrane, played by Ernest Clark, to choose an experienced leader for a special squadron of Lancasters that will drop the bouncing bombs once they are ready. This of course is Wing Commander Guy Gibson, who accepts the challenge. The names, faces and background of some of the aircraft captains and flight commanders chosen for 617 Squadron, as well as some of the wing commander's own crew, are rapidly introduced through various conversations in different locations, after which training in low flying at night begins from Scampton while Gibson is called away to be told first of the weapon by

Wallis and then of the target by Cochrane. That there remain technical problems is illustrated by a sequence in which Wallis and Gibson witness the failure of the first full-scale test bombs to survive impact with the water when dropped. Difficulties, though, are overcome, with Gibson inventing a spotlight system to allow pilots to judge their height at a level too low for altimeters to work, a crude but effective bombsight being produced and Wallis redesigning the bomb casings so that the next set of full-scale test drops show the weapon is finally ready for use.[63]

The second half of the film deals with the day and night of the raid itself. Gibson briefs the crews on their mission, and they disperse afterward to eat, read, play games and lounge about until it is time to go out to their aircraft. The wing commander learns that his boon canine companion, a black Labrador, has been accidentally run over but stays focused on the task at hand. He leads the crews as they head towards the motor transport that will ferry them to the dispersal points where their aircraft sit waiting. After a farewell from Cochrane, Gibson and his crew board, engines are started up, and the first three Lancasters take off together.[64] A mixture of day-for-night aerial photography and studio cockpit shots combined with special effects allows the audience to follow the low-level journey of three-plane formations and some of the individual bombers as they speed over the enemy-held Dutch coast and on towards the Möhne dam. They encounter dangers ranging from electricity pylons to searchlights and flak, the latter shown bringing down one of the Lancs in a crashing fireball. Action sequences in the air alternate with brief scenes on the ground set in the 5 Group operations room at Grantham, where Wallis, Cochrane, Harris and Whitworth, played by Derek Farr, anxiously await news of the attack's progress by wireless.[65]

Having reached the target area, Gibson confirms by radio that seven other aircraft have made it this far and begins the attack in the face of fire from flak guns mounted on the Möhne dam's sluice towers. His own bouncing bomb scores a hit, but the explosion does not breach the dam. The next Lanc to have a go, flown by Flight Lieutenant 'Hoppy' Hopgood, played by John Fraser, drops the bomb too late, causing it to skip over the dam, explode and destroy the overflying bomber. Two more bomb runs are made, first by 'Micky' Martin, then by 'Dinghy' Young, played by Richard Leech, with first Gibson and then Martin as well providing covering fire despite damage to the latter's plane. Both times the bombs seem to explode where they should, but once again without result. Back at Grantham the mood is increasingly gloomy as the lack of progress is relayed to Wallis and the others by wireless code word. A fifth bomb run, this time flown by Flight Lieutenant David Maltby, played by George Baker, seems to produce the same result; but then the dam wall gives way, and Wallis is suddenly the subject of congratulation.[66]

In a fictional story this would have been the single great climax, but, staying more or less true to the facts, Gibson is then shown leading the Lancasters which have not yet dropped their bombs to attack the secondary target, the Eder dam. Though this dam is undefended, the terrain makes the bomb run and pull-out trickier. The first attempt, flown by Flight Lieutenant Dave Shannon, played by Ronald Wilson, has to be aborted; the second, in a Lancaster skippered by Squadron Leader Henry Maudslay, played by Richard Thorp, ends in a fiery crash. The news filtering back to Wallis and the others at Grantham is once again uniformly bad. Shannon tries again with more success, yet the dam holds; but the last bomb, dropped from the Lancaster piloted by Flying Officer Les Knight, played by Denys Graham, does the job and the Eder dam collapses. Once more there is cause for celebration back at Grantham, the success of the raid then being illustrated through a mixture of special effects and actual footage of surging water and flooded industrial areas.[67]

The fast-paced double climax of *The Dam Busters* is followed by a slower denouement, the tired crews landing back at base, the success of the raid, pronounced in a voiceover version of a BBC communiqué, balanced by the admission that eight of the aircraft failed to return, subsequent scenes of empty chairs at breakfast in the mess and the juxtaposition of the lucky ones in their billets and of silent rooms whose occupants will never return. The rather sombre mood continues outside as Gibson confirms to a distraught Wallis that a total of fifty-six men have been lost on the operation. Gibson stresses to Wallis that the men concerned would have volunteered even if they had known how bad things would be, and the film ends with the wing commander determinedly heading off to write the necessary letters of condolence to the next of kin.[68]

Publicity for the production emphasized the extent to which *The Dam Busters* was going to be an authentic recreation of past events. The man who had been the station commander at the time served as historical advisor, and a good deal of time and effort was put into talking with and consulting others involved in the actual operation. A number of former Bomber Command aircrew later remarked how true to life some of the dialogue and actions in the script were. Richard Todd in particular took great pains to try and dress and move as he had been told Gibson had done; and photos were distributed to the press showing how much alike some of the actors were to their role models once in costume and makeup.[69]

Nonetheless, the film was at variance with the record in a number of respects. At the time of shooting the bouncing bombs used on the raid were still on the secret list, which meant the mock-ups attached to the bomb bays bore little resemblance to the real thing.[70] Despite the length of the film and the size of the cast, certain developments were altered or simplified for comprehension or dramatic effect. The idea for an attack on the Ruhr dams and the development of a suitable weapon, for instance, was more of a team effort than a single misunderstood genius overcoming petty bureaucratic obstacles. Gibson was less central to who else flew with 617 Squadron than he is made out to be; the invention of the special dual-spotlight system to judge low-level height over water was not quite the Eureka moment depicted on screen; and coverage of the failed attack on the crucial third dam, the Sorpe, is so minimal as to be virtually absent.[71] As for representation among the lead players, Barnes Wallis understood that Michael Redgrave was inventing a character rather than mimicking him, and while some of those who had met Guy Gibson thought Richard Todd had got the part uncannily right, others knew that the real man was rather more volatile and troubled than the understated sensitive-yet-determined character depicted on screen.[72]

At least some of these and other departures from recorded events were, it should be noted, almost inevitable given that *The Dam Busters* was in the end supposed to be an appealing drama rather than a factual documentary. As Robert Clark explained to Barnes Wallis, a 'somewhat simplified treatment of highly complicated issues' was necessary since 'we have so little time in which to make [them] clear to an uninstructed audience' and because 'our film cannot hold interest unless we present "living" people whose feelings an audience can share': thus, 'the many personal touches (by tacit admission fictional) introduced to this end'.[73] Wallis fully grasped the point and in public neatly bridged the fact-fiction gap by stating that while no single scene was entirely accurate, 'the whole thing adds up to the truth'.[74]

In terms of representing the nature and effectiveness of wartime strategic bombing by the RAF, this meant implying that striking at enemy manufacturing capacity remained the main goal of Bomber Command but that the dams raid represented a switch from bombing entire industrial towns to hitting specific targets vital to the enemy war-production process. Within the first five minutes of *The Dam Busters*, Wallis uses a simile in explaining to the family doctor, played by Charles Carson, why area bombing is too imprecise to properly undermine German industry: 'It's like trying to kill a giant by firing at his arms and legs with thousands of pea-shooters.' As for the effect on the morale of the enemy civilian population, if British spirits had not collapsed under the weight of the *Luft waff e*'s bombs during the Blitz a few years earlier, why should German morale collapse? 'You know what happened when they tried to wipe out London', Wallis warns. In a later scene Harris, briefing his group commanders, concludes by saying of what is supposed to be a typical forthcoming raid: 'I want a maximum effort tonight and see if we can't get a real knock at Essen.' The clear implication here, of course, is that thus far area bombing has not yielded the expected results. What is really needed, as Wallis has put it metaphorically to the family physician, is 'a clean bullet through the heart'. A precisely delivered attack on the dams, it is thus insinuated, will deliver this kind of *coup de grâce*. When Gibson briefs the assembled crews for the raid later in the film, he is a little more circumspect about what is supposed to happen – 'tonight, you're going to have the chance to hit the enemy harder, and more destructively, than any small force has done before' – but after the breaching of the dams the audience sees footage and hears a BBC announcement which indicate the raid has been a complete success, the flood of water released by the breached dams sweeping all before it, including bridges, locomotives, factories and power stations. Though the film ends on a fairly downbeat note, reflecting the high aircrew losses sustained, the overall message is that Bomber Command in a single night had delivered a carefully aimed blow that significantly hastened the demise of the Third Reich. In *Appointment in London*, area bombing and precision attacks are more or less elided; in *The Dam Busters*, the latter seems to be replacing the former. That area bombing rather than precision strikes remained the dominant strategy of Bomber Command, if not 617 Squadron, for the final two years of the war, is the opposite of the impression left by the new film.

In other ways, *The Dam Busters* was more closely aligned to *Appointment in London*. Each picture featured flyers from Australia but virtually none from the

Celtic fringe or northern England. Both also emphasized individual leadership rather than collective effort and shared a tendency to divide uniformed characters according to importance along both rank and class lines. The new film, though, took these trends a bit further. Barnes Wallis manages to overcome the roadblocks placed in his way by a small army of civil-servant bureaucrats, committees being depicted as more of a hindrance than a help in developing and testing the weapon. Guy Gibson, like Tim Mason, is an experienced wing commander who has the accent and manners of a home-counties, upper-middle-class Englishman, is admired by his men, decides what they need in the way of training and recreation and leads them in battle, but in Gibson's case without any signs of the combat fatigue exhibited by Mason or any need for female companionship.[75] As characters, the other commissioned flyers in *The Dam Busters* have less screen time and dialogue than in *Appointment in London*, further emphasizing the centrality of Gibson.[76] In both films, non-commissioned aircrew are shown as part of the background but rarely heard from. When casting for *The Dam Busters* took place, there may even have been an effort to separate ranks by appearance, with the more clean-cut faces getting to be officers while tough-looking types became NCOs.[77] As for the other ranks on the ground, Gibson is more at ease with his batman, played by Harold Goodwin, than Mason is with Aircraftsman Ackroyd in *Appointment in London*, but the gulf between lower-class groundlings and genteel senior aircrew officers is, if anything, even more apparent through their respective accents and facial features.[78]

All this, it is worth stressing, was not simply a reflection of the historical reality, despite a contrary claim by director Michael Anderson.[79] Half the men who flew on the raid did not hold commissions; and while only two of them were pilots, neither involved in the attack on the Möhne or Eder, it certainly ought to have been possible, say, to flesh out the role of flight engineer John Pulford, the sole NCO in Gibson's own crew. As it is, as played by Robert Shaw, Pulford has less than a dozen Lancashire-accented lines, mostly echoing brief instructions issued to him by Gibson in the cockpit. Interestingly, while the rest of the crew, all officers, address Gibson as 'skipper' in the air, Pulford defers to rank, commenting 'nice work, sir' after they drop the first bomb.[80]

Of course the author of the source material, Paul Brickhill, had been himself a commissioned pilot during the Second World War, while the screenwriter, R. C. Sherriff, had also held a commission – in his case in the infantry – during the First World War. The underlying perspective, then, was that of middle-class officers.[81] Yet author background is only a partial explanation for the class hierarchy of leaders and followers present in *The Dam Busters* (or indeed *Appointment in London*). John Wooldridge, after all, while ending up a highly decorated wing commander, had begun his flying career in the RAF as a humble sergeant, and Terence Rattigan, at one point a contender to write the screenplay for *The Dam Busters*, though an RAF officer during his wartime service and famous for the upper-middle-class sensibilities of his post-war stage characters, had proved himself capable of co-scripting the cross-class *Journey Together* as well as the much more bourgeois *Way to the Stars* towards the end of the war.[82]

But that had been in an earlier time permeated by a different ethos. The austerely collectivist 1940s, in which Labour leaders had held the dominant position in domestic affairs and the perceived interests of the wider community had seemed to take priority over those of the individual, had given way to the increasingly consumerist 1950s, with much talk – though only limited action – by the governing Conservatives about setting people free from state interference in order to advance their personal interests. The one-nation conservatism assumed by the Tories in this decade was at root paternalistic, and without the pressures of war to promote a progressive cross-class agenda, the socio-functional hierarchy was left largely unchallenged.[83] Hence well-bred commissioned heroes could be celebrated and bureaucracies denigrated, as in *The Dam Busters*, rather than the other way round as in, for instance, the earlier *Cage of Gold*.[84]

After a further delay involving the settlement of a lawsuit by Gibson's widow, who claimed that use had been made of her former husband's memoir without copyright authorization, *The Dam Busters* premiered at the Empire Theatre, Leicester Square, amidst a blaze of publicity, twelve years on from the actual raid, in the spring of 1955.[85] That it was very much in tune with the times in Britain was demonstrated by how, in the words of R. C. Sherriff, *The Dam Busters* 'hit the bullseye'.[86] One or two newspaper critics thought Richard Todd a little wooden as Guy Gibson, but even they liked the film.[87] In the broadsheets *The Dam Busters* was described as a 'skillful treatment' (*Daily Telegraph*) and a 'film of unusual merit' (*The Times*).[88] The mass-circulation press tended to be considerably less restrained. 'It's a picture to rave about' (*Daily Mirror*); 'one of the best British war films of them all' (*Daily Express*); 'the finest flying picture ever made' (*Reynolds News*); 'perhaps the best war picture to come our way since the real show ended' (*Daily Sketch*); 'a fine picture that can proudly take its place among Britain's best of all time' (*Evening News*).[89] 'If there has been a better war picture', enthused the reviewer for the *Star*, 'then I must have missed it'.[90] Even the communist *Daily Worker* thought it 'straightforward, honest and remarkably fresh'.[91] Cinemagoers agreed when the film went on general release, *The Dam Busters* going on in the UK to be the biggest box-office attraction of the year.[92]

The film also met with a positive response in the dominions, though not in the United States, where attempts by the distributor to recut sections to make it more palatable for local audiences did nothing to make up for the absence of a romantic subplot or American characters.[93] In the UK, though, *The Dam Busters* continued to elicit popular enthusiasm of almost seismic proportions. 'Absolutely true to the feelings of the 1950s', as one admirer later reflected, adding that it was also 'sufficiently true to the facts of 1939 to 1945'.[94] After initial success on the big screen, the film went on to become a fixture on the small screen after BBC-TV acquired the broadcasting rights in the early 1970s; television success followed in the 1980s by VHS tape sales and, in the new century, those of digital video and Blu-ray discs.[95] That the film had become an icon in British popular culture decades after it was made was demonstrated by the way familiarity was assumed – indeed essential to understanding – in a pair of television adverts promoting a brand of beer.[96] *Appointment in London*, by way of contrast, came to be almost completely overshadowed by *The Dam Busters*.[97] Though autobiographical novels were published by ex-aircrew through the fifties that emphasized the stresses and strains of bombing operations and occasionally class conflict, on screen at least the public preferred to remember strategic bombing by the RAF in unambiguously positive terms: '*The Dam Busters* is the way the British public wanted to remember their bomber war', as historian Mark Connelly later concluded.[98]

Given the huge success of *The Dam Busters*, logically Associated British might have considered a follow-up film along the lines of 'what the Dambusters did next' based on the later chapters of the Brickhill history of 617 Squadron to which they already held the screen rights.[99] However, there were a number of problems with any potential sequel from within ABPC or, if the rights had been sold on, by another studio.[100]

Despite the box-office success of *The Dam Busters*, Associated British was under pressure. Like other film production companies dependent on the domestic box office, it was starting to feel the effects of the popular drift towards television and away from the cinema. While in 1955 just over 1.18 billion cinema tickets were purchased, by 1957 that figure was only 915.2 million, a drop of over 266 million; and in 1960, only 500.8 million tickets were sold. In the meantime, the annual number of television licenses issued had jumped by over 2.8 million.[101] In January 1958, Robert Clark was replaced by managing director C. J. Latta and assistant head of production James Wallis, with a mandate from Warners (the largest ABPC shareholder) to boost sagging profits by shifting film production at Elstree into low-budget comedies and concentrating on relatively low-cost television productions. The strategy worked in terms of the company's profit margin; but it meant that a comparatively big-budget film production sequel to *The Dam Busters* was impossible.[102]

Just as importantly, there were no longer enough airworthy Lancasters in Britain to repeat the aerial spectacle of *The Dam Busters*. While happy enough to hire out men and equipment to various production companies making films involving the RAF through the mid-fifties, the Air Ministry did not try and link the Bomber Command of the war in the public mind with the contemporary V-Force in the way the US Air Force did with respect to the wartime Eighth Air Force and Strategic Air Command.[103] It cannot have helped that a few years after *The Dam Busters* was released, an internal study found that it and other films had no influence on recruits' attitudes towards the RAF.[104] In any event, there appears to have been little hesitation in sending the handful of airworthy Lancs still in RAF hands to the scrapyard in the summer and autumn of 1956.[105]

This development did not, however, entirely prelude cinematic references to the bomber boys and their work later in the decade. In *Battle of the V-1*, for instance, a low-budget feature from Eros Films released in 1958 that made little impression at the box office, the Peenemünde Raid was recreated with footage drawn from, among other sources, *Target for Tonight* and *Journey Together*.[106] The stock-film option, though, simply would not do for a major flying picture seeking to replicate the box-office success of *The Dam Busters*, especially in the context of competition from television. With only a single Lancaster remaining in anything approaching airworthy condition, at least in the UK, it would take some years to work out a new means of combining RAF wartime bombing as a central plot device and mass box-office potential.[107]

Notes

1 On disbandment of the RAF film production unit see Keith Buckman, 'The Royal Air Force Film Production Unit', *Historical Journal of Film, Radio and Television* 17 (1997), 221. On the winding up and replacement of the Ministry of Information in 1946 by a very different though still initially controversial body see Mariel Grant, 'Towards a Central Office of Information: Continuity and Change in British Government Information Policy, 1939-51', *Journal of Contemporary History* 34 (1999), 49-63.
2 On Air Ministry terms for assisting Wardour Street see TNA, AIR 2/12261, Form of agreement between Air Ministry and film companies for the grant of facilities, 1946-56.
3 Winston S. Churchill, *The Second World War: Closing the Ring* (Boston, MA: Houghton Mifflin, 1951), 517. On the background to this statement and the chapter from which it came see David Reynolds, *In Command of History: Churchill Fighting and Writing the Second World War* (London: Allen Lane, 2004), 396-7.
4 Among the features reissued were *The Big Blockade* in 1947 and both *One of Our Aircraft Is Missing* and *Journey Together* in 1949. Stephen Guy, 'After Victory: Projections of the Second World War and Its Aftermath in British Feature Films, 1946-1950' (PhD diss., University of London, 2002), 199.
5 The three RAF features in the early 1950s were *Angels One Five* (Templar, 1952), *Appointment in London* (Mayflower, 1953) and *Malta Story* (Thea, 1953). See TNA, AIR 2/7400, D of Ops(1)/6271, 1 June 1952 summary of requests approved or received for consideration by the RAF Participation Committee, May 1952, attached PC(52)4, f. 6. The next wave of features focusing on the wartime RAF were *The Purple Plain* (Two Cities, 1954), *The Sea Shall Not Have Them* (Eros, 1954), *The Dam Busters* (ABPC, 1955) and *Reach for the Sky* (Pinnacle, 1956). Among the signs back in 1950 that combat films set in the recent conflict could do well was the success of *They Were Not Divided* (1950) from Two Cities, which dealt with the Guards armoured division and, with specific reference to air combat pictures, the success of the Twentieth Century-Fox import *Twelve O'Clock High* (1949). See *Kinematograph Weekly*, 14 December 1950, 9-10. On box-office accounts for *Landfall* see Vincent Porter, 'The Robert Clark Account: Films Released in Britain by Associated British Pictures, British Lion, MGM, and Warner Bros., 1946-1957', *Historical Journal of Film, Radio and Television* 20 (2000), 490. On RAF participation in *Landfall* see TNA, AIR 2/12261, encl. 22A, Agreement on Film 'Landfall', 9 April 1949; Mark Ashley, *Flying Film Stars: The Directory of Aircraft in British World War Two Films* (Walton-on-Thames: Red Kite, 2014), 107-9.
6 Wooldridge flew Manchesters with 207 Squadron and Lancasters with 106 Squadron before going on to fly Mosquitos. On the latter period see John de Lacy Wooldridge, *Low Attack: The Story of Two Royal Air Force Squadrons from May, 1940 until May, 1943* (London: Sampson, Low, Marston, 1944).
7 On Setton, Baring and Westerly see Sue Harper and Vincent Porter, *British Cinema of the 1950s: The Decline of Deference* (Oxford: Oxford University Press, 2007), 177-8.

8 Original budget information on *Appointment in London* from Film Finances, Realised Film Box 41, kindly provided by James Chapman, Professor of Film Studies, University of Leicester.
9 See BFI Library, *Appointment in London* pressbook, 2–3; *Today's Cinema*, 29 May 1952, 5, 21 July 1952, 10; *Kinematograph Weekly*, 10 July 1952, 64; *Picturegoer*, 26 July 1952, 10–11; TNA, AIR 20/7400, R.A.F. Facilities for feature film "An Appointment in London" – about Bomber Command, 9 October 1951. The Lincolns based at RAF Upwood bore a strong enough resemblance to the Lancaster to be used in long shots. See Trevor Popple, 'Appointment in London', *After the Battle* 206 (2000), 42–3. A fifth, unserviceable Lancaster was also provided for ground shots. See Simon D. Beck, *The Aircraft-Spotter's Film and Television Companion* (Jefferson, NC: McFarland, 2016), 27. On Leacock as director see Philip Leacock, BFI screenonline, accessed 6 December 2012, http://www.screenonline.org.uk/people/id/513363/; Philip Leacock in Brian McFarlane, *An Autobiography of British Cinema* (London: Methuen, 1997), 352.
10 The part of Eve Canyon was written by John Wooldridge for his wife, Margaretta Scott, but by the time shooting began she was pregnant, so the part went to Dinah Sheridan. Margaretta Scott in McFarlane, *Autobiography of British Cinema*, 517.
11 Bryan Forbes was a bit dismissive in describing *Appointment in London* as a 'well-constructed tearjerker' but admitted to being happy with his fee and co-star billing. Bryan Forbes, *Notes for a Life* (London: Collins, 1974), 217–18. Forbes had played an RAF officer in *The Wooden Horse* (London Films, 1950) who, to judge by a sketch hanging by his bunk and a nightmare he is briefly shown to experience, crashed a Wellington and is suffering some trauma as a result. He had not enjoyed being among the cast of that film at all. Ibid., 190–2.
12 A number of newspaper reviewers noticed the family resemblance. See *Daily Herald*, 13 February 1953; *Daily Telegraph*, 16 February 1953; *Illustrated London News*, 7 March 1953. Though they shared a theme and were each scripted by veteran bomber unit leaders, *Twelve O'Clock High* and *Appointment in London* differed in that while Brigadier General Frank Savage, USAAF, ultimately suffers a nervous breakdown, Wing Commander Tim Mason, RAF, manages to cope with the stress without cracking up. On the making of *Twelve O'Clock High* see Allan T. Duffin and Paul Matheis, *The 12 O'Clock High Logbook* (Boalsburg, PA: Bear Manor, 2005), 51–95.
13 4/10 was pretty close to the C-in-C's estimate of 1/3 during the worst periods for Bomber Command. Arthur Harris, *Bomber Offensive* (London: Collins, 1947), 267.
14 Jonathan Falconer, *RAF Bomber Command in Fact, Film and Fiction* (Stroud: Sutton, 1996), 91.
15 Peter Finch was originally cast and when he was unable to play the part of Bill Brown, he recommended Bill Kerr. *Australian Women's Weekly*, 1 October 1952, 61.
16 On belief in jinxed squadrons, see e.g. Campbell Muirhead, *Diary of a Bomb Aimer*, ed. Philip Swann (Barnsley: Pen and Sword Aviation, 2009), 41. On footprints-on-the-ceiling, see e.g. Don Charlwood, *No Moon Tonight* (Manchester: Crécy, 2000), 53. Wooldridge himself may have made an appearance briefly in *Appointment in London* as one among a group of new pilots for 188 Squadron late in the film.
17 See Neil Rattigan, 'The Last Gasp of the Middle Class: British War Films of the 1950s', in *Re-Viewing British Cinema, 1900–1992*, ed. Wheeler Winston Dixon (Albany: State University of New York Press, 1994), 150.
18 The station commander, played by Ian Hunter, introduces Peter Greeno to Eve Canyon, for example, as being 'from nowhere in particular', and his fitter, played by Sam Kydd, seems to find him more approachable than he does, say, Tim Mason.

19 The three working-class parts in *Appointment in London* in RAF blue were the senior engineering NCO, played by Campbell Singer; Greeno's fitter, played by Sam Kydd; and Brown's bomb aimer, played by Michael Ripper.
20 Dirk Bogarde was particularly happy to play upper-middle-class Tim Mason as the part broke from the working-class youth roles that the Rank Organization still wanted to cast him in. Dirk Bogarde, *Snakes & Ladders* (London: Chatto and Windus, 1978), 134–5.
21 Though the name of the climactic target is not mentioned, one reviewer assumed that this must be the Peenemünde raid of 17/18 August 1943. *The Times*, 16 February 1953. The post-raid photograph of the initial 'Meltzheim' target is in fact of Brest harbour in the wake of German attempts to render it unusable in the summer of 1944. RAF Ministry of Defence, Bomber Command, accessed 3 December 2012, http://www.raf.mod.uk/bombercommand/images/3121-49.jpg.
22 It is unclear if actual footage from *Target for Tonight* was used in *Appointment in London*, but even if not, the close resemblance is striking.
23 On the wartime footage see Falconer, *RAF Bomber Command*, 92.
24 *Kinematograph Weekly*, 12 February 1953, 16, 18.
25 See e.g. *The Times*, 16 February 1953; *Daily Worker*, 14 February 1953; *Tribune*, 13 March 1953; see also *Evening Standard*, 12 February 1953; *Spectator*, 13 February 1953; *Monthly Film Bulletin*, March 1953, 30.
26 *Sunday Graphic*, 15 February 1953; *Evening News*, 12 February 1953; *Daily Sketch*, 13 February 1953, *Daily Mail*, 13 February 1953; On *Appointment in London* as a box-office winner see *Kinematograph Weekly*, 17 December 1953, 10.
27 John Coldstream, *Dirk Bogarde: The Authorized Biography* (London: Weidenfeld and Nicolson, 2004), 195–6. Though the review in the leading US trade paper was quite positive (see *Variety*, 25 February 1953), the fact that Mac Baker loses out in competition with Tim Mason for the affections of Eve Canyon would not have gone down well with American audiences. On Commonwealth reaction, see e.g. *News* [Adelaide], 14 September 1954; *Age* [Melbourne], 8 October 1954; *Globe and Mail* [Toronto], 9 June 1953.
28 See Martin W. Bowman, *Legacy of the Lancasters* (Barnsley: Pen and Sword Aviation, 2013), 7.
29 Hilary St. George Saunders, *Per Ardua: The Rise of British Air Power, 1911–1939* (Oxford: Oxford University Press, 1944). On Richards and the commissioning of the three-volume narrative history see Denis Richards and Hilary St. George Saunders, *Royal Air Force, 1939–1945*, box-set edition (London: HMSO, 1993), copyright page, iv.
30 On the complicated writing and publication history of the trilogy see Denis Richards, *It Might Have Been Worse: Recollections, 1941–1996* (London: Smithson Albright, 1998), 97–126. On the critical response, see e.g. *Times Literary Supplement*, 8 January 1954, 19; 16 April 1954, 243; 8 October 1954, 639.
31 Denis Richards, *Royal Air Force, 1939–1945: The Fight at Odds* (London: HMSO, 1953), 239–40.
32 Ibid., 377.
33 Denis Richards and Hilary St. George Saunders, *Royal Air Force, 1939–1945: The Fight Avails* (London: HMSO, 1954), 118; see e.g. ibid., 136, 286, 382.
34 Hilary St. George Saunders, *Royal Air Force, 1939–1945: The Fight Is Won* (London: HMSO, 1954), 9–10, 32, 370.
35 Ibid., 381–4.

36 Ibid., 386.
37 Ibid., 387.
38 BBCWA, R9/8/2, Audience Research: Television Weekly Summary, 8 November 1954–14 February 1955; see also *The Times*, 11 February 1955. *War in the Air* also did well in Canada. See *The Times*, 30 September 1955. On the making of the series see BBCWA, T6/293–294, T6/301, T6/310; TNA, AIR 2/12866; see also BFI Library, *War in the Air* pressbook.
39 Robert Saundby had previously played himself back in 1941 in *Target for Tonight*.
40 Interestingly, the narrator does not quote the rest of the directive – 'and the undermining of the morale of the German people to the point where their armed resistance is fatally weakened'. Robert Saundby, *Air Bombardment: The Story of Its Development* (New York: Harper and Row, 1961), 145.
41 'Oboe' was explained to viewers in part through a staged conversation between Robert Saundby, who had been Harris's deputy, and Don Bennett, who had led the Pathfinders.
42 For the dam-busters raid, the BBC was able to use some exterior footage from the forthcoming ABPC film *The Dam Busters*.
43 Film Distributors' Association, UK cinema admissions, 1935 to date, accessed 17 March 2017, http://www.launchingfilms.com/research-databank/uk-cinema-admissions; Broadcasters Audience Research Board, TV ownership, January 1956, accessed 17 March 2017, http://www.barb.co.uk/resources/tv-ownership/.
44 See James Chapman, 'Our Finest Hour Revisited: The Second World War in British Feature Films since 1945', *Journal of Popular British Cinema* 1 (1998), 63–75; Sue Harper and Vincent Porter, 'Cinema Audience Tastes in 1950s Britain', *Journal of Popular British Cinema* 2 (1999), 66–82; Nicholas Pronay, 'The British Post-Bellum Cinema: A Survey of the Films relating to World War II Made in Britain between 1945 and 1960', *Historical Journal of Film, Radio and Television* 8 (1988), 39–54; John Ramsden, 'Refocusing the "People's War": British War Films of the 1950s', *Journal of Contemporary History* 33 (1998), 35–63.
45 See Stephen Dando-Collins, *The Hero-Maker: A Biography of Paul Brickhill* (North Sydney, NSW: Vintage, 2016), 233–4, 237. On Clark and ABPC see Vincent Porter, 'Outsiders in England: The Films of Associated British Picture Corporation, 1948–59', in *British Cinema, Past and Present*, ed. Justine Ashby and Andrew Higson (London: Routledge, 2000), 152–65.
46 See e.g. on both Operation Chastise and Operation Margin – a precision-bombing disaster – James Holland, *Dam Busters: The Race to Smash the Dams, 1943* (London: Bantam, 2012).
47 See TNA, AIR 2/5546, Encl. 13C 'The Dam'; L. Tom Perry Special Collections, Harold B. Lee Library, Brigham Young University, Howard Hawks Collection, MSS 1404, Box 5, Folder 2, Dams script, 9 September 1943, Folder 1, Dahl to Hawks, 6 December 1943; Donald Sturrock, *The Storyteller: The Authorized Biography of Roald Dahl* (New York: Simon and Schuster, 2010), 220–1.
48 Falconer, *RAF Bomber Command in Fact, Film and Fiction*, 104–5. Gibson had written his memoir at the urging of the Air Ministry in 1944 – see Richard Morris, *Guy Gibson* (London: Viking, 1994), 221–6 – but was subsequently killed in action. On speculation that Tim Mason was modelled on Guy Gibson, see ibid., 314; Falconer, *RAF Bomber Command in Fact, Film and Fiction*, 92. It has also been suggested that Mason was based on Leonard Cheshire: see Bowman, *Legacy of the Lancasters*, 7. It is quite possible, however, that Wooldridge based Mason on himself: see Coldstream,

Dirk Bogarde, 195. On interest by Ealing Studios see Jonathan Falconer, *Filming the Dam Busters* (Stroud: Sutton, 2005), 34.
49 Stephen Dando-Collins, *The Hero Maker: A Biography of Paul Brickhill* (North Sydney, NSW: Vintage, 2016), 233–4, 237, 276.
50 Ibid., 237, 241, 243, 256. See also Surrey History Centre, R. C. Sherriff Papers, 2332/3/6/31/7, 'The Dam Busters': First Draft Outline Treatment, 10 November 1951.
51 Dando-Collins, *Hero Maker*, 241.
52 Falconer, *Filming the Dam Busters*, 70–1; John Ramsden, *The Dam Busters* (London: I.B. Tauris, 2003), 34. The camera planes were a Varsity trainer and a Wellington trainer from the RAF, the latter itself filmed as a prelude to the bomb-testing sequences. Falconer, *Filming the Dam Busters*, 75, 85–8, 97.
53 Others considered for the part of Barnes Wallis included Jack Hawkins and Lawrence Olivier. See *News Chronicle*, 2 June 1954.
54 Inclusion, however, did not necessarily mean a positive attitude to the film. Arthur Harris felt that the script of *The Dam Busters* made him far more hostile to the concept of the attack than he remembered being. RAF Museum, Hendon, Harris Papers, 85/5, Harris to Whittaker, 30 January 1954. The record suggests his memory was faulty.
55 Robert Shaw, who played Gibson's flight engineer, John Pulford, earned £500 over four weeks on *The Dam Busters*. John French, *Robert Shaw: The Price of Success* (London: Nick Hern, 1993), 35. Aside from Gibson and Wallis, there were thirty-six credited roles in *The Dam Busters*. The size of *The Dam Busters* cast was more than double that of *Appointment in London* (compare Falconer, *Filming the Dam Busters*, 153–4 with BFI Library, *Appointment in London* pressbook).
56 Dando-Collins, *Hero Maker*, 262. On budgets see Ramsden, *Dam Busters*, 34.
57 On Redgrave's need for money see Corin Redgrave, *Michael Redgrave: My Father* (London: Richard Cohen, 1995), 57. In all, it was estimated that paying the artists and extras consumed 15 per cent of the budget, or about £30,000. See *News Chronicle*, 3 June 1954.
58 See Falconer, *Filming the Dam Busters*, 42; Richard Todd, *In Camera* (London: Hutchinson, 1989), 62.
59 This also held true for *Appointment in London*, which used three of the same aircraft. All that was done was to add green camouflage patterns on top of the upper-surfaces' existing post-war sea grey paintjob, perhaps with an occasional splash of khaki for close-ups. The propeller spinners were also left grey in both films rather than repainted the black they would have been during the war. See Martin Derry and Neil Robinson, *Avro Lancaster, 1945–1965: In Military Service* (Barnsley: Pen and Sword Aviation, 2014), 2, 748; Falconer, *Filming the Dam Busters*, 72, 76.
60 As the film's editor, Richard Best, put it: 'ABPC was not the sort of company to waste money on over-shooting.' Falconer, *Filming the Dam Busters*, 135–6.
61 See Ramsden, *Dam Busters*, 34–52, 96, 99–101, *passim*; Richard Todd in McFarlane, *Autobiography of British Cinema*, 565; see also J. C. Scutts, 'The Dam Busters', *After the Battle* 10 (1975), 46–8. On consultations, see e.g. Imperial War Museum, Lambeth [hereafter IWM], 25948, J. V. Hopgood Papers, JVH 5, W. A. Whittaker to G. Hopgood, 15 January 1954; W. A. Whittaker to Hilda Taerum, 13 January 1954, quoted in Ted Barris, *Dam Busters: Canadian Airmen and the Secret Raid against Nazi Germany* (Toronto: HarperCollins, 2018), 321–2.
62 On this section of the film see Ramsden, *Dam Busters*, 54–65.
63 On this section of the film see ibid., 65–76.

64 For the sake of authenticity, the take-off sequence was filmed at Kirton-in-Lindsey as Scampton, the station from which the actual raid was launched when it was still a grass airfield, now had concrete runways. Falconer, *Filming the Dam Busters*, 109.
65 On this section of the film see Ramsden, *Dam Busters*, 77–86.
66 Ibid., 86–9.
67 Ibid., 89–90.
68 Ibid., 91–4.
69 See BFI Library, *The Dam Busters* pressbook; Ramsden, *Dam Busters*, 45, 82; Richard Todd in McFarlane, *Autobiography of British Cinema*, 565; Todd, *In Camera*, 62, 66. On authentic dialogue, see e.g. Bill Grierson, *We Band of Brothers* (Hailsham: J&KH, 1997), 132; IWM, 27800/6, Ernie Lummis.
70 Falconer, *Filming the Dam Busters*, 73.
71 Though the film was more or less faithful to the way Brickhill, and to an extent Wallis himself, portrayed the matter, the idea for an attack on the dams and the promotion and development of the weapon involved plenty of other people. See Ramsden, *Dam Busters*, 25–6; see also e.g. IWM, 7462/36, Frederick Winterbotham. In the film it is Gibson and Whitworth who decide who will fly with 617 Squadron, and by implication Gibson's entire previous crew volunteer to go with him to Scampton. In fact, only Flight Lieutenant Robert Hutchinson, his wireless operator, went with him from his old crew at 106 Squadron, and while he chose some of them, Gibson did not know that many of the pilots or crews selected for the new squadron. Holland, *Dam Busters*, 154–5, 159; see e.g. Les Munro in Tony Iveson and Brian Milton, *Lancaster: The Biography* (London: Deutsch, 2009), 98. In the film, Gibson invents the bombsight after a eureka moment at a theatrical show, whereas in the book it is Micky Martin who experiences this epiphany, and in fact it was a scientist who came up with the idea after Gibson had asked the Ministry of Aircraft Production to solve the problem. The screenplay covers only the force attacking the Sorpe dam through mention in Gibson's briefing to the assembled crews and through messages to Grantham which suggest things are not going well for the force involved. The two aircraft which managed to drop their bombs on the Sorpe without success are not shown. See Ramsden, *Dam Busters*, 73, 79, 84.
72 On Todd getting Gibson right, see e.g. Ronald Walker in *News Chronicle*, 17 May 1955. On Todd idealizing Gibson, see e.g. George 'Johnny' Johnson, *The Last British Dambuster* (London: Ebury, 2014), 139; see also Max Arthur, *Dambusters: A Landmark Oral History* (London: Virgin, 2008), 27–38. On Michael Redgrave and Barnes Wallis see Michael Redgrave, *In My Mind's Eye: An Autobiography* (London: Weidenfeld and Nicolson, 1983), 196.
73 Science Museum Research Centre, Barnes Wallis Papers, BNW, D9/8, Whittaker to Wallis, 21 November 1952.
74 Dando-Collins, *Hero Maker*, 256; see also *News Chronicle*, 2 June 1954.
75 See Andrew Spicer, *Typical Men: The Representation of Masculinity in Popular British Cinema* (London: I.B. Tauris, 2001), 32. Gibson had in fact a rather complicated romantic life: see Morris, *Guy Gibson*, 43–6, 49, 61–2, 72–3, 127–34, 135, 159. That *The Dam Busters* does not hint even at the latter was due to the influence of screenwriter R. C. Sherriff, a lifelong bachelor who did not want any 'feminine influence' intruding into the masculine world of 617 Squadron. *News Chronicle*, 1 June 1954; see Robert Wales, *From Journey's End to the Dam Busters: The Life of R. C. Sherriff, Playwright of the Trenches* (Barnsley: Pen and Sword Military, 2016), 278–9.

76 On the character and class homogeneity of the skippers chosen see Christine Geraghty, *British Cinema in the Fifties: Gender, Genre and the 'New Look'* (London: Routledge, 2000), 184.
77 See Robert Shaw in Leonard Mosley, *The Battle of Britain: The Making of a Film* (London: Weidenfeld and Nicolson, 1969), 138; see also Michael Anderson in Ramsden, *Dam Busters*, 68. It is indicative of the class/rank divide in the film that Patrick McGoohan adopted a thrust-out lower lip and cockney accent for the tiny part of a RAF sergeant policeman. See Roger Langley, *Patrick McGoohan: Danger Man or Prisoner?* (Sheffield: Tomahawk, 2007), 43.
78 See also Ramsden, *Dam Busters*, 69.
79 See BFI Library, Michael Anderson, 1967 BBC interview TS.
80 Robert Shaw was not happy with his part and showed it in his interactions with Richard Todd and other actors on set. See Todd, *In Camera*, 70; Robert Shaw in Mosley, *Battle of Britain*, 138. On the NCO-officer aircrew ratio in 617 Squadron for the raid see Dambusters, The Crews, accessed 25 March 2017, http://www.dambusters.org.uk/the-dam-raids/the-crews/.
81 On Brickhill and his works see Dando-Collins, *Hero Maker*. On Sherriff and his works see Wales, *From Journey's End to the Dam Busters*.
82 On Rattigan see Geoffrey Wansell, *Terence Rattigan* (London: Fourth Estate, 1997). On Wooldridge see biography in Jonathan Falconer, *The Bomber Command Handbook, 1939-1945* (Stroud: Sutton, 1998), 219-20.
83 On the ideology and practice of Conservatism in this period, see e.g. Kevin Jeffreys, *Retreat from the New Jerusalem: British Politics, 1951-64* (New York: St. Martin's, 1997); John Ramsden, *The Age of Churchill and Eden, 1940-1957* (London: Longman, 1995). On the general character of two decades compare Peter Hennessy, *Never Again: Britain, 1945-51* (London: Cape, 1992); and David Kynaston, *Austerity Britain, 1945-51* (London: Bloomsbury, 2007) with Peter Hennessy, *Having It So Good: Britain in the Fifties* (London: Allen Lane, 2006); and David Kynaston, *Family Britain, 1951-57* (London: Bloomsbury, 2009).
84 In *Cage of Gold* collectivist spirit is shown to be praiseworthy while the individualist war hero becomes the villain, while in *The Dam Busters* bureaucracy is portrayed as the enemy of progress by Barnes Wallis and Guy Gibson remains an unblemished war hero. On the middle-class ethos of British films in the 1950s see Ramsden, 'Refocusing "The People's War"', 56; Rattigan, 'Last Gasp of the Middle Class', 143-53; see also Harper and Porter, *British Cinema of the 1950s*, 255. Only in a few low-budget comedies such as *Worm's Eye View* (Byron, 1951) and *On the Fiddle* (Coronado, 1961), both based on pieces written by R. F. Delderfield built around his own wartime RAF experiences in the ranks, did the cynicism towards authority of the RAF rank and file take centre stage. See R. F. Delderfield, *For My Own Amusement* (New York: Simon and Schuster, 1972), 278-81 277, 307-22; *Worm's Eye View* (London: Samuel French, 1948); *Stop at a Winner* (London: Hodder and Stoughton, 1961). Even in this context it is worth noting that in *The Night We Dropped a Clanger*, a successful but low-budget farce released by Rank in 1959 starring Brian Rix as an impossibly accomplished upper-crust wing commander sporting the Pathfinder badge plus the VC and bar, as well as his hapless doppelganger, a dim-witted lower-class aircraftsman, the role reversal at the heart of the plot ends with each man returning happily to his original role and class. On *The Night We Dropped a Clanger* see Brian Rix, *My Farce from My Elbow: An Autobiography* (London: Secker and Warburg, 1975), 172, 178. A more subversive

figure was Matt Braddock, also VC and bar, an ultra-competent NCO bomber pilot featured in the boys' comic *The Rover* as constantly upstaging foolish commissioned upper-class types. See e.g. George Bourne, *I Flew with Braddock* (London: D. C. Thomson, 1959); see also Michael Paris, *Warrior Nation: Images of War in British Popular Culture, 1850-2000* (London: Reaktion, 2000), 234-5.
85 See Ramsden, *Dam Busters*, 97-8, 102-5.
86 R. C. Sherriff, *No Leading Lady: An Autobiography* (London: Gollancz, 1968), 349.
87 See *Evening Standard*, 19 May 1955; *Manchester Guardian*, 18 May 1955; see also *Film and Filming*, July 1955, 14; *Monthly Film Bulletin*, June 1955, 82-3; John Gillett, 'Westfront 1957', *Sight and Sound* 27 (1957/8), 126-7.
88 *The Times*, 17 May 1955; *Daily Telegraph*, 21 May 1955; see also *Sunday Times*, 22 May 1955; *Observer*, 22 May 1955; *New Statesman*, 21 May 1955; *Spectator*, 20 May 1955.
89 *Evening News*, 19 May 1955; *Daily Sketch*, 19 May 1955; *Reynolds News*, 22 May 1955; *Daily Express*, 20 May 1955; *Daily Mirror*, 20 May 1955; see also *News Chronicle*, 17 May 1955; *Evening News*, 17 May 1955; *Daily Express*, 20 May 1955; *Sunday Express*, 22 May 1955; *Sunday Dispatch*, 22 May 1955; *Illustrated London News*, 28 May 1955.
90 *Star*, 20 May 1955.
91 *Daily Worker*, 21 May 1955.
92 *Kinematograph Weekly*, 15 December 1955, 4. On *The Dam Busters* as the big picture of the year, see e.g. Allen Eyles in *Enter the Dream-House: Memories of Cinemas in South London from the Twenties to the Sixties*, ed. Margaret O'Brien and Allen Eyles (London: MOMI, 1993), 165.
93 Ramsden, *Dam Busters*, 113-19; see also Wales, *From Journey's End to The Dam Busters*, 295. On positive Commonwealth responses, see e.g. *The Argus*, 31 March 1956; *Globe and Mail*, 22 July 1955. On outrage in the UK about the reediting of *The Dam Busters* by Warners for the US release, see e.g. *The Times*, 19 November 1955; see also TNA, AIR 2/12261, Encl. 83A, 84A, November 1955. This was seen as overblown in the United States. See *Washington Post*, 25 November 1955.
94 Fred Inglis, 'National Snapshots: Fixing the Past in English War Films', in *British Cinema of the 1950s: A Celebration*, ed. Ian MacKillop and Neil Sinyard (Manchester: Manchester University Press, 2003), 44.
95 A special anniversary edition was released in the UK on DVD in 2010 and on Blu-ray in 2015. On *The Dam Busters* on UK television see Ramsden, *Dam Busters*, 119-20. That it had become a fixture on British television is illustrated by the scene in which the Bob Geldorf character vacantly sits watching it in the film version of Pink Floyd's *The Wall* (MGM, 1982).
96 See *The Independent*, 18 February 1994; Mark Robinson, *100 Greatest TV Ads* (London: HarperCollins, 2000), 94-5; Ramsden, *Dam Busters*, 123.
97 See Mark Connelly, *Reaching for the Stars: A New History of Bomber Command in World War II* (London: I.B. Tauris, 2001), 144; see also e.g. Angus Calder, *Disasters and Heroes: On War, Memory and Representation* (Cardiff: University of Wales Press, 2004), 136, and Rupert Matthews, *RAF Bomber Command at War* (London: Hale, 2009), 220, where *The Dam Busters* is stated confidently to be the *only* film made about Bomber Command.
98 Connelly, *Reaching for the Stars*, 147. It is worth noting that when Don Bennett, who rose during the war to lead 8 Group, published a volume of memoirs – D. C. T. Bennett, *Pathfinder: A War Autobiography* (London: Muller, 1958) – in which he was overtly critical of various aspects of how Bomber Command had evolved, reviewers

dismissed the criticism as the product of a difficult antipodean personality. See e.g. *The Times*, 10 July 1958; *Spectator*, 25 July 1958, 147; *Times Literary Supplement*, 25 July 1958, 420; *New Statesman*, 2 August 1958, 148–9; *Journal of the Royal United Services Institution*, 1 November 1958, 607–8. The often quite gritty autobiographical novels by former members of Bomber Command included Henry Archer and Edward Pine, *To Perish Never* (London: Cassell, 1954); Ray Ollis, *101 Nights* (London: Cassell, 1957); Miles Tripp, *Faith Is a Windsock* (London: Peter Davies, 1952); and John Watson, *Johnny Kinsman* (London: Cassell, 1955). There was also the bestselling novel *Room at the Top* by John Braine – who had served in the Royal Navy rather than the RAF – in which lower-class former Wellington observer Joe Lampton not only resents the competition for the romantic attentions of upper-middle-class Susan Brown posed by a decorated upper-middle-class squadron leader, Jack Wales, but also has occasional vivid memories of aircrew being burnt alive or smashed by flak and admits at one point that he was glad to be captured rather than killed. See John Braine, *Room at the Top* (London: Eyre and Spottiswoode, 1957), 23, 128, 161–2, 230. It was perhaps a sign that the hierarchical ethos of the decade was finally wearing thin that when this novel was turned into a highly successful feature by Romulus Films in 1959, scriptwriter Neil Paterson, diverging from the source material in which the sense of inferiority and resentment in the protagonist are self-generated, has Jack Wales (John Westbrook) consciously humiliate Joe Lampton (Laurence Harvey) in several scenes by playing the class-and-rank card. See Margaret Butler, *Film and Community in Britain and France: From* La Règle du Jeu *to* Room at the Top (London: I.B. Tauris, 2004), 106; see also Neil Sinyard, *Jack Clayton* (Manchester: Manchester University Press, 2000), 45. Lampton nonetheless still struck many as a far from sympathetic character because of his eagerness to pay virtually any price in order to enjoy the fruits of an upper-middle-class lifestyle. See e.g. *The Times*, 24 January 1959.

99   The phrase is borrowed here from the title of a 2014 TV documentary and the subsequent book: see John Nichol, *After the Flood: What the Dambusters Did Next* (London: Collins, 2015).

100 This did not mean, of course, that elements from *The Dam Busters* could not be refashioned without the rights to the Brickhill book, as was the case with the first *Star Wars* film. See Will Brooker, *Star Wars* (London: BFI, 2009), 37, 56; James Chapman, *War and Film* (London: Reaktion, 2008), 230–3.

101 Film Distributors' Association, UK cinema admissions 1935 to date, accessed 17 March 2017, http://www.launchingfilms.com/research-databank/uk-cinema-admissions; Broadcasters Audience Research Board, TV ownership, January 1956, accessed 17 March 2017, http://www.barb.co.uk/resources/tv-ownership/; Stuart Hanson, *From Silent Screen to Multi-Screen: A History of Cinema Exhibition in Britain since 1896* (Manchester: Manchester University Press, 2007), 99.

102 Porter, 'Outsiders in England', 163.

103 See Steve Call, *Selling Air Power: Military Aviation and Popular Culture after World War II* (College Station: Texas A&M University Press, 2009); Lawrence H. Suid, *Guts & Glory: The Making of the American Military Image on Film*, revised and expanded edition (Lexington: University Press of Kentucky, 2002), 109–15, 210–22, 229. The efforts of the Air Ministry were more invested in Fighter Command and the Battle of Britain. See Gary Campion, *The Battle of Britain, 1945–1965: The Air Ministry and the Few* (Basingstoke: Palgrave, 2015).

104 TNA, AIR 32/479, The Influence of Films on Recruits' Attitudes to the Service, 29 April 1959.

105 Falconer, *Filming the Dam Busters*, 155–6; *The Times*, 16 October 1956.
106 On the footage in *Battle of the V-1* see Ashley, *Flying Film Stars*, 156. The film is not mentioned as being among the successes of the year by Josh Billings in his summary for *Kinematograph Weekly*, 17 December 1959, 6–7.
107 On the single airworthy Lancaster in Britain, at this point belonging to the College of Aeronautics, see Lancaster PA474, Battle of Britain Memorial Flight, accessed 31 March 2017, http://www.raf.mod.uk/bbmf/theaircraft/lancasterpa474.cfm. Lancs continued to serve in a maritime reconnaissance role in Canada and France into the early 1960s. See Derry and Robinson, *Avro Lancaster*, Part 2.

Figure 3.1 Poster for *633 Squadron* (Mirisch, 1964).

Chapter 3

FIGHTERS: THE 1960s

As the new decade began to unfold, the list of potential pitfalls in developing another Bomber Command picture that could potentially replicate the success of *The Dam Busters* only seemed to lengthen. What the bomber boys and those who led them had accomplished during the war came under scrutiny both in print and on stage, while the limitation of having only a single airworthy Lancaster to use for filming purposes was exposed in a pair of major cloak-and-dagger features. Nonetheless, within ten years of the premiere of that mid-fifties triumph a new Bomber Command feature appeared on the big screen that was sufficiently successful at the international level to spawn a sequel before the decade was out.

An early sign that established narratives and authority figures were starting to become less sacrosanct appeared in the satirical stage revue *Beyond the Fringe*. In a series of comedy sketches, young Oxbridge graduates Alan Bennett, Peter Cook, Jonathan Miller and Dudley Moore took on sacred cows ranging from Scotland Yard to the Church of England. Among their targets was the way in which the struggle against Hitler had come to be viewed through rose-tinted glasses in a multipart piece entitled 'The Aftermyth of War', which included a none-too-subtle dig at Bomber Command:

SENIOR RAF OFFICER [Peter Cook]: Perkins! Sorry to drag you away from the fun, old boy. War's not going very well, you know.
JUNIOR RAF OFFICER [Jonathan Miller]: Oh, my God!
SENIOR RAF OFFICER: We are two down, and the ball's in the enemy's court. War is a psychological thing, Perkins, rather like a game of football. And you know how in a game of football ten men often play better than eleven – ?
JUNIOR RAF OFFICER: Yes, sir.
SENIOR RAF OFFICER: Perkins, we are asking you to be that one man. I want you to lay down your life, Perkins. We need a futile gesture at this stage. It will raise the whole tone of the war. Get up in a crate, over to Bremen, take a shufti, don't come back. Good-bye, Perkins. God, I wish I were going too.
JUNIOR RAF OFFICER: Good-bye, Sir—or perhaps it's *au revoir*?
SENIOR RAF OFFICER: No, Perkins.[1]

Given how many of their fellows had been lost on operations, at least some ex-Bomber Command personnel found this a bit offensive; but the sketch, and indeed the show, proved to be a huge box-office success after *Beyond the Fringe* opened in London in the second week of May 1961.[2]

Much more serious in every sense were the four volumes of the official history, *The Strategic Air Offensive against Germany 1939–1945*, many years in gestation, which appeared simultaneously six months later. The Air Ministry, as noted in Chapter 2, had already sponsored a three-part popular account of the RAF at war. These new volumes formed part of a different, much more detailed and scholarly set of tomes produced under the auspices of the Cabinet Office aiming to record, for policy purposes, precisely what had happened and why both on the home front and the various campaigns on land, at sea and in the air through privileged access to official records. The two authors chosen after a rather convoluted search to deal with strategic bombing, the distinguished diplomatic historian Charles Webster and a former Lancaster navigator and historian who had recently written his doctoral thesis on the subject, Noble Frankland, had both insisted from the start that for the sake of accuracy and academic credibility the work they produced should not be subject to official interference or censorship. As some both inside and outside the Air Ministry had feared, the resulting fully referenced volumes contained pieces of embarrassing data and some unsettling conclusions.[3]

The difficulties faced by Bomber Command in the early war years had been touched on before but never revealed in such detail. A special report undertaken in the summer of 1941, for instance, revealed that only a third of the aircraft dispatched had gotten within 5 miles of the intended target.[4] As for area bombing in later years, this definitely had not achieved its primary aim of effectively dislocating and destroying the war-related industries of the Third Reich: 'Huge areas in many great towns all over Germany were severely stricken and some were devastated', to be sure, 'but the will of the German people was not broken nor even seriously impaired and the effect on war production was remarkably small'.[5] At the same time over 55,000 Bomber Command aircrew had been killed in the course of the war.[6] As for the dams raid, its effects had been limited by the failure to breach the Sorpe; and even if it too had collapsed, 'it is probable that no crippling or very prolonged effect would have been obtained'.[7] Only in the last year of the war, as Allied armies closed in on the Reich and overran its forward air defences while American long-range fighters decimated the enemy air arm, did strategic bombing contribute directly to final victory through attacks on enemy fuel production and various precision strikes.[8] Arthur Harris, meanwhile, despite the efforts of Charles Portal as chief of air staff to get him to change his focus, had continued to concentrate on more general area bombing of urban centres.[9] Churchill, it was revealed, once a strong supporter of the campaign, had in the last phases of the war begun to question the mass destruction of cities such as Dresden.[10]

All this, and more besides, did not go down at all well with those who thought that an official history ipso facto ought to be supportive of its subject, and that the authors of *The Strategic Air Offensive* had unfairly maligned the wartime leadership of Bomber Command. Thoughtful observers who took the time to read through the volumes could find little fault with either the very measured language used throughout or the evidence and logic deployed; but this did not stop Frankland – Webster having died some months before publication – from being pilloried in large swathes of the patriotic press for having supposedly claimed that the huge wartime human and material investment in Bomber Command had resulted only in costly failure.[11]

Perhaps not surprisingly, retired senior RAF officers were often among the most critical reviewers. Philip Joubert, for example, having helped craft a more positive view of strategic bombing in the BBC-TV *War in the Air* series some years earlier, claimed in the pages of the *Daily Telegraph* that the conclusions were 'biased and unfair'. Robert Saundby, former deputy to Harris at Bomber Command (whose own book on air bombing, published just after the new official history, took a line similar to that of the Air Ministry volumes of the previous decade and was completely overshadowed), found it 'disappointing' and claimed to readers of the *RAF Review* that it did 'much less than justice to a great and successful operation of war'.[12] This did not stop the massive work from becoming the go-to reference source for anyone writing on the subject, not least among those predisposed to view the campaign as a waste of effort.[13]

The Strategic Air Offensive against Germany, as at least one reviewer had noted, criticised area bombing on practical rather than on ethical grounds.[14] Frankland himself made it clear afterward that in his view Bomber Command had no moral case to answer.[15] Not so a young self-taught historian by the name of David Irving, who less than two years later published *The Destruction of Dresden*, detailing the hugely destructive raids of February 1945 in which, he asserted, 135,000 people had been killed in what constituted 'the biggest single massacre in European history'.[16] Decades later, the highly partisan fashion in which Irving approached historical research would be fully revealed, and it is now generally accepted that the death toll was 25,000 or less.[17] The firestorm was real enough, however, and at the time *The Destruction of Dresden* was first published in the spring of 1963 it was hailed as revealing 'an operation unworthy of our history' (*Observer*), mounted against a target 'of no military or industrial significance' (*Spectator*) and 'one of those crimes against humanity whose authors would have been arraigned at Nuremberg if that Court had not been perverted into a mere instrument of Allied vengeance' (*New Statesman*).[18] 'I was not in any way responsible for the decision to make a full-scale air attack on Dresden', Saundby felt compelled to write after reading the book, adding: 'Nor was my Commander-in-Chief, Sir Arthur Harris.'[19]

A much less defensive attitude was apparent in how the bombing war was handled in the first television documentary series chronicling the role of certain Commonwealth dominions. Produced in 1961 by Artransa Park Television and directed by Alex Ezard for broadcast on Channel 7, *ANZAC* indicated Australian aircrew in Bomber Command had, at very high risk, been 'carrying the war deep into the heartland of the enemy'.[20] In *Canada at War*, meanwhile, produced by the National Film Board and broadcast by the CBC in the spring of 1962, Bomber Command in general and 6 Group (RCAF) in particular were shown to be grinding down the enemy war effort by bombing the Ruhr industries, setting back the Nazi rocket programme at Peenemünde, helping prepare for D-day through 'precision bombing' and striking heavy and presumably effective blows at cities like Hamburg and Berlin. Aircrew losses and fear are touched on in the script written by Donald Brittain and narrated by Bud Knapp, but concerning the loss of German civilian life and property, blame is placed entirely on Hitler.[21]

Back in the UK, moreover, the shadows being cast on the wartime record of Bomber Command in print did not mean that RAF air attacks were, as a subject, now necessarily too controversial for commercial success – especially with a young male audience. In popular war comic series like Air Ace Picture Library, the bomber boys were still shown as part of what developed into a 'tremendous striking force', able to 'rain blow after blow upon the Third Reich', smashing up factories as well as precise targets like the battleship *Tirpitz*.[22] Indeed, in light of the box-office success of *Sink the Bismarck!* at the start of the decade, it might have seemed natural for film producers to think about a feature on the latter operation by 617 Squadron of dam busters fame.[23]

Such a potential project, though, while able to avoid controversial aspects of the bombing war by concentrating once again on a precision raid, faced seemingly insurmountable challenges at a technical level. In the early years of the decade, it was all very well to appropriate footage from *Target for Tonight* to represent the bomber from which an eminent scientist accidentally parachutes to earth on German soil in the cheap-but-cheerful prisoner-of-war comedy *Very Important Person*.[24] It was quite another to contemplate doing so for a 'Sink-the-Tirpitz!'-type production in the context of rather better financed and much more successful international war films of the period such as *The Great Escape* that aimed at a global mass audience in which full use of colour on location formed an integral part of the anticipated attraction.[25] Yet the fact that there was only a single airworthy Lancaster in the UK – PA474, in this period a flying testbed operated by the College of Aeronautics – with which to conduct colour shooting created serious problems.[26] In various big cloak-and-dagger features of the period it was found easier to use scale models than to actually film PA474 aloft in the brief scenes in which Lancasters appeared.[27] That, though, would not suffice in any new flying epic where a bombing operation would be central rather than peripheral to the plot and model work would have to be at best ancillary to full-scale aerial photography for the sake of credibility. *Appointment in London* and *The Dam Busters* had been possible thanks to a handful of flyable Lancasters. For a widescreen colour picture, one Lanc simply would not do.[28]

There was, however, an option that did not involve stock footage or heavy reliance on a single aircraft and model work. Through a mixture of luck and foresight the Mirisch Corporation, an independent film production company based in the United States, had acquired the film rights to *633 Squadron* by author Frederick E. Smith soon after publication in the mid-1950s.[29] An air gunnery instructor through much of the war, Smith had written a novel that incorporated aspects of people he had known, personal research into settings and elements of various war operations including some of the exploits of 617 Squadron as well as efforts to knock out a heavy-water plant in Norway vital to German atomic research.[30] *633 Squadron* followed the trials and tribulations of a fictional elite Bomber Command squadron being reequipped with Mosquitos and specially trained for an ultimately successful but terribly costly precision strike in the spring of 1943 against a hydro facility protected by not only guns and fighters but also an overhanging rock face at the end of a cliff-lined Norwegian fjord.[31]

According to Smith, his publisher, Hutchinson, had not been very impressed by *633 Squadron*; but from the Mirisch perspective, the story had a lot of potential to be translated onto the big screen. It was set in wartime England, and if hiring and filming took place in the UK then this American company could take advantage of an exhibition tax – the famous Eady Levy – aimed at supporting local film production.[32] It featured Mosquitoes, and around the turn of the decade there were still just enough of these twin-engine aircraft in flying condition to credibly represent the squadron of the title. The machines described in the book, moreover, were fighter bombers that engaged in dogfights and strafing runs as well as bomb drops, thereby extending the range of potentially exciting aerial scenes. The plane would also have relative novelty value on screen, having appeared only tangentially in two previous British war pictures.[33] In contrast to *The Dam Busters*, the story contained a romance involving the squadron commander and the sister-in-exile of a Norwegian resistance fighter. Since it was about a raid on a single and highly important industrial target, the controversies surrounding the ethics and effectiveness of area bombing could be neatly sidestepped. Finally, it was at heart a work of fiction rather than history, which would make it easier to make any necessary alterations to the plot when crafting the screenplay since there could be no quibbling from veterans or critics about screen distortions of recorded events.[34]

Nonetheless, it took several years for *633 Squadron* to reach the production stage. As Walter Mirisch later explained, while there were limits to what could be done in order for the film to qualify for financial support from the British Film Production Fund, 'I wanted to stock it with as much American talent as I could' in order to maximize transatlantic box-office potential.[35] In late 1958, it was reported that John Sturges would direct a screenplay to be crafted by Rod Serling.[36] By the autumn of 1959, the word was that Dean Martin would take on the starring role.[37] After that, however, the project 'remained relatively inactive', according to Walter Mirisch, until James Clavell was contacted and 'wrote a good script'.[38]

The resulting screenplay departed from the source material in several important respects. The story was simplified through the elimination of various episodes and of subplots involving secondary characters. There were also a few additions, including a Gestapo torture scene that Smith had never written.[39] Perhaps because of another film in development centring on the actual commando attacks made on the heavy-water plant, the target was changed to a rocket fuel facility and the date advanced from 1943 to 1944.[40] In addition, there were significant character alterations. Mirisch had no interest in exploring issues of class, so every flyer in the film was made an officer. In the book, the central figure was Squadron Leader Roy Grenville, an experienced Englishman commanding the title unit. In line with the aim of using an American actor in the lead role for box-office purposes, he became Wing Commander Roy Grant, an ex-Eagle Squadron pilot: a part that was eventually altered somewhat after lead actor Cliff Robertson wanted changes and Mirisch persuaded blacklisted writer Howard Koch – then resident in England – to do some last-minute script doctoring.[41] Another major character created by Smith, a big blond Norwegian resistance leader by the name of Finn Bergman, was given the first name Erik by Clavell to avoid possible audience confusion over his nationality, and eventually played by the rather small and dark American actor George Chakiris.[42]

Efforts were also made at the scripting stage and later to solve the perennial problem of distinguishing one flyer from another in quickly shifting cockpit shots when heads and faces were mostly covered by flying helmets, goggles and oxygen masks by making the other lead pilots aurally or visually distinctive from Grant. Gillibrand, a Canadian in the book, became an Australian, a role which antipodean native John Meillon spoke with an unmistakable accent in the distinctive dark-blue uniform of the RAAF. Scott and Singh, neither present in the novel, were played respectively by English actor John Bonney with an artificial-hook right hand and Indian-born actor Julian Sherrier with the requisite Sikh facial hair and, on the ground, turban.[43]

The screenplay for *633 Squadron* took care to focus on the *The Dam Busters* elements that had drawn Mirisch to the book in the first place. The target is vital to the war effort, physically difficult to hit, requires special training and specialized weapons and the assault is preceded by a detailed pre-mission briefing where the crews are finally let in on the secret. Multiple attacks by individual aircraft, generating heavy losses through fire from the ground, seemingly all fail until something vast and apparently immovable is seen to suddenly give way and crash earthward: 'it's gone!' (*Dam Busters*) / 'it's going!' (*633 Squadron*). The connection between the two films became even more obvious through the inclusion in both of shots of the organizers of the attack waiting tensely back at headquarters for code-word news of how the operation is going to be relayed to them.[44] Even the endings are similar, the losses sustained being justified in conversation between two characters in terms of success and heroic determination.[45]

The opening credits of the film, like those of *The Dam Busters*, are displayed against an aerial cloudscape. There was even an effort to imply that *633 Squadron* too was based on historical events. The screenplay is listed as being drawn from 'the novel' by Frederick E. Smith; and later, in tiny letters, appears the standard legal disclaimer to the effect that all characters and events depicted in the film are fictitious and any resemblance to actual actions and events 'coincidental and unintentional'. But at the end of the opening credits, in screen-filling font, the following sentence appears: 'This story is inspired by the exploits of the Royal Air Force and the Commonwealth Mosquito air crews during World War II.'[46] Some later print ads for the film went further, stating authenticity was 'the keynote' and that *633 Squadron* was based on a 'fantastic true story'.[47] All this left at least some in the audience a little unsure as to the provenance of the plot.[48]

633 Squadron nonetheless was an updated version rather than a straight copy of *The Dam Busters*. There was much less stiff-upper-lip stoicism about the human cost of war, with Grant unable to say anything to comfort the distraught newly married wife of one of his pilots when her husband, after a crash-landing in which the Mosquito catches fire, is left faceless and blind.[49] In quite marked contrast to the celibate and uncomplicated enthusiasm of the screen version of Guy Gibson, the officer preparing to lead the squadron into battle in *633 Squadron* is portrayed not only as capable of amorous intent but also as a someone whose war experiences have made him cynical and fatalistic. By the time this new film was moving towards production, more than half a decade on from the old, a certain degree of distrust of authority figures and suspicion of war in general had become much more publicly acceptable.[50]

Walter Grauman, an American television director who had flown B-25s during the war and was eager to break into feature films, signed a contract for *633 Squadron*, as did Austrian actress Maria Perschy, who would play the female lead Hilde Bergman, sister of Erik and romantic interest for Grant. Two other Americans, Lewis Rachmil and Bob Relyea, would help supervise production in Britain on behalf of Walter Mirisch, though the producer of record would be an Englishman, Cecil Ford. The rest of the team were also from the UK, including Ron Goodwin, who produced a highly memorable score; production designer Michael Stringer; special effects wizard Tom Howard; director of photography Ted Scaife; editor Bert Bates; and second-unit director Roy Stevens. The majority of the supporting cast was also British and included familiar faces such as Harry Andrews, Barbara Archer, Donald Houston, Angus Lennie and Michael Goodliffe.[51]

Making arrangements for the acquisition, modification and servicing of the necessary planes took some time, even after Film Aviation Services Ltd and technical advisor Hamish Mahaddie – recommended by the Air Ministry – were brought on board. On a fairly modest budget of $1.3 million, shooting in widescreen Panavision using Deluxe colour stock was scheduled to begin in the autumn of 1962; but delays in obtaining enough airworthy Mosquitoes (mostly former target tugs) meant that it was not until the summer of the following year that cast and crew were able to start shooting at a Royal Air Force communications squadron airfield near Bovingdon and above the Wash and various Scottish lochs complete with a B-25 camera plane, a pair of Me-108 trainers to stand in for Me-109 fighters and a grand total of eleven Mosquitoes: five that could fly, four others that could be used as background or in crash staging and two more disassembled for cockpit footage.[52] Post-shoot work caused additional delay so that while the credits list the film as a product of 1963, it was not until the late spring of 1964 that *633 Squadron* hit the big screen on both sides of the Atlantic, starting with a Leicester Square premiere on behalf of the RAF Benevolent Fund.[53]

Reviews in the upmarket press were generally dismissive. In the *New York Times* the plot of *633 Squadron* was said to be 'overblown' and the script 'turgidly routine'.[54] In London the film was written off in the *Guardian* as 'completely without interest, cliché-ridden and dull' and skewered in the *Observer* as 'bone-headed' and a 'travesty' of what the war had really been like for those involved.[55] 'It's hard to imagine who would actually want to see this sort of film', sniffed *The Times*.[56]

In fact *633 Squadron* went on to appeal to a great many cinemagoers, especially in Britain where it ranked somewhere between the seventh and fourteenth most popular film of the year.[57] The dialogue was indeed full of clichés, as more downmarket dailies such as the *Express* confirmed; and few reviewers at any level had anything positive to say about the decision to cast George Chakiris as a Norwegian.[58] Yet as trade publications correctly understood in predicting box-office success rather than failure for *633 Squadron*, these weaknesses would be overshadowed by breathtakingly exciting scenes of aerial action.[59] Many critics of the script and dialogue more or less conceded that this was indeed the case. It was a 'spectacular flying film' (*Evening Standard*) that 'packed a powerful pictorial punch' (*Daily Mail*), with aerial combat sequences 'among the most exciting I have ever seen' (*Daily Herald*).[60] Even the veteran reviewer Dilys Powell of the *Sunday Times*, approaching her sixty-third birthday, wrote that 'there are some flying sequences here which are exciting enough to make me forget the hokum'.[61]

Within six months, *633 Squadron* had made a tidy overall profit of $400,000.[62] It would go on to become a regular fixture on television in the following decades, familiar enough, especially in the context of its score, to form the backdrop to several British TV ads forty-odd years later.[63] Back in the mid-1960s, the success of *633 Squadron* prompted Mirisch to develop a series of Second World War combat films using the same basic template: a modest per-picture budget of $1 million plus not-too-expensive American leads and British locations, crews and supporting casts. Among these, at the end of the decade, would be a de facto sequel to *633 Squadron*.[64]

On the stage as well as on the page, meanwhile, Bomber Command continued to be subjected to critical scrutiny. The subject of quite intense and often public arguments about truth, censorship and libel, the controversial Rolf Hochhuth play *Soldiers*, finally performed in London in late 1968, debated the ethics of fire-raising raids through imaginary conversations between, among others, Winston Churchill, his pro-bombing chief scientific advisor, Lord Cherwell, and a public opponent of the policy, Bishop Bell, in which the latter holds the moral high ground.[65] Predictably, Arthur Harris, when he heard about the play, felt that once again Bomber Command was being maligned.[66] Most of the debate, however, focused not on bombing but on the conspiracy-theory claim that Churchill had connived in a plot to kill Polish leader General Sikorski through a successfully staged 'accidental' plane crash.[67] Meanwhile, in a sometimes rather convoluted analysis of wartime strategic bombing aimed at the general reader published in Britain in 1968 and the United States in 1969, journalist Anthony Verrier, while making use of new interviews, essentially echoed the position taken by Webster and Frankland concerning the failure of area bombing.[68] At the end of the decade, Frankland himself wrote a heavily illustrated sixty thousand-word summary of his original conclusions in a volume of a popular series that sold nearly a quarter-million copies.[69]

Yet in other media a more positive message continued to prevail. The cloak-and-dagger feature film *Operation Crossbow*, for example, released in 1965 and quite successful at the box office, included a brief recreation of a Bomber Command operation codenamed Hydra, in which a heavy bomber force successfully struck the important rocket research facility at Peenemünde in August 1943.[70] The cover art of a war comic in the popular Commando series, 'Low-Level Lanc', published in June 1967, suggested that an RAF heavy bomber was capable of dropping a high-explosive load precisely on target.[71] At a more elevated level there was the fifty-minute BBC-TV documentary *Fifty Years of the R.A.F.*, in which the history of the service was chronicled in almost entirely positive terms, including the Second World War as fought by Bomber Command. It was conceded in the programme that 'Bomber Command lost more aircrew in the Second World War than the British Army did officers in the First', but area bombing was discussed only in reference to the first thousand-bomber raid, judged as the start of 'a campaign without parallel in human history'. Much more time was spent outlining the attack on the dams, described in the narration as 'the most accurate raid of the war' and as one which had dealt 'a heavy blow' to German industry.[72] Just under ten million people watched when *Fifty Years of the R.A.F.* was broadcast on BBC-1 on 28 March 1968, and subsequent audience research indicated that watchers were 'highly appreciative'.[73]

There would likely continue to be, in short, a willing audience for any successor to *633 Squadron* despite the critics. The formula Mirisch had developed meant that Oakmont, a subsidiary production company, would have to work with a smaller budget and people drawn from television. Lewis Rachmil would once again be producer, while another American, Boris Sagal, would be brought in as director.[74] This time the star would be an Englishman rather than an American; but it was no accident that David McCallum was best known for co-starring in the hit American TV series *The Man from U.N.C.L.E.*, several episodes of which Sagal had directed.[75] British players known for their television work in the UK, such as David Buck and Suzanne Neve, would round out the cast.[76]

As for the plot, there was nothing more to draw from the *633 Squadron* novel by Frederick E. Smith, and there were as yet no sequels.[77] Even to use the squadron number might cause Oakmont copyright difficulties with the author, who had not been involved in creating the first screenplay and was ambivalent about what had been done to his original story.[78] It was nevertheless still possible for the designated scriptwriters, Donald Sandford and Joyce Perry, both with a background in American television, to adopt half the original title for *Mosquito Squadron* and develop a screenplay that mirrored various elements of, and was set shortly after, the big raid of the earlier film.

Once more the plot revolved around a do-or-die special mission with links to actual events. This time the aim is for '641 Squadron' to use a new special bomb to destroy the entrance to an underground facility in France where the Germans are developing a new 'V' weapon and also free a group of RAF prisoners being held hostage in the adjacent French chateau by breaching the outer wall. The skip bomb in question, codenamed 'highball', had been developed by Barnes Wallis as a smaller version of the mine used to breach the dams, and though various problems meant that it was never used in anger, a special unit of Mosquitoes, 618 Squadron, had been formed to operate it.[79] Underground work at Mimoyecques on the mountings for the third of the secret German retaliatory weapons, a very high-velocity cannon, had been halted due to hits from another Barnes Wallis bomb, the 'Tallboy', delivered by 617 Squadron in July 1944.[80] An even more direct historical reference point was Operation Jericho, mounted some months before by Mosquitoes of 140 Wing led by P. C. 'Pick' Pickard of *Target for Tonight* fame. This particular airstrike had knocked down a wall of a prison at Amiens in order to free French Resistance fighters before they were due to be shot.[81] These were all episodes with great cinematic potential – indeed the last had been the subject of a French feature made over twenty years earlier – and combining them in a fictional manner doubtless offered the possibility of trebling audience excitement. This time, though, there was no attempt in the titles or promotional material to suggest *Mosquito Squadron* was not at heart a work of fiction.[82]

There were plenty of other similarities between the screenplays of *Mosquito Squadron* and *633 Squadron*. As in the earlier film, a senior officer – in this case Air Commodore Hufford played by Charles Gray – coldheartedly pushes the mission forward despite the mounting risks involved. Once again, romantic and ethical dilemmas form subplots. In *633 Squadron*, the central character becomes attached to Hilde Bergman, and is then full of self-loathing at the need to kill her brother Erik, with whom she was emotionally very close. In *Mosquito Squadron*, the pilot leading the raid becomes involved with the wife of his best friend and then has to cope with the news that the husband has not in fact been killed in action but instead is being held hostage in the chateau due to be bombed out of existence whether or not the adjacent tunnel is hit or the wall breached. There are gunfight scenes in each between German troops and members of the resistance, and in both films the officer leading the squadron crash-lands but survives. Roy wears an Eagle Squadron patch while Quint sports Canada flashes on his uniform, but the second name given to the David McCallum character is virtually identical to that given to Cliff Robertson: Munroe versus Munro. There is even a new secondary character in *Mosquito Squadron* with a claw hand.[83]

There were now fewer Mosquitoes to draw on, in part because three of them had been intentionally broken up or destroyed during the filming of *633 Squadron*. Nonetheless, six were eventually tracked down, four in flyable condition, along with a couple of Anson transports and – as a camera plane – a Shackleton maritime reconnaissance patrol aircraft courtesy of the Royal Aircraft Establishment. The Ministry of Defence once again allowed Bovingdon to be used for location shooting, along with Minley Manor, a country house that could credibly stand in for a French chateau.[84] A more limited budget, however, allowed for less filmed aerial spectacle, which in turn meant that, as well as dispensing with Panavision while keeping Deluxe, a fair amount of action footage from *633 Squadron* had to be recycled.[85]

Shooting took place in the summer of 1968, and the film was more or less complete by the end of the year. Normally a spring or summer release date would have been chosen, but likely because of the widely anticipated rollout of a much bigger British war picture centring on the wartime Royal Air Force, *Battle of Britain*, also distributed through United Artists, in September of 1969, *Mosquito Squadron* was not released as part of a double bill until the summer of the following year in the United States and the late autumn in the UK.[86]

The trade reviews were not particularly upbeat concerning the prospects of *Mosquito Squadron*, though *Boxoffice* commented that 'the production values and aerial shots are quite good'.[87] The film had its defenders in the popular press. 'An entertaining, action-filled war drama' was the verdict of the *Sunday Express*; 'plenty of dramatic excitement', opined the *Daily Mirror*. 'Quite exciting in an old-fashioned sort of way', admitted the critic for the *Guardian*.[88] The majority of reviews, however, were decidedly negative. It was 'a very ordinary wartime melodrama' (*Telegraph*), with 'too much talk and too little action' (*The Times*).[89] *Mosquito Squadron* received particularly harsh treatment at the hands of Ian Christie in the pages of the *Daily Express*. He wrote that the characters 'seemed to me to be played by cardboard dummies', adding that it was perhaps just 'the dull, ponderous direction of Boris Sagal that gave the characters their unbelievable, synthetic qualities'.[90] In the *New York Times*, the film was dismissed as a 'dud'.[91] Box-office performance was poor enough for United Artists to stop backing the Mirisch formula.[92] *Mosquito Squadron* had the usual afterlife on television, but it is worth noting in light of the love triangle written into the script that even *Australian Women's Weekly* awarded it a mere two stars out of a possible five a dozen years later.[93]

Despite the challenges presented by the disappearance of period aircraft and growing doubts about the wartime achievements of Bomber Command, the Mirisch organization, thanks in part to cooperation from within Whitehall, had developed in the first half of the 1960s a successful strategy for a film about RAF bombing that avoided controversy while generating international audience appeal. A second try in the latter 1960s was significantly less profitable – doubtless partly due to lower production values but also perhaps because some of the dialogue and sentiments expressed in *Mosquito Squadron* seemed more dated than those in *633 Squadron*. In contrast to Roy Munro's modern American cynicism, Quint Munroe – technically Canadian but brought up by middle-class English stepparents – gloomily exhibits the kind of romantic inhibition and dedication to duty more typical of pictures of the 1940s like *Brief Encounter* than more contemporary British films such as *I'll Never Forget What's'isname* in which a near-namesake middle-class central character, Andrew Quint, rebels against conformity in spectacular though ultimately unsuccessful fashion.[94] For someone like *Sunday Times* critic Dilys Powell, born at the beginning of the century, the throwback approach could simply appear as a 'fair try at recreating the emotions of the early 1940s'.[95] To someone like Tom Milne on the other hand, born a quarter century later and writing for the *Observer*, the result was 'the sort of film one can't believe they still makes these days, all stiff-upper-lip and noble sentiments'.[96]

633 Squadron had indicated that it was possible to present Bomber Command in a way that would entertain younger audiences twenty years after the events described, and *Mosquito Squadron* that drawing on the models of the past without adequate adaptation to contemporary mores was a recipe for failure. If and how the RAF bombing war would be presented on screen three decades on, when approximately a third of British teens and adults had been born after the fighting ceased and had grown up in an evolving social world, remained to be seen.[97]

Notes

1. Alan Bennett, Peter Cook, Jonathan Miller and Dudley Moore, *Beyond the Fringe* (New York: Random House, 1963), 45.
2. On the development and success of *Beyond the Fringe* see Humphrey Carpenter, *That Was Satire That Was* (London: Gollancz, 2000), 91–126. On distaste among some Bomber Command veterans, see e.g. Tony Iveson in Patrick Bishop, *Bomber Boys: Fighting Back, 1940–1945* (London: HarperPress, 2007), xxv–xxvi.
3. On the long and complicated prepublication history of *The Strategic Air Offensive against Germany* see Sebastian Cox, 'Setting the Historical Agenda: Webster and Frankland and the Debate over the Strategic Bombing Offensive against Germany, 1939–1945', *Contributions to the Study of World History* 106 (2003), 147–59; Noble Frankland, *History at War: The Campaigns of an Historian* (London: DLM, 1998), 40–113.
4. Charles Webster and Noble Frankland, *The Strategic Air Offensive against Germany, 1939–1945: Volume I* (London: HMSO, 1961), 178.
5. Ibid., *The Strategic Air Offensive against Germany, 1939–1945: Volume III* (London: HMSO, 1961), 288.
6. Ibid., 286–7.
7. Ibid., *II*, 289, 172, 178.
8. Ibid., *III*, 288–9.
9. Ibid., 76–94.
10. Ibid., 112.
11. See Frankland, *History at War*, 114–25.
12. *Royal Air Forces Quarterly*, 1, 4 (1961), 266; *Daily Telegraph*, 13 October 1961. On the former deputy AOC-in-C's own more upbeat interpretation see Robert Saundby, *Air Bombardment: The Story of Its Development* (London: Chatto and Windus, 1961). Not surprisingly, this met with a more positive response in RAF circles: see review in *Royal Air Forces Quarterly*, 1, 4 (1961), 334.
13. See e.g. David Divine, *The Blunted Sword* (London: Hutchinson, 1964), 207. The official history, it should be noted, was by no means flawless analytically: see Peter Gray, *The Leadership, Direction and Legitimacy of the RAF Bomber Offensive from Inception to 1945* (London: Continuum, 2012), 257–9.
14. See C. P. Stacey review in *International Journal* 17, 3 (1962), 307–8.
15. See Noble Frankland, 'Some Reflections on the Strategic Air Offensive, 1939–1945', *Journal of the Royal United Services Institution* 107, 626 (1 May 1962), 99.
16. David Irving, *The Destruction of Dresden* (London: Kimber, 1963), 234.
17. On problems with Irving's figures for Dresden see Richard J. Evans, *Lying about Hitler: History, Holocaust, and the David Irving Trial* (New York: Basic, 2001), 149–84.
18. Richard Crossman in *New Statesman*, 3 May 1963, 684; Richard Gott in *Spectator*, 14 June 1963, 782; Harold Nicolson in *Observer*, 5 May 1963. Crossman was instrumental in negotiations for a memorial in Dresden, as he put in his diary on 17 July 1963, 'to be presented by Coventry Cathedral, to commemorate the Germans killed in the raid'. *The Backbench Diaries of Richard Crossman*, ed. Janet Morgan (London: Hamish Hamilton and Jonathan Cape, 1985), 1015. A previous indictment of an earlier firestorm raid by American author Martin Caidin, *The Death of Hamburg* (New York: Ballantine, 1960) was largely ignored by reviewers on both sides of the Atlantic.

19 Robert Saundby foreword to Irving, *Destruction of Dresden*, 5. This was true insofar as Bomber Command HQ was acting on directives from higher up the chain of command. See Webster and Frankland, *Strategic Air Offensive*, III, 101–9. Later in the decade, Dresden would become a stick with which to beat supporters of American bombing in Vietnam. See Melden E. Smith, Jr., 'The Strategic Bombing Debate: The Second World War and Vietnam', *Journal of Contemporary History* 12 (1977), 183.
20 See *ANZAC* (Artransa Park Television, 1961), Episode 9, 'RAAF over Europe'. The series was not always well received: see *Australian Women's Weekly*, 27 December 1961, 19.
21 See *Canada at War* (NFB, 1962), Episode 6, 'Turn of the Tide'; Episode 8, 'New Directions'; Episode 12, 'V Was for Victory'. On the development and positive critical reception of this major documentary series see CBC Archives, Toronto, 'Canada at War' and 'Productions – Canada at War' files.
22 *Blast Bomb* (Air Ace Picture Library no. 76, November 1961), Introduction; *Fighter! Fighter!* (Air Ace Picture Library no. 39, February 1961), Introduction; *Target Tirpitz* (Air Ace Picture Library no. 54, June 1961). On the rise of British war comics see James Chapman, *British Comics: A Cultural History* (London: Reaktion, 2011), 95 ff.
23 On the success of *Sink the Bismarck!* (Twentieth Century-Fox, 1960) see *Kinematograph Weekly*, 15 December 1960, 8. An attack on the *Tirpitz* had, to be sure, already been the subject of a naval war epic, *Above Us the Waves* (London Independent Producers, 1955), but the midget submarines involved had only damaged the enemy battleship in 1943, not sunk it as Lancasters of 617 Squadron did in 1944.
24 On the making of *Very Important Person* (Independent Artists, 1961) see Ken Annakin, *So You Wannabe a Director?* (Sheffield: Tomahawk, 2001), 127–8.
25 See comment by Walter Grauman in BFI Library, *633 Squadron* pressbook, and Ed Schenpf, '633 Squadron', *Air Classics* 2 (1964), 44. The great exception to the full-colour international war-film rule was *The Longest Day* (Twentieth Century-Fox, 1962). Black-and-white stock was deliberately chosen in this instance to try and infuse the film with a more 'authentic' look: that is, make it appear similar to wartime monochrome combat footage and thus more credible as a cinematic recreation of a recent historical event. See George F. Custen, *Twentieth Century's Fox: Darryl F. Zanuck and the Culture of Hollywood* (New York: BasicBooks, 1997), 361.
26 On the history of Lancaster PA474 from 1945 through the mid-1960s see Jarrod Cutter, *The Battle of Britain Memorial Flight: 50 Years of Flying* (Barnsley: Pen and Sword Aviation, 2007), 159.
27 PA474 was scheduled to appear in *The Guns of Navarone* (Highroad Productions, 1961), *The Heroes of Telemark* (Benton Film Productions, 1965) and *Operation Crossbow* (MGM-British, 1965) but in the end was not used except for one short landing scene in the latter. See TNA, AIR 2/16547; Mark Ashley, *Flying Film Stars: The Directory of Aircraft in British World War Two Films* (Walton-on-Thames: Red Kite. 2014), 172, 198, 206.
28 As Chapter 4 indicates, an attempt to marry up shots of PA474 with shots of specially developed scale models that could actually fly was eventually tried for the small screen, but even in this case it was clear which were appearing at any given point, and the contrast would have been even more glaring on the big screen. On the differing attitude to accuracy of RAF detail in television and film production see T. G. Hamish Mahaddie, *Hamish: The Memoirs of Group Captain T. G. Mahaddie* (London: Ian Allan, 1989), 119.

29 Walter Mirisch, *I Thought We Were Making Movies, Not History* (Madison: University of Wisconsin Press, 2008), 201; Frederick E. Smith, *The Final Absurdities: An Autobiography, Volume 3* (Bicester: Emissary, 2012), 10.

30 The plot of the novel suggests that the war operations Smith drew on included the dams raid, the sinking of the *Tirpitz* in a fjord in northern Norway through the dropping of Tallboy 'earthquake' bombs as well as various attempts to disrupt heavy water production at the Vemork Norsk Hydro plant in south-eastern Norway: see *Flight International*, 15 August 1963, 260. On his wartime service see Frederick E. Smith, *A Youthful Absurdity: An Autobiography, Volume 1* (Bicester: Emissary, 2010). On researching *633 Squadron* – including approaching the Air Ministry for a fictional squadron number – see ibid., *Author's Absurdities*, 159, 191–9; Frederick E. Smith to Doug Deaton, 26 January 1966, in Doug Deaton, 'Bitten by a Mosquito', Vintage Wings of Canada, accessed 15 May 2017, http://www.vintagewings.ca/VintageNews/Stories/tabid/116/articleType/ArticleView/articleId/518/633-Squadron.aspx.

31 Frederick E. Smith, *633 Squadron* (London: Hutchinson, 1956).

32 See Mirisch, *I Thought We Were Making Movies*, 201. On the UK arms of Hollywood production companies taking advantage of the opportunities presented by the Eady levy in this period see Jonathan Stubbs, 'The Eady Levy: A Runaway Bribe? Hollywood Production and British Subsidy in the Early 1960s', *Journal of British Cinema and Television History* 6 (2009), 1–20.

33 The Mosquito had featured briefly in *The Man Who Never Was* (Sumar, 1956) and at slightly greater length in the ground-attack role in *The Purple Plain* (Two Cities, 1954), set in the Far East.

34 The book's author, to be sure, was unhappy with the way in which a major subplot involving a Canadian pilot and his navigator did not appear in the script – see Smith to Deaton, 26 January 1966, in Deaton, 'Bitten by a Mosquito', note 30 above – but as the screen rights had been sold he had absolutely no control over what was done to his story: see Smith, *Author's Absurdities*, 199–200.

35 Mirisch, *I Thought We Were Making Movies*, 201.

36 *New York Times*, 1 December 1958.

37 *Australian Women's Weekly*, 30 September 1959, 68.

38 Mirisch, *I Thought We Were Making Movies*, 201.

39 That adding a torture scene involving a female Nazi interrogator was a calculated addition is suggested by the later appearance of *Ilsa, She Wolf of the SS* (Aetaes, 1975) and other money-spinning Nazi sexploitation films. In the film *633 Squadron* subplots in the novel involving a Canadian pilot and his English navigator and an intelligence officer and his wife were cut, as were various characters considered extraneous to the plot, such as the brigadier and two flight commanders, and the squadron's transition from Boston light bombers to Mosquito fighter bombers.

40 The competing film was *The Heroes of Telemark* (Benton, 1965).

41 Mirisch, *I Thought We Were Making Movies*, 203.

42 Mirisch cast Chakiris because he had a contract option on him dating back to the hit musical *West Side Story* (Mirisch/Seven Arts, 1961) – see Mirisch, *I Thought We Were Making Movies*, 201 – and perhaps also because of the trend in recent war-film productions to cast pop idols such as Paul Anka (*The Longest Day* [Twentieth Century-Fox, 1962]) and James Darren (*The Guns of Navarone* [Highroad, 1961]) to broaden audience appeal.

43 As the production team may have known through, e.g., their technical advisor, there were wartime precedents for these two characters in the form of fighter pilots James 'One-Armed Mac' MacLachlan and Mohinder Singh Pujji.
44 'Vesuvius' as code word for success in *633 Squadron* was true to the novel, while 'Nigger' in *The Dam Busters* was true to history: though whether or not to delete or alter the latter became an issue as time passed and standards changed. See John Ramsden, *The Dam Busters* (London: I.B. Tauris, 2003), 51. George Lucas would borrow the down-the-fjord attack from *633 Squadron* in staging the climactic canyon-trench assault on the Death Star in *Star Wars* (Lucasfilm, 1977). The *633 Squadron* waiting-for-news-at-headquarters scene was not present in the Smith novel and likely borrowed for the screenplay directly from *The Dam Busters* film.
45 In *The Dam Busters*, the exchange written by R. C. Sherriff is between a philosophically professional Guy Gibson, played by Richard Todd, and an angst-laden Barnes Wallis, played by Michael Redgrave. See Ramsden, *Dam Busters*, 93. While it is true that Grant is not on hand at the end of *633 Squadron*, having been shot down on the raid, it is not quite the case that 'unlike in *The Dam Busters*, no character is on hand to justify the high loss of life' (Jeremy Havardi, *Projecting Britain at War: The National Character in British World War II Films* [Jefferson, NC: McFarland, 2014], 180). As written by James Clavell, it is the prime architect of the raid, Air Vice-Marshal Davis, played by Harry Andrews, who offers pragmatic consolation to the upset intelligence officer, Squadron Leader Frank Adams, played by Michael Goodliffe, adding that despite nobody returning 'you can't kill a squadron'. It is possible to interpret these words as 'empty bombast' (Robert Murphy, *British Cinema and the Second World War* [London: Continuum, 2000], 243), especially given Davis's body language once back in his staff car and the alternative version provided in the press synopsis – 'Men who do what they have done, never die. Their memory will live forever!' (BFI Library, *633 Squadron* one-page press synopsis). However, the swelling background music when the words are uttered indicates that the audience is meant to take them as both sincere and profound. Patrick Gibbs, in reviewing the film, commented that the final scene would have been better suited 'to ironic rather than heroic treatment'. *Daily Telegraph*, 6 June 1964.
46 Use of the phrase 'World War II', standard in the United States, rather than 'Second World War', then more common in the United Kingdom, was likely a matter of the former taking up less space than the latter.
47 See *Toronto Daily Star*, 11 July 1964; *Western Herald* [NSW], 11 August 1967.
48 See e.g. *Daily Worker*, 6 June 1944; Deaton, 'Bitten by a Mosquito'; marquee picture in Smith, *Final Absurdities*, 48.
49 The young pilot was Pilot Officer Bissell, played by Scott Finch, and his wife a WAAF sergeant, nee Mary Blake, played by Suzan Farmer. This was one of the scenes not in the book.
50 See e.g. Carpenter, *That Was Satire*, and the successful Joan Littlewood 1963 musical black comedy on Britain in the First World War: Theatre Workshop, *Oh, What a Lovely War* (London: Bloomsbury Metheun Drama, 2014), less successfully extended to the Second World War in the Richard Lester film *How I Won the War* (Petersham, 1967). On the contrast between Sherriff's Guy Gibson and Clavell's Roy Grant see Havardi, *Projecting Britain at War*, 180.
51 On choosing a director and producers see Mirisch, *I Thought We Were Making Movies*, 201–2. Harry Andrews, who played Air Vice-Marshal Davis, had played supporting roles in 1950s British war films from *The Red Beret* (Warwick, 1953) through *Ice Cold in*

Alex (ABPC, 1958). Barbara Archer had already developed her barmaid character in *In the Wake of a Stranger* (Crescent, 1959) and *Libel* (MGM, 1959). Donald Houston had recently played an RAF pilot opposite Richard Burton in *The Longest Day* (Twentieth Century-Fox, 1962), while Angus Lennie, who played Grant's navigator, Hoppy Hopkinson, had also put on RAF flyer's uniform in the 1963 Mirisch hit *The Great Escape*, which James Clavell had scripted. As for Michael Goodliffe, he had played a similar RAF intelligence officer role in *The One That Got Away* (Julian Wintle, 1957).

52 See Ashley, *Flying Film Stars*, 190–6; Simon D. Beck, *The Aircraft-Spotter's Film and Television Companion* (Jefferson, NC: McFarland, 2016), 173–4; Jonathan Falconer, *RAF Bomber Command in Fact, Film and Fiction* (Stroud: Sutton, 1996), 94–5; Mahaddie, *Memoirs*,117; Mirisch, *I Thought We Were Making Movies*, 202, 204; TNA, AIR 2/16547, J. Crewdson to R. R. Goodbody, 31 March 1964; *Flight International*, 15 August 1963, 260.

53 On the premiere see Smith, *Final Absurdities*, 47–50.

54 *New York Times*, 25 June 1964.

55 *Observer*, 7 June 1964; *Guardian*, 5 June 1964; see also *Sunday Telegraph*, 7 June 1964.

56 *The Times*, 4 June 1964.

57 *The Times*, 1 January 1965; see Mirisch, *I Thought We Were Making Movies*, 204.

58 On criticism of clichés see *Daily Express*, 4 June 1964; *Daily Herald*, 5 June 1964; *Daily Mail*, 2 June 1964; also *Evening Standard*, 4 June 1964; *Evening News*, 4 June 1964; *New Statesman*, 5 June 1964, 886. On the miscasting of George Chakiris, see e.g. *Variety*, 3 June 1964; *Evening Standard*, 4 June 1964; *Daily Express*, 4 June 1964; *Punch*, 17 June 1964, 904; *Toronto Daily Star*, 11 July 1964.

59 See e.g. *Boxoffice*, 22 June 1964; *Variety*, 3 June 1964.

60 *Daily Herald*, 5 June 1964; *Daily Mail*, 2 June 1964; *Evening Standard*, 4 June 1964; see also e.g. *Daily Express*, 4 June 1964; *Daily Worker*, 6 June 1964; *Evening News*, 4 June 1964; *Globe and Mail*, 11 July 1964; *Punch*, 17 June 1964, 904; *New Statesman*, 5 June 1964, 886; *Washington Post*, 2 July 1964.

61 *Sunday Times*, 7 June 1964.

62 On the box-office gross for *633 Squadron* see *Variety*, 6 January 1965. On it doing better-than-average business see *Boxoffice*, 5 April 1965, B31.

63 See *Evening Standard*, 4 September 2002; *Campaign*, 30 July 2010, 3; Smith, *Final Absurdities*, 50.

64 Films in the series included *Attack on the Iron Coast* (1967) and *Submarine X-1* (1968). Mirisch, *I Thought We Were Making Movies*, 204

65 See Rolf Hochhuth, *Soldiers: An Obituary for Geneva*, trans. Robert David MacDonald (London: Andre Deutsch, 1968), 83–6, 89–91, 141–51, 187–237. On the debate inside and outside the National Theatre on whether or not to stage *Soldiers*, and development of the New Theatre production, see Dominic Shellard, *Kenneth Tynan: A Life* (New Haven: Yale University Press, 2003), 306–14.

66 Churchill College Archives, Oliver Lyttelton Papers, CHAN II 4/13, Part I, Harris to Chandos, 18 April 1967, f. 80; see Tynan to Harris, 30 March 1967, in *Kenneth Tynan Letters*, ed. Kathleen Tynan (London: Weidenfeld and Nicolson, 1994), 393–4.

67 See e.g. David Frost, *An Autobiography* (London: HarperCollins, 1993), 409–16; *Observer*, 1 December 1968; Carlos Thompson, *The Assassination of Winston Churchill* (Gerrards Cross: Colin Smythe, 1969). Though there were some decent reviews (see e.g. *The Times*, 13 December 1968; *New Statesman*, 20 December 1968), the London production at the New Theatre closed after a short run (see Shellard, *Kenneth Tynan*,

314). Because of the National Theatre's decision not to proceed, the premiere of *Soldiers* in English occurred in Canada, where it was lauded in both the *Toronto Star* (28 February 1968) and *Globe and Mail* (29 February 1968) but condemned in the magazine *Maclean's* (1 April 1968, 95).
68 Anthony Verrier, *The Bomber Offensive* (London: Batsford, 1968/New York: Macmillan, 1969); see *The Listener*, 25 July 1968, 118; *New Statesman*, 26 April 1968, 553-4.
69 Frankland, *History at War*, 127. See Noble Frankland, *Bomber Offensive: The Devastation of Europe* (New York: Ballantine, 1969/London: Macdonald, 1970).
70 *Operation Crossbow* (MGM-British, 1965). On box-office success see *The Times*, 31 December 1965.
71 *Low-Level Lanc*, Commando 263, June 1967 [re-released as 927, April 1975]. The story, to be sure, suggested that a low-level attack of this sort was unacceptably high-risk in nature, but as always with comics it was the images rather than the text that were most striking.
72 TNA, AIR 20/10307, BBC 'Fifty Years of the R.A.F.' script, 27-32.
73 Ibid., Television Coverage – RAF 50th Anniversary, minute by P. M. Brothers, 25 April 1968.
74 *Boxoffice*, 29 April 1968, E6.
75 On *The Man from U.N.C.L.E.* see John Abbott, *Cool TV of the 1960s: Three Shows That Changed the World* (Bloomington, IN: CreateSpace, 2015), 29-192.
76 David Buck was familiar from the supernatural anthology series *Mystery and Imagination* (ABC/Thames, 1966-8), while Suzanne Neve was known for a supporting role in the BBC adaptation of *The Forsythe Saga* (BBC-TV, 1967).
77 Smith would eventually publish eight other '633 Squadron' novels, but the first two of these, *Operation Rhine Maiden* and *Operation Crucible*, only appeared under the Cassell imprint in 1975.
78 Smith, *Final Absurdities*, 44. '633 Squadron' was, however, mentioned as a unit in a briefing scene in *Mosquito Squadron*, indicating that the new film inhabited the same pseudo-factual wartime world as its predecessor.
79 See Des Curtis, *A Most Secret Squadron: The First Full Story of 618 Squadron* (London: Grub Street, 2009).
80 John Nicol, *After the Flood: What the Dambusters did Next* (London: Collins, 2015), 139-43.
81 Jack Fishman, *And the Walls Came Tumbling Down* (London: Macmillan, 1983).
82 The earlier French film on the Amiens Raid had been *Jéricho* (Sacha Gordine, 1945).
83 The character with the hook hand was Flight Lieutenant Douglas Shelton, played by David Dundas, another well-known face from television.
84 See Ashley, *Flying Film Stars*, 215-16; Beck, *Aircraft-Spotter's Film and Television Guide*, 146-7; Falconer, *RAF Bomber Command in Fact, Film and Fiction*, 95-6. Cliff Robertson, a pilot and aviation enthusiast as well as an actor, had been unhappy at the way in which vintage Mosquitoes had been wilfully destroyed in *633 Squadron*. Di Freeze, *In the Cockpit with Cliff Robertson* (Denver: Freeze Time Media, 2013), 15.
85 In addition, the opening pre-credit sequence of *Mosquito Squadron* was lifted from *Operation Crossbow* (MGM-British, 1965).
86 Some of the aircraft used for *Battle of Britain* had been based at Bovingdon at the same time *Mosquito Squadron* was being filmed. See Ashley, *Flying Film Stars*, 216.
87 *Boxoffice*, 15 June 1970, 39; see also e.g. *Variety*, 8 July 1970, 14.

88 *Daily Mirror*, 5 November 1970; *Sunday Express*, 8 November 1970; see also e.g. *Daily Mail*, 6 November 1970; Monthly *Film Bulletin*, March 1970, 57.
89 *The Times*, 6 November 1970; *Observer*, 8 November 1970; *Daily Telegraph*, 6 November 1970.
90 *Daily Express*, 5 November 1970; see also e.g. *Sun*, 5 November 1970.
91 *New York Times*, 2 July 1970.
92 *Variety*, 26 August 1970, 6.
93 *Australian Women's Weekly*, 30 June 1982, 122–3.
94 Andrew Quint was played by Oliver Reed. *I'll Never Forget What's'isname* (Scimitar, 1967).
95 *Sunday Times*, 8 November 1970; see also Cecil Wilson (b. 1909) in *Daily Mail*, 6 November 1970.
96 *Observer*, 8 November 1970; see also e.g. Fergus Cashin (b. 1924) in *Sun*, 5 November 1970. One leading film scholar of younger vintage went further, arguing 'that the conventions it relies on are those of Victorian melodrama'. Murphy, *British Cinema and the Second World War*, 243.
97 See UK population pyramid, 1975, accessed 24 May 2017, http://www.populationpyramid.net/united-kingdom/1975/.

Figure 4.1 Cast members contemplate one of the radio-controlled Lancaster models used in *Pathfinders* (Warboys, 1972).

Chapter 4

PATHFINDING: THE 1970s

A quarter century after the end of the war, the challenge of finding enough of the right multiengine period aircraft still in airworthy condition for a big-screen aviation film involving wartime Royal Air Force (RAF) bombing had gotten harder as the few remaining examples came into private hands and were dispersed at home and overseas. *Mosquito Squadron* was the last time four examples of this aircraft type would be filmed together flying in formation, and though Lancaster PA474, as it underwent refurbishment at Waddington, still might be used for static shots with permission from the Ministry of Defence (MoD), a single example could not stand in for a group in the way three or more could.[1] On the big screen, at least, small-scale models would appear too obviously fake unless used very sparingly indeed and, if possible, only when intercut with shots of the real thing.[2]

Not that a new Bomber Command feature was in prospect. There was, to be sure, no shortage of new source material to work with. *Bomber*, for instance, a well-researched novel by the popular spy writer Len Deighton chronicling a fictitious RAF raid on a German town based on an actual attack on Krefeld in the spring of 1943 that became a bestseller after publication in the autumn of 1970 was the sort of book, one reviewer commented, which 'could make a film'.[3] In the latter part of the previous decade, independent producer Harry Saltzman had already brought three of the author's novels to the big screen and while working on the epic *Battle of Britain* had provided help in researching *Bomber*.[4] *Battle of Britain*, though, had failed to recoup its costs, and Saltzman subsequently got into major financial difficulties.[5] *Bomber* was also not the sort of story that the MoD would have been keen to support, questioning as it does the human cost and ultimate worth of area bombing in graphic fashion and suggesting that class and rank trumped skill and experience among heavy-bomber crews.[6] Yet even if Saltzman had not got into serious debt, and PA474 had been made available to him or to some other prospective producer, it is highly unlikely that a film version of *Bomber* would have materialized. Aside from a problem of finding enough period aircraft, such a production would have involved a large cast and contained essential plot features such as the destruction of an entire town that would be either hugely expensive or physically impossible to generate.[7]

Hollywood studios, to be sure, had greater financial and technical resources. They, however, were only interested in bankrolling projects that had box-office potential in the American market: and even then, the film version of the semiautobiographical satiric novel by Kurt Vonnegut, *Slaughterhouse-Five*, released by Universal in 1972, involved cutting back heavily on some of the aerial and ground imagery in the book related to the destruction of Dresden. In any event, dealing with events from the perspective of a captured GI, and without the occasional references to Bomber Command and British servicemen present in the book, this slick but sterile film made only a tepid impression when released in the UK.[8]

Even the initially successful Mirisch formula of 'solidly predictable' British colour productions made on limited budgets yet crafted for their transatlantic market appeal had been abandoned as no longer profitable at the start of the decade after *Mosquito Squadron* did less-than-average business at the box office.[9] This was an early indicator of a wider negative trend in UK film production in the context of shifting social habits and economic turmoil in the 1970s that also made a new Bomber Command feature difficult to contemplate. Hollywood studios, overextended, cut back on British productions, while the number of active domestic players dwindled. The annual total of features made in Britain from 1972 through 1980 shrank every year but one, and the overall annual rate of production more than halved.[10] Cinema admissions continued to decline annually, with eighty-one million fewer tickets being sold in the UK at the end of the 1970s than at the start.[11]

In this climate it might be possible for Ken Russell to decide that the father of the title figure in *Tommy*, his mid-seventies screen musical version of the rock album by The Who, should be a decorated Lancaster pilot, as only a couple of studio shots of a Lancaster cockpit were required.[12] It was quite another thing for filmmakers to contemplate a big aerial war drama, especially after the box-office failure of the star-studded and expensive Anglo-American battle epic *A Bridge Too Far*.[13] It was a sign of the times that though he wrote and successfully published two sequels to *633 Squadron* in the middle of the decade, Frederick E. Smith was still waiting for someone to make an offer for the film rights several years on.[14]

Television, meanwhile, seemed to be going from strength to strength. The number of households possessing TV sets rose year in and year out, and by the mid-1970s an estimated 90 per cent of the population watched television as their main leisure pursuit and more than half the licenses being purchased were for colour reception.[15] Advertising revenue flowed in to the regional Independent Television (ITV) franchises, and both they and BBC-TV continued to generate a range of new drama series to meet audience demand. The war years, furthermore, became the setting for some of the most successful of these offerings.[16] Thus the bomber boys seemed to have more of a future on the small screen than on the big screen, and in the seventies featured not only in a major new documentary series but also in television plays and series episodes. There was also a notably ambitious, if ultimately unsuccessful, attempt to create a popular series centring on an elite Bomber Command squadron, *Pathfinders*.

The apparent inability of the Establishment to deal effectively with various problems Britain was facing around the turn of the decade – including inflation, industrial decline and growing class strife made manifest through militant strike action – tended to undermine faith in its past as well as present executive efforts. The resulting sense of disillusionment was to some extent reflected in how critically various writers now approached the wartime record of Bomber Command or the experiences of the bomber boys and how the public responded to their efforts.[17]

Mention has already been made of the bestselling novel *Bomber* by Len Deighton; and even in the pages of patriotic war comics area bombing occasionally might be termed 'wasteful in bombs and human life'.[18] Those writing successfully for television also tended to take a somewhat jaundiced line on aircrew experience. In 'Return Flight', the second piece in the BBC2 supernatural anthology series *Dead of Night*, written by Robert Holmes and broadcast on 12 November 1972, for instance, a charter airline pilot hears the ghostly intercom exchanges of the crew of a Lancaster hit by anti-aircraft fire, one among them reported to have had his legs blown off.[19] Aired two weeks later on BBC1, the second episode of the prisoner-of-war drama *Colditz* written by Ian Kennedy Martin, to take another example, has commissioned but lower-middle-class Wellington pilot Simon Carter – David McCallum, last seen wearing RAF blue in *Mosquito Squadron* and now sporting a moustache and darker hair – getting no support from his commanding officer over technical issues and showing signs of combat fatigue. Carter is shot down and is captured – a better fate than that of his Welsh rear gunner, Tom Morris, played by Brian Godfrey, who is so frightened that he drinks from a hip flask when aloft and is killed by flak.[20]

This rather gritty approach was already evident in various segments of the long-running *A Family at War* from Granada Television, a series which chronicled the wartime experiences of the lower-middle-class Ashton family of Liverpool on the ITV network between mid-April 1970 and mid-February 1972. One of the sons, Dave, played by Colin Campbell, signs up for aircrew duties and becomes a navigator-bomb aimer, first as non-commissioned officer on Wellingtons and later as a commissioned officer on Lancasters and Fortresses.[21]

In an episode set in September 1940, writer Julian Sands highlights the way in which fear has bred superstition among crews and also how death on operations can be both arbitrary and grisly. The new rear gunner of the Wellington crew in which Dave Ashton serves, played by Gordon Griffen, is said to have had half his head blown off and the wireless operator, played by Michael Harbour, is shown on screen badly burned in a friendly fire incident after a raid on Magdeburg.[22] Sixteen months on, in December 1941, writer John Stevenson has Dave, on leave with his family, decline to go to the pictures with his schoolboy son, Peter, played by Alan Guy, in order to see what can be inferred to be *Target for Tonight*, since he is trying to forget about bombing for a couple of days. He later emphasizes to a rather incredulous Peter that just like everyone else, he is scared when flying on operations.[23]

By January 1942, in an episode written by Geoffrey Lancashire, Dave is having to deal with muted scepticism from his father, played by Colin Douglas, about the efficacy of night bombing, as well as the loss of mates, while in an episode written by series-creator John Finch set in June 1943, another RAF friend, played by John

Alkin, admits to being on the verge of losing his nerve before viewers learn he has been killed in a fiery crash-landing.[24] Finch also wrote an episode set in March 1945 in which several members of Dave's crew are shown getting wounded or killed in action by flak. In the next episode, written by Alexander Baron and set the following month, pilot Derek Robbins, played by Richard Thorpe, has to be taken off operations late in his tour because he is getting twitchy. A doctor, played by Mike Murray, comments to Dave (in hospital because of a road accident) that 'we've had a lot of your chaps through here; I've seen them smashed by cannon shells; pulled out of wrecks looking more like cat's meat than human beings.'[25]

Though very popular at home and sometimes overseas,[26] in the context of many hours of scheduled broadcasting and limited license fee (BBC) or advertising (ITV) revenue, these series were not generously funded. The number of actors, size of studio sets, amount of location work and time spent rehearsing and shooting were therefore often strictly circumscribed, and videotape – more economical than film – was used for interior scenes. The money available for *A Family at War* in particular was 'very tight', John Finch remembered, with each fifty-minute episode budgeted at a mere £12,500.[27] Naturally enough, the drive for cost savings affected production values. 'It bears the unmistakable look of having been done on the cheap', commented Stanley Reynolds in *The Times*.[28]

As far as the stories mentioned above are concerned, aircraft interior mock-ups were pretty rudimentary, and aerial footage was initially borrowed from *Target for Tonight*.[29] The relative proximity to the Granada studios in Manchester of a semi-operable Lancaster in private hands, NX611, located at Blackpool Airport at the time, allowed it to be employed as an exterior static prop for a single episode of *A Family at War*.[30] In order to include at least a bit of freshly shot aerial footage before the series ended, John Finch had to have Dave Ashton serving with a radio countermeasures squadron in a couple of episodes to allow three B-17 photographic mapping planes in the possession of the French *Institut Géographique National* based at Creil to be used. Even then, what could be afforded in order to make these machines resemble those used by the RAF squadron in question was extremely circumscribed.[31]

Independent producer Gerald Brown, who in his mid-twenties had worked as a technician on *The Dam Busters* and was the son of a bomber pilot, thought he could do better. If his company, Toledo Films, could raise enough money then it ought to be possible to create an entirely new dramatic Bomber Command series, 'unsurpassed in its excitement and dramatic spectacle' that could turn a profit by being sold to television companies not only domestically but also overseas.[32]

According to the pitch made by Toledo the new series, initially to be called *The Pathfinders*, would contain a total of twenty-six episodes in two groups. Each story would contain dramatized versions of real events, mostly drawn from the memories of former members of the elite Bomber Command target-marking Pathfinder Force (PFF).[33] The focus would be on operations from a PFF station resembling Warboys, which the technical advisor to the series, Group Captain (retd.) Hamish Mahaddie, had commanded toward the end of the war. Stock footage would be dispensed with entirely, only colour film would be used and location shooting would take place on the Continent as well as in and over England.[34]

Studio space could be rented from EMI-MGM at Elstree and permission to film once more at nearby Bovingdon as well as at another care-and-maintenance airfield, West Malling, obtained from the MoD along with limited use of Lancaster PA474 based at Waddington. With no other airworthy Lancasters to draw on, a squadron of largish radio-control scale-model Lancasters could be built at a cost of £2,000 each and used for both aerial and ground shots. A full-scale mock-up or two, using scrap parts where possible, could be assembled for close-up and medium-shot exterior and interior filming.[35]

As for the cast, the idea was to use young guest players as flyers of varying rank from the Commonwealth as well as various parts of the UK for stand-alone stories in which they would interact with a core set of older characters who would appear in most episodes. Among the latter would be two faces familiar from cinematic depictions of Bomber Command. Wing Commander Angus McPherson, the commander of the fictional 697 Squadron operating from the equally fictional Oakwood bomber station, would be played by Robert Urquhart, who had appeared in *Mosquito Squadron*.[36] The station medical officer, initially called McAllister but eventually dubbed 'Doc' Saxon, would be acted by Jack Watling, now silver-haired but still quite recognizable from his major role in *Journey Together* back in the forties.[37]

Obtaining financial backing for Warboys Film Productions, the company set up by Toledo for the making of what came to be called simply *Pathfinders*, was a major headache for Gerald Brown. Though willing to include at least one Yank-in-the-RAF role, he was unable to generate interest in the United States, where the TV market for aerial war drama had already been saturated in the mid-sixties by QM Productions' successful episodic version of the American bomber-film classic *Twelve O'Clock High*.[38] Some upfront money was apparently provided by the Italian broadcaster RAI, while eventually the City firm Midland Montagu invested in the series and the London-area weekend ITV franchise Thames Television agreed to buy the resulting product.[39] To get to this point while starting production, however, Brown and a business associate had been forced to sell or mortgage their houses, and stress had taken a serious toll on the former's marriage. A projected budget of £1 million was cut back to £350,000, and plans for the second set of thirteen episodes shelved.[40] Some of the major characters and stories had to be axed and stock footage – taken during the war or shot later for films such as *The Dam Busters* and *Battle of Britain* – resorted to, even though much of it was in monochrome.[41]

The remaining episodes, with screenplays developed by half a dozen different writers, included an unexploded-bomb story, a shot-down-and-on-the-run adventure, a tale of pilot rivalry, a prisoner-of-war drama, a yarn centring on aircrew superstition, another on strained relations between a new skipper and crew and several tales with major cloak-and-dagger elements. Nonetheless among what were billed as 'stories of heroism, tragedy, triumph and humour' were episodes which tackled controversial issues head-on: the ethics of area bombing and the psychological and physical toll of bombing operations.[42]

In 'Codename – Gomorrah', civilian scientists express moral qualms about the use to which a new on-board navigation device will be put. 'H2S – Home Sweet Home – what a hideously ironic nickname that is', Dr Evelyn Roberts, played by Sally Bazely, reflects at one point, adding, 'Picture of happy family peacefully sleeping and then quite suddenly being blasted into the fire of an aerial bombardment.' Her colleague, the irascible Scot Dr Malcolm Woolley, played by Mike Pratt, is more outspoken, pointing out to the group captain he works for that a city like Hamburg contains over a million innocents and that Bomber Command was bulldozing morality by preparing to 'put the bloody boot in!'. Observing the firestorm below as Hamburg is struck, pathfinder navigator Peter Parr, played by Donald Douglas, remarks, 'Looks pretty horrifying', adding, 'I hope they don't do the same to us.'[43]

The price aircrew can pay for flying operations is graphically illustrated in several instances. At the end of 'Sitting Ducks' an aircraft captain, despite his displays of superb airmanship in managing to nurse a severely crippled Lancaster back to base, is killed before he can escape an explosion after he successfully crashlands.[44] In the final episode, 'In the Face of the Enemy', set mostly in a hospital ward, one of the two central characters, navigator Flight Lieutenant John Benson, played by Ray Brooks, is shown blind, missing one leg and with extensive burns on both his face and hands. During the same episode the psychological burden of a bomber pilot holding in his hands the lives of six other men is highlighted as Flying Officer David Warwick, played by Dennis Waterman, refuses to fly a Lancaster on operations: 'I can't take that sort of responsibility!' Doc Saxon at one point opines his is a case of lack of moral fibre (LMF), but a civilian psychiatrist played by Susan Jameson argues that LMF is just 'a convenient stamp' and not a medical diagnosis at all.[45]

Storyline diversity was matched by the geographic range of characters on display in the course of the series. Featured in various episodes were characters from various Commonwealth countries as well as a Yank-in-the-RCAF.[46] From within the British Isles the Irish, Welsh and Scots were all represented alongside Englishmen from various regions.[47] There was also variation in rank among aircrew, with non-commissioned officers being featured as frequently as commissioned officers. In several instances, moreover, commissioned pilots of good breeding are shown to disadvantage compared to lower-middle-class aircrew.[48]

Pathfinders, however, came to praise Bomber Command rather than to bury it.[49] More often than not the boys of 697 Squadron seem to stand in for 617 Squadron, successfully knocking out precise targets such as a radar site or a jet propulsion development facility.[50] Moreover it was notable that, among the English at least, in virtually every episode pilot characters were middle-class officer types while gunner characters were mostly lower-class flight sergeants.[51] In 'Operation Gomorrah', Woolley's scruples are overborne by the total-war philosophy of the man he works for, Group Captain Mark Foss. Played by Paul Massie, the coldly fanatical Foss is determined to use H2S to hit 'shipyards, submarine bases, armaments, munitions' in Hamburg as well as wreck enemy morale: 'If we can raise *that* [city] to the ground the German people could never take it because next it would be Berlin.' The failure of the subsequent campaign against Berlin in 1943–4 is never alluded to.[52] Instead, the Hamburg firestorm is portrayed as 'a vital step', in the words of a BBC announcement, on the road to aerial victory, and thus in moral terms a necessary evil.[53] As for 'In the Face of the Enemy', the bloody-minded but absolute refusal of Benson, despite his wounds, to allow the better educated and psychologically conflicted Warwick to justify his refusal to fly as anything other than cowardice – 'as far as I'm concerned . . . you don't even exist' – finally forces the latter to do his duty: 'I'll fight!' The overall thrust of *Pathfinders* is that the elite of Bomber Command were brave, resourceful and effective in helping win the war.[54]

Gerald Brown summed up his creation thus: 'This is a British production, made to enhance British prestige, as well as make money.' It remained to be seen if all this constituted something that the critics and viewing public wanted to watch when *Pathfinders*, complete with brassy title-theme score by Malcolm Lockyer, aired at 7.00 pm each Wednesday evening on Thames Television between the last week of September 1972 and late January 1973.[55]

Bernard Davies, reviewing for the trade in the *Television Mail*, thought it something of a throwback but concluded that 'it's a quite a likeable series'.[56] After watching the first episode, James Thomas gave it the green light in the pages of the *Daily Express*: 'it looks to me as if with this series all systems are go.'[57] Most newspaper and periodical reviews, however, were negative. In the *Guardian*, Nancy Banks-Smith damned its makers for their 'naïveté, their stock types', and their formulaic approach.[58] Patrick Campbell then weighed in for *Television Today*, describing the second episode as a reversion to the war films of the forties and fifties with 'entirely predictable' storylines and dialogue.[59] T. C. Worsley, writing for the *Financial Times*, agreed that *Pathfinders* was 'a badly dated new series'.[60] Even in the *Daily Mail*, Peter Black thought the whole idea misguided: 'You simply cannot produce a fiction series on this subject at this stage', he argued. Given what was now known about area bombing, a 'simple action series about Bomber Command is not on'.[61] In the *Observer*, Clive James wrote off the entire exercise as 'frightful'.[62]

Such critical carping would not have mattered much to Thames Television or other ITV regional broadcasters who had purchased *Pathfinders* for subsequent airing if the series had been a hit with viewers. Weekly ratings, however, indicated it was not. The drama was never among the top ten in the London area and thereafter only rarely broke into the top ten in other regions. In central Scotland, it occasionally garnered small Scottish Television audiences of between 400,000 and 430,000, while in south-west England it managed only between 350,000 and 370,000 at best.[63] There were a couple of overseas sales; but when asked earlier by journalist Philip Phillips if the gamble on producing *Pathfinders* and then selling it to make a profit for Toledo had paid off, Gerald Grant immediately replied: 'It hasn't!'[64]

Thus *Pathfinders*, despite the title, had not found the route to success. Thankfully for Thames, which had also committed to making a very expensive in-house documentary series on the Second World War and was deep in the red by the end of the following year, this did not mean that the public had finally lost interest in the subject.[65] Rather, as the subsequent success of twenty-six part *The World at War* demonstrated, it was a matter of presentation as well as content.[66]

The brainchild of the Thames director of features, Jeremy Isaacs, the idea behind *The World at War* was to tell the story of the conflict on a global scale not only through narration (by Laurence Olivier) over assembled wartime footage (plus occasional contemporary background shots) but also through the memories of participants at all levels in filmed interviews. The twenty-six episodes, each dealing with a different period or aspect of the conflict within an overlapping chronological framework, would be about earth-shattering events from the perspective of ordinary people as well as decision makers from all sides. The overarching theme, fully reflected in the grim images and mournful music written by Carl Davis contained in the famous title sequence used for each episode, would be the pity of war. The hope was that the story of the war told at the human level would draw in viewers and keep them watching once they had seen an episode.[67] Broadcast on Wednesday evenings between the end of October 1973 and the second week of May 1974, *The World at War* was a great success with audiences, regularly drawing in more than six million viewers each week in the UK and successfully sold both to Commonwealth countries and the United States.[68]

It was in the twelfth episode, titled 'Whirlwind' and broadcast on 24 January 1974, that writer Charles Douglas Home and producer/director Ted Childs tackled strategic bombing. The gritty, uncompromising tone is set in the opening pre-title sequence, in which, against close-up aerial footage of PA474 taken head-on and broadcast in black and white, the audience hears Hamish Mahaddie bluntly sum up the ethos of area bombing: 'If you couldn't get the Kraut in his factory, it was just as easy to knock him off his bed; and if old granny Schicklgruber in the street next door got the chop that was hard luck.' The problems faced by Bomber Command in the early war years are illustrated post-titles by contrasting cheery sequences from *Target for Tonight* with the realities of early night bombing. Arthur Harris explains in an interview the shift to area attacks, beginning with fire raids on Lubeck and Rostock and moving on to the Hamburg firestorm and then the campaign against Berlin. The cost to Bomber Command is chronicled through comments from former bomber pilots, while the human toll on the ground is illustrated through post-raid footage and the extremely graphic recollections of various German eyewitnesses such as former Hamburg fire-service chief Hans Brunswig. As for the effectiveness of the air campaign, the dams raid was of little real consequence and the assault on Berlin resulted in the loss of a thousand bombers. While former Nazi armaments minister Albert Speer is shown on camera explaining that the need to defend against the bombing absorbed a lot of resources and manpower, and the former head of Bomber Command is shown forcefully arguing that the attacks against the enemy capital constituted a major contribution to final victory – 'Harris did not and does not concede defeat', as Olivier comments – the fact was that enemy morale never irreparably cracked and war industries continued to function into the spring of 1944.[69] An estimated 6.6 million people tuned in.[70]

The *World at War* retuned to area bombing in two later segments. In the sixteenth episode, 'Inside the Reich: Germany, 1940–1944', written by Neal Ascherson, produced by Philip Whitehead and broadcast on 20 February 1974, the Hamburg firestorm and other big raids are mentioned in the narration, but a British woman married to a German who experienced the raids reflects on camera in an interview that they brought people together rather than breaking their will.[71] An estimated 6.6 million people watched this episode.[72] Towards the end of the series, 'Nemesis: Germany, February–May 1945', produced by Martin Smith and aired on 3 April 1974, has a pre-title sequence detailing the Dresden firestorm, complete with harrowing testimony from a German survivor and contemporary film footage, writer Stuart Hood having Laurence Oliver explain drily that this was 'a severe case of over-bombing'. Despite the carnage, damage to war production was slight, and the railway was in operation within three days.[73] By this point, 6.75 million viewers were tuning in.[74]

That people were more interested in the experiences and perspectives of those who had been directly involved than in what were perceived as tired and insufficiently quizzical simulacra was also evident in the success in print of two separate analyses of the costliest single-night attack for Bomber Command of the entire war that were based largely on interviews with survivors. *The Nuremberg Raid*, by popular military historian Martin Middlebrook, and *The Bombing of Nuremberg*, by journalist and former bomber aircrew member James Campbell, were both published in hardback in late 1973. They each garnered favourable reviews and went into mass-market paperback editions in subsequent years.[75]

Relying on the voices of those who were there suited the aural as well as the visual media. Author and historian Norman Longmate scripted an hour-long BBC radio documentary piece entitled *The Bombers* that utilized interviews with both senior figures and junior participants in explaining – and in this case defending – the course of the strategic air campaign. It was broadcast on Radio 4 in the spring of 1978 and met with a positive response.[76]

The following year *Bomber Command* appeared, a book by the journalist-historian Max Hastings that garnered much greater attention. Drawing on records that only the official chroniclers had seen before their public release under the thirty-year rule as well as his own interviews, Hastings, who grew up amid the heroic images of the fifties but was disillusioned by what he had recently read and heard, went further than most of his predecessors in arguing that the 'cost of the bomber offensive in life, treasure and moral superiority over the enemy tragically outstripped the results that it achieved'.[77] The book met with predictable hostility from senior RAF reviewers after it was published in the autumn of 1979 but was otherwise well received by critics and the public, its author, as an older authority noted a trifle enviously, 'soon accorded the role of leading expert on the subject of the bomber offensive'.[78]

As for small-screen dramas involving the bomber boys, nobody was about to try and resurrect the formula that had so signally failed in *Pathfinders*. Instead, representations were confined to a couple of one-off television plays and a multipart ghost story at the end of the decade.

The first play, written by Geoffrey Lancashire and broadcast late on Saturday, 2 June 1979, was a seventy-minute offering in the ITV Playhouse anthology series that was entitled *The Purple Twilight*. This involved a pilot, played by William Franklyn, about to ditch in a Lancaster in 1944, having possible future lives rather than his past flash before his eyes. The bomber was an enabling device rather than central to the plot, but according to Franklyn being able to use the static Lancaster on display at the RAF Museum at Hendon (R5868) made the flying scenes 'totally convincing'.[79] Critical verdicts, though, were mixed, ranging from 'Hokum but gripping' (Judith Cook, *Western Mail*) to 'interesting but in the end hopelessly muddled' (Philip Porter, *Sunday Telegraph*).[80] *The Purple Twilight* was not widely seen.[81]

Many more people watched the second multi-episode but untitled adventure of the ITV science-fiction fantasy series *Sapphire & Steel* on the same network at 7.00 pm on Tuesdays – barring a period of industrial action – between the end of July and early November 1979. Starring Joanna Lumley and David McCallum (a decade on from *Mosquito Squadron*) in the title roles acting as extraterrestrial temporal operatives, this particular story, written by series creator P. J. Hammond, involved efforts to thwart a dark force preying on the resentments of various men who had unfairly lost their lives in the past. The latter include the ghost of an RAF bomber pilot, played by David Cann, who had been treated as jinxed by his fellow flyers because his crew all 'bought it' in the course of their tour and was himself killed in a fiery crash aboard a defective aircraft just before he was due to go on extended leave. Set in a studio-built abandoned railway station, the story required very little in the way of service props beyond uniforms and flying kit. Around 20 per cent of the TV-watching audience tuned through the eight episodes.[82]

The second seventy-minute TV play, broadcast as part of BBC2 Playhouse at 9.35 pm on Wednesday, 21 November, centred on an RAF hospital ward where a non-aircrew 'erk', played by David Threlfall, suffering from frostbite, finds himself thrown in with a shell-shocked Lancaster crew of NCOs who nightmarishly 'fly ops' together each evening. *The Brylcreem Boys*, written by Peter Durrant, was described in the *Guardian* as an original and moving tour de force but criticized in *Television Today* for sloppy development and limited ambition.[83] Either way, *The Brylcreem Boys* also did not leave a mark on the ratings charts when it was first aired or when it was rebroadcast ten months later.[84]

Nonetheless, both these plays, as well as the insertion of a pilot into a *Sapphire & Steel* story, indicated that Bomber Command was still seen as a potential dramatic setting and subject for television – a phenomenon which makes sense given the continuing public if not critical enthusiasm for war subjects in general and the ongoing battles in print surrounding the bombing campaign in particular.[85] They also suggested that, with the right sort of plotting, television productions need not be comparatively expensive in the manner of *Pathfinders* nor obtrusively fake due to the continuing absence of enough airworthy period aircraft of the right type.[86]

Notes

1. On Lancaster PA474 *c.* 1967–72, see e.g. Lancaster PA474, RAF BBMF, accessed 25 May 2017, https://www.raf.mod.uk/bbmf/theaircraft/lancasterpa474.cfm. On *Mosquito Squadron* as the last time four Mosquitoes were filmed in the air together, and subsequent dispersal, see Mark Ashley, *Flying Film Stars: The Directory of Aircraft in British World War Two Films* (Walton-on-Thames: Red Kite, 2014), 191–4, 219–20.
2. On more or less successful intercutting of model aircraft for the big screen see *633 Squadron* (Mirisch, 1964). On the credulity limits of scale-model aircraft on the big screen even for a few seconds, see e.g. *The Heroes of Telemark* (Benton, 1965).
3. *South China Morning Post*, 19 October 1970. *Bomber* 'received a large number of long, detailed and mostly very laudatory reviews' (J. Gathorne-Hardy in *London Magazine*, 1 February 1971, 97) and was later chosen by Anthony Burgess as one of the best ninety-nine novels published in English since 1939 (Anthony Burgess, *99 Novels: The Best in English Since 1939: A Personal Choice* [New York: Summit, 1984], 107); see also Angus Calder, *Disasters and Heroes: On War, Memory and Representation* (Cardiff: University of Wales, 2004), 68. Deighton, too young to have fought in the war, undertook a good deal of research for the novel (see Len Deighton foreword to Jonathan Falconer, *RAF Bomber Command in Fact, Film and Fiction* [Stroud: Sutton, 1996], vii–ix; Digby Diehl interview of Len Deighton, *Los Angeles Times*, 9 January 1972).
4. On help from Saltzman with *Bomber* see Len Deighton foreword to Falconer, *Bomber Command in Fact, Film and Fiction*, vii–viii. The spy novel screen adaptations on which they had previously collaborated through Saltzman's Lowndes Productions were *The Ipcress File* (1965), *Funeral in Berlin* (1966) and *Billion Dollar Brain* (1967).
5. On *Battle of Britain* not making money see James Chapman, *Past and Present: National Identity and the British Historical Film* (London: I.B. Tauris, 2005), 253. On Saltzman's financial plight causing production cancellations in the 1970s, see e.g. Tony Richardson, *The Long-Distance Runner: An Autobiography* (New York: Morrow, 1993), 273.
6. Len Deighton, *Bomber* (London: Cape, 1970). The book, very much an anti-war novel, details what happened on the ground when the bombs rain down – on the wrong target in this instance – as well as what it was like aboard a Lancaster facing flak and night fighters, and shows a well-bred commissioned flight commander named Sweet lording it over one of the central characters, a highly competent but non-commissioned and lower-middle-class pilot named Lambert. Curiously, the officer leading the squadron is – as in the film-script version of *633 Squadron* – a Wing Commander Munro. It is worth noting that by this point arguing that Bomber Command under Harris went too far was fairly common, military theoretician and historian Basil Liddell Hart, concluding in his last, posthumously published book that 'the British pursued area-bombing long after they had any reason, or excuse, for such indiscriminate action'. Basil Liddell Hart, *The Second World War* (London: Cassell, 1970), 612.
7. A radio adaptation of *Bomber* was much more feasible in logistical and overall cost terms, and one was finally mounted by the BBC and broadcast on Radio 4 in February 1995. See Falconer, *RAF Bomber Command in Fact, Film and Fiction*, 105.
8. On tepid British reviews of the film version of *Slaughterhouse-Five*, see e.g. *New Statesman*, 3 November 1972, 650; *Spectator*, 4 November 1972, 719–20; *Sight and*

Sound, Fall 1972, 232–3. The book, released in 1970 in Britain, had garnered more positive responses. See e.g. *Observer*, 22 March 1970; *Guardian*, 10 December 1970. Former RAF aircrew might be less enamoured: see e.g. Arch Whitehouse in *New York Times*, 18 May 1969.

9   The phrase 'solidly predictable' in relation to the Mirisch formula is drawn from Robert Murphy, *Sixties British Cinema* (London: BFI, 1992), 260. On United Artists abandoning backing for inexpensive Oakmont war films see *Variety*, 26 August 1970, 6. *Mosquito Squadron* did what one industry observer described as at best 'ho-hum' business (*Variety*, 8 July 1970), and was not among those features released in 1969–70 that broke even or made a profit (*Boxoffice*, 7 June 1971, 30–4).

10 Justin Smith, 'Glam, Spam and Uncle Sam: Funding Diversity in 1970s British Film Production', in *Seventies British Cinema*, ed. Robert Shail (Basingstoke: Palgrave, 2008), 67, Table 1.

11 UK cinema admissions, 1979, 1970, Film Distributor's Association, accessed 17 March 2017, http://www/launchingfilms.com/research-databank/uk-cinema-admissions. On how domestic filmmakers coped with the difficult production funding climate of the 1970s, see Sian Barber, *The British Film Industry in the 1970s: Capital, Culture and Creativity* (Basingstoke: Palgrave, 2013).

12 Ken Russell, the writer/director/co-producer of *Tommy* (RSO, 1975), having served in the post-war RAF as an aircraftsman, decided that the 'Captain Walker' of the album should be a Lancaster skipper, 'Group Captain Walker' (played by Robert Powell) who goes missing-presumed-killed but returns unexpectedly to his wife (played by Ann-Margret), badly burned, after the end of the war, only to be murdered by her lover (played by Oliver Reed). See BFI Library, *Tommy* press synopsis, 2; Ken Russell, *Directing Film: From Pitch to Première* (London: Batsford, 2000), 45; see also Ken Russell, *A British Picture: An Autobiography* (London: Southbank, 2008), 66–71.

13 On *A Bridge Too Far* see A. T. McKenna, 'Joseph E. Levine and *A Bridge Too Far* (1977): A Producer's Labour of Love', *Historical Journal of Film, Radio and Television* 31 (2011), 211–27.

14 Frederick E. Smith, *The Final Absurdities: An Autobiography, Volume 3* (Bicester: Emissary, 2012), 146. Other new Bomber Command novels written with cinematic potential in mind that did not make it to the screen in this decade included Spencer Dunmore, *Bomb Run* (New York: Morrow, 1971), and James Campbell, *Maximum Effort* (London: Alison and Busby, 1975).

15 Joe Moran, *Armchair Nation: An Intimate History of Britain in Front of the TV* (London: Profile, 2013), 202; TV Ownership, 1965–80, Broadcasters Audience Research Board, accessed 17 March 2017, http://www.barb.co.uk/resources/tv-ownership/.

16 On the popularity of 1970s drama series set in the Second World War see Lez Cooke, *British Television Drama*, 2nd ed. (London: Palgrave, 2015), 121. Successful series included *Manhunt* (LWT, 1970), *A Family at War* (Granada, 1970–2), *Colditz* (BBC, 1972–4), *Secret Army* (BBC, 1977–9), *Danger U.X.B.* (Euston/LWT, 1979) and *Enemy at the Door* (LWT, 1978–80). See Tisi Vahimagi (comp.), *British Television: An Illustrated Guide*, 2nd ed. (Oxford: Oxford University Press, 1996), 188, 190, 202, 237, 247. On ITV franchises making money for shareholders in the 1970s see Jack Williams, *Entertaining the Nation: A Social History of British Television* (Stroud: Sutton, 2004), 38.

17 On the turmoil of the 1970s in the UK, see e.g. Andy Beckett, *When the Lights Went Out: Britain in the Seventies* (London: Faber, 2009); Dominic Sandbrook, *State of Emergency: The Way We Were: Britain, 1970–1974* (London: Allen Lane,

2010); Dominic Sandbrook, *Seasons in the Sun: The Battle for Britain, 1974–1979* (London: Allen Lane, 2012).

18 *Hail of Steel*, Commando 459, February 1970, 17. Typically, however, the problems of area bombing were still overborne in the Commando Comics universe through successful day and night precision strikes. See ibid., 21–54; *Sky of Flame*, Commando 597, November 1971, 42; *A Stirling Called Satan*, Commando 869, September 1974, 56; *Everything under Control*, Commando 1194, January 1978, 36–49.

19 'Return Flight', *Dead of Night* (BBC2), tx. 12 November 1972. On critical reaction see *Sunday Telegraph*, 19 November 1972.

20 *Colditz*, 'Missing, Presumed Dead', by Ian Kennedy-Martin, tx. 26 October 1972.

21 On the genesis and success of *A Family at War* see Michael Cox in *Granada Television: The First Generation*, ed. John Finch (Manchester: Manchester University Press, 2003), 98–9; John Finch, Introduction to the Series, A Family at War, accessed 31 May 2017, http://www.afamilyatwar.com/Finch%20Intro.htm; see also BFI Library, *A Family at War* Granada press release, November 1970, 3; Mark Connelly, ' "We Can Take It!" Britain and the Memory of the Home Front', in *Experience and Memory: The Second World War in Europe*, ed. Jörge Echternkamp and Stefan Martens (Oxford: Berghahn, 2010), 63.

22 *A Family at War*, 'One of Ours', tx. 14 July 1970; see also Kathleen Baker, *A Family at War* (St. Albans: Mayflower, 1970), 112.

23 *A Family at War*, 'A Hero's Welcome', tx. 30 December 1970; see also Jonathan Powell, *A Family at War: To the Turn of the Tide* (St. Albans: Mayflower, 1971), 77.

24 *A Family at War*, 'The Lucky Ones', tx. 6 October 1943; 'Lend Your Loving Arms', tx. 13 January 1971; see also Roy Russell, *A Family at War: Towards Victory* (London: Severn House, 1976), 8–9, 14.

25 *A Family at War*, 'Breaking Point', tx. 22 December 1971; 'The Lost Ones', tx. 29 December 1971; see also Russell, *Family at War*, 108–28.

26 *A Family at War* had consistently high and sometimes chart-topping viewing figures in the UK (see Michael Cox in Finch, *Granada Television*, 99) and came out top in a New Zealand poll (see *Broadcast*, 12 October 1973, 6). It was also a surprise smash hit in Sweden and Denmark (see Denis Forman, *Persona Granada: Some Memories of Sydney Bernstein and the Early Days of Independent Television* [London: Andre Deutsch, 1997], 276; *Sun*, 30 March 1971). *Colditz* garnered even higher audience figures across the UK (see S. P. MacKenzie, *The Colditz Myth: British and Commonwealth Prisoners of War in Nazi Germany* [Oxford: Oxford University Press, 2004], 14, 19).

27 John Finch to Michael Cox, October 2003, A Family at War, John Finch, accessed 27 May 2017, http://johnfinch.com/a-family-at-war/; see Forman, *Persona Granada*, 277.

28 *The Times*, 14 October 1971.

29 See *A Family at War*, 'One of Ours', tx. 14 July 1970; *A Family at War*, 'The Forty-Eight Hour Pass', tx. 9 December 1970; *Colditz*, 'Missing, Presumed Dead', tx. 26 October 1972. In 'Return Flight', *Dead of Night*, tx. 12 November 1972, there is a brief shot of a Lancaster in the sky, but the equally brief interior shots show the geodetic construction of a Wellington – possibly some of the same sets used in 'Missing, Presumed Dead'.

30 *A Family at War*, 'The Lucky Ones', tx. 6 October 1971.

31 *A Family at War*, 'Breaking Point', tx. 22 December 1971; 'The Lost Ones', tx. 29 December 1971. On the IGN Fortresses see BFI Library, *A Family at War* Granada press release, 1972, 2; *Sun*, 22 December 1971; *Daily Mirror*, 26 June 1971; Key Aero

Network, Aviation Forum, Historic Aviation, B-17s in 'A Family at War', accessed 30 May 2017, http://forum.keypublishing.com/showthread.php?140051-B-17s-in-A-Family-at-War. One such Fortress that had briefly stood in for a Bomber Command aircraft is the hugely successful French comedy *Le grande vadrouille* (Corona, 1966), on which see Réne Fournier Lanzoni, *French Comedy on Screen: A Cinematic History* (Basingstoke: Palgrave, 2014), 92.

32   BFI Library, *Pathfinders* press material, Background to the Production; See *Sun*, 20 May 1972; *Variety*, 5 May 1971, 38.

33   Adapting stories from real Bomber Command veterans would presumably help the series avoid the sort of criticism levelled by some ex-RAF personnel at the Len Deighton's novel *Bomber*, which though a bestseller did not strike them as true to life as far as wartime aircrew were concerned. See e.g. Noble Frankland in *RUSI Journal*, 1 March 1974, 74; Robert Kee in *Observer*, 20 September 1970, and *The Listener*, 18 February 1971, 207–8. The definite article 'The' was dropped by the time the *Pathfinders* title credits were designed.

34   BFI Library, *Pathfinders* press material, A Background to the Series; *Variety*, 5 May 1971, 38.

35   Simon D. Beck, *The Aircraft-Spotter's Film and Television Companion* (Jefferson, NC: McFarland, 2016), 230; Falconer, *RAF Bomber Command in Fact, Film and Fiction*, 107; *Sun*, 20 May 1972; Aircraft, Airfields and Airshows, Avro Lancaster B.1 – PA474, accessed 2 June 2017, http://www.airshowspresent.com/avro-lancaster-b1-pa474.html; see *Pathfinders* Lancaster mock-up and scale-model photos in third picture section, T. G. Mahaddie, *Hamish: The Memoirs of Group Captain T. G. Mahaddie* (London: Ian Allan, 1989).

36   In *Mosquito Squadron*, Robert Urquhart, uncredited, had played an army intelligence officer, Major Kemble, killed on a recce flight.

37   BFI Library, *The Pathfinders* pressbook, 1971, Main Characters of the Pilot Episode. Other semi-regulars were Julian Orchard as the padre ('Jonah Man', 'Nightmare', 'In the Face of the Enemy') and Jack May as the intelligence/engineering officer ('Into the Fire', 'Fog', 'Sweets from a Stranger').

38   On the *Pathfinders* pitch in the United States see *Variety*, 5 May 1971, 38. On the sense there that it was an unnecessary recycling of the *Twelve O'Clock High* series see *Variety*, 11 October 1972, 42. On the *Twelve O'Clock High* television series of the mid-sixties – which had been broadcast in the UK on Anglia TV in in 1967–8 – see Allan T. Duffin and Paul Matheis, *The 12 O'Clock High Logbook* (Boalsburg, PA: BearManor, 2005), 96–162; Johnathan Fetter, *Quinn Martin, Producer: A Behind-the-Scenes History of QM Productions and Its Founder* (Jefferson, NC: McFarland, 2003), 46–61.

39   *Financial Times*, 25 September 1972; *Times*, 18 May 1972; *Variety*, 5 May 1971, 38.

40   *Sun*, 20 May 1972; *Variety*, 5 May 1971, 38.

41   In the original concept an actor representing the PFF head, Air Vice-Marshal Don Bennett, would be one of the core cast. Other more fictional recurring characters were also either cut entirely (e.g. Squadron Leader David Ring) or reduced to a single episode (e.g. Flight Lieutenant David Copeland, played by Basil Moss). On the original prospectus of stories and characters see BFI Library, *The Pathfinders* promotional pamphlet, 1971. Bennett was thanked for his cooperation and introduced in the opening credits of the first episode, 'Into the Fire', as the father of the Pathfinders, 'a man whose utter professionalism in every department of airmanship set the example that made the Pathfinders what he intended them to be – the elite of Bomber Command'. Bennett's memoir was republished in paperback with

cover art adapted from *Pathfinders*: Donald Bennett, *Pathfinder: A War Autobiography* (London: Sphere, 1972).
42 BFI Library, *The Pathfinders* press material, Background to the Production, 1972.
43 'Codename – Gomorrah', tx. 13 December 1972.
44 'Sitting Ducks', tx. 15 November 1972.
45 'In the Face of the Enemy', tx. 25 January 1973.
46 The Yank-in-the-RCAF was Flight Lieutenant Logan Crossley, played by Ed Byrnes, in 'Sitting Ducks', tx. 15 November 1972. RAAF flight sergeant and navigator Joe Carson, played by Mark McManus, was central to the plot of 'Jonah Man', tx. 1 November 1972. Australian aircrew also featured in 'Into the Fire', tx. 27 September 1972; 'One Man's Lancaster', tx. 8 November 1972; 'Sitting Ducks', tx. 15 November 1972; and 'Nightmare', tx. 17 January 1973; while a Canadian and a South African appeared briefly in, respectively, 'Fog', tx. 11 October 1972, and 'Sitting Ducks', tx. 15 November 1972.
47 Scotland was represented by Robert Urquhart in the recurring role of Wing Commander Angus McPhearson and also by Mike Pratt as Dr Malcolm Woolley in 'Codename – Gomorrah', tx. 13 December 1972; while other episodes featured aircrew Welshmen ('For Better for Worse', tx. 4 October 1972; 'Jonah Man', tx. 1 November 1972; 'Nightmare', tx. 17 January 1973) and an Irishman ('Into the Fire', tx. 27 September 1972). As for the English, they included several cockneys (e.g. 'Jonah Man', tx. 1 November 1972; 'One Man's Lancaster', tx. 8 November 1972) and at least one Northerner ('Nightmare', tx. 17 January 1973).
48 In 'One Man's Lancaster', tx. 8 November 1972, written by Chris Penfold based on a story by J. B. Hughes, sports car-driving Squadron Leader Jim Stanton, played by Anthony Valentine, is an unsympathetic character in comparison to the NCO crew he adopts and their regular skipper – as is son of a war hero Pilot Officer David Warwick, played by Dennis Waterman in 'In the Face of the Enemy' written by Tony Barwick, in comparison to lower-middle-class Flight Lieutenant John Benson, played by Ray Brooks.
49 See e.g. *Sun*, 20 May 1972.
50 See 'For Better for Worse', tx. 4 October 1972; 'Sitting Ducks', tx. 15 November 1972; 'Sweets from a Stranger', tx. 10 January 1973.
51 An exception was the episode 'Jonah Man', written by Bruce Stewart, in which Bob Starling, the flight engineer, takes over from the skipper after a freak accident: a role played by Colin Campbell, who had already demonstrated his aerial skills in *A Family at War*. An example of the gunner type was Flight Sergeant Bob Broome, played as a cockney by Roy Holder in 'Sitting Ducks', tx. 15 November 1972, written by Chris Penfold.
52 On the failure of the post-Hamburg campaign against the German capital see Martin Middlebrook, *The Berlin Raids: R.A.F. Bomber Command Winter 1943–44* (London: Viking, 1988).
53 'I knew he'd crack before we'd finished', Foss observes of Woolley after the latter drinks himself into insensibility rather than face the consequences of the attack, to which Roberts replies: 'There are some kinds of success some men would prefer to do without. This is such a success. And Woolley is such a man.' 'Codename – Gomorrah', tx. 13 December 1972.
54 See e.g. *Air Mail*, Summer 1971, 28.
55 *Pathfinders* subsequently aired in 1973–4 on other regional ITV franchises.
56 *Television Mail*, 20 October 1972, 14.

57 *Daily Express*, 28 September 1972.
58 *Guardian*, 28 September 1972.
59 *Television Today*, 12 October 1972.
60 *Financial Times*, 11 October 1972.
61 *Daily Mail*, 29 September 1972.
62 *Observer*, 13 February 1977; see also Clive James, *Clive James on Television: Criticism from the Observer, 1972-1982* (London: Picador, 1991), 8 October 1972, 25; *Television Today*, editorial, 26 October 1972. It is worth noting that when the BBC ran a profile of Bomber Harris on November 1972 as part of its series on *The Commanders*, some critics complained that it glossed over controversial issues like firebombing. See *The Listener*, 21 December 1972, 871; James, *On Television*, 30.
63 JICTAR ratings for South West, 2-8 September 1974, *Television Times*, 19 September 1974; JICTAR ratings for South West, 5-11 August 1974, *Television Times*, 22 August 1974; JICTAR ratings for Central Scotland for week ending 4 February 1973, *Television Today*, 15 February 1973; JICTAR ratings for Central Scotland for week ending 11 February 1973, *Television Today*, 22 February 1973; JICTAR ratings for Central Scotland for week ending 11 March 1973, *Television Today*, 22 March 1973; see JICTAR ratings for London, *Television Today*, 12 October 1972-11 January 1973. *Pathfinders* was also shown on Southern Television, Ulster Television and Channel Television through the mid-seventies, where it never broke into the top ten regionally.
64 *Sun*, 20 May 1972. *Pathfinders* was shown in Australia on TCN9 (see *Australian Women's Weekly*, 28 November 1973, 15) and in Hong Kong on RTV English (see *South China Morning Post*, 21 February 1975). A paperback novelization of the initial episodes of the series was also written by William Ray Buck writing as William Buchanan for Sphere: William Buchanan, *Pathfinder Squadron* (London: Sphere, 1972).
65 On Thames Television's overall financial problems see *Television Today*, 20 December 1972. On the cost of *The World at War*, which grew from a projected £400,000 to £900,000, see *World at War - Making the Series: 30th Anniversary Retrospective.*
66 Ibid. For work on this iconic series see James Chapman, 'Television and History: The World at War', *Historical Journal of Film, Radio and Television* 31 (2011), 247-75; Taylor Dowling, *The World at War* (London: BFI Palgrave, 2012).
67 See *World at War - Making the Series: 30th Anniversary Retrospective*; Jeremy Isaacs, *Look Me in the Eye: A Life in Television* (London: Little Brown, 2006), chapter 7.
68 See JICTAR ratings, *Television Times*, 10 January-16 May 1974. *The World at War* was shown on Channel 9 in Australia and on PBS in America.
69 The analytical thrust of the 'Whirlwind' episode reflected the views of Noble Frankland, chief historical advisor to *The World at War* in his capacity as director of the Imperial War Museum. See Noble Frankland, *History at War: The Campaigns of an Historian* (London: DLM, 1998), 188-90; see also Mark Arnold-Foster, *The World at War* (London: Thames Metheun, 1981), 265-74.
70 JICTAR ratings for week ending 24 February 1974, *Television Times*, 7 March 1974, 14. It was perhaps a sign of how, at least among intellectuals, the pendulum had swung against the policy of area bombing that one highly educated viewer thought that this episode had not taken sides. See Douglas Johnson in *New Society*, 31 January 1974, 268.
71 Christabel Bielenberg in 'Inside the Reich: Germany 1940-1944', *The World at War*, tx. 20 February 1974.
72 *Broadcast*, 8 March 1974, 27.

73 'Nemesis: Germany, February–May 1945', *The World at War*, tx. 23 April 1945.
74 *Broadcast*, 22 April 1974, 21.
75 James Campbell, *The Bombing of Nuremberg* (London: Alison and Busby, 1973); Martin Middlebrook, *The Nuremberg Raid* (Allen Lane, 1973). See OCLC, accessed 6 June 2017, http://www.worldcat.org, for subsequent publication history. For favourable comparative reviews, see e.g. *Guardian*, 27 December 1973; *Observer*, 13 January 1974. In their concluding remarks, Campbell argued that Bomber Command achieved a good deal (184–5), while Middlebrook – whose book ultimately had a much longer active publishing history – stated that area bombing failed to become the war winner Harris had promised (292–3).
76 *The Bombers*, tx. radio 4, 5 April 1978; see *The Listener*, 6 April 1978, 425–7; ibid., 13 April 1978, 474.
77 Max Hastings, *Bomber Command* (London: Michael Joseph, 1979), 352.
78 Frankland, *History at War*, 128. On other reactions see Max Hastings, 'The Controversy over Bombers & Bombing', *Encounter* 59, 2 (1982), 62–6. *Bomber Command* was soon issued and then periodically reissued in paperback. See OCLC World Cat, Max Hastings, Bomber Command, accessed 7 June 2017, http://www.worldcat.org. This was in contrast to a critique published seven years earlier, H. R. Allen's *The Legacy of Lord Trenchard* (London: Cassell, 1972), which tended to be dismissed as sloppy and polemical and was not republished. See e.g. Noble Frankland review in *Journal of the Royal United Services Institution*, 1 December 1972, 66–7; Alfred Price in *The Times*, 7 February 1973.
79 William Franklyn in *High Flyers: 30 Reminiscences to Celebrate the 75th Anniversary of the Royal Air Force*, ed. Michael Fopp (London: Greenhill/RAF Museum, 1993), 86; see BFI Library, *The Purple Twilight*, ITC pressbook; *Evening Standard*, 9 February 1972.
80 *Sunday Telegraph*, 10 June 1979; *Western Mail*, 9 June 1979; see also *Daily Telegraph*, 4 June 1972.
81 See *Television Today*, 7 June 1979, 30; JICTAR ratings, May 28–June 3, *Television Today*, 7 June 1979, 21.
82 Richard Callaghan, *Assigned! The Unofficial and Unauthorised Guide to* Sapphire & Steel (Prestatyn: Telos, 2009), 67.
83 See *Television Today*, 29 November 1979, 39; *Guardian*, 19 December 1979; *Guardian*, 5 September 1981; see also *Sunday Times*, 25 November 1979; *Morning Star*, 21 November 1979; *Daily Mail*, 21 November 1979.
84 See JICTAR ratings, 19–25 November 1979; *Television Today*, 6 December 1979, 17.
85 Like film critics in the 1950s, TV critics in the 1970s sometimes thought there was too much concentration on the Second World War. See e.g. *Guardian*, 25 November 1972; *The Listener*, 7 December 1972, 806. As in earlier decades, non-aircrew types were generally relegated to comedies, in this case a TV series about National Service days, *Get Some In!* (Thames, 1975).
86 'The Brylcreem Boys', set in a hospital ward, only used a bit of archival footage of taxiing Lancasters in the closing credits, while 'The Purple Twilight', as noted, made creative use of the static R5868, thus avoiding the costs of borrowing the flyable PA474.

Figure 5.1 John Thaw and Robert Hardy in *Bomber Harris* (BBC, 1989).

Chapter 5

CHIEFS: THE 1980s

The controversies surrounding area bombing in general and the firestorm raids in particular showed no signs of abating forty-plus years on from the actual wartime events. Almost two decades after David Irving had first drawn widespread attention to the event in Britain, another British writer, Alexander McKee, published *Dresden 1945: The Devil's Tinderbox*, which in retrospect seemed both intemperate and factually confused but at the time was lauded by, among other prominent figures, novelist David Lodge and popular military historian John Keegan.[1]

Meanwhile, an ongoing lack of suitable aircraft continued to impose major constraints on what could be portrayed on screen in relation to Bomber Command at war. Thus, for example, the opening episode of *Airline*, a nine-part Yorkshire Television drama aired at the start of 1982 which chronicled the efforts of a demobilized NCO bomber pilot – Jack Ruskin, played by Roy Marsden – to set up a private air charter company, has the protagonist ending his RAF service flying a Dakota transport plane (of which there were still many operating) rather than a wartime heavy bomber (of which there was at the time of filming only one airworthy example).[2]

That it was still possible to develop something new about Bomber Command that would resonate with the viewing public, however, was demonstrated by two successive drama-documentaries that appeared on British television at the start and in the middle of the new decade. That the subject of area bombing was, if anything, growing even more controversial as time passed was evident in the varying reactions to another pair of TV drama plays of the latter 1980s that had as their subject the man most commonly associated with that policy, Arthur Harris.

That there was a public appetite for personal stories about Bomber Command at this time was evident in the ongoing success of new books by Martin Middlebrook recreating, through interviews with those involved, various Bomber Command raids prior to Nuremberg.[3] As the wartime crews started to age and began to reflect on their youth, a new set of war memoirs, some destined to become classics, also appeared in print.[4]

Among the first was a volume by Jack Currie detailing the experiences of the Lancaster crew he skippered on his first tour of operations in 1943–4.[5] This became the basis of a half-hour BBC docudrama, *The Lancaster Legend: A Pilot's Story*, in which Currie is shown reflecting on his younger days at his former base at Wickenby while showing the audience what it was like to serve inside and fly a Lanc (PA474 and crew, courtesy of the RAF Battle of Britain Memorial Flight). A sense of the times was generated through selective scenes in which young actors played crewmembers, and through liberal use of rare colour footage from a film about operations shot by the commander of another Lancaster base around the same time Currie was working through his tour.[6] Produced by Douglas B. Smith with some narration by Richard Todd of *Dam Busters* film fame, *Lancaster Legend* won the Royal Television Society award for best regional programme after its initial BBC North showing in February 1980, prompting a general network broadcast in June that year. Most critics and other viewers who tuned in agreed that this was a very fine piece of work.[7]

A variety of other documentaries dealing with Bomber Command appeared in the following years. To mark the fortieth anniversary of the dams raid, one of the ITV affiliates, Yorkshire Television, had sponsored a documentary, *Operation Chastise: The Dams Raid Relived*, which explored both positive and negative aspects of the raid.[8] A couple of years later another forty-years-on documentary, *Dresden: Forgotten Anniversary*, broadcast on Channel 4, sought to put this most controversial of area bombing raids in its full historical context using a script developed by Noble Frankland.[9] The next month *Bomber*, from Anglia TV, brought together former crew members of 7 Squadron and paired them up for conversation with veterans of the *Luftwaffe* in Germany.[10]

A few years on, Howard Griffiths produced what the *Sydney Morning Herald* described as a 'revealing and moving' documentary portrait of Bomber Command at war based on veteran interviews entitled *Wings of the Storm* that was broadcast both in Australia (ABC) and the UK (Channel 4). Containing extracts from an interview with Don Bennett, *Wings of the Storm* was by no means uncritical of the way in which Harris had conducted the bomber offensive.[11] More universal condemnation was on display around the same time in *Return to Dresden*, an award-winning short film by Martin Duckworth sponsored by the National Film Board of Canada, which followed a group of former crew members visiting the city as its opera house was finally restored. Many of those involved were peace activists, and some of their words and actions did not go down well with more patriotic ex-aircrew. 'Not too long ago I watched on TV an ex-airgunner who had been invited to visit the city of Dresden', an amazed 75 Squadron veteran, David Golombeck, wrote in a letter to the Bomber Command Association, 'and in an interview he actually apologised to two housewives for taking part in the raid!'[12]

Also of note was *One of Our Bombers Is No Longer Missing*, a narrated programme covering the recovery of a Wellington that had crashed into Loch Ness back in 1940, which BBC2 first broadcast almost exactly forty-five years after the accident.[13] This was one of the first examples of the wartime wreck excavation genre that would become commonplace on twenty-first-century British television.[14] Commando comics meanwhile, continued to issue illustrated stories in which night bombers struck at specific factories.[15] A more contemporary and interactive form of entertainment directed at male youngsters emerged during the middle of the decade in the form of a desktop computer flight-simulation game which focused on the dam busters.[16]

Meanwhile, a good deal of notice was taken of another television film project in which the docudrama elements deployed in parts of *Lancaster Legend* were more omnipresent. This was the fifty-minute *Letters from a Bomber Pilot*, directed by filmmaker David Hodgson, a poignant narrative based around the wartime correspondence of his older brother, Bob Hodgson, who had volunteered for aircrew in 1941 and flown Wellingtons as a sergeant until killed in action over Holland one night in 1943. 'Much has been made of our wartime heroes', the younger Hodgson wrote of men like Guy Gibson. 'But many were like Bob: they did what they were asked and died unacknowledged.' Those who had lost their lives as members of Bomber Command were not mere 'statistics of war'; they were 'men of the highest calibre' who deserved to be remembered, even if the success of the campaign in which they fought 'is clearly open to question'.[17]

Along with contextual voiceover narration, the film consisted of a mixture of period clips and recreated scenes in which Bob Hodgson, played by Hugh Laurie, interacts with his crewmates and others, often as Laurie reads extracts from Bob's letters in voiceover or to camera. Broadcast in the London area on Thames Television on 18 June 1985, the low-key *Letters from a Bomber Pilot* met with a positive critical response from across the political spectrum. Sean Day-Lewis, for example, called it a 'moving tribute', full of 'tactful and evocative dramatisation' in the *Daily Telegraph*, while Stewart Lane of the *Morning Star* hailed it as 'a remarkably moving story which captures much of the spirit of ordinary people without jingoism or flag-waving'.[18] Though it did not win, *Letters from a Bomber Pilot* was sufficiently well regarded to be put forward as the Independent Television entry for the prestigious Prix Italia.[19]

A few months earlier a major contribution to the scholarly debate over the strategic air offensive had appeared under the title *The Right of the Line*, a comprehensive and well-received survey of RAF wartime operations against Nazi Germany and fascist Italy. Best known for seeking to rehabilitate the reputation of Douglas Haig as commander of the British Expeditionary Force on the Western Front in the First World War, journalist-historian John Terraine might have been expected to have defended the conduct of the strategic bombing campaign. Instead, he reiterated the main criticisms already levelled by Webster and Frankland in the early 1960s and again by Max Hastings in the late 1970s, arguing that the effort Bomber Command put into destroying German cities grew out of all proportion to the results achieved in terms of winning the war.[20]

Filmmakers' attention, meanwhile, had been drawn towards the high command in the wake of the death of the man most commonly associated with area bombing, Arthur Harris, in April 1984. The obituaries were generally respectful, as were a pair of post-mortem studies which appeared in bookshops some months later; but as Andrew Wilson put it in the *Observer*, 'Harris will always be the symbol for a part of the British war effort about which many people have very mixed feelings.'[21] During his long retirement, the former C-in-C had continued to defend his record and that of those who served under him with vigour when he thought it necessary;

and there are indications that at least some of those thinking about writing, staging or publishing material about his wartime career during his lifetime were inhibited by the possibility that he might resort to legal action.[22] Since the dead cannot be libelled, the disappearance of this particular Sword of Damocles seems to have emboldened both Channel 4 and BBC executives to sponsor the production in the latter eighties of one-off television plays about Harris's role at Bomber Command HQ – a setting, perhaps not coincidentally, that had the major advantage of not requiring period aircraft.[23]

Channel 4, set up earlier in the decade with a mandate to provide alternative perspectives and forms of programming compared to what was then being broadcast by ITV and the BBC, had developed a track record for funding unorthodox and sometimes radical independent projects. Under chief executive Jeremy Isaacs and his commissioning editors, a number of productions were developed under the auspices of groups run exclusively by women.[24] The latter included members of the Barefoot Video collective (Su Braden, Trudi Davies, Claire Hunt and Kim Longinotto), who were given the green light to develop *Fireraiser*, a docudrama about the now deceased head of Bomber Command adapted from a script by stage activist Albert Hunt drawing on his early mixed-media theatrical piece, *The Destruction of Dresden*.[25] The resulting fifty-minute film made use of wartime footage, the recollections of firebombing survivor Erika Woollams, the thoughts of the left-wing intellectual Ernest Mandel and some on-camera commentary by Hunt. The central feature, though, was veteran entertainer Max Wall playing Sir Arthur Harris – complete with costumes and props – explaining to camera the development of area bombing.[26]

Hunt's well-known opposition to the bombing of civilians in combination with the anti-establishment stance of many others involved in its making made it unlikely that what was initially titled *Bomber Harris Explains* and eventually *Fireraiser* would portray those responsible for the formulation and implementation of Bomber Command area attacks in a positive light. 'We feel that it is important that following generations can re-examine the past and look behind the myths that surround the Second World War', as the makers later stated, adding, 'We think that it is important for people to be able to look critically at the actions of their leaders and recognise the mistakes of the past.'[27]

When word got out in the summer of 1987 of what was afoot, the Bomber Command Association, a five thousand-strong veterans group which sought among other things to uphold the honour of wartime RAF heavy bomber aircrew and their commanders, was so sure that a hatchet job – 'another attempt to denigrate our highly respected commander'[28] – was in the works that a protest was sent to the Independent Broadcasting Authority and the prime minister's office concerning what was expected to be a portrait of a 'cold-blooded killer'.[29] Though the makers argued that the image they were creating was not unfair, it became clear to the commissioning editor and Isaacs when the completed film was handed over to Channel 4 in mid-October 1987 that *Fireraiser* was indeed a highly partisan piece of filmmaking.[30]

Its targets included Hugh Trenchard (for having organized the RAF bombing of Arab civilians in the 1920s), Anthony Eden (for advocating the wartime bombing of smaller as well as larger German cities while foreign secretary) and Winston Churchill (for promoting the Bomber Command offensive in general as prime minister and in particular for urging the firebombing of Dresden). It was Arthur Harris, though, who was the focal point for attack in *Fireraiser*. As played by Wall based on the script by Hunt, the head of Bomber Command is a leader who is willing, indeed eager, to wipe out entire German urban populations in order to win the war and keep down the rabble. There are signs of class-based antisemitism – 'of course, a lot of people think that Hitler had the right idea, you know; get rid of the Jewboys, crack down on the unions, put an end to strikes' – and even a hint that Harris may have been the devil incarnate in his final lines: 'Perhaps my best years have gone; but I wouldn't want them back; not with the fire in me now.'[31]

The chief executive of Channel 4 had major reservations about the completed product, later admitting that some of what had been sponsored in the way of programming on his watch was 'terrible . . . naïve, tendentious, partial'.[32] Quite apart from the portrayal of Harris, there were various highly combustible lines of argument in *Fireraiser*. On more than one occasion, for example, on-camera comments are made equating the firebombing of Dresden and the Nazi extermination camps. 'They [residents of Dresden sheltering in cellars] must have died like the Jews in the gas chambers', Hunt comments, 'struggling for breath'. There was also a suggestion that saturation air attacks had been designed as much to eliminate the possibility of post-war political resurgence by the German workers as to win the war against Hitler. 'I have at least a suspicion that this complete decomposition of society as a result of mass bombing was a deliberate purpose of the military leaders in the West', states Mandel at one point. 'They were obsessed with the image of what had happened in Germany at the end of the First World War, with the German revolution. One of the ways to avoid that was this massive bombing in order to destroy the possibility of collective action by the mass of the people.' Through the commissioning editor, Isaacs made it known in January 1988 that *Fireraiser* was not acceptable in its current form.[33]

The filmmakers agreed to make cuts to the Mandel material, but in the meantime Jeremy Isaacs had been replaced at Channel 4 by Michael Grade. 'Soon', the new chief executive recalled, 'letters began to arrive on my desk from Air Force types claiming that we intended to desecrate the memory of a great wartime leader'.[34] While controller at BBC1 earlier in the decade, Grade has faced charges of left-wing bias in his handling of television plays dealing with the 1982 Falklands War and the 1917 Étaples Mutiny, and expected to have to 'once again come out fighting in defence of free speech and Channel 4's duty to state minority viewpoint'.[35] On viewing a rough cut of *Fireraiser* for the first time, however, his opinion radically changed:

> To my astonishment, as I watched the programme, I felt more and more strongly that it was unfair to Harris. Quotations from his speeches were put into his

mouth, which, I suppose, was barely permissible though people don't normally talk in private with the vehemence they use in public orations. What worried me more were the passages of scripted dialogue that were intercut with eye-witness testimonies from survivors [sic – in fact only one] of the Dresden firestorm. The result was a damning indictment of Harris because the criticisms of him were drawn from real life while some of his side of the argument was fictional.[36]

In his eyes, this was all just meretricious 'agitprop television'. *Fireraiser*, due to be broadcast in February 1988 on the anniversary of the bombing of Dresden, was pulled from the schedule, Grade making it clear that 'under no circumstances' was it to be shown on Channel 4.[37]

The chief executive was prepared to face the understandably vexed filmmakers in person. 'When we met Michael Grade the following week', Kim Longinotto recalled, 'he stressed that the decision was entirely his and was because of the film's mix of documentary and fiction. He said it was dishonest to have a real character played by an actor mixed in with archive footage.' The implication was that 'the audience might confuse the acted parts with the real Harris'.[38] Given that at the start of *Fireraiser* Max Wall introduces himself with the words 'I'm not really Sir Arthur Harris, am I? No, I'm just an actor trying to depict Harris', this seemed a suspect line of argument to those who supported the film. Those involved in the making of *Fireraiser*, along with allies such as Alan Sapper, the general secretary of the Association of Cinematography, Television and Allied Technologies union, made public their certainty that Grade had given way to pressure from the Establishment. As he himself later wrote in frustration, 'No one would believe I had banned the film strictly on professional grounds.'[39]

Fireraiser was not, however, the only attempt in the latter eighties to dramatize the tenure of Arthur Harris as head of Bomber Command. In July 1987 it had been announced that the BBC would be developing, with in-house producer Innes Lloyd and writer Don Shaw, a television play on the subject that would span ninety minutes and be broadcast in the spring of 1988. The two men had collaborated a decade earlier on a three-part BBC portrait of another controversial wartime leader, Orde Wingate, and felt they were up to the challenge of tackling Harris. According to Shaw, the goal was to 'awaken the audience to the realities of war' by showing the C-in-C 'as he really was – warts and all' in the context of the times and without thrusting a 'moral judgement' on the audience. Some observers voiced their fears that the end result, *Bomber Harris*, eventually completed and ready to air in the late summer of 1989, nonetheless, would be another hatchet job. Shaw, though, was so certain of his underlying objectivity that he went on record to say that there would also be some viewers who would think the play was too sympathetic towards its subject.[40]

The script was indeed even-handed in a number of respects. Positive as well as negative aspects of Harris as C-in-C Bomber Command would appear in what was far from a one-note portrayal of the kind on display for the small audiences that saw *Fireraiser* in special public showings after it was pulled by Channel 4.[41]

Area bombing, it is made clear early on in *Bomber Harris*, was a policy handed to the C-in-C by the Air Ministry, albeit one he is shown to be determined to carry out to maximum effect. 'Progressively, and systematically', he announces to his group commanders, 'we are going to take apart every industrial city, street by street, block by block, until the Boche surrenders'. Harris is also portrayed as fully aware of the price of his relentless campaign to wipe out through blast and fire entire urban areas, agreeing with the chaplain at Bomber Command HQ that the effect of the Hamburg firestorm was 'terrible' – indeed 'ghastly' – for the civilian population and indicating the burden of sending aircrews to their doom during the subsequent assault on the Berlin. 'Do you know how many men I've lost?' he rhetorically asks the RAF's principal medical officer at one point, having earlier predicted to Churchill that he would likely lose five hundred aircraft in raids over the German capital. His sense of responsibility is further emphasized when Bomber Command is then diverted by the Air Ministry to attack targets which the C-in-C regards as worthless strategically. 'I've had it up to here seeing my old lags shot up, burnt, and drowned', Harris angrily complains to the chief of the air staff, adding, 'I want to get it over'.

That last point is, for him, the *raison d'être* for Bomber Command. In seeking to build up his heavy bomber force and use it exclusively against large urban targets – often in the face of attempts from various quarters to shift the focus of the air campaign – Harris is shown as relentless in his belief that area bombing, if conducted on a sufficient scale, will produce victory sooner and at less cost to the Allies than through any other means by bludgeoning the enemy to death. 'War is a battle between heavyweights', he argues to the chief of air staff at one point, going on to assert that 'the winner is the one that clobbers hardest with the maximum effort in the minimum time'. For Harris, under the conditions of total war – what one of his staff officers describes as 'a complete breakdown in civilization' where ethical considerations do not apply – the ends justify the means. 'The only thing that matters is you win', he quietly reflects in conversation with the American air commander Carl Spaatz at the end of play: 'You bloody well win.'[42]

That there is no feasible alternative to night incendiary area attacks if airpower is to be used as a decisive strategic weapon is suggested by discussion of various ineffectual or counterproductive propaganda leaflets devised by the Political Warfare Executive and by the shocked reaction of American air general Ira Eaker to the huge losses suffered by the US Eighth Air Force in attempting daylight precision bombing against Schweinfurt and Regensburg ('You were right', he concedes to Harris). The C-in-C is shown as more supportive of the fleetingly covered dams raid than he actually was, while the disaster at Nuremberg roughly ten months later is briefly put down to bad luck without acknowledging the responsibility of Harris in launching the attack under questionable circumstances. As for the ultimate inability of the campaign to deliver the early victory repeatedly promised, multiple references to smaller-than-requested numbers of aircraft being distributed to Bomber Command and the refusal of the Americans to adopt the RAF approach to strategic bombing despite British pleas leave open the possibility that Harris failed not because his logic was flawed but because he simply never had sufficient strength to generate a German collapse.[43]

Churchill is shown to back Harris and his campaign repeatedly, hoping that Bomber Command can deliver an early victory, and aware that attacking German cities can perhaps placate Stalin concerning the latter's demands for a second front. Shaw adds yet another dimension to the argument in favour of the night bombing campaign by suggesting that the prime minister thinks Bomber Command can slow down the development of new Nazi weapons of mass destruction, perhaps even an atomic bomb. It is also emphasized that Churchill rather than Harris is the man who presses for Dresden to be bombed in order to assist the Russians in the last months of the war before suddenly distancing himself from the raid – and Harris – in its aftermath.[44]

At the same time the screenplay did not make the C-in-C Bomber Command out to be quite the sort of figure one of those who served under him praised as 'this incredible man who did so much to win the war'.[45] While the massive raids on Cologne and Hamburg are portrayed as successes, with stirring music to accompany wartime footage of RAF bombers, the subsequent assaults on Berlin which Harris doggedly pursues are shown in terms of cumulative failure: the wartime footage now accompanied by the subdued notes of Beethoven's moonlight sonata, the C-in-C appearing and sounding increasingly tired and – for the only time – enemy footage of crashed RAF bombers being projected on screen. 'Bert, show me the whirlwind you promised, show me the photographs', says the chief of air staff, adding, 'You're defeated, Bert, and you won't admit it.'[46]

Harris is also shown to be openly insubordinate when crossed by higher authority, and a bit over the top in some of his pronouncements. As Churchill notes early on, the C-in-C Bomber Command is clearly 'a fanatic'. More significantly, though no post-raid German newsreel-type footage of destroyed homes and burnt civilian bodies is deployed (the visual effects of city bombing are confined to the perspective of RAF cameramen in bombers flying many thousands of feet above at night), on no less than four separate occasions the case against area bombing on ethical grounds is made. In the first, Harris quotes a statement made by Great War veteran Richard Stokes in the House of Commons to the effect that 'a growing volume of opinion in this country considers the indiscriminate bombing of civilian centres' is 'morally wrong'. In the second, the chaplain at Bomber Command HQ, John Collins, protests to Harris in reference to the firebombing of Hamburg that 'there are moral limits, surely'. In a later scene the minister for aircraft production, Stafford Cripps, speaking at the invitation of Collins to an assembly of staff officers, argues that aircrew should be allowed to stand down if their assigned tasks conflict with their personal ethics and that there ought to be 'some difference between what we are prepared to do and what the enemy is prepared to do' if Britain wants to occupy the moral high ground.[47] Finally, towards the end of the script, Collins gets to respond to the talk on the ethics of bombing made by Weldon through the public observation that it really ought to have been titled 'the bombing of ethics': for Collins, it is morally impossible to defend 'wholesale slaughter'.[48]

On top of all that, the domain which the C-in-C rules appears, visually, almost completely cut off from normal human activity thanks to designs by David Myerscough-Jones lit by Clive Thomas and made full use of by director Michael Darlow. 'Relatively minimalist, theatrical set designs very carefully lit create the impression that Bomber Command headquarters operated from subterranean bunkers permanently illuminated by artificial light', as Mark Connelly has noted. Thus, 'Harris and his almost entirely masculine team . . . drift around offices and control rooms like medieval monks caught up in their devotions oblivious to all else'. Harris and his acolytes therefore come across almost as 'creatures of the night shadows'.[49]

Yet when all was said and done, *Bomber Harris* was more sympathetic than critical of this most controversial of British war leaders. 'Don's Shaw's script found for Sir Arthur every time', in the opinion of TV critic Gavin Millar.[50] Thus those who admired the former C-in-C, such as his daughter and several of his former wartime assistants at Bomber Command HQ, thought that the television play gave an excellent account of Harris's character and thinking.[51]

The tilt towards an ultimately more positive than negative portrayal can be attributed to the attitudes of a number of figures. The historical advisor for the play, Norman Longmate, some years earlier had produced a book on the bomber offensive which, while being no means uniformly uncritical, had as often as not given Harris the benefit of the doubt.[52] Shaw himself seems to have believed that too much criticism had been levelled at Harris *ex post facto* and out of context and thought that the bombing offensive, at least indirectly through drawing resources away from the Eastern Front, contributed to the winning of the war.[53] That producer and director were in accord with the writer in terms of sympathy is made clear through certain casting decisions.[54]

The choice of actors appears to have depended in almost all cases on a mixture of physical resemblance to the person being played and ability to project certain character traits. Similarities in appearance and the kinds of roles they had previously played, for instance, made Bernard Kay and Frederick Treves the right men to impersonate, respectively, a stolidly supportive Robert Saundby at Bomber Command HQ and an avuncular but politically astute Charles 'Peter' Portal as Harris's superior at the Air Ministry.[55] John Nettleton, to take another example of a fine English character actor, was a perfect fit for the C-in-C's personal staff officer if the peacetime Oxford philosophy don T. D. 'Harry' Weldon was meant to be smoothly detached in manner and pronouncement.[56] If the prime minister was to be both larger than life and at the same time rather calculating, then balding, round-faced Robert Hardy was the obvious choice for Winston Churchill, having already played the part to widespread acclaim for an ITV drama series, *Winston Churchill: The Wilderness Years*, made at the start of the decade.[57]

Opponents of the indiscriminate bombing of German civilians were also cast carefully in terms of appearance and manner but, in combination with script and direction, in such a way as to undermine their characters' positional credibility.[58] Thus, the thespian attributes that would later allow Roger Llewelyn to play Sherlock Holmes – aquiline nose, high cheekbones, precise diction – also made him the right actor for the part of Canon John Collins should the Bomber Command HQ chaplain be meant to project his ethical objections to firebombing with a degree of high-strung clerical certitude.[59] Similarly, if another supporter of not suspending moral judgement in time of war, minister for aircraft production Stafford Cripps, was meant to come across as overly ethereal in his ethical pronouncements, then Charles Kay, an actor with a strong line in pedantic roles, was perfect.[60]

The most crucial piece of casting, of course, both in terms of shaping the part and drawing in an audience, was for the title role. Lloyd had planned originally to sign up Anthony Hopkins to play the C-in-C Bomber Command, but instead the role of Arthur Harris went to John Thaw.[61] 'I was very grateful for the offered the part because it was not the sort of thing I would have expected', Thaw subsequently commented, adding, doubtless because of differences in everything from voice and appearance to politics and experience between the actor and his subject, that playing Harris 'was a challenge'.[62]

Yet, this particular thespian brought with him a number of key advantages from the perspective of Lloyd and Darlow. Though lacking any service background, he had proven that he could play a man in uniform convincingly as the star of a military police procedural series, *Redcap*, back in the mid-sixties. An air of toughness and decisive authority on the small screen had been heavily reinforced in the latter seventies playing a flying-squad detective inspector in *The Sweeney*. 'I think it's the way I look', Thaw explained during production of *Bomber Harris*: 'Ever since I came into television I've tended to be given what the press call tough-guy roles.'[63] Yet, just as importantly, the actor had in the eighties projected a degree of fallibility, even vulnerability, in the title role of the long-running *Inspector Morse*. Above all, the characters played by Thaw were almost never out-and-out villains and usually on the side of the angels. 'I've tried to play it as it was', the actor explained, 'without leaning one way or the other. That's what the script does.'[64] But with Thaw starring as the C-in-C, audiences were being primed to give Harris the benefit of the doubt.

It was Thaw, indeed, who drew most critical praise before and after *Bomber Harris* was aired on BBC1 starting at 8.35 pm on Saturday, 2 September 1989. His was a 'compelling' (Peter Waymark in *The Times*) or 'corking' (Alan Coren in the *Mail on Sunday*) performance – in any case a role 'played to perfection', according to Michael Thompson-Noel of the *Financial Times*.[65] Max Hastings, to be sure, argued in the pages of the *Sunday Times* magazine that from a historical perspective both the play and the portrayal of Harris were 'unsubtle' and elided the documented record too much: but he admitted that he was anyway 'somewhat dubious' about television films which sought to portray events which many of those living at the time could recreate more accurately than any post-war playwright.[66] In all, 7.6 million people watched *Bomber Harris* when it premiered, the view that 'an absorbing argument was presented with style' (*Plays and Players*) being affirmed by repeats and its nomination in the best single drama category at the BAFTA awards.[67]

Those who sought to defend the record of Bomber Command and its commander were, for the time being, appeased. But that controversy was not about to disappear any time soon was evident in Granada developing and airing roughly three months after *Bomber Harris* a documentary about bomber crews who could no longer stand the stress and refused to continue operational flying. *Whispers in the Air* was judged 'interesting and extremely moving' even in the pages of the patriotic *Daily Mail*, with Harris coming under fire for his inflexible attitude towards those judged lacking in moral fibre (LMF).[68] The skirmishes of the eighties, though, would prove to be only a prelude to the full-scale battles of the nineties.

Notes

1 It was symptomatic that McKee thought Irving's account 'was so historically balanced and precise that I felt he had failed to bring out the full and terrible truths of the story as I had understood it'. Alexander McKee, *Dresden 1945: The Devil's Tinderbox* (London: Granada, 1983), xxix; see John Keegan review in *New Statesman*, 6 August 1992, 22; David Lodge review in *London Review of Books*, 21 October 1982, 18; see also W. L. Webb review in *Guardian*, 2 September 1982; Albert Hunt review in *New Society*, 10 June 1982, 60. On the weaknesses of the book, first published in 1982 by Souvenir, see Mark Connelly, *Reaching for the Stars: A New History of Bomber Command in World War II* (London: I.B. Tauris, 2001), 154–5. A more temperate and balanced new analysis of the bombing war by US academic historian Lee Kennett, *A History of Strategic Bombing* (New York: Scribner's, 1982), appears to have been ignored outside the United States. See I. B. Holley, Jr, review in *Military Affairs* 48 (1984), 91.
2 The single airworthy heavy bomber was Lancaster PA474 of the RAF Battle of Britain Memorial Flight, useful enough when a story involved only one aircraft: see e.g. *TV Times*, 3 July 1980, 26. On the Dakotas used in *Airline*, see Simon D. Beck, *The Aircraft Spotter's Film and Television Companion* (Jefferson, NC: McFarland, 2016), 225–6. The central character in *Airline*, Jack Ruskin, a highly skilled non-commissioned pilot from a relatively humble background who has a problem with the class hierarchy of the RAF and BOAC, bears something of a resemblance to Sam Lambert, the protagonist in Len Deighton's novel *Bomber* (London: Cape, 1970).
3 See Martin Middlebrook, *The Battle of Hamburg: Allied Bomber Forces against a Germany City in 1943* (London: Allen Lane, 1980); *The Peenemünde Raid: The Night of 17–18 August 1943* (London: Allen Lane, 1982); *The Berlin Raids: RAF Bomber Command, Winter 1943–1944* (London: Viking, 1988). Leaving aside US publishers, *The Battle of Hamburg* was issued in paperback by Penguin in 1980 and reissued in 1984 and 1988; *The Peenemünde Raid* was issued in paperback by Penguin in 1982; and *The Berlin Raids* was issued in paperback by Penguin in 1990.
4 Popular memoirs by former Bomber Command aircrew in this period included Murray Peden, *A Thousand Shall Fall: The True Story of a Canadian Bomber Pilot in World War Two* (Sttitsville, ON: Canada's Wings, 1979), a second edition of which appeared in 1981, was reprinted in 1982, followed by an updated edition in 1986 (Toronto: Stoddart) and a new edition in 1988 (Toronto: Stoddart). Walter Thompson's *Lancaster to Berlin* (London: Goodall, 1985) was first reprinted in 1987, and Tom Sawyer's *Only Owls and Bloody Fools Fly at Night* (London: Kimber, 1982) was reprinted in paperback (Manchester: Goodall) in 1987.
5 Jack Currie, *Lancaster Target: The Story of a Crew Who Flew from Wickenby* (London: New English Library, 1977).

6 Originally titled *Prelude to Victory*, this 16 mm effort by the CO of RAF Hemswell, H. I. Cozens, was used in several documentaries after it was released in the early 1980s and was issued on videocassette with a new narration under the title *Night Bombers* in 1982. See *The Times*, 16 October 1982; Air Commodore Iliffe Cozens, accessed 3 September 2012, http://ftfmagazine.lewcock.net; Brian Johnson and H. I. Cozens, *Bombers: The Weapon of Total War* (London: Thames Methuen, 1984), 7; W. E. Jones, *Bomber Intelligence* (Leicester: Midland Counties, 1983), 222; Prelude to Victory, Imperial War Museum, accessed 19 August 2012, http://www.iwm.org.uk. It was broadcast on ITV in 1986. *Observer*, 14 September 1986.
7 See *Broadcast*, 23 June 1980, 9; *Observer*, 8 June 1980; *Television Today*, 17 July 1980, 20; *Times*, 13 June 1980, 27; *Daily Telegraph*, 14 June 1980. The success of *Lancaster Legend* prompted a paperback reissue of *Lancaster Target* by Goodall in 1981.
8 BFI Library, *Operation Chastise: The Dams Raid Relived*, Yorkshire Television press release, July 1983. Questions about the raid had been posed in print by historian John Sweetman in his book *Operation Chastise: The Dams Raid: Epic or Myth* (London: Jane's, 1982).
9 See Noble Frankland, *History at War: The Campaigns of an Historian* (London: DLM, 1998), 193–4; *Times*, 13 February 1985; *Guardian*, 13 February 1985; *Daily Mirror*, 13 February 1985.
10 See *Television Today*, 12 July 1984, 19; Ralph Edwards, *In the Thick of It: The Autobiography of a Bomber Pilot* (Upton: Images, 1994), 185.
11 *Sydney Morning Herald*, 26 December 1987, Spectrum, reviews, 30. *Wings of the Storm* was broadcast on Channel 4 in the UK. *Guardian*, 7 November 1987.
12 David Golombeck letter, *Bomber Command Association Newsletter* 8 (1988), 1; see review in *Cinema Canada*, December 1986, 18. On *Return to Dresden* (NFB, 1986), see interview with Martin Duckworth, 24 June 2009, Montreal Serai, accessed 4 November 2017, https://montrealserai.com; *Peace Magazine*, December 1986–January 1987, 41; *Toronto Star*, 14 October, 9 November 1986; *Globe and Mail*, 22 October 1986; *Ottawa Citizen*, 24 September 1986. On this film and a similarly accusatory BBC piece on the 1944 bombing of Le Havre see also Harry Yates, *Luck and a Lancaster: Chance and Survival in World War II* (Shrewsbury: Airlife, 1999), 144–6.
13 *Guardian*, 30 December 1985, 14 July 1986.
14 See Simon W. Parry, *Spitfire Hunters: The Inside Stories behind the Best of the TV Aircraft Digs* (Walton-on-Thames: Red Kite, 2010).
15 See e.g. 'Air Gunner', *Commando Comics* 1473, December 1980, 39; 'A Boy's Hero', *Commando Comics* 1653, November 1982, *passim*.
16 *The Dam Busters* (U.S. Gold, 1984–6). See Dam Busters, accessed 25 August 2017, http://spectrumcomputing.co.uk/index.php?cat=96&id=0001229.
17 David Hodgson, *Letters from a Bomber Pilot* (London: Thames Methuen, 1985), 88, 7.
18 *Morning Star*, 15 June 1985; *Daily Telegraph*, 19 June 1985; see also *Times*, 15 June 1985; *Sunday Telegraph*, 16 June 1985; *Guardian*, 19 June 1985; *Daily Express*, 19 June 1985; *Daily Mirror*, 19 June 1985; *Observer*, 23 June 1985; *Mail on Sunday*, 23 June 1985; *Sunday Telegraph*, 23 June 1985; *Times Educational Supplement*, 26 June 1985, 25.
19 *Sunday Times*, 30 June 1985.
20 John Terraine, *The Right of the Line: The RAF in the European War, 1939–1945* (London: Hodder and Stoughton, 1985). For reviews, see e.g. *Daily Mail*, 21 March 1985; *The Times*, 21 March 1985; *Observer*, 14 April 1985; *Spectator*, 30 March 1985, 23–4. A prominent Canadian historian was expressing even greater doubts at this

time: see Desmond Morton, *A Military History of Canada* (Edmonton: Hurtig, 1985), 205–7.
21 *Observer*, 8 April 1984; see also e.g. *The Times*, 7 April 1984; *Guardian*, 7 April 1984. Polarized reactions to the post-mortem books – *'Bomber' Harris: The Authorised Biography* (London: Cassell, 1984) by a former BCHQ staff officer, Dudley Saward, and the somewhat less hagiographic *Bomber Harris and the Strategic Bombing Offensive* (London: Arms and Armour, 1984), by the popular military writer Charles Messenger – which sought to defend Harris indicate how right Wilson was. See e.g. Murray Sayle in *Spectator*, 28 July 1984, 23–5, and letter in response from Paul A. Tomlinson, *Spectator*, 15 September 1984, 26.
22 See e.g. Churchill Archives Centre, Oliver Lyttelton Papers, CHAN II 4/13, Part I, Lovell White King to National Theatre Board, 5 January 1967, f. 130; Harris to Chandos, 18 April 1967, f. 80; ibid., Part II, Chandos to Tynan, 18 April 1967, f. 233. It is noteworthy that Len Deighton in his novel *Bomber* never referred to Harris by name – only as 'the C.-in-C.' – and offered no other identifying features. The stated hobbies of his senior staff officer, by way of contrast, echoed those of the real Robert Saundby. Len Deighton, *Bomber* (London: Cape, 1970), chapter 2. Only when the novel was adapted for radio by the BBC a decade after Harris's death was this cautiousness dropped and the C-in-C directly named. *Bomber* (dir. Adrian Bean, 1994).
23 On the dead not being subject to libel laws, see e.g. Duncan Walker, Can you say anything about the dead?, 28 June 2005, BBC News, accessed 26 August 2017, http://news.bbc.co.uk/1/hi/magazine/4630243.stm.
24 See Maggie Brown, *A License to Be Different: The Story of Channel 4* (London: BFI, 2007), 84, 85, 89, 90; Dorothy Hobson, *Channel 4: The Early Years and the Jeremy Isaacs Legacy* (London: I.B. Tauris, 2008), 13–14, 48–50, 61–2, 87–9. For the chief's own account see Jeremy Isaacs, *Storm over 4: A Personal Account* (London: Weidenfeld and Nicolson, 1989).
25 *Fireraiser* (Barefoot, 1987), end credits. On *The Destruction of Dresden* see Clive Barker, 'Rampant Pacifism: The Work of the Bradford College of Art Group, 1967–1973', in *Acts of War: The Representation of Military Conflict on the British State and Television since 1945*, ed. Tony Howard and John Stokes (Aldershot: Scolar, 1996), 102–4; Albert Hunt, *Hopes for Great Happenings: Alternatives in Education and Theatre* (London: Eyre Methuen, 1976), 83–95.
26 *Fireraiser* was accurately described by television writer Jane Harbord ahead of the projected transmission date as 'a mix of drama, documentary and archival material' (*Broadcast*, 8 January 1988, 8). Max Wall had served in the RAF during the war, though on the ground rather than in the air. See Max Wall with Peter Harris, *The Fool on the Hill* (London: Quartet, 1975), 122–8.
27 Twentieth Century Vixen in *Index on Censorship* 17 (1988), 16.
28 W. F. Thomson letter, *Daily Mail*, 17 August 1987; see *Bomber Command Association Newsletter* 6 (1988), 1.
29 *Daily Mail*, 12 August 1987; see Michael Grade, *It Seemed Like a Good Idea at the Time* (London: Macmillan, 1999), 338.
30 On Barefoot Video arguing that what was being created was not in any way unfair see Trudi Davies comment in *Daily Mail*, 12 August 1987. On *Fireraiser* being judged highly partisan, see e.g. *Variety*, 8–14 February 1988, 152.
31 Though some commentators thought the choice of vaudevillian Max Wall to play Arthur Harris a mistake – see e.g. *Daily Mail*, 17 August 1987, 22 January 1988 – he

turned in a quite impressive performance. Issues of historical accuracy aside, Harris in *Fireraiser* is a fine study in disdainful menace.
32 Jeremy Isaacs, *Look Me in the Eye: A Life in Television* (London: Little, Brown, 2006), 365.
33 *Index on Censorship* 17 (1988), 6; *Guardian*, 23 January 1988.
34 Grade, *It Seemed Like a Good Idea*, 338–9; see also ibid., 220 ff.
35 Grade, *It Seemed Like a Good Idea*, 339. On the Falklands and Étaples controversies see ibid., 220–7; Mihar Bose, *Michael Grade: Screening the Image* (London: Virgin, 1992), 187–95.
36 Grade, *It Seemed Like a Good Idea*, 339.
37 *Index on Censorship* 17 (1988), 16; Grade, *It Seemed Like a Good Idea*, 339.
38 *Index on Censorship* 17 (1988), 16.
39 Grade, *It Seemed Like a Good Idea*, 339; see *Index on Censorship* 17 (1988), 6; *Guardian*, 23 January 1988; Bose, *Michael Grade*, 229.
40 *Broadcast*, 31 July 1987, 8.
41 On special showings of *Fireraiser*, see e.g. *Index on Censorship* 17 (1988), 16; *Guardian*, 3 February 1988; *Broadcast*, 25 August 1989, 11.
42 On Shaw arguing that this was Harris's position see *Guardian*, 10 August 1989.
43 See Mark Connelly, 'Bomber Harris: Raking Through the Ashes of the Strategic Air Campaign Against Germany', in *Repicturing the Second World War: Representations in Film and Television*, ed. Michael Paris (Basingstoke: Palgrave, 2007), 168–70.
44 On Churchill seeing the air campaign as an alternative to the second front, his worries about a Nazi atomic bomb, and being the prime mover behind the Dresden attack before backtracking, see e.g. Henry Probert, *Bomber Harris: His Life and Times* (Toronto: Stoddart, 2001), 146–7, 317–9, 320–1.
45 W. F. Thomson in *Daily Mail*, 17 August 1987.
46 In the several of the early interludes of wartime footage used to denote operations that Harris has set in motion, *Target for Tonight* once more features.
47 On what the minister for aircraft production actually said see Stafford Cripps, *Towards Christian Democracy* (New York: Philosophical Library, 1946), 91–101; see also Peter Clarke, *The Cripps Version: The Life of Sir Stafford Cripps, 1889–1952* (London: Allen Lane, 2002), 374.
48 See L. John Collins, *Faith under Fire* (London: Leslie Frewin, 1966), 89.
49 Connelly, 'Bomber Harris', 174.
50 *The Listener*, 7 September 1989, 39.
51 Probert, *Bomber Harris*, 151; Connelly, 'Bomber Harris', 174; *Radio Times*, 23 September 1989, 77.
52 Norman Longmate, *The Bombers: The RAF Offensive against Germany, 1939–1945* (London: Hutchinson, 1983).
53 See *Radio Times*, Second World War Supplement, 2 September 1989, 34.
54 The importance of casting choices is made clear in Connelly, 'Bomber Harris'.
55 Frederick Treves had Portal's balding pate and 'specialised in playing men in positions of authority' (*Guardian* obituary, 3 February 2012) while Bernard Kay sported Saundby's strong eyebrows and moustache as well as thespian 'gravitas' (*Guardian* obituary, 25 December 2014).
56 John Nettleton was already familiar to television viewers as the Machiavellian cabinet and then former cabinet secretary Sir Arnold Robinson in the popular BBC political satire *Yes, Minister* (1980–4) and its sequel, *Yes, Prime Minister* (1985–8).
57 *Winston Churchill: The Wilderness Years*, eight episodes (Southern Television, 1981).

58 See e.g. John Dugdale review in *The Listener*, 31 August 1989, 39.
59 For the views and manner of the actual BCHQ chaplain on area bombing see John L. Collins, *Faith under Fire* (London: Frewin, 1966), 69, 88–9, ff.
60 The offensively pedantic roles played by Bernard Kay included the public school headmaster Alcock in the BBC series *To Serve Them All My Days* (1980-1) and the Archbishop of Canterbury in *Henry V* (BBC Films, 1989).
61 *Broadcast*, 31 July 1987, 8; Connelly, 'Bomber Harris', 174.
62 *Radio Times*, Second World War Supplement, 2–8 September 1989, 35; see also Stafford Hildred and Tim Ewbank, *John Thaw: The Biography* (London: Deutsch, 1998), 121–2.
63 *Guardian*, 10 August 1989.
64 *Radio Times*, Second World War Supplement, 2–8 September 1989, 34–5.
65 *Financial Times*, 6 September 1989; *Mail on Sunday*, 10 September 1989; *The Times*, 2 September 1989; see also *Sunday Times*, 10 September 1989; *Guardian*, 4 September 1989.
66 *Sunday Times* magazine, 3 September 1989, 15.
67 *Plays and Players*, November 1989. On the BAFTA nomination see *Television Today*, 22 November 1990, 18; on viewing figures see *Broadcast*, 22 September 1989, 27. On the second BBC showing see BFI Library, BBC press release, *Bomber Harris*, 13 February 1990.
68 *Daily Mail*, 29 November 1989; see ibid., 28 November 1989; *Guardian*, 29 November 1989. Not everyone agreed, however, that LMF had been treated fairly in *Whispers in the Air*: see James Hampton, *Selected for Aircrew: Bomber Command in the Second World War* (Walton-on-Thames: Air Research, 1993), 146, 150. Commando Comics, interestingly, suggested that fear was a natural reaction that did not necessarily denote cowardice. See *A Man Afraid*, Commando 1727, August 1983.

Figure 6.1 Avik, played by Jason Scott Lee, lands amidst the Dresden firestorm in *Map of the Human Heart* (Working Title, 1993).

Chapter 6

MARTYRS: THE 1990s

With the passage of roughly fifty years, it might have been expected that the arguments about the wartime record of Bomber Command – on moral grounds, concerning military effectiveness, or a mixture thereof – would start to diminish. Time, after all, is supposed to heal all wounds. Yet the last decade of the twentieth century was to witness a sharp escalation rather than a gradual diminution of controversy. Arguments over the efficacy and ethics of area bombing would reach a new crescendo in the run-up to and aftermath of the fiftieth anniversary of the end of the Second World War in print, on screen and even on the streets.

In the latter case, the focal point was a statue of the man who had led the force due to be placed outside the Royal Air Force (RAF) church of St. Clement Danes in central London. The Bomber Command Association, a veterans group, had argued that since a statue of the famous wartime chief of Fighter Command, Hugh Dowding, had been erected in front of the church in the latter 1980s, Bomber Command ought to be represented in similar fashion with a bronze of its best known leader, Arthur Harris. The RAF had no objections, and the Queen Mother, as royal patron, agreed to unveil the statue – paid for through popular subscription rather than out of the public purse – at a service of reconciliation and remembrance. News of the project drew in the necessary donations but also sparked protest. Civic leaders from cities that had undergone firestorm raids publicly voiced their disquiet, as did prominent figures in the peace movement in Britain. The press was split, with doubts being expressed in certain left-of-centre broadsheets and jingoistic support trumpeted in right-wing tabloids.[1] Protesters were present and vocal when the ceremony nonetheless took place on schedule at the end of May 1992, and subsequently the Harris statue was defaced several times.[2]

Lack of consensus about the bombing war was also evident in a new round of television documentaries. There were some that took a traditional line but others that were distinctly revisionist in tone.

Albert Hunt, in the wake of the *Fireraiser* cancellation, had developed a more subtle documentary approach to Bomber Command in collaboration with producer Martin Cook. *The Flying Schoolboys and the Wild Sow* – a reference to what one veteran described RAF aircrew as being and the *Luftwaffe* code term for bomber-hunting fighters not reliant on radar – initially appeared as an exercise in putting together old combatants to those viewers who watched it before midnight on Channel 4 at the end of January 1990. But as Hugh Herbert of the *Guardian* noted, what 'seemed on the surface to set off being about old enemies meeting and sharing memories and wine and reliving shared dangers' evolved into a film about 'the morality of area bombing'. Dresden, including the harrowing testimony of survivor Erika Woollams, featured prominently.[3]

More prominent was another documentary, *Battle of the Bombers*, produced by Helen Bettinson as part of the long-running BBC *Timewatch* series. A studio audience composed of advocates for and against the area campaign was selected to watch the programme and then participate in a live discussion moderated by Jonathan Dimbleby during the evening of 7 April 1993. The BBC received about a hundred calls from viewers protesting an overly critical stance towards the RAF – one viewer asserting that *Battle of the Bombers* was 75 per cent pro-German and only 25 per cent pro-British – and the broadcast discussion was extremely heated. 'Instead of a balanced debate', one of those asked to contribute to the documentary acidly recalled, 'there then followed a general shouting match, mostly about the bombing of Dresden, between very excited contenders, none of whom seemed to know anything at all about the bomber offensive'.[4]

In the anniversary sweepstakes, the dams raid could serve as a celebratory counterbalance to such downbeat commemoration. Thus ITV screened, in the aftermath of the inevitable small-screen showing of the 1955 film in May 1993, a documentary entitled *Dambusters!*, written by Central Television journalists Derek Braithwaite and Brian Collins, in which some of those who had flown on the attack and some of those who had experienced the aftermath were interviewed.[5] Yet even in this largely valedictory piece the question 'was it really worth the immense loss of life incurred' was nonetheless posed, and thirteen months later a rather more revisionist account appeared in the *Secret History* series on Channel 4. *The Dambusters Raid*, produced by Chris Haws and directed by Alex Beetham, featured interviews with participants on both sides and also historians but took a more critical approach to the planning, execution and aftermath of the strike. 'The Möhne and Eider dams were rebuilt; the Sorpe had survived; and the devastation had little lasting effect', the narrator explains, adding, 'the dambusters raid has become legend; but was it really worthwhile?' Judging by how the documentary was advertised and responded to by critics when it was broadcast by Channel 4 in June 1994, the answer seemed to be only in terms of public morale.[6]

The BBC, meanwhile, had been working out a way to dramatize *Bomber*, Len Deighton's bestselling novel in which both the physical ghastliness and apparent futility of RAF area attacks were underlined. The problem with trying to mount a screen version of *Bomber* had been the huge costs involved in set building and the absence of airworthy Lancasters. Turning the book into a radio play rather than a big- or small-screen epic neatly circumvented these problems, the visual element being confined to pictures in the *Radio Times* of some of the players dressed in period uniforms standing next to a static Lancaster (R5868) in the RAF Museum at Hendon.[7] The aural-only version of *Bomber*, however, adapted by Joe Dunlop, produced by Jonathan Ruffle and directed by Adrian Bean at the BBC's Maida Vale studios, did not lack ambition. Involving a cast of three dozen people, including both major and minor characters plus Tom Baker as commentator, the play was organized to recreate the roughly twenty-four hours of events chronicled in the book in segmented real time. The result was aired on Radio 4 through the afternoon, evening and late hours of 18 February 1994 to mark the fiftieth anniversary of the Dresden firestorm. Critical reaction was mixed. It was described on the one hand as 'tension-filled' and 'deeply moving' by Moira Petty for *The Stage*, and writing for the right-wing *Daily Mail* Linda O'Callaghan argued without irony that Bean and Ruffle 'deserve medals'.[8] Martin Hoyle, on the other hand, judged in the *Financial Times* that 'gimmicks' like mixing documentary interviews into the dramatic narrative were a mistake, this particular technique only emphasizing that voices such as that of Sam West were those of trained thespians, not real people.[9] Overall, however, the project was retrospectively judged a 'huge success' with the public.[10]

Bomber Command was also putting in a limited appearance on the big screen through a pair of romantic dramas. Neither would be seen by a mass audience, but both indicated sometimes acute awareness on the part of their makers of the human costs of the strategic bombing campaign.

Written, directed and coproduced by filmmaker Aaron Kim Johnson with help from the National Film Board of Canada and the Commonwealth Air Training Plan Museum in his native Manitoba, *For the Moment*, set in 1942, was principally about relationships between young men from Canada, Australia, Britain and elsewhere being trained as aircrew and young women from the surrounding communities. The film did, however, stress that the chances of survival for those who successfully passed through training and joined the strategic air offensive were poor. The local Anderson family has to deal with the loss of their son, Dennis, a freshly minted navigator played by Kelly Proctor who, it turns out, has been killed on only his second op. 'Do you know what the average life expectancy of a bomber pilot is?' aspiring Australian flyer Lachlan Currie, played by Russell Crowe, rhetorically asks his distraught Canadian mate Johnny Crouch, played by Peter Outerbridge, after the latter's fiancée breaks off their marriage plans: 'It's six bloody weeks, Johnny!' Though nicely acted, beautifully photographed and able to make use of various grounded and airworthy examples of training aircraft such as the Tiger Moth and Anson still in Western Canada to add more than a touch of authenticity, *For the Moment* was a small regional production that, while garnering some positive reviews across Canada in the autumn of 1993 in a theatrical run, only appeared elsewhere on videocassette several years later.[11]

Several months before *For the Moment* premiered, a considerably more ambitious romantic drama had appeared in cinemas around the world in which Bomber Command played a more direct role. This was *Map of the Human Heart*, an epic tale shot in Canada and England on a decidedly non-epic budget from a story idea from New Zealand director Vincent Ward developed by Australian writer Louis Nowra about the complicated relations between a mixed-race Inuit, boy and man; a Métis, girl and woman; and an older, male Caucasian cartophile at various junctures between the thirties and the sixties.[12] Almost half of the film was set in England during the last year of the Second World War, at which point Avik, played by Jason Scott Lee, is a flight sergeant bomb aimer in a multinational

Lancaster crew; Albertine, played by Anne Parillaud, is a commissioned photographic interpreter in the Women's Auxiliary Air Force; and Walter Russell, played by Patrick Bergin, is a group captain at the Air Ministry. A love triangle develops in which Avik competes with Walter for the affections of Albertine, a struggle that Walter wins by default when he decides not to intervene and prevent Avik's crew from having to fly a compulsory post-tour operation to Dresden on which they are shot down.[13]

Given that a number of scenes were set in and around bombers both on the ground and in the air, Ward and his co-producer Tim Bevan had to find period aircraft or the means to represent them. They might have looked to the Battle of Britain Memorial Flight for access to PA474, but as the bulk of the shoot took place in Canada rather than England, the filmmakers turned instead to the Canadian Warplane Heritage Museum outside Hamilton, Ontario, which owned its own restored Lancaster, FM213.[14] This plane featured in a number of exterior and interior shots, but for depicting attacks on Berlin and the climactic raid on Dresden the filmmakers used a mixture of full-scale replicas and restorations of various portions of the Lancaster, model work and various special effects at a studio in Montreal.[15] The results were generally impressive, particularly since the flying sequences were at night, allowing for a certain amount of impressionism rather than precise depiction of what a city under attack looked like from the air.[16] Air force uniforms, flying kit and dialogue also, for the most part, provided an aura of authenticity.[17]

The attack on Dresden, which in many ways serves as the climax of *Map of the Human Heart*, was an event that Ward strongly felt to be 'a primitive act of savagery'.[18] Avik thus wonders why Bomber Command is being sent to the city since 'there's just civilians there'. Walter explains to him that the idea is to break the enemy's will to fight – and that he, personally, is seeking revenge for the emotional pain inflicted by a former lover who still resides there. Later, as the firestorm rages below and bombs are released, a horrified Avik asks, 'What have we done?' A fighter attack graphically illustrates how a bomber can be transformed into a burning, uncontrollable hulk filled with dead and wounded men, and though Avik is bodily thrown out wearing a parachute as his Lancaster begins to explode, he descends into a streetscape where everything is ablaze and in which the howling wind is capable of ripping off a child's clothes and melting radiographic film in an instant.[19]

When *Map of the Human Heart* was released in the spring of 1993, critical reaction tended towards admiration for the stunning visuals – not least with respect to the firestorm sequences – combined with disappointment with plot and dialogue elements.[20] Though it did comparatively well in the director's home country, in global terms box-office receipts were rather disappointing for such a monumental undertaking.[21] 'You get the impression that the director is not a Bomber Harris fan', Anne Billson wrote drily for the *Sunday Telegraph*; but by this point, those intent on defending the reputation of Bomber Command were focusing their attention almost exclusively on another Canadian production: an ambitious small-screen docudrama that proved the most controversial attempt yet seen to grapple with the bombing war.[22]

This was the work of the McKenna brothers, documentary filmmaker Brian and television journalist Terence. Having collaborated on a film for the Canadian Broadcasting Corporation (CBC) about the courage and suffering of ordinary Canadian servicemen and the incompetence of some of their senior commanders in the First World War titled *The Killing Ground* in the late 1980s, they had turned their attention by the start of the 1990s to the Second World War.[23] The aim was to remind people that by its very nature warfare is, as Brian McKenna put it, 'just this thrashing, bloody insanity'.[24] More specifically, he sensed that some of the more uncomfortable truths about Canada at war had been suppressed for decades, particularly with reference to the courage and suffering of ordinary servicemen and the heartless ineptitude of those who led them from on high.[25]

This seemed to be true for, among other wartime events, the participation of the Royal Canadian Air Force (RCAF) in the strategic bombing campaign. This story, Brian McKenna thought, 'had never had a public airing in Canada'.[26] There were other tales to tell as well in an ambitious series of one hundred-minute films financed to the tune of $2.8 million by no less than four different entities, including the National Film Board as well as the CBC, and collectively dubbed *The Valour and the Horror* (shades of the famously controversial film by Marcel Ophüls about French collaboration with the Nazis, *The Sorrow and the Pity*); but prominent among them would be *Death by Moonlight: Bomber Command*.[27]

Convinced that 'deliberate bombing of German civilians' was morally indefensible, the brothers were 'determined to tell the truth as we found it'.[28] In practice this meant approaching the subject from an inductive rather than deductive perspective based on the conviction that, under the direction of a ruthless and blinkered RAF commander, the aerial campaign waged by Bomber Command had been highly unethical, unacceptably costly and largely ineffective.[29]

Death by Moonlight would touch on a wide range of subjects ranging from cultural prejudices to the policies applied to psychological casualties. There would be critical discussion of specific operations, including the attack on the dams, the Hamburg firestorm and the Nuremberg disaster. The perspective of Germans in relation to area bombing would be included, but the main thrust would be on the destruction of cities and those in them as the C-in-C's idée fix and on the Canadian bomber crews martyred in 'catastrophic' numbers in pursuit of a secret policy to massacre German civilians, 'most of them women and children'.[30]

In terms of structure and form, *Death by Moonlight* would follow the pattern laid out for the series as a whole. The recollections and reactions of two veterans, wartime RCAF pilots Doug Harvey and Ken Brown, would be recorded as they revisited airfields in England and the locations and people they bombed in Germany. In order to avoid turning off younger audience members by giving the impression that the film was 'just a bunch of old guys talking', a small cast of actors would speak 'the documented words' of both the leaders and the led in full wartime costume against semi- or fully staged wartime backdrops, including Lancaster FM213. The actor and veteran approaches would be knitted together through the addition of archival footage, a soundtrack largely composed of extracts from Fauré's *Requiem* and voiceover narration written by Brian and spoken by Terence.[31]

First broadcast by CBC Television on the evening of Sunday, 19 January 1992, *Death by Moonlight* attracted 1,677,000 viewers and impressed TV critics, the picture it painted being described using terms such as 'harrowing' (*Edmonton Journal*), 'shattering' (*Globe and Mail*) and 'devastating' (*Ottawa Citizen*).[32] It soon became apparent, however, that many of those who had fought in Bomber Command under Harris were deeply upset by what they perceived as a distorted and biased account of their wartime service.[33] A second broadcast on the CBC cable news channel two months later that was followed by a rather one-sided studio debate between Brian McKenna and a couple of upset vets only made matters worse. Over the following days, weeks, months and years, outraged veterans sought redress via individual letters of protest and collective action through the Royal Canadian Legion, the National Council of Veterans Associations, the Senate Subcommittee on Veterans Affairs and eventually a newly formed group of Bomber Command veterans eager to defend their reputation, the Bomber Harris Trust. The uproar was such that both the CBC ombudsman and the chairman of the Canadian Radio-television and Telecommunications Commission (CRTC) were asked to judge whether *The Valour and the Horror* as a whole had violated broadcasting standards in the spring and summer of 1992, the Senate of Canada held public hearings on the same subject in the autumn and winter, and in July 1993 a class-action lawsuit was lodged in Ontario against practically everyone involved in the production.[34]

The unedifying no-holds-barred war of words that resulted, into which various historians were drawn, witnessed victories and defeats for each side.[35] Though the CRTC eventually ruled that the series had not violated broadcasting standards concerning truthfulness and the lawsuit along with a subsequent appeal were ruled inadmissible, those who thought that the McKennas had played fast and loose with the facts could point to the conclusion of the Senate subcommittee that the filmmakers had indulged in sloppy research and displayed 'serious bias' – and that of the CBC ombudsman that 'the series as it stands is flawed and fails to measure up to the CBC's demanding policies and standards' concerning accuracy.[36] For their part, the brothers could take solace from the way in which the media almost unanimously opined that an unacceptable attempt was being made to stifle freedom of expression and from a Gemini award for top documentary of the year in Canada.[37]

A new front in this confrontation opened across the Atlantic once it became known in the summer of 1993 that Channel 4 planned to broadcast *The Valour and the Horror* the following year.[38] The Bomber Command Association was keen to suppress *Death by Moonlight* and in June 1994 persuaded their royal patron, the Queen Mother, to write a letter expressing her 'concern'.[39] Channel 4, however, despite this and several hundred letters of complaint from ex-aircrew, decided to press on regardless.[40] Aired on the first Sunday evening of August, the film was treated roughly in the press. 'Goebbels could not have made a better job of this travesty of the truth', Andrew Roberts thundered in the *Daily Mail*, while TV critic Tom Sutcliffe informed readers of the *Independent* that *Death by Moonlight* was a 'leaden' and 'simple-minded' affair. Even Nancy Banks-Smith in the *Guardian* disliked the 'resentful commentary' and the 'relentless requiem'.[41] Channel 4 received a barrage of complaints, and a special *Right to Reply* programme was laid on in which veterans and historians effectively pointed out what was wrong with the McKenna version of the bomber war.[42]

Brian McKenna vigorously insisted throughout the controversy that research for the series had been 'bulletproof' and that *Death by Moonlight*, along with the rest of *Valour and the Horror*, was a completely legitimate form of investigative journalism that exposed dark truths about Canada's Second World War.[43] He also took repeated exception to the label 'docudrama', arguing that 'we didn't take license with the facts' in using 'dramatic techniques' since the actors spoke the documented words of the figures they represented.[44]

The research, however, was selective and partisan, when transferred to script form often simplified for narrative compression, and when translated onto film contained questionable or erroneous dramatic editing choices. Robert Dale, played by Hamish McEwan in a couple of brief scenes, had indeed been a navigator on the weather recce flight preceding the Nuremberg raid; but the words spoken by McEwan had never been uttered by Dale – they turned out to have been scripted on the basis of a secondary account.[45] A less peripheral figure played by Janne Mortil, WAAF sergeant Mary 'Bubbles' Moore, speaks prose adapted from a poem, a fictional short story and an interview with the author, a former WAAF officer.[46] Most central of all to *Death by Moonlight* was Arthur Harris, played by Graham Campbell, who makes pronouncements that at various junctures involve multiple elisions and sentences refashioned from the words of others.[47]

The anger that drove critics to uncover these and other faux pas was doubtless partly a reaction to segments of the narration clearly designed to *épater la bourgeoisie*, such as describing Barnes Wallis as 'an eccentric scientist' and the Avro Lancaster as 'an efficient killing machine'.[48] The strength of the reaction, though, was in large part driven by the choice of actors in the staged sequences and the way they were directed to deliver their lines.[49]

Figures who reflected the filmmakers' point of view concerning the campaign, such as scientist Freeman Dyson, were played as pleasant in both word and aspect, in the case of Dyson by actor Andrew Gillies. Those who held views antithetical to their values, on the other hand, such as Marvin Fleming and Arthur Harris himself, were played as villainously malevolent. In the hands of actor Mark Burgess, Fleming looked and sounded 'demonic', while actor Graham Campbell turned the head of Bomber Command into someone 'who could go on as Richard III without rehearsal'.[50] Even some of those who otherwise strongly supported *Death by Moonlight* thought that this was going too far. Before the series aired, researcher D'Arcy O'Connor, who had spoken with Fleming before his death, protested in a letter to the McKennas that the portrayal of the wing commander by Burgess was very unfair, since 'I just know he wouldn't have delivered those details [on firebombing] with such gloating malice'.[51] The real Freeman Dyson had no quarrel with how he was depicted but in a post-broadcast letter to O'Connor complained that 'Harris was a far more complicated and more interesting character than the puppet who appears in the film'.[52]

As the debate over *Death by Moonlight* raged on in the media, new books on the subject of area bombing did little to draw a line under the Bomber Command debate. An illustrated volume based on the series sold well but attracted a good deal of scorn from those who disputed the McKenna version of events.[53] Those who defended the C-in-C and strategic bombing were in turn sometimes treated with a certain amount of scepticism. *Reap the Whirlwind*, for instance, in which Spencer Dunmore and William Carter chronicled the story of Canada's 6 Group, was critiqued in one review as 'a bit too inclined to give Harris the benefit of the doubt'.[54] Similarly *The Hardest Victory*, in which Denis Richards, co-author of the official popular history of the RAF published in the mid-fifties, again sought to make a positive case, was judged by one knowledgeable reviewer as having not dealt effectively 'with the overarching issues of morality and strategic effectiveness'.[55] On the other hand, *Ethics and Airpower in World War II*, a condemnation of RAF area bombing by an American scholar, Stephen A. Garrett, was judged in some circles to be too 'biased' to be considered in any way definitive; while another American work, *The Holocaust and Strategic Bombing*, which equated these phenomena, was condemned as 'fundamentally flawed' by a number of senior scholars.[56]

Crucible of War, the massive, multi-author third volume in the official history of the RCAF, covering the war years, which appeared around the middle of the decade, inevitably was judged in the context of the *Valour and the Horror* imbroglio. The ten chapters devoted to Bomber Command in essence did not differ that much from the British official history of the campaign published more than thirty years earlier concerning the failure of area bombing to seriously weaken morale or fatally undermine war production until the last six months or so of the air campaign. The language, though, was in some instances much starker – the big attacks on Hamburg being described, for example, as 'a terror campaign, pure and simple'[57] – and horrific accounts from firestorm survivors as well as beleaguered aircrew were also included.[58] As a result, the volume was compared to *The Valour and the Horror*: admiringly by Brian McKenna and disparagingly by critics such as Jack Granatstein who opined that the volume 'too often seems like nothing so much as the TV series with footnotes'.[59] A few years later, back in the UK, the *Daily Mail* took heart from an introduction to the published version of the post-war British Bombing Survey written by the senior historian at the RAF Air Historical Branch that highlighted the entrenched bias against area bombing and its chief author.[60]

Meanwhile, it had been recognized on both sides of the Atlantic that writing critiques, submitting protests and launching lawsuits against *Death by Moonlight* might not be sufficient means to prevent defeat in what some regarded as a life-or-death battle for the reputation of Bomber Command. The small screen was a powerful medium, so perhaps images ought to be fought with images through the development of programming that either directly refuted what was being claimed or offered wider contextualization and more balanced perspectives. Thus no less than four separate broadcasting projects were initiated by those keen to avoid *The Valour and the Horror* becoming, as one concerned veteran put it, 'the definitive television record' of the events portrayed.[61]

The first to appear on the small screen was the work of Jeannie Muldoon, a member of the Royal Canadian Legion branch in London, Ontario, who decided to create a local documentary that would allow Bomber Command veterans to 'express their concerns' about *Death by Moonlight*. Introduced and narrated by Peter Desbarats, dean of journalism at the University of Western Ontario, *On the Wings of Valour: In Defense of Bomber Command*, was broadcast in the last quarter of 1992 on a number of regional cable community channels across Canada but was largely ignored by the press.[62]

Another, more or less simultaneous attempt was undertaken by the War Amps charity at the behest of its chief executive officer and anti-McKenna crusader, Cliff Chadderton. Over the course of eight months, a seventy-minute video was assembled 'which challenges at least twenty errors of fact or interpretation'. The result, *Bulletproof? You Be the Judge!*, was completed in late 1992 and consisted of point-by-point rejoinders through narrated select quotes from the limited array of published primary and secondary sources available in the War Amps library. The production values were low, the retorts were in places not obviously pertinent and lead commentator Chadderton did himself no favours by pointedly remarking at the start that Max Hastings' book did not 'really belong' in the corpus of serious work on Bomber Command. The video was distributed to cable television companies across Canada in the hope that it would be broadcast but does not appear to have achieved its makers' aim. 'We have no idea if or when it will be scheduled', a spokesman stated the following January, adding that *Bulletproof* would remain 'available on loan to anyone who requests it'.[63]

The third, and ultimately much more effective, effort to counterbalance *The Valour and the Horror* on screen was initiated around the same time by journalist Anderson Charters and filmmaker Richard Nielsen, who put together a proposal for a new documentary series on Canada in the Second World War. To get the project off the ground they asked Barney Danson, a former minister of national defence and Normandy veteran who had heartily disliked *The Valour and the Horror*, to act as de facto sponsor. Danson in turn reached out to his contacts in politics, the professions and the business world and formed a fundraising and advisory body that raised $1.2 million from the private sector and secured a further $600,000 from Telefilm Canada and the National Film Board. This allowed Charters and Nielsen, through the latter's production company, Norflicks, to develop a six-part series, *No Price Too High*, with the help of various collaborators in 1993–4.[64]

Co-written by Nielsen with James Wallen and narrated by journalist Arthur Kent, *No Price Too High* employed various conventional documentary techniques, such as voiceover reading of wartime letters and other first-person accounts as well as on-camera commentary by military historian Terry Copp. Among many other subjects related to Canada's war it contextualized strategic bombing, pointing out that it was the enemy who had first begun mass aerial assaults on civilians and arguing that the combined bomber offensive had done much to win the war. The big Allied raids had forced the enemy to divert a huge amount of manpower and material to try and defend the skies over Germany, and thus, as Copp put it, 'the bomber offensive was one of the decisive factors in the defeat of Nazi Germany'.

A book of the same title was published a year later that dealt with the issues raised at greater length.⁶⁵

Critical reaction was quite positive after *No Price Too High* premiered on a Canadian cable channel in the late summer of 1995, was subsequently picked up by border stations of the US broadcasting system in 1996 and was finally aired across Canada by the CBC in 1998. It was hailed as 'a top-notch series' in the *Calgary Herald*, for example, and described as, respectively, 'a triumph' and 'excellent television' by different reviewers in the pages of the *Globe and Mail*.⁶⁶

On the other side of the Atlantic, members of the Bomber Command Association had been busy developing their own televisual riposte to *The Valour and the Horror* ('disgraceful') as well as to the Harris statue protestors.⁶⁷ It was they who sponsored Alex Beetham, filmmaker son of the chairman, Sir Michael Beetham, to develop through Cinecam Productions an alternative documentary version of the wartime RAF strategic air campaign, *Bomber Command: Reaping the Whirlwind*. The goal, as the president of this veterans organization explained, was to present 'a true picture of what happened' for current and future generations through television so as 'to reach the maximum audience'.⁶⁸

Utilizing a combination of wartime footage, audio interviews with some of those involved, and linking female-voice narration, Alex Beetham deftly sought to put area bombing in context. For years after Dunkirk, aerial attack by night was the only means Britain had of directly carrying the war to Germany. While *Target for Tonight* had exaggerated the effectiveness of the early bombing campaign, it nevertheless remained true that Bomber Command had been trying hard to hit precise targets until losses and photographic evidence indicated that very little was being achieved at high cost. It was Churchill's scientific advisor, Lord Cherwell, who had persuaded the cabinet to shift the RAF strategic air offensive towards mass area bombing before Harris had even been appointed to head Bomber Command. Harris himself believed the total destruction of German industry from the air would win the war without the need for a land invasion, while the campaign gave Churchill something to show Stalin that indicated that Britain was indeed opening a Second Front against Germany in the summer of 1942. The directive issued by the combined chiefs of staff at Casablanca at the beginning of 1943 had confirmed enemy war industries to be among the five priority targets of a combined bomber offensive. Successful raids on cities such as Hamburg were devastating, but unlike the government, Harris never made any bones about the fact that civilians were being killed in area attacks. Moreover, alongside important precision strikes such as the dams raid and Peenemünde, Bomber Command in general was starting to achieve much greater accuracy through Pathfinder and other techniques; and though the cost was high, increases in German war production were far below their target levels thanks to constant bombing in 1943–4. Bomber Command played a major part in the success of the Allied invasion of France the following spring and summer, and the subsequent return to area bombing by Harris in 1944–5, though subject to much later criticism, was in his mind necessary to bring the war to a close as quickly as possible. As for Dresden, this had been a target that Harris had been reluctant to hit, but he had eventually done so on orders from Churchill and Eisenhower. The prime minister had then issued his notorious memo decrying wanton destruction, which the C-in-C had rightly viewed as an attack on a policy Churchill had overseen and approved of for years. Harris, it was implied, as someone who refused to deny that bombing meant mass urban destruction, was – and would continue to be in the post-war decades – used as a scapegoat for decisions made by more calculating figures.

Channel 4, having endured a lot of abuse for having aired *The Valour and the Horror*, agreed to schedule *Bomber Command: Reaping the Whirlwind* for broadcast in the late summer of 1996.[69] Television reviewers seem to have thought that Beetham had made a good case for Bomber Command in general and Arthur Harris in particular. 'It is hard to watch the archive film, and listen to the testimony of veterans', wrote Hilary Mantel for the *Observer*, 'without feeling that Harris has been the victim of injustice'. The *Daily Mail* thought Channel 4 had finally 'done the right thing', and even *Guardian* critic Stuart Jeffries conceded that the programme 'had an important argument to make'. At the same time, there was a sense in some circles that the moral case against area bombing had not been properly addressed.[70]

As had been the case with both *The Valour and the Horror* and *No Price Too High*, a book was published to follow up in print the small-screen presentation of *Reaping the Whirlwind*. In *Bomber Command, 1939–1945*, a lavishly illustrated work published by the trade press HarperCollins in the spring of 1997, Richard Overy, then professor of modern history at King's College London, sought to get past the 'great many distortions and illusions' that 'litter the popular view' of the RAF area bombing campaign, and 'show the whole record', complete with the experiences and perspectives of those who fought, and 'make it clear who was responsible for taking the decisions that affected Bomber Command'.[71] Overall, the bombing campaign had assisted the war on land and sea a great deal at various junctures, had served as an important political and psychological weapon, had contributed to the defeat of the *Luftwaffe* and done a good deal of indirect and direct damage to German war production. 'The critical question is not so much "What did bombing do to Germany?", but "What could Germany have achieved if there had been no bombing?"' If the enemy had been left unmolested, D-Day might have been an impossibility. In broad comparative combat terms, aircrew losses in Bomber Command were not exceptionally high. As for the death of large numbers of German civilians, it was thought at the time that the bombardment of places like Rotterdam and Warsaw and the Blitz had stripped Germany of the moral right to wall off its population from aerial danger. All in all, 'Bomber Command made a larger contribution to victory in Europe than any other element in Britain's armed services'.[72] Like the series, the associated book was seen as a 'fine story so well and so honestly told' by those who were 'outraged by the mawkish revisionism and hand-wringing' over the RAF's wartime bomber offensive.[73]

Overheated rhetoric may have been one of the motives for Canadian filmmaker Robert Linnell, whose father had been killed in action flying a Halifax over Berlin, to avoid overtly contentious issues in making a new documentary miniseries on Bomber Command entitled *Warriors of the Night*. 'I hadn't seen anything that I felt really told the story of, you know, the tactics and technology', he subsequently explained, 'so I sort of thought this might be a good story to tell'.[74] Using archival footage, new interviews and surviving aircraft examples, such as Lancaster FM213 from the Canadian Warplane Heritage Museum, the low-profile series framed the bombing war chiefly in terms of a seesaw battle of men and machines rather than strategic controversies. The fact that *Warriors of the Night*, when broadcast on the Discovery Channel in Canada to mark the forty-fifth anniversary of Victory in Europe, was viewed as basically uncontroversial by the critics, as were a number of new book titles, perhaps suggested to some at the time that the debate over Bomber Command was finally cooling down as the century came to an end. If so, the first years of the twenty-first century were to prove that the interpretation of wartime events over Germany still had the power to generate strong emotional responses.[75]

Notes

1 See Max Hastings, 'The Lonely Passion of Bomber Harris', *MHQ* 6, 2 (1994), 5–6; Peter Jacobs, *Stay the Distance: The Life and Times of Marshal of the Royal Air Force Sir Michael Beetham* (London: Frontline, 2011), 263–4; Maurice Weaver, 'A Storm Cast in Bronze', *Daily Telegraph*, 28 May 1992.
2 See *Daily Telegraph*, 1 June 1992; *Daily Mail*, 1 June, 21 and 30 October 1992. The involvement of various peace organizations in the Harris statue affair possibly may have been an indirect result of the end of the Cold War, causing a partial redirection in effort on the part of groups that had previously focused on denouncing nuclear weapons. See Kate Hudson, *CND – Now More Than Ever: The Story of a Peace Movement* (London: Vision, 2005), chapter 6.
3 *Observer*, 30 January 1990; see also *Times*, 29 January 1990.
4 Noble Frankland, *History at War: The Campaigns of an Historian* (London: DLM, 1998), 193–4; see *Daily Telegraph*, 8 April 1993.
5 See BFI Library, *Dambusters!* programme information, 1993. On airing *Dambusters!* after the 1955 film, see e.g. *Observer*, 16 May 1993.
6 See e.g. *Times*, 18 June 1994; *Observer*, 19 June 1994; *Irish Times*, 18 June 1994.
7 *Radio Times*, 24 February 1995, 18–19.
8 *Daily Mail*, 18 February 1995; *The Stage*, 9 March 1995, 27; see also *Times*, 18 February 1995.
9 *Financial Times*, 25 February 1995; see also *Times*, 18 February 1995.
10 *Guardian*, 11 March 1995. Interestingly, Spencer Dunmore had long before begun work on a radio play for the Canadian Broadcasting Corporation along similar lines – 'I thought the conversations across the intercom of a bomber crew might be an interesting device' (*Toronto Star*, 10 December 1971) – before deciding to turn the work into a novel, *Bomb Run* (London: Davies, 1971), written and published around the same time as Deighton's work.
11 For positive initial reviews of *For the Moment*, see e.g. *Calgary Herald*, 7 October 1994; *Hamilton Spectator*, 2 December 1994; *Toronto Star*, 11 November 1994. There were some Canadian critics, though, who judged it rather clichéd: *Globe and Mail*, 11 November 1994; *MacLean's*, 28 November 1994, 86; *Ottawa Citizen*, 11 November

1994. Critics in the United States were also of two minds: see e.g. *Chicago Tribune*, 19 April 1996; *Los Angeles Times*, 19 April 1996; *New York Times*, 19 April 1996.
12 BFI Library, *Map of the Human Heart* production plot synopsis.
13 The chronology of the film is a little off, since the Dresden raid appears to take place in the summer of 1944 rather than early in 1945. On the origins and making of *Map of the Human Heart* see Louis Nowra, *Shooting the Moon: A Memoir* (Sydney: Picador, 2004), 104–35; 'The Fever: The Making of *Map of the Human Heart*', *Australian-Canadian Studies* 11, 1–2 (1993), 113–38; also *Venue* magazine (Bristol), 9–29 July 1993, 6–7. On the work of the director see Stephanie Rains, 'Making Strange: Journeys through the Unfamiliar in the Films of Vincent Ward', in *New Zealand Filmmakers*, ed. Ian Corinch and Stuart Murray (Detroit: Wayne State University Press, 2007), 273–88.
14 See Bette Page, ed. *Mynarski's Lanc: The Story of two famous Canadian Lancaster Bombers KB726 & FM213* (Erin, ON: Boston Mills, 1989).
15 See Vincent Ward in *Edmonton Journal*, 21 May 1993. The replicas were subsequently donated to the Bomber Command Museum of Canada in Nanton, Alberta. See Bomber Command Museum of Canada, accessed 29 September 2017, http://www.bombercommandmuseum.ca. On the development of the museum see Ted Barris, *Dam Busters: Canadian Airmen and the Secret Raid against Nazi Germany* (Toronto: HarperCollins, 2018), 331–43.
16 See Jeremy Clarke in conversation with Vincent Ward, *What's On*, 2 June 1993, 13.
17 There were occasional lapses, such as a reference to an army rather than air force rank.
18 *Venue* [Bristol], 9–23 July 1993, 6.
19 Subsequent sequences in which Avik, against the odds, is able to make his way out of Dresden without being captured and lynched were cut. See e.g. Nowra, *Shooting the Moon*, 28.
20 See *The Times*, 3 June 1993; *Guardian*, 3 June 1993; *Independent*, 4 June 1993; *Daily Mail*, 4 June 1993; *Evening Standard*, 3 June 1993; *Morning Star*, 5 June 1993; *Observer*, 6 June 1993; *Mail on Sunday*, 6 June 1993; *Sunday Times*, 6 June 1993; *Today*, 4 June 1993. See also *Sunday Express*, 6 June 1993; *Independent on Sunday*, 6 June 1993; *Chicago Tribune*, 14 May 1993; *Christian Science Monitor*, 19 April 1993; *Los Angeles Times*, 23 April 1993; *Vancouver Sun*, 14 May 1993; *Boxoffice*, 1 June 1993, 38; *Ottawa Citizen*, 14 May 1993; *Calgary Herald*, 21 May 1993; *Toronto Star*, 14 May 1993; *Globe and Mail*, 14 May 1993; *South China Morning Post*, 28 November 1993; *Sight and Sound*, 1 June 1993, 6; John Downie, 'Seeing Is Not Believing', *Illusions*, 1 July 1993, 4–6; J. A. Wainwright, 'Australia North: The Gaze from Above/Down Under in *Map of the Human Heart*', *Australian-Canadian Studies* 12, 2 (1994), 29–38.
21 *Map of the Human Heart* opened well in New Zealand (*On Film*, 1 May 1993, 6) but earned only $2,806,881 in North America. Map of the Human Heart, Box Office Mojo, accessed 29 September 2017, http://www.boxofficemojo.com.
22 *Sunday Telegraph*, 6 June 1993.
23 Anne Collins, 'The Battle over "The Valour and the Horror"', *Saturday Night*, May 1993, 46–7; CUA, McKenna Papers, HA 1154, The Producers Response to the Critics, Appendix A, Brief to the Senate Sub-committee on Veterans Affairs, by Brian McKenna, 3–4.
24 James Hale and Peter Milner, 'Vision and the Revision', *Legion*, June 1992, 8
25 See Collins, 'Battle', 47.
26 *Gazette* [Montreal], 10 June 1992. On television, the *Canada at War* series had touched on Bomber Command three decades earlier; but to McKenna this was the authorized official version rather than the uncomfortable truth now being uncovered.

See CUA, Brian McKenna Papers, HA 1154, The Producers Response to the Critics, Appendix A, Brief to the Senate Sub-committee on Veterans Affairs, by Brian McKenna, 2.

27 *The Valour and the Horror* was produced in a partnership between the CBC, the NFB and the independent production company Galafilm, with additional funding from Telefilm. Monica McDonald, 'Producing the Public Past: Canadian History on CBC Television, 1952–2002' (PhD diss., York University, 2007), 215; Collins, 'Battle', 48. The initial plan for *The Valour and the Horror* appears to have been for three films that would approach Canada's Second World War chronologically (see CUA, McKenna Papers, HA 1152, Valour: Promotional Material, The Valour and the Horror: Canada and the Second World War, n/d). As the project evolved, a more thematic approach was taken, with a film devoted to Canadian soldiers during and after the fall of Hong Kong to the Japanese (*Savage Christmas: Hong Kong 1941*) and another to Canadian troops during D-Day and its aftermath (*In Desperate Battle: Normandy 1944*) as well as – as already noted – area bombing in *Death By Moonlight: Bomber Command*. The director had plans for a second trio of films to be made in the wake of the broadcast of the first on Canada's navy, Canadian women at war and Canadians in Fighter Command (see HA 1154, *The Valour and the Horror II*, planning document, 16 March 1992; *Vancouver Sun*, 10 January 1992). In the wake of the bitter controversy surrounding the first set of films, however, only *War at Sea: The Black Pit* (NFB, 1995) was made; and under tighter supervision. McDonald, 'Producing the Public Past', 239. On the title and thematic similarities between *The Valour and the Horror* and *The Sorrow and the Pity* see Neil Cameron, 'The Bombing of Brian McKenna', *Discourse: The Journal of the St. Lawrence Institute for the Advancement of Learning* 12 (Summer 1993), 3.

28 CUA, McKenna Papers, HA 1155, Brian McKenna, Notes for St. Thomas Annual History Lecture, 21 October 1993, 12; HA 3515, P112; Brian McKenna, 'Second World War Reflections: Connections to the War Still Vibrate', *Compass: A Jesuit Journal* 12 (March/April 1994), 19.

29 See CUA, McKenna Papers, HA 1147, Galafilm, Inc. *The Valour and the Horror*, post-production script including final narration, *Death by Moonlight: Bomber Command*, by Brian McKenna, October 1990. An example of the filmmakers trying to elicit responses from interviewees to support a priori conclusions can be found in HA 1154, TS D'Arcy O'Connor telephone interview with Ken Brown, 3 September 1990; see also on this issue Teresa Iacobelli, '"A Participant's History?": The Canadian Broadcasting Corporation and the Manipulation of Oral History', *Oral History Review* 38 (2011), 331–48.

30 CUA, McKenna Papers, HA 1147, Galafilm Inc., *The Valour and the Horror*, post-production script including final narration, Brian McKenna, October 1990, 1, 46, ff.; see MacDonald, 'Producing the Public Past', 219–20.

31 The phrase 'documented words' was used in the introduction to each episode in repeats and on videocassette. At the start of the initial broadcast, it was explained that the words actors speak 'have been taken from letters and diaries, and interviews'. CUA, McKenna Papers, HA 1147, Galafilm, Inc., *The Valour and the Horror*, post-production script including final narration, *Death by Moonlight: Bomber Command*, by Brian McKenna, October 1990. On 'just a bunch of old guys talking', see Collins, 'Battle', 48; see also *Gazette* [Montreal], 11 November 1992.

32 *Ottawa Citizen*, 12 January 1992; *Globe and Mail*, 11 January 1992; *Edmonton Journal*, 17 January 1992; see also e.g. *Chronicle Herald* [Halifax], 11 January 1992; *Maclean's*,

13 January 1992, 48; *Toronto Star*,12 January 1992; *Vancouver Sun*, 10 January 1992; *Windsor Star*, 10 January 1992. On audience size see CUA, McKenna Papers, HA 1147, *Valour and the Horror* Neilsen ratings.

33 See e.g. Clayton Moore, *Lancaster Valour: The Valour and the Truth* (Warrington: Compaid, 1995), 167; Les Morrison, *Of Luck and War: From Squeegee Kind to Bomber Pilot in World War II* (Burnstown, ON: GSPH, 1999), 148; Jack Singer, *Grandpa's War in Bomber Command* (Ottawa: War Amps, 2012), vi; Harry Yates, *Luck and a Lancaster: Chance and Survival in World War II* (Shrewsbury: Airlife, 1999), 144. It should be noted, though, that some veterans supported the McKenna version of Bomber Command at war. See e.g. Joseph Aaron Freidman interview, The Memory Project, accessed 20 January 2018, http://www.thememoryproject.com; George H. Laing, Harold MacDonald, James Oran, et al. in CUA, McKenna Papers, HA 1154, The Producers Respond to the Critics, Appendix C, Comments from Veterans, May 1993; Barris, *Dam Busters*, 345.

34 The text of the lawsuit claim can be found in Bomber Harris Trust, *A Battle for Truth: Canadian Aircrews Sue the CBC over Death by Moonlight: Bomber Command* (Agincourt, ON: Ramsay, 1994), 3–184. The Senate hearings can be found in Senate of Canada, Standing Committee on Social Affairs, Science and Technology, Proceedings of the Subcommittee on Veterans Affairs, 25 June 1992–6 November 1992, 3:1–9A:355. Though no longer available, the formal submissions on *The Valour and the Horror* to the CRTC and CBC from the National Council of Veterans Associations were for many years mounted on the War Amps website: Submission to Keith Spicer, Chairman, CRTC, 4 May 1992; Final Submission to Ombudsman, CBC, 20 July 1992, accessed 3 October 2012, http://www.waramps/ca/newsroom/archives/valour/home.html. On other complaints to the CRTC see *Globe and Mail*, 25 April 1992. On protest from the Royal Canadian Legion see letter from Dominion President J. W. Jolleys, *Calgary Herald*, 12 April 1992; *Legion*, July/August 1992, 4–5. On other efforts at coordination, see e.g. *Calgary Herald*, 6 May 1992; *Ottawa Citizen*, 1 September 1992. On the failure of the CBC *Newsworld* broadcast in March to settle matters see William Morgan, 'Report of the CBC Ombudsman', in *The Valour and the Horror Revisited*, ed. David J. Bercuson and S. F. Wise (Montreal and Kingston: McGill-Queen's University Press, 1994), 62. On individual protest letters to the press by bomber veterans, see e.g. Tom Farley and Eric Yaxley letters, *Ottawa Citizen*, 8 February 1992, Donald G. Miller letter, ibid., 28 November 1992.

35 Those who wrote or spoke in support of the McKennas specifically in reference to *Death by Moonlight* included Max Hastings and John Keegan (see *Globe and Mail*, 26 June 1992; Max Hastings, 'The Lonely Passion of Bomber Harris', *MHQ* 6, 2 [1994], 58; CUA, McKenna Papers, HA 1154, Death by Moonlight: Bomber Command, the Producers Response to the Critics, May 1993, 19). Those who spoke or wrote against it included Martin Middlebrook (letters to the editor, *Sitrep: Newsmagazine of the Royal Canadian Military Institute*, vol. 51, no. 1, January 1992, 2), Denis Richards (see William Morgan, 'Report of the CBC Ombudsman', in Bercuson and Wise, *Valour and the Horror Revisited*, 62) and William Carter (see Senate of Canada, Standing Committee on Social Affairs, Science and Technology, Proceedings of the Subcommittee on Veterans Affairs, 25 June 1992, 3:13). Various other high-profile Canadian historians, military and otherwise, also became involved in the debate about *The Valour and the Horror*, including Pierre Berton and Terry Copp (see e.g. *Toronto Star*, 4 June 1992), Sidney Wise and David Bercuson (see S. F. Wise, 'The Valour and the Horror: A Report for the CBC Ombudsman', in Bercuson and Wise, *Valour*

and the Horror Revisited, 3–30; David J. Bercuson, 'The Valour and the Horror: An Historical Analysis', in ibid. 31–58), Michael Bliss (see Michael Bliss, *Writing History: A Life* [Dundurn: Toronto, 2011], 311), Desmond Morton (see *Toronto Star*, 19 November 1992; Desmond Morton, 'As I See It: Horror, Valour, and the CBC', *Canadian Social Studies* 28, 2 [Winter 1994], 57–8) and Jack Granatstein (see J. L. Granatstein, *Who Killed Canadian History?* [Toronto: Harper Perennial, 2007], 14).

36 Morgan, 'Report of the CBC Ombudsman', in Bercuson and Wise, *Valour and the Horror Revisited*, 72; Senate of Canada, Standing Committee on Social Affairs, Science and Technology, Subcommittee on Veterans Affairs, Proceedings, 4 February 1993, 10:34.

37 On *Valour and the Horror* winning the Gemini award for best TV documentary of 1992 see *Globe and Mail*, 8 March 1993. On the media rally behind the McKennas, see e.g. *Globe and Mail*, 12–14, 20, 25 November 1992; Knowlton Nash, *The Microphone Wars: A History of Triumph and Betrayal at the CBC* (Toronto: McClelland and Stewart, 1994), 527–35; see also Wayne Skeene, *Fade to Black: A Requiem for the CBC* (Vancouver: Douglas and McIntyre, 1993), 199–205; on this phenomenon see Morton, 'As I See It', 57–8; Ted Byfeld in *Alberta Report*, 23 November 1993, 60. On the dismissal of the lawsuit on appeal see Ken McDonald, 'Justice Denied', *Airforce*, 75th Anniversary Issue, Fall 1998, 84–5. On the CRTC ruling see *Globe and Mail*, 19 December 1992. *Death by Moonlight* was also received well by critics when broadcast some years later in Australia: see *The Age*, 25 August 1995; *Sydney Morning Herald*, 21 August 1995.

38 See BFI Library, Channel 4 *The Valour and the Horror* press material, Summer 1993.

39 See *The Times*, 27 June 1994.

40 See *Guardian*, 5 August 1994; *Daily Telegraph*, 5 August 1994.

41 *Guardian*, 8 August 1994; *Independent*, 8 August 1994; *Daily Mail*, 6 August 1994; see also e.g. Sean Day-Lewis review in *Sunday Telegraph*, 7 August 1994; Peter Patterson review in *Daily Mail*, 8 August 1994.

42 See *Bomber Command Association Newsletter*, October 1994, 9; *Flarepath* [Bomber Harris Trust newsletter], 4, September 1994, 2; *Financial Times*, 17 August 1994.

43 *Gazette* [Montreal], 10 June 1992. 'We were determined to apply our experience covering war and revolution', Brian McKenna explained, 'to a story 50 years old'. CUA, McKenna Papers, HA 1155, Notes for the St. Thomas Annual History Lecture, 21 October 1993. See also Cameron, 'Bombing of Brian McKenna', 6.

44 Hale and Milner, 'Vision and the Revision', 7; CUA, McKenna Papers, HA 1154, The Producers Response to the Critics, Appendix A, Brief to the Senate Sub-committee on Veterans Affairs, by Brian McKenna, 6.

45 See Peter W. Kitcher, *The Valour and the Horror: The True Story* (Belleville, ON: Kitcher, 2005), 180–2; MacDonald, 'Producing the Public Past', 233–4.

46 See Bomber Harris Trust, *Battle for Truth*, 126–8; MacDonald, 'Producing the Public Past', 234.

47 On refashioning the written words of others see Kitcher, *Valour and the Horror*, 148–51; Bomber Harris Trust, *Battle for Truth*, 174–5. On elisions see Bomber Harris Trust, *Battle for Truth*, 112, 116, 156; see also e.g. CUA, McKenna Papers, HA 1152, yellow highlights on Martin 'Joe' Favreau interview TS, 22 October 1990.

48 See Bomber Harris Trust, *Battle for Truth*, 140; Kitcher, *Valour and the Horror*, 81.

49 See e.g., on the portrayal of Arthur Harris, Donald G. Miller letter, *Ottawa Citizen*, 28 November 1992; John Turnbull in Senate of Canada, Standing Committee on Social

Affairs, Proceedings of the Subcommittee on Veterans Affairs, 4 November 1992, 7:20; Nancy Banks-Smith review in *Guardian*, 8 August 1994.
50 *Guardian*, 8 August 1994; S. F. Wise, 'The Valour and the Horror: A Report for the CBC Ombudsman', in Bercuson and Wise, *Valour and the Horror Revisited*, 27; see also e.g. Dan McCaffrey, *Battlefields in the Air: Canadians in the Allied Bomber Command* (Toronto: James Lorimer, 1995), ix.
51 CUA, McKenna Papers, HA 1151, Valour: Prebroadcast Reaction Fall 91, D'Arcy to Brian and Terry, 18 July 1991.
52 Ibid., HA 1155, Dyson to O'Connor, 5 April 1992.
53 On negative reactions to Merrily Weisbord and Merilyn Simonds Mohr, *The Valour and the Horror: The Untold Story of Canadians in the Second World War* (Toronto: HarperCollins, 1991), see e.g. *Ottawa Citizen*, 20 June 1992; Gilbert Drolet review of book and series in *Canadian Defence Quarterly*, June 1992, 55-7. On good sales, see e.g. *Calgary Herald*, 8 February 1992.
54 David Bennett review of Spencer Dunmore and William Carter, *Reap the Whirlwind: The Untold Story of 6 Group, Canada's Bomber Force of World War II* (Toronto: McClelland and Stewart, 1991) in *Ottawa Citizen*, 15 February 1992; see also W. A. B. Douglas review in *Canadian Historical Quarterly* 74 (1993), 300-1; Stephen J. Harris review in *Canadian Defence Quarterly* 22, 3 (1992), 53-4. On Carter's negative view of *Death by Moonlight*, see e.g. *Globe and Mail*, 26 June 1992.
55 John Buckley review of Denis Richards, *The Hardest Victory: RAF Bomber Command in the Second World War* (London: Hodder and Stoughton, 1994) in *History* 82 (1997), 375; see also e.g. Vincent Orange review in *Journal of Military History* 60 (1996), 177-8. Its author suspected that *Hardest Victory* was generally ignored by the British press: see Denis Richards, *It Might Have Been Worse: Recollections, 1941-1996* (London: Smithson Albright, 1998), 236. The book did, though, have defenders: see Michael Beetham review in *Bomber Command Association Newsletter* 27 (1994), 3. Other advocates in the case for the defence of Bomber Command in this period included Walter J. Boyne, *Clash of Wings: Air Power in World War II* (New York: Simon and Schuster, 1994), 355-7; James Hampton in *Selected for Aircrew: Bomber Command in the Second World War* (Walton-on-Thames: Air Research, 1993), 309-61; McCaffrey, *Battlefields in the Air*, 169-73.
56 Stephen J. Katz review of Erik Markusen and David Kopf, *The Holocaust and Strategic Bombing: Genocide and Total War in the Twentieth Century* (Boulder, CO: Westview, 1995) in *International History Review* 17 (1996), 712. See also Gerhard Weinberg review of same in *American Historical Review* 102 (1997), 90 (the latter's own view was that area bombing, while it failed to achieve its primary aim, was inevitable and did contribute indirectly to Allied victory. Gerhard L. Weinberg, *A World at Arms: A Global History of World War II* [New York: Cambridge University Press, 1994], 580); Philip S. Meilinger review of Stephen A. Garrett, *Ethics and Airpower in World War II: The British Bombing of German Cities* (New York: St. Martin's, 1993) in *Armed Forces and Society* 21 (1994), 159 (see also Daniel T. Kuhl review in *Technology and Culture* 40 [1999], 448-50). It is important to note that all these works generated some positive as well as negative reviews (see e.g. Robert Bathurst review of Garrett, *Ethics and Airpower*, in *Journal of Peace Research* 31 [1994], 361-2). Alan J. Levine's attempt at a balanced overview, *The Strategic Bombing of Germany, 1940-1945* (Westport, CT: Praeger, 1992), was judged to have 'both assets and liabilities' (Kenneth P. Werrell review, *Journal of American History* 80 [1993], 1145).

57 Brereton Greenhous, Stephen J. Harris, William C. Johnston, William G. P. Rawling, *The Crucible of War, 1939–1945: The Official History of the Royal Canadian Air Force, Volume III* (Toronto: University of Toronto Press, 1994), 725. Lead author Brereton Greenhous went further in a pre-publication interview for television: 'I would say that what they were out there to do [in Bomber Command under Harris] was to terrorize the German population at large by bombing their residential areas, and killing and maiming as many civilians as they could.' CBC Prime Time News, 18 May 1994.
58 See Greenhous et al., *Crucible of War*, 696–7, 857, ff.
59 Jack Granatstein review in *Quill & Quire*, June 1994, 41 (though see also *Alberta Report*, 20 June 1994, 7); see Brian McKenna review in *Gazette* [Montreal], 9 July 1994; see also *Globe and Mail*, 19 May 1994. On the mixed reaction to *Crucible of War* see Tim Cook, *Clios's Warriors: Canadian Historians and the Writing of the World Wars* (Vancouver: UBC Press, 2006), 230–1; see also Bercuson and Wise, *Valour and the Horror Revisited*, Appendix, 181–5.
60 *Daily Mail*, 15 February 1998; see Sebastian Cox introduction to British Bombing Survey Unit, *The Strategic Air War against Germany, 1939–1945* (London: Frank Cass, 1998).
61 Barney Danson with Curtis Fahey, *Not Bad for a Sergeant: The Memoirs of Barney Danson* (Toronto: Dundurn, 2002), 267; see also Michael Beetham foreword to Richard Overy, *Bomber Command, 1939–1945* (London: HarperCollins, 1997), 7.
62 *Ottawa Citizen*, 1 December 1992; See Ernest J. Dick, '"The Valour and the Horror" Continued: Do We Still Want Our History on Television?', *Archivaria* 35 (Spring 1993), 268 n. 17.
63 *Toronto Star*, 12 January 1993 (see also *Hamilton Spectator*, 15 September 1993); BULLETPROOF? You Be the Judge, transcript, f. 1, accessed 3 October 2012, http://www.waramps.ca/newsroom/archives/valour/home/html; *Bulletproof? You Be the Judge!* prod. Cliff Chadderton (War Amps, 1992). A booklet on the subject was also produced: see H. Clifford Chadderton, *The Morality of Bomber Command in World War II* (Ottawa: War Amps, 1992). In all, twenty-one public and university libraries across Canada appear to have acquired copies. See OCLC 30705389, OCLC WorldCat, accessed 15 October 2017, http://www.worldcat.org. Efforts to get school boards to show *Bulletproof* if *Valour and the Horror* was to be shown met with limited success. *Ottawa Citizen*, 15 September 1993.
64 See Danson, *Not Bad for a Sergeant*, 267–9; Barney Danson foreword to Terry Copp with Richard Nielsen, *No Price Too High: Canadians and the Second World War* (Toronto: McGraw-Hill Ryerson, 1996), 7–8; *Globe and Mail*, 4 July 1992, 11 March 1993, 24 November 1994; Norflicks Productions, No Price Too High, accessed 30 September 2017, http://www.norflicks.com/npth.html.
65 Terry Copp in 'The Air War' segment, Episode 4, 'Alton Was a Poet', *No Price Too High* (Norflicks, 1995); see also Copp and Nielsen, *No Price Too High*, 113–19, 208–10, ff. On the previous journalistic travails of the narrator of *No Price Too High* see Arthur Kent, *Risk and Redemption: Surviving the News Network Wars* (Toronto: Viking, 1996).
66 *Globe and Mail*, 18 November 1996, 16 May 1998; *Calgary Herald*, 11 March 1997; see Danson, *Not Bad for a Sergeant*, 268–9.
67 *Sunday Telegraph*, 25 September 1994. It should be noted that not all veterans were willing to defend area bombing in the manner of the Bomber Command Association: see e.g. Peter Johnson, *The Withered Garland: Reflections and Doubts of a Bomber* (London: New European, 1995).

68 Michael Beetham foreword to Overy, *Bomber Command*, 7; see ibid., 6; *Sunday Telegraph*, 25 September 1994.
69 See BFI Library, Channel 4 press kit for *Bomber Command: Reaping the Whirlwind*.
70 *Guardian*, 11 September 1996; *Daily Mail*, 11 September 1996; *Observer*, 8 September 1996; see also e.g. *Daily Mirror*, 10 September 1996; *Daily Mail*, 10 September 1996.
71 Overy, *Bomber Command*, 11.
72 Ibid., 183-92. The souvenir video for the RAF Museum at Hendon, produced in 1997, narrated by Ken Rees, also indicated that Bomber Command's heavy bombers had been effective, the Halifax dropping 'an awesome 230,000 tons' of bombs while 'the Lancaster was truly one of those aircraft that won the war'. *Royal Air Force Museum Souvenir Video* (Aviacam, 1997).
73 John Barraclough in *RUSI Journal* 143 (1998), 81-2; see also *Independent*, 23 October 1997.
74 *The Gazette* [Montreal], 30 April 1999.
75 On reviews of *Warriors of the Night* see ibid.; *Globe and Mail*, 4 May 1999. A pair of general works dealing with air power during the world wars aimed respectively at students – John Buckley, *Air Power in the Age of Total War* (London: UCL Press, 1999) – and the general public – Williamson Murray, *War in the Air, 1914-45* (London: Cassell, 1999) – also appeared, both suggesting that the indirect effect of the area bombing campaign on the Nazi war effort had been significant but neither generating much in the way of critical controversy (see e.g. on Buckley, review by Vincent Orange in *Journal of Military History* 63 [1999], 1028-9; Michael Sherry review in *International History Review* 22 [2000], 492-4). Commando comics, meanwhile, continued to suggest that night bombing involved striking at industrial targets: see *The Final Mission*, Commando 2896, October 1995, 11; *Night of Reckoning*, Commando 3009, December 1996, 46.

Figure 7.1 Edward Woodward and Christopher Plummer in *Night Flight* (BBC, 2002).

Chapter 7

VETERANS: THE 2000s

The first dozen or so years of the new millennium witnessed a variety of established and innovative approaches to representing Bomber Command. A host of new volumes on area bombing tended either to condemn or defend what had been done to German cities. Commemorations of the bomber boys in print and in documentary form, on the other hand, tended to concentrate on the trials and tribulations as well as triumphs of the men reaching the end of their lives who had once flown over Germany sixty-odd years in the past. These diverging perspectives also were evident in how Harris and the bomber boys were represented in screen dramas.

There were plenty of new books and articles appearing in print which concentrated on the civilian victims of area bombing and in many cases condemned the policy as immoral and even a war crime.[1] Some school texts in England, furthermore, tended to situate the destruction of Dresden in particular within a negative ethical framework.[2] There were also television documentaries which emphasized the costs to women and children of area bombing. Twenty months into the new decade, *Bombing Germany*, aired on BBC2 as part of the *Timewatch* series, explored in detail the development of policies which culminated in what were shown as indiscriminate and horrific attacks on places like Würtzburg in the last months of the war.[3] Almost seven years later, even a programme like *Last of the Dambusters* on Channel 5, mainly devoted to the location and excavation of the remains of a Lancaster that had taken part in the dams raid, ended with one of the few surviving aircrew who flew the raid meeting some of those he had bombed and wondering of it had all been worth it.[4] This sort of thing left other Bomber Command veterans feeling 'deeply betrayed', in the words of one former Lancaster pilot.[5]

Yet it is important to keep in mind that there were an equivalent number of new works appearing which argued, implicitly or explicitly, that contextual and utilitarian issues ought to be considered when assessing the record of Arthur Harris and Bomber Command.[6] Area attacks against the Ruhr Valley, one author convincingly argued, had been far more effective than earlier bombing surveys had indicated.[7] There was even attempts to strip away some of the myths around the targeting and bombing of Dresden.[8] In addition, a succession of new single- and multivolume popular studies appeared in which the sympathetic focus was on the experiences of the bomber crews themselves rather than on those they had bombed.[9] Much of what appeared on the small screen in the first years of the new century, what was more, was as often as not either carefully neutral or more often overtly sympathetic towards Bomber Command veterans.[10]

In light of the sound and fury that had greeted *Death by Moonlight*, it was not entirely surprising that when the CBC produced a new television history of Canada at the start of the new decade, care was taken to avoid being overtly provocative concerning Bomber Command in the episode dealing with the Second World War, entitled *The Crucible*, broadcast in the second half of 2001. Against the backdrop of some of the wartime colour footage of Lancasters at RAF Hemswell shot by Henry Cozens, the narrator, Maggie Huculak, notes that 'massive nighttime air assaults on German cities' resulted in the loss of almost ten thousand Canadian aircrew and that nearly 'half a million civilians are killed in the immense firestorms'. That was it, the whole segment on Bomber Command occupying under two minutes of screen time. An initial suggestion that a comparison be made with the London Blitz in order to emphasize the sheer scale of the destruction meted out to German cities was quietly ignored.[11]

A desire to avoid a new confrontation with veterans groups was also evident a few years later in the decision, in the wake of complaints, to reword a text panel dealing with the bombing war in the new Canadian War Museum.[12] A pro-veteran stance was evident on television in *Bomber Boys: The Fighting Lancaster*, a four-part 'reality history' series picked up by several cable channels in which the recollections of surviving aircrew were juxtaposed with the efforts of a group of young male descendants going through a recreation of wartime aircrew training.[13] Also popular on Canadian television around Remembrance Day sixty years on was *Last Flight to Berlin*, an elegiac documentary in which filmmaker Robert Linnell traced the wartime journey of Lloyd Linnell, the father he never knew, from joining the RCAF as a trainee pilot to being shot down in a Halifax bomber by a night fighter near the German capital.[14]

Meanwhile, on the other side of the Atlantic, *Bomber*, an episode in the *Battlefields* documentary series, broadcast on BBC2 a few months after *Bombing Germany*, concentrated on the men who had flown rather than on those who had been bombed and in the end put forward the case for the secondary effects of bombing in relation to winning the war.[15] For the sixtieth anniversary of the dams raid, Channel 4 aired a new two-part programme in which traditional documentary elements were linked to an effort by modern RAF aircrew to fly the same operation via a computer simulation.[16] Towards the end of the following year the same channel also broadcast *Bomber Crew*, a television event in which interviews with veterans were mixed in with the filmed efforts of five young volunteers – grandchildren of men who had flown over the Reich – to complete wartime-style training and pilot a Lancaster.[17]

There was also something of a split in viewpoint in small-screen drama. On the one hand, near the turn of the millennium, *Night Flight* underlined the psychological stresses Bomber Command aircrew endured without referencing the ethics or effectiveness of area attacks. On the other hand, in the latter part of the first decade of the new century, both *Dresden* and *Into the Storm* concentrated on the destruction being wrought and those held to be responsible for it.

Night Flight, a 2002 two-part television drama lasting in total 160 minutes, was penned by William Ivory, whose father had served as a wartime navigator with 50 Squadron and whose uncle had been killed flying over Germany. Having established his screenwriting credentials with the comedy series *Common as Muck*, the Nottingham-born Ivory was keen to develop a fictional story that would highlight the lasting human dimensions of having been part of a Lancaster crew. 'What our airmen went through was terrifying and horrendous, and to try and sweep it under the carpet like some dirty little secret does them a disservice', he explained in an interview in reference to the critical tendency towards area bombing, adding, 'The point is that they were trying to win the war and they were doing a job like everybody else.'[18]

Tentatively titled *Ready Steady Go* and *Night and Day* before *Night Flight* was settled on, this was to be a story set in both the contemporary world and in wartime which revolved around various members of a single Lancaster crew and explored issues of fear, friendship, romance and class – and, above all, how the traumas of the past can be resurrected in the present. The major leading actors, Christopher Plummer and Edward Woodward, ably supported by Barbara Flynn among others, formed the cast in the present-day sequences, in which prosperous retiree and former bomber pilot Harry (Plummer) is forced to confront deeply buried truths through the unexpected appearance of his crew's down-on-his-luck former mid-upper gunner Vic (Woodward) accompanied by middle-aged spiv Ted Atwell, played by Kenneth Cranham, supposedly the son of their dead rear gunner but in fact the product of a wartime affair between Harry and the also long deceased rear gunner's wife, Pam. What happens now, however, is conditioned by what happened then. Drawing both on his own research and conversations with his father and others, Ivory sought to explain some of the problems facing Harry and Vic in the present through an examination of their lives in 1943. This meant exploring the difficulties the young Harry – played as well-educated, competent, yet emotionally high-strung by Alex Newman – has reconciling his bonds with the uncomplicated Yorkshireman, Tommy Atwell, played by Andrew Lee Potts, and the attractive and empathetic Pam Atwell, a Women's Auxiliary Air Force (WAAF) sergeant played by Liverpudlian Christine Tremarcio, in the context of what the producer of *Night Flight*, Hilary Salmon, described as the 'utterly terrifying' business of flying a heavy bomber to and from targets in the Third Reich.[19]

The representative all-NCO crew 'Flash' Harry skippers includes, along with Tommy and a very scared Londoner, Vic (played as a young man by Chris Lennard), a flight engineer from the south (played by Alex Palmer), a Geordie bomb aimer (played by Christian Steel), a Mancunian navigator (played by Andy Sheridan), a Canadian radio operator (played by Christian Malcolm) and an English flight engineer (Alex Palmer). Though Harry Peters is distinctly upper-middle class, Ivory chose not to make him a commissioned officer, perhaps in order to make more credible the off-duty social interaction that goes on with the other non-commissioned types necessary for the plot. Thanks to his own research and talks with his father, Ivory was able to include many other true-to-life elements ranging from start-up procedures and superstitious beliefs to the strain of having an operation scrubbed just before take-off or – in one of the most effective sequences in the film – how terrifying a surprise attack by night fighters could be.[20]

The original choice for director, Phil Davis, bowed out when the BBC curtailed the spending limit. With a tight budget of £2.5 million, Nicholas Renton was nonetheless able to shoot period scenes at RAF Halton and at the former RAF airfield at East Kirkby, home of the Lincolnshire Aviation Heritage Centre and Lancaster NX611, restored to the point where it could taxi. For airborne work, footage of PA474 of the Battle of Britain Memorial Flight would be used, while aircraft interiors would be shot in and around mock-ups built at Bray Studios, notably the climactic night-fighter attack sequence in which Tommy is killed. A limited number of special effects also would be incorporated.[21] Once the younger cast members were chosen, they were introduced to what it was like to crew a Lancaster through listening to wartime recordings of their real-life counterparts over the target. Both film technicians and cast also benefitted from chats with Bomber Command veterans.[22]

Just over four million people, 18.5 per cent of those watching television, tuned in when *Night Flight* was broadcast on BBC1 during the latter part of the evening of 1 February 2002, but critical reaction was sharply divided.[23] Some reviewers simply hated it. In the *Daily Mail*, for instance, Peter Patterson described it as 'tedious, disorienting, and interminable'. Writing for *The Times*, Paul Hoggart concurred, calling it 'slow' and 'boring'.[24] Some aircrew, what was more, were disappointed: it was 'a shambles', according to the chairman of the Bomber Command Association. 'Although written by the son of a wartime bomber navigator, [*Night Flight*] presented an incoherent, disjointed story of a Lancaster aircrew', Tony Iveson went on to write, 'with scant reference to reality in behaviour, dress and discipline – in the air and on the ground'.[25] Yet there were other, much more favourable, reactions. 'Many issues are addressed intelligently', Mike Bradley argued in the *Observer*, going on to list 'the terrible physical and psychological conditions endured by wartime aircrew, the deaths of fellow combatants, the search for love and the repression of emotions, the intensity of relationships in times of war and how they change as time passes'. It might be 'over-ambitious' and 'a little too long', but it was 'rewarding all the same'. In contrast to his colleague Peter Patterson, Nigel Andrew gave his opinion to *Daily Mail* readers that despite some weaknesses, *Night Flight* 'takes us on an exhilarating, gripping and emotionally involving ride'.[26]

Shorn of the retrospective element, the emotional stresses induced by heavy bomber operations among aircrew were also at the heart of *The Haunted Airman*, written, produced and directed by Chris Durlacher four years later in 2006 for BBC4. This was an adaptation of the classic occult potboiler by Dennis Wheatley, *The Haunting of Toby Jugg*, to be broadcast on Halloween in the seventy minutes before midnight, that contained the requisite number of scary images but which diverged significantly from the original plot. Instead of a crippled, fearful fighter pilot battling a satanic cult, the story now centred on a psychologically as well as physically damaged bomber pilot, played by Robert Pattinson, grappling with a combination of impotence and post-traumatic stress disorder as a result of an attack on Cologne: 'It was one of the big bombing raids against the factories and goods yards; but it was also at a time when we'd catch the housewives in their beds.'[27]

Press reviews of *The Haunted Airman* were mixed, though not on account of the insertion of the area bombing controversy. Indeed, John Dugdale wrote for the *Sunday Times* that this was 'a potentially potent theme' mishandled, while Martin Skegg opined in the *Guardian* that is was 'the most interesting aspect' of the film which in the end was undermined by a tawdry denouement.[28]

Earlier in the year Channel 4 had acquired the rights to broadcast a much bigger production, *Dresden*, written by Stefan Kolditz and directed by Roland Suso Richter.[29] This two-part, 160-minute television collaboration, led by teamWorx and costing more than €10 million to make, had netted over thirteen million viewers when first aired in Germany on ZDF.[30] Those involved in crafting *Dresden*, such as co-producer Nikolaus Kraemer, whose original idea it was, calculated correctly that people would be drawn in to a disaster story featuring a forbidden romance in the context of a historic cataclysm in the same way they had for the Hollywood blockbuster *Titanic*; hence the central plotline following the unlikely but passionate affair between local hospital nurse Anna Mauth and wounded Lancaster pilot Robert Newman.[31] From the start, meanwhile, there had been plans to market *Dresden* outside the homeland, which meant being careful not to suggest that those under the bombs all had been blameless victims or that those responsible for the destruction of the city were simply terror flyers.[32]

Prior the Dresden raid, local farmers and Hitler Youth are depicted trying to murder several downed British airmen, various authority figures are shown to be corrupt or malevolent throughout, and the plight of the Jews is highlighted through a 'mixed-race' couple desperately trying to survive in the city. The hero, played by English actor John Light, among other things steers a German boy away from committing suicide. Other aircrew are depicted as relatable human beings displaying emotions ranging from happiness, fear and sadness to, ultimately, a desire for revenge and unease at destroying a beautiful city and its inhabitants. The C-in-C himself is given the opportunity to make the case for unleashing Bomber Command on Dresden. In the Bomber Command operations room, Arthur Harris, vigorously played by English actor Christian Rodska, explains to his staff that cities in eastern Germany need to be hit in order to disrupt the movement of enemy troops and show the Russians that Britain is 'still in the game'. When his deputy, Robert Saundby, played by English actor Pip Torrens, suggests that attacking synthetic oil plants would be more effective than yet more area attacks – 'bombing their cities has not succeeded in breaking the morale of the population let alone got them to send the regime packing' – Harris retorts that the real problem is that 'the Germans have lost the war, they just refuse to give in', implying that brute force needs to be applied in order to extract a surrender before the enemy are able to deploy new weapons of mass destruction such as poison gas or even a suspected atomic bomb. In a later scene, when Saundby launches another line of counterargument, making, in a roundabout way, the case that 'we're in danger of inheriting a completely destroyed country', Harris replies, 'The sooner this war ends, the fewer people will die.'[33]

Though the end results were by no means flawless, the production team had also gone to considerable lengths to achieve authenticity for the British as well as German scenes. British actors and dialogue – dubbed for German audiences but deployed in the original for Anglosphere release – were used for all the Bomber Command sequences, there was proper attention to detail in the reproduction of RAF uniforms and flying kit, and the scenes involving Lancasters on the ground and in the air over Germany were made to look more realistic through blending together excerpts from the Cozens film, other wartime footage, new shots involving cockpit and fuselage mock-ups and extensive computer-generated imagery.[34]

Nonetheless, there were still aspects of the miniseries that might cause offense with veterans and others if and when Channel 4, having acquired the rights, decided to broadcast *Dresden* in the UK. For one thing, the firestorm sequences were fairly graphic, showing as they did men, women and children being asphyxiated in shelters and catching fire amid an inferno being whipped up by RAF bombs. For another, while the case both for and against area bombing is made through the C-in-C Bomber Command and his deputy, choice of actor and direction indicate that audience sympathy was meant to tilt towards the latter rather than the former. An improbably tall, thin and morally aware Robert Saundby is clearly getting uncomfortable with the scale of wanton destruction being meted out by Bomber Command. The more physically accurate and forceful Arthur Harris, on the other hand, seems to gain some deep personal satisfaction from being able to order the destruction by blast and fire of entire cities.[35]

Dresden eventually aired in Britain on the sixty-fourth anniversary of the raid, but starting at midnight. Doubtless as intended, given the late-night scheduling, reaction was limited, the few critics who watched it tending to focus on the romantic element rather than moral issues. According to Sophie Heath of the *Daily Mail*, it was an 'epic' account of an historical event 'with a love story at its core'. *The Sun* gave it three out of four stars.[36]

Later that same year the BBC broadcast *Into the Storm*, a 98-minute co-production with the American cable television company HBO directed by Thaddeus O'Sullivan dramatizing the wartime premiership of Winston Churchill.[37] It, like *Dresden*, addressed the issue of responsibility for area attacks, albeit relatively briefly. About halfway through the film, there is a scene written by Hugh Whitemore set in the Cabinet War Rooms in which Harris, played by Michael Pennington, discusses RAF night bombing with the prime minister, played by Brendan Gleeson, and the deputy prime minister, Clement Attlee, played by Bill Paterson. Attempts to hit specific targets at night, the C-in-C explains, have failed – 'We're killing more cows than Germans' – leaving area bombing as the only viable option. This, Attlee retorts, would involve the morally dubious tactic of targeting civilians, including women and children. Churchill, however, having already stated that night bombing was 'the only thing that we can do to hurt Germany' and help the Russians, overrides his deputy, arguing military necessity should trump the ethical qualms of 'psalm-singing defeatists'. 'Let 'em have it, Harris', he tells him pugnaciously, adding, 'Never maltreat the enemy by halves.'³⁸

Towards the end of the film Churchill becomes visibly depressed while watching a newsreel describing the destruction of Dresden, subsequently lamenting how war has become a matter of 'entire communities, women and children included, pitted against one another in brutish mutual extermination'. That the C-in-C Bomber Command never develops any qualms about enemy civilian casualties is made evident not only in his puzzlement at the PM's reaction to the Dresden footage but also in an earlier scene in which he tells a slightly shocked Chief of the Imperial General Staff, Alan Brooke, played by Geoffrey Kirkness, a story about himself: 'I was on my way home the other evening, got stopped for speeding. "You might have killed someone," said the copper. "My dear young man", I said, "I kill thousands of people every night"'.³⁹

Harris was mostly overlooked in this case by the critics, perhaps because there was little new being portrayed about him and he appears only briefly. Yet they certainly picked up on what Whitmore was saying about the central protagonist. In the *Independent on Sunday*, for instance, Tim Walker remarked on how the drama revealed the PM's ruthless side, including a willingness to encourage Harris to 'readily bomb' German cities 'full of innocents' in order to beat the enemy down.⁴⁰ Critical opinion on this generally sympathetic warts-and-all effort was more divided than in the United States, but when *Into the Storm* was broadcast in the UK on the evening of Monday 2 November 2009 on BBC2, no less than 2.5 million people – six hundred thousand more than usual for that channel at this time – were watching.⁴¹

Anyone looking for a truly upbeat projection of Bomber Command operations on screen might have taken heart from the news a few years earlier that a cinematic remake of *The Dam Busters* was in the works. After Mel Gibson and Icon Films had apparently toyed with the idea, Peter Jackson of *Lord of the Rings* fame announced in 2006 that he would be producing a new *Dam Busters* film in New Zealand through WingNut Films with director Christian Rivers on a budget of somewhere between £16 and £20 million. The goal, he explained, was to be as 'authentic as possible' given technical information not available in the 1950s, yet at the same time get 'as close to the spirit of the original [film] as possible'.⁴² Interviews were conducted, pre-production work began and Stephen Fry was commissioned to write a script which he completed with the assistance of copious nicotine jags towards the end of the year.⁴³ It seemed over the following months and years, with full-scale Lancaster replicas being built and a fuss being made about whether or not to give the canine that would play Gibson's dog a less politically incorrect name, that the film would shortly begin shooting.⁴⁴ Other projects, however, began to loom larger for Jackson, and the production eventually was put on indefinite hold.⁴⁵

As the seventieth anniversary of the Second World War unfolded, the balance of informed opinion concerning the efficacy or inefficacy of wartime bombing seemed to swing in favour of the latter when historian Richard Overy, who had devoted much of his academic career to the subject and previously gone on record defending Bomber Command, published his widely praised magnum opus in which he deployed a vast trove of evidence to show that it had in fact achieved very little.[46] Yet screen documentaries now tended more towards celebration of iconic achievements and, above all perhaps, respect for the now quite elderly survivors who had flown against fearful odds so many decades ago.[47]

The wartime exploits of 617 Squadron were once again extolled around the anniversary year of the dams raid in programmes with descriptive titles or subtitles such as *Building the Bouncing Bomb* (Channel 4), *Dambusters Declassified* (BBC2) and *Race to Smash the German Dams* (BBC2), not to mention, afterward, *What the Dambusters Did Next* (Channel 5).[48] As television critic Vicki Power commented in the *Telegraph*, the story 'continues to exert a firm grasp over our collective imaginations', a stirring tale which, as Stuart Jeffries pointed out in the *Guardian*, meant avoiding having to grapple with 'the bombing of German civilians in [places like] Dresden and Pforzheim'.[49]

There were in addition several more general documentaries about Bomber Command that also involved interviews with veterans and focused mostly on the multiple hazards bomber aircrew had faced. These included *Into the Wind*, shown on Yesterday, and *Bomber Boys Revealed* on Channel 5. These were well received, especially *Bomber Boys* on BBC1, fronted by Scottish actor Ewan McGregor and his ex-RAF pilot brother, Colin, which drew almost 4.6 million viewers.[50]

Four months after *Bomber Boys* was broadcast, the unveiling of a new monument to Bomber Command became the occasion for yet more television tributes. Over the years, many veterans had developed a strong belief that they and their commander had been deliberately ignored once the war was won. It was sometimes bitterly noted that Harris had not been raised to the peerage in the same way as other wartime commanders, and that no campaign medal had been struck for Bomber Command aircrew.[51] Some of the criticism of the bombing campaign, furthermore, had on occasion been taken quite personally.[52] There was also awareness that, in contrast to others who had struggled through the war, the bomber boys had no monument in the capital: 'where's our memorial?' as Douglas Radcliffe, secretary of the Bomber Command Association, had put it. Thanks to donations totalling around £6.5 million from a variety of sources, a large-scale monument to those who had given their lives flying for Bomber Command, complete with a massive seven-man ensemble statue, was ready to be unveiled by Queen Elizabeth II within Green Park in late June 2012.[53]

The occasion, which was attended by over six thousand veterans and families of those killed, featured the dropping of eight hundred thousand poppies by Lancaster PA474 and was recapitulated for viewers in *A Tribute to Bomber Command* later in the day on BBC2.[54] The same evening Yesterday premiered *Who Betrayed the Bomber Boys?*, narrated by Stephen Fry, in which it was argued that those Harris had called his 'old lags' were ignored after the war for reasons of political expediency. It drew 70 per cent more viewers than usual to Yesterday, and the reviews were excellent.[55] Three days later ITV1 broadcast *Bomber Command*, a program along similar lines narrated by John Sergeant which also featured interviews with veterans. It too garnered mostly positive press, and though slightly fewer people watched the channel in the time slot than usual, the documentary drew 2.46 million viewers.[56] However, not everyone was happy with either the intent or the form of the new monument. 'There is some question as to whether it should have been built at all', architectural critic Rowan Moore wrote for the *Observer*, adding that it was 'a work of wishing away, of ignoring time, place and moral difficulty'. In the *Evening Standard*, veteran journalist Simon Jenkins argued that what was really needed was 'a humbler memorial, somewhere in London, to the hundreds of thousands of German civilians . . . whom we killed with so little compunction'. The debate over the wartime record of Bomber Command, in short, was by no means laid to rest in the soil of Green Park.[57]

Even those who questioned the morality of area bombing, however, conceded that, as Andrew Mueller put it in the *Guardian*, it was not 'the fault of the air crews who waged the campaign', over 40 per cent of whom had been killed.[58] That such a loss rate was pretty horrendous was something that everyone could agree on, and was at the heart of a fifteen-minute dramatic piece, *Lancaster*, from Red Dog Films and Polymath Pictures, that appeared the following year. Directed by Philip Stevens and produced by Tom Walsh for the people of Lincolnshire and later a wider internet audience, the high-production-value short film, bookended by interview footage and accompanied by a fine score from Lee Gretton, followed an ultimately fatal night sortie by a typical heavy bomber crew using actors, footage shot inside NX611, and occasional computer-generated imagery.[59] Homage to the veterans, in short, unlike to their simulacra in bronze, did not provoke controversy.

Notes

1 See e.g. Hermann Knell, *To Destroy a City* (Cambridge, MA: Da Capo, 2003); W. G. Sebald, *On the Natural History of Destruction* (London: Hamish Hamilton, 2003); Jörge Friedrich, *The Fire: The Bombing of Germany, 1940–1945* (New York: Columbia University Press, 2006); A. C. Grayling, *Among the Dead Cities: Was the Allied Bombing of Civilians in WWII a Necessity or a Crime?* (London: Bloomsbury, 2006); Randall Hansen, *Fire and Fury: The Allied Bombing of Germany, 1942–45* (Toronto: Doubleday, 2008); Keith Lowe, *Inferno: The Devastation of Hamburg, 1943* (London: Viking, 2007); *Terror from the Sky: The Bombing of German Cities in World War II*, ed. Igor Primoratz (Oxford: Berghahn, 2010); see also e.g. Donald Bloxam, 'Dresden as a War Crime', in *Firestorm: The Bombing of Dresden, 1945*, ed. Paul Addison and Jeremy Crang (London: Pimlico, 2006), 180–208. In addition, the Bomber Command failures of the early war years – and the problems of a film like *Target for Tonight* – were highlighted in the darkly comic novel *Damned Good Show* (London: Cassell, 2002) by Derek Robinson (see review by Mark Connelly in *Times Literary Supplement*, 20 December 2002, 20).

2 Keith A. Crawford and Stuart J. Foster, *War, Nation, Memory: International Perspectives on World War II in School History Textbooks* (Charlotte, NC: Information Age, 2008), chapter 3.

3 On positive remarks regarding *Timewatch: Bombing Germany* (BBC2, tx. 29 August 2001), written and produced by Detlef Siebert, see e.g. *Independent*, 26 August 2001; *Daily Telegraph*, 24 August 2001; *The Times*, 24 August 2001; *Guardian*, 23 August 2001; *Independent*, 19 August 2001; *TV Times*, 24 August 2001.
4 On *Last of the Dambusters* (C5, tx. 17 June 2008) see *The Times*, 17 June 2008; *Daily Mail*, 17 June 2008; *Daily Mirror*, 17 June 2008; *Guardian*, 14 June 2008; Simon Perry, *Spitfire Hunters* (Walton-on-Thames: Red Kite, 2010), 79–104. This would not be the only crash excavation programme featuring a Bomber Command veteran: see e.g. press release on Episode 1, Series 1, *War Digs with Harry Andrews*, tx. 13 May 2012, Discovery UK, accessed 4 August 2018, https://press,discovery.com/uk/know/programs/war-digs-harry-andrews/.
5 Royan Yule, *On a Wing and a Prayer* (Derby: Derby Books, 2012), 161; see also e.g. Tony Iveson comments on *Timewatch: Bombing Germany* in *Bomber Command Association Newsletter*, October 2001, 2; Bill Lucas letter in *Daily Telegraph*, 29 August 2001. If they had known about it they likely would have disapproved of the plot premise of a small independent comedic film, *Bomber*, involving as it did the desire of a former RAF pilot – played by Benjamin Whitrow – to make a road journey to a town in Germany and apologize for having bombed the place during the war. *Bomber* (dir. Paul Cotter, 2009) press kit, accessed 19 August 2012, http://www.filmmovement.com/downloads/press/BOMBER-Press_Kit.pdf.
6 See e.g. Mark Connelly, *Reaching for the Stars: A New History of Bomber Command in World War II* (London: I.B. Tauris, 2001); Robin Neillands, *The Bomber War: Arthur Harris and the Allied Bomber Offensive, 1939–1945* (London: John Murray, 2001); Henry Probert, *Bomber Harris: His Life and Times* (Toronto: Stoddart, 2001); Simon Read, *The Killing Skies: RAF Bomber Command at War* (Stroud: Spellmount, 2006); Randall T. Wakelam, *The Science of Bombing: Operational Research in RAF Bomber Command* (Toronto: University of Toronto Press, 2009); see also David L. Bashow, 'The Balance Sheet: The Costs and Gains of the Bombing Campaign', *Canadian Military History* 15, 3&4 (2006), 43–70, and on a broader canvas, Michael Burleigh, *Moral Combat: A History of World War II* (London: Harper, 2010), chapter 19.
7 Adam Tooze, *The Wages of Destruction: The Making and Breaking of the Nazi Economy* (London: Allen Lane, 2006), 597 ff.
8 See Mark Taylor, *Dresden: Tuesday 13 February 1945* (London: Bloomsbury, 2004); see also the less successful Marshall De Bruhl, *Allied Airpower and the Destruction of Dresden* (New York: Random House, 2006).
9 See e.g. David L. Bashow, *No Prouder Place: Canadians and the Bomber Command Experience 1939–1945* (St. Catherines, ON: Vanwell, 2006); Patrick Bishop, *Bomber Boys: Fighting Back, 1940–1945* (London: HarperCollins, 2007); Martin Bowman, *RAF Bomber Command: Reflections of War*, 5 vols. (Barnsley: Pen and Sword Aviation, 2011–14); Max Lambert, *Night after Night: New Zealanders in Bomber Command* (Auckland: HarperCollins, 2005); Hank Nelson, *Chased by the Sun: Australians in Bomber Command in World War II* (Sydney: ABC, 2002); Peter Rees, *Lancaster Men: The Aussie Heroes of Bomber Command* (Crows Nest, NSW: Allen and Unwin, 2013); Andrew R. B. Simpson, *'Ops': Victory at All Costs: On Operations over Hitler's Reich with the Crews of Bomber Command: Their War – Their Words* (Pulborough: Tattered Flag, 2012); John Sweetman, *Bomber Crew: Taking on the Reich* (London: Little, Brown, 2004); Kevin Wilson, *Bomber Boys: The RAF Offensive of 1943* (London: Weidenfeld and Nicolson, 2005); *Men of the Air: Doomed Youth of Bomber Command, 1944* (London: Weidenfeld and Nicolson, 2007); *Journey's End: Bomber*

Command's Battle from Arnhem to Dresden and Beyond (London: Weidenfeld and Nicolson, 2010).

10   Commando Comics, meanwhile, still emphasized precision attacks by Bomber Command: see e.g. *Automatic Pilot*, Commando 4043, October 2007. A drawn history of the bombing war published in the United States was rather more dubious about the achievements of the RAF area bombing campaign. See Wayne Vansant, *Bombing Nazi Germany: The Graphic History of the Allied Air Campaign That Defeated Hitler in World War II* (Minneapolis, MN: Zenith, 2013).

11   See Monica MacDonald, 'Producing the Public Past: Canadian History on CBC Television, 1952-2002' (PhD diss., York University, 2007), 259. The accompanying book of the series – Don Gillmor, Achille Michaud and Pierre Turgeon, *Canada: A People's History: Volume Two* (Toronto: McClelland and Stewart, 2001) – ignored Bomber Command altogether. On the making of the series see Mark Starowicz, *Making History: The Remarkable Story behind* Canada: A People's History (Toronto: McClelland and Stewart, 2003): see in particular page 41 in possible reference to *The Valour and the Horror*.

12   On this controversy see David J. Bercuson, 'The Canadian War Museum and Bomber Command: My Perspective', *Canadian Military History* 20, 3 (2011), 55-62; Robert Bothwell, Randall Hansen and Margaret MacMillan, 'Controversy, Commemoration, and Capitulation: The Canadian War Museum and Bomber Command', *Queen's Quarterly* 115 (2008), 367-87; David Dean, 'Museums as Conflict Zones: The Canadian War Museum and Bomber Command', *Museum and Society* 7 (2009), 1-15.

13   On positive reactions to *Bomber Boys: The Fighting Lancaster* (Frantic Films, 2005), see e.g. *Gazette* [Montreal], 11 November 2005; *Globe and Mail*, 10 November 2005; on the series see also *Winnipeg Free Press*, 11 July 2006. The term 'reality history' – which can also be applied to *Bomber Crew* (see note 17 below) – is drawn from Jerome de Groot, *Consuming History: Historians and Heritage in Contemporary Popular Culture* (London: Routledge, 2009), chapter 11.

14   See e.g. *Edmonton Journal*, 9 November 2005; *Toronto Star*, 9 November 2005. The War Amps organization also brought out for community use the two-hour *Boys of Kelvin High: Canadians in Bomber Command* that year, in which the sacrifices made by volunteers from one particular high school in Winnipeg were chronicled within a narrative framework which emphasized the importance of what they were doing. *The Boys of Kelvin High* (prod. Cliff Chadderton, 2005).

15   On positive remarks concerning *Bomber* (BBC2, tx. 9 October 2001) in the *Battlefields* series written and presented by military historian Richard Holmes, see e.g. *Times*, 9 October 2001; *Sunday Times*, 7 October 2001.

16   See *Broadcast*, 4 April 2003, 22; *Daily Telegraph*, 8 April 2003; *Times*, 8 April 2003; *Independent*, 8 April 2003; *TV Times*, 8 April 2003, 23; *Independent*, 6 April 2003.

17   Critical reaction to *Bomber Crew* (C4 tx. 27 November-20 December 2004) varied: see e.g. *Observer*, 28 November 2004; *Times*, 29 November 2004; *Independent*, 30 November 2004; *Daily Telegraph*, 30 November 2004; *Evening Standard*, 30 November 2004; *Daily Mail*, 20, 27, 30 November 2004; *Guardian*, 30 November, 4 December 2004; *Evening Times* [Glasgow], 29 November 2004. See also James Taylor and Martin Davidson, *Bomber Crew* (London: Hodder and Stoughton, 2004).

18   *The Times* magazine, 2 February 2002, 51.

19   Hilary Salmon in British Film Institute Library, *Night Flight* BBC pressbook; see *Radio Times*, 2 February 2002, 40-3. On *Night and Day* as a working title see *Daily*

Telegraph, 29 October 2001; on *Ready Steady Go* as a working title see *The Stage*, 5 October 2000.

20 On photographing *Night Flight* see Kerry Anne Burrows, 'Night Flight', *Eyepiece* 22, 5 (2001), 15–16. On Ivory's research and talks with his father see *Daily Mail*, 1 February 2002; *Radio Times*, 2 February 2002, 42–3; *The Times* magazine, 2 February 2002, 51–2. On engine start-up procedures, see e.g. Yule, *On a Wing and a Prayer*, 53. On the strain of last-minute scrubs, see e.g. IWM 27800/6, Ernie Lummis interview; C. Wade Rodgers, *There's No Future in It* (Rodgers: Orford, TAS, 1988), 54. On the importance of talismans and rituals see S. P. MacKenzie, 'Beating the Odds: Superstition and Human Agency in RAF Bomber Command. 1942–1945', *War in History* 22 (2015), 382–400. On night-fighter attacks, see e.g. Bob Porter, *The Long Return* (Burnaby, BC: Porter, 1997), 55–7; Peter Russell, *Flying in Defiance of the Reich* (Barnsley: Pen and Sword Aviation, 2007), 1. Other true-to-life elements in *Night Flight* included the off-duty rabbit-shooting sequence: see e.g. Thomas G. Quinlan, *Corkscrew to Safety* (Bognor Regis: Woodfield, 2011), 98. On the commissioned–non-commissioned social divide in the RAF see Brereton Greenhous, Stephen J. Harris, William C. Johnston and William G. P. Rawling, *The Crucible of War, 1939–1945: The Official History of the Royal Canadian Air Force, Volume III* (Toronto: University of Toronto Press, 1994), 49 ff.

21 See Burrows, 'Night Flight', 15–16; *Daily Telegraph*, 29 January 2002. On Phil Davis bowing out see *The Stage*, 5 October 2000.

22 See *Radio Times*, 2 February 2002, 42; *Eyepiece*, 22, 5 October 2001, 15; *Bradford Target*, 2 February 2002.

23 *Broadcast*, 5 February 2002.

24 *Times*, 4 February 2002; *Daily Mail*, 4 February 2002; see also e.g. *Birmingham Evening Mail*, 6 February 2002; *Financial Times*, 3 February 2002.

25 Tony Iveson in *Bomber Command Association Newsletter*, April 2002, 2.

26 *Daily Mail*, 2 February 2002; *Observer*, 28 January 2002; see also *Sunday Times*, 27 January 2002; *Evening Standard*, 7 February 2002; *Broadcast*, 8 February 2002; *TV Times*, 2 February 2002; *Tribune* [Blackpool], 8 February 2002.

27 *The Haunted Airman* (BBC, 2006); see Dennis Wheatley, *The Haunting of Toby Jugg* (London: Hutchinson, 1948). On Chris Durlacher see his website, accessed 4 April 2018, http://chrisdurlacher.net. On Dennis Wheatley see Phil Baker, *The Devil Is a Gentleman: The Life and Times of Dennis Wheatley* (Sawtry: Dedalus, 2009).

28 *Guardian*, 28 October 2006; *Sunday Times*, 29 October 2006. For other negative reviews, see e.g. *Financial Times*, 31 October 2006. For positive reviews, see e.g. *Evening Standard*, 31 October 2006; *Observer*, 29 October 2006; *The Times*, 31 October 2006. War and mental trauma were also at the heart of the award-winning novel *Day* by A. L. Kennedy (London: Cape, 2007), which focusses on the experienced and memories of a rear-gunner sergeant.

29 Ed Meza, 'C4 takes "Dresden"', *Variety*, 4 April 2006.

30 David F. Crew, 'Sleeping with the Enemy? A Fiction Film for German Television about the Bombing of Dresden', *Central European History* 40 (2007), 117; Wilfried Wilms, 'Dresden: The Return of History as Soap', in *Collapse of the Conventional: German Film and Politics at the Turn of the Twenty-First Century*, ed. Jaimey Fisher and Brad Prager (Detroit: Wayne State University Press, 2010), 139.

31 See Paul Cooke, '*Dresden* (2006), TeamWorx and *Titanic* (1997): German Wartime Suffering as Hollywood Disaster Movie', *German Life and Letters* 61 (2008), 279–94.

32 See 'Making of' Featurette, 2-disc DVD Region 1 version of *Dresden* (Koch, 2006); see also Crew, 'Sleeping with the Enemy', 122. It was significant that Richard Overy, then a known defender of Bomber Command, was brought on board as one of the historical advisors. See Bas von Benda-Beckmann, *German Historians and the Bombing of German Cities: The Contested Air War* (Amsterdam: Amsterdam University Press, 2015), 222; see also Overy in 'Making of' Featurette, 2-disc DVD Region 1 version of *Dresden* (Koch, 2006).

33 The real Saundby, it is worth noting, only later in life came to regret the attack on Dresden.

34 On the GCI, mock-ups and use of English actors for all the British parts for the sake of authenticity, see 'Making of' Featurette, 2-disc DVD Region 1 version of *Dresden* (Koch, 2006). An Afro-Caribbean crewmember is even shown momentarily in a briefing scene, possibly a nod to the rear gunner of a Lancaster that flew on the raid and is shown in a photograph replicated in Taylor, *Dresden*. On Harry McCalla see Miles Tripp, *The Eighth Passenger* (London: Macmillan, 1969). On blending the Cozens film with new footage to add to a sense of authenticity see Griseldis Kirsch, 'Memory and Myth: The Bombings of Dresden and Hiroshima in German and Japanese TV Drama', *Contemporary Japan* 24 (2012), 62. In addition to the use of out-of-place USAAF combat footage, flaws ranged from showing an aircrew NCO wearing corporal rather than sergeant stripes and aircraft flying in formation at night to a poor mid-upper turret mock-up and placing the door on the wrong side of a Lancaster fuselage mock-up.

35 As in *Death by Moonlight*, the fact that Harris employed a cigarette holder is used in *Dresden* to give him the air of a Bond film villain. The vaguely Rhodesian accent that Rodska employed for the role also makes Harris sound sinister. The fact that Pip Torrens did not resemble Saundby may have been due to the erroneous use of a comparison photo of Hugh Dowding, head of Fighter Command in 1940. See 'Making of' Featurette, DVD 2-disc Region 1 version of *Dresden* (Koch, 2006).

36 *Daily Mail*, 16 February 2009; see *The Sun*, 14 February 2009; see also e.g. *Sentinel* [Stoke-on-Trent], 16 February 2009. On lack of audience impact see *Broadcast*, 22 February 2008, 50–1. On *Dresden* see also Linda Robertson, 'Marketing the Bombing of Dresden in Germany, Great Britain, and the United States', in *A Companion to the War Film*, ed. Douglas A. Cunningham and John C. Nelson (Oxford: Wiley Blackwell, 2016), 234–52.

37 *Into the Storm* was a follow-on to the earlier co-production *Gathering Storm* (HBO/BBC, 2002), also written by Hugh Whitemore, dealing with Churchill's efforts against the appeasement of Hitler in the mid-1930s. On the HBO-BBC collaborations see Janet McCabe and Kim Akass, 'It Is Not TV, It's HBO's Original Programming', in *It's Not TV: Watching HBO in the Post-Television Era*, ed. Marc Leverette, Brian L. Ott and Cara Louise Buckley (London: Routledge, 2008), 91.

38 This exchange was a fair representation of the positions of Churchill and Harris concerning the bombing campaign in 1942, though some of the language was borrowed from other contexts and both the discouraging surveys and the shift to area bombing predated the arrival of Harris as C-in-C Bomber Command. Less in line with the known facts was having Attlee – who was in fact a strong supporter of bombing (see Richard Overy, *The Bombing War: Europe, 1939–1945* [London: Allen Lane, 2013], 244) – express moral qualms.

39 After being used in *Death by Moonlight*, this story was held up for criticism as being apocryphal (see Monica MacDonald, 'Producing the Public Past: Canadian History

on CBC Television, 1952–2002' [PhD diss., York University, 2007], 232). One of the sources Brian McKenna had consulted, however, replicated it as fact (see Max Hastings, *Bomber Command* [London: Michael Joseph, 1979], 135), and someone who worked with Harris subsequently indicated hearing the tale from the C-in-C himself (see James Pelly-Fry, *Heavenly Days: Recollections of a Contented Airman* [Manchester: Crécy, 1994], 255). Churchill did indeed express dismay on seeing a film of bomb damage, albeit not of Dresden. See Ralph Bennett, *Behind the Battle* (London: Pimlico, 1999), 170.

40 *Independent on Sunday*, 8 November 2009; see also e.g. *The Times*, 2 November 2009; *Scotland on Sunday*, 8 November 2008.
41 *Broadcast*, 3 November 2009. On negative reviews, see e.g. *Sunday Times*, 8 November 2008. On more positive responses, see e.g. *Guardian*, 1 November 2009. For laudatory American reviews, see e.g. *Washington Post*, 30 May 2009.
42 Peter Jackson to film Dam Busters, BBC News, 31 August 2006, accessed 13 September 2012, http://news.bbc.co.uk/2/hi/entertainment/5301998.stm.
43 On writing the script see Stephen Fry, *The Fry Chronicles* (London: Michael Joseph, 2010), 59–62. On interviews see *New Zealand Herald*, 2 September 2006.
44 See Susan Ottaway, *Guy Gibson VC: The Glorious Dambuster* (Hampshire: Speedman, 1994), 171; Charles Foster, Dambusters Remake: Quiet Progress, 8 November 2011, Dambusters Weblog, accessed 12 December 2012, https://dambustersblog.com/2011/11/08/dambusters-remake-quiet-progress/; Dam Buster Dog Renamed for Movie Remake, BBC News, 10 June 2011, accessed 17 February 2013, https://www.bbc.com/news/uk-england-lincolnshire-13727908.
45 See e.g. *Independent*, 5 August 2015; Dambusters remake shoved to the back of the queue, again, 25 October 2016, Dambustersblog, accessed 9 December 2017, http://dambustersblog.com/2016/10/25.
46 Overy, *Bombing War*. On the change of mind see Max Hastings in the *Sunday Times*, 29 September 2013. On praise for the book see also e.g. Richard J. Evans in *Guardian*, 28 October 2013; John Gooch in *Times Literary Supplement*, 20 September 2013. There were still books being published in this decade, however, which argued the contrary position. See e.g. David L. Bashow, *Soldiers Blue: How Bomber Command and Area Bombing Helped Win the Second World War* (Kingston, ON: Canadian Defence Academy Press, 2011); Kenneth Harder, *The Key to Survival: Bomber Command in World War II* (Maidstone: George Mann, 2006).
47 This was also true on the stage: writer Billy Ivory paid homage to his deceased father, a former navigator in 50 Squadron, in his new play *Bomber's Moon*, first produced in 2010 – see William Ivory on *Bomber's Moon*, University of Nottingham, 11 May 2010, accessed 6 June 2018, https://www.youtube.com; Michael Billington review, *Guardian*, 7 April 2014, accessed 30 May 2018, https://www.theguardian.com/stage/2014/apr/07/bombers-moon-review-william-ivory-park-theatre – while Trevor Nunn successfully revived Terence Rattigan's *Flare Path* in 2011 – see Michael Billington review, *Guardian*, 13 March 2011, accessed 14 December 2017, https://www.theguardian.com/stage/2011/mar/13/flare-path-terence-rattigan-review; Charles Spencer review, 14 March 2011, *Telegraph*, accessed 14 December 2017, https://www.telegraph.co.uk/culture/theatre/theatre-reviews/8380218/Flare-Path-Theatre-Royal-Haymarket-review.html.
48 See *What the Dambusters Did Next* (C5, tx. 26 May 2014); *Dam Busters: The Race to Smash the German Dams* (BBC2, tx. 8 November 2011); *Dambusters Declassified* (BBC2, tx. 17 October 2010); *Dambusters: Building the Bouncing Bomb* (C4, tx. 2

May 2011). See also John Nicol, *After the Flood: What the Dambusters Did Next* (London: Collins, 2015); and John Sweetman, *The Official Dambusters Experience* (London: Carlton, 2013). The RAF was happy to support commemoration of the raid in 2013 (see e.g. Morgan Johnson epilogue to George 'Johnny' Johnson, *The Last British Dambuster* [London: Ebury, 2014], 291) while the following year the attention given to PA474 of the Battle of Britain Memorial Flight increased as a result of a summer visit by the only other Lanc then in flying condition, FM213 of the Canadian Warplane Heritage Museum, formation flying that included a mock 'dambuster' bomb run over Derwent Reservoir. See e.g. *Daily Mail*, 21 September 2014; see documentary *Reunion of Giants* (dir. Morgan Elliott, 2015).

49   *Guardian*, 27 May 2014; *Daily Telegraph*, 5 November 2011.
50   On audience figures for *Bomber Boys* (BBC, 2012) see *Broadcast*, 6 February 2012. On praise for the programme see *Sunday Telegraph*, 5 February 2012; *Sunday Times*, 12 February 2012; *Mail on Sunday*, 5 February 2012; *Daily Express*, 6 February 2012; *Sun*, 4 February 2012; *Financial Times*, 4 February 2012; *Observer*, 5 February 2012; *Independent*, 6 February 2012. On praise for *Bomber Boys Revealed* (Channel 5, 2011) see *Daily Mail*, 29 October 2011. On *Into the Wind* (Electric Egg, 2010), shown on Yesterday on 31 March 2012, see Into the Wind, accessed 9 February 2013, http://www.intothewind.co.uk. Over in Canada, the elegiac *Boys of Kelvin High* was in 2012 rereleased to community channels in Manitoba by the War Amps. Boys of Kelvin High, accessed 19 August 2012, http://kelvin100.com/.
51   See e.g. Bill Grierson, *We Band of Brothers* (Hailsham: J&KH, 1997), 328; Arthur White, *Bread and Butter Bomber Boys* (Upton-on-Severn: Square One, 1995), 2. Though there was some truth to all this, the linked issues of a peerage and a campaign medal were in fact more complicated than many realized. See Peter Gray, 'A Culture of Official Squeamishness? Britain's Air Ministry and the Strategic Air Offensive Against Europe', *Journal of Military History* 77 (2013), 1349–77; Henry Probert, *Bomber Harris: His Life and Times* (Toronto: Stoddart, 2001), 344–51, 360.
52   See e.g. Yule, *On a Wing and a Prayer*, 161.
53   Robin Gibb, Jim Dooley, Gordon Rayner, Steve Darlow and Sean Feast, *The Bomber Command Memorial: We Will Remember Them* (Hitchin: Fighting High, 2012), 9, ff. There had been smaller monuments at the Australian War Memorial in Canberra since 2005 (see Bomber Command Memorial, Australian War Memorial, accessed 15 December 2016, https://www.awm.gov.au), at what is now the Bomber Command Museum of Canada since 2005 (see Canada's Bomber Command Memorial, Bomber Command Museum of Canada, accessed 15 December 2017, http://www.bombercommandmuseum.ca/memorialgranite.html), and at the Auckland Memorial Museum since 2010 (see *New Zealand Bomber Command Association Newsletter*, October 2015, 5).
54   Wimbledon apparently ruled out live coverage by the BBC. See *Sunday Times*, 24 June 2012.
55   On audience figures for *Who Betrayed the Bomber Boys?* (Mediacam, 2012) see *Broadcast*, 29 June 2012. On positive reviews, see e.g. *Daily Telegraph*, 29 June 2012; *Metro*, 29 June 2012; *The Times*, 29 June 2012; *Guardian*, 28 June 2012. Needless to say, veterans liked it: see e.g. *New Zealand Bomber Command Association Newsletter*, August 2012, 5.
56   On audience figures for *Bomber Command* (ITV, 2012) see *Broadcast*, 4 July 2012. For positive reviews, see e.g. *Independent*, 4 July 2012; *Sun*, 22 July 2012; *Sunday Telegraph*, 1 July 2012.

57 Simon Jenkins, 'Defacing a park is not the way to honour war dead', 19 June 2012, *Evening Standard*, accessed 7 April 2018, https://www.standard.co.uk/comment/comment/defacing-a-park-is-not-the-way-to-honour-war-dead-7865854.html; Rowan Moore, Bomber Command memorial – review, 23 June 2012, *Guardian*, accessed 7 April 2018, https://www.theguardian.com/artanddesign/2012/jun/24/bomber-command-memorial-london-review. On debating the memorial see also e.g. Keith Lowe versus Patrick Bishop, How should we remember the men of bomber command?, 28 June 2012, *History Extra*, accessed 7 April 2018, https://www.historyextra.com/period/second-world-war/bomber-command-memorial-men-remember/; Christoph Ehland, 'London Remembers: The Bomber Command Memorial and Recent Memories of War in the British Capital', in *London post-2010 in British Literature and Culture*, ed. Oliver von Knebel Doeberitz and Ralf Schneider (Leiden: Brill Rodopi, 2017), 147–54.

58 *Guardian*, 3 July 2012.

59 See *Lancaster* on Vimeo, accessed 11 December 2017, https://vimeo.com; Tom Walsh portfolio, *Lancaster*, accessed 11 December 2017, http://www.tomwalsh/lancaster; *Lincolnshire Echo*, 13 December 2013; Film recreates Lancaster bomber crew's last flight, 14 May 2013, *Telegraph Online*, accessed 11 December 2017, http://www.telegraph.co.uk. The theme of sacrifice was also evident in the three veteran-interview films made later by Jabberwocky and released in November 2014 to help support the upkeep of the Bomber Command monument. See *Gordon*, *Doug*, and *Harry*, Ads of the World, accessed 12 December 2017, http://www.adsoftheworld.com/campaign/raf-bomber-command-jabberwocky-11-2014; RAF Bomber Command at Just Giving, accessed 12 December 2017, https://www.justgiving.com/.

CONCLUSION

That the long campaign fought under the direction of Sir Arthur Harris became a subject of popular controversy while the exploits of Fighter Command in its finest hour continued to be celebrated over the last seventy-odd years seems beyond dispute.[1] However, in light of the fact that the number of post-war screen dramas devoted to Bomber Command remains neck and neck with the figure for Fighter Command, the concomitant assumption that the bomber boys have been shunned on screen compared to the fighter boys is rather more questionable.[2]

During the war itself the bombing of the Third Reich generated little debate, partly due to the strong popular desire to hit back and also because of official obfuscation and guided cinema and other publicity that aimed to present Bomber Command as waging a necessary and effective battle against an uncompromising enemy.[3] As the war receded into the ever-more-distant past, however, even within the RAF the bombing of the Reich became more problematic to celebrate than the earlier defensive victory over English skies.[4] Yet as indicated, despite the potentially controversial subject matter – and the consequent higher-than-average chance of critical and/or commercial failure – plus various technical challenges, a succession of filmmakers accepted the risks and found ways to project Bomber Command dramatically on screen in the second half of the twentieth century and beyond.[5]

Representing aircraft of the right type in sufficient number has been a consistent problem in production planning. Initially, while it was possible to arrange shooting on and over airfields, there were plenty of bureaucratic hurdles to surmount, and wartime operations and security considerations naturally took precedence.[6] Within ten years the number of period bombers had dwindled to a handful, and over the next quarter century the shortage of airworthy machines had grown too acute to allow even for type substitution.[7] Within the last ten years or so computer-generated imagery has developed qualitatively to a point where it can represent more or less convincing simulacra of the real thing, though it has yet to be applied fully in the case of Bomber Command.[8] Model work and optical effects might be employed, along with insertions of wartime footage – the latter providing an enduring afterlife for the films of Harry Watt and Henry Cozens.[9] If the focus was exclusively on the commanders rather than the flyers, then it was possible to do without aircraft entirely.[10] Nonetheless, having only one or two restored Lancasters and usually only a single airworthy example to work with on either side of the Atlantic has tended over the past forty-odd years to make associated camerawork a matter of close-ups and medium shots rather than panoramic vistas, and likely contributed to a preference for storylines that focus on the members of an individual bomber crew.[11]

A recurring motif in Bomber Command screen dramas over the past eighty years has been the variety of distant places from which the Bomber Boys are shown to have come. Those hailing from beyond the British Isles are more often than not cast in supporting rather than leading roles, exceptions occurring only when a film is being made for an international audience. In certain instances, moreover, foreign voices and faces seem to have been inserted merely to add a little aural and visual variety.[12] Nonetheless, the fact remains that Australian and Canadian characters make an appearance of one sort or another in over a dozen films, as do, on rarer occasions, New Zealanders plus the occasional Afrikaner, Pole, Sikh, Jamaican or Yank. The underlying message, with only one or two exceptions, is one of international harmony in pursuit of a common cause.[13]

The depiction of regional and class variation among aircrew from within the UK has been much more sporadic. This is especially true of the Celtic fringe, Scottish and Welsh characters appearing only three times each and an Ulsterman only once. The north-south divide in England has been given somewhat better coverage, but it is noticeable that every single British skipper down the decades seems to have had a middle-class upbringing in the Home Counties.[14] This is true even on the rare occasions when the aircraft captain wears chevrons on his sleeves rather than the rings of an officer.[15] Indeed, those from further afield in Britain have almost invariably been portrayed as non-commissioned types, also something true for working-class airmen on the comparatively rare occasions they have put in an appearance. In almost all cases, a common attitude of professionalism trumps regional and class difference.[16]

This has not meant, however, that Bomber Command aircrew have been portrayed as flawless. Visible fear and stress, while for obvious reasons absent from the wartime pictures, grew in prominence as the ethos of the stiff upper lip gradually gave way in the post-war decades to self-examination and emotional expression. Initially this was mainly a matter of hinting at the psychological burdens of command, but by the last quarter or so of the twentieth century fear of death, emotional as well as physical trauma, and the possibility of combat refusal or mental collapse among the bomber boys became an accepted – indeed almost cliché – part of the average aircrew drama.[17]

Even long after the war, though, and in spite of the of the lively debate in print and elsewhere, it has been rare in crew-focused dramas for the ethics and efficacy of area bombing to be mentioned, let alone for its effects to be depicted.[18] For the most part, questions of morality have been confined to a different set of films in which Sir Arthur Harris is one of the central characters. Perhaps not surprisingly with such a lightning-rod figure, projected depictions have ranged from an uncompromisingly committed warrior to something approaching the devil incarnate; though as noted earlier it was the former image that prevailed on British television.[19] Screenplays which centre on the bomber boys themselves have mostly depicted precision or special raids, concentrated on the trials and tribulations of a crew or at most a squadron and ignored the broader command strategy and its consequences for those on the ground.[20]

The approach seems to be what filmmakers – at least in countries which contributed significant human and other resources to mounting the bomber offensive – have learned will be sufficiently anodyne on highly sensitive matters such as targeting yet at the same time gripping enough in terms of emotional identification for audiences to be drawn in while at the same time avoiding copious amounts of outrage. In simple terms, it has made sense in terms of viewership ratings or ticket sales to try and shift the mantle of victimhood from the bombed to the bombers.[21]

Those in the industry have sometimes calculated incorrectly as to what critics and audiences will decide is acceptable dramatic viewing. Productions on occasion have been written off at birth as either completely out of sync with the times or treated as vastly more controversial than anticipated.[22] Nonetheless, an attempt has always been made to assess what the public at a particular time will generally embrace rather than ignore or reject, and the big successes have been those screen dramas which tend to match up best with a popular sense of who the bomber boys were and what they did.[23] It is illustrative that the only big-budget Bomber Command film currently in prospect is a remake of *The Dam Busters* – rather than, say, an epic screen version of the novel *Bomber* – and that controversy has swirled around whether or not to rename Gibson's dog rather than over the unrepresentative nature of the bombing attack at the centre of the story.[24]

It may be that as fewer and fewer active veterans remain to comment publicly on how their wartime years are represented, the sometimes quite heated debates over the record of the bomber boys will become less polarized or even fade away. The stated purpose of the International Bomber Command Centre (IBCC) opened in May 2018 outside Lincoln is to serve 'as a point of recognition, remembrance, and reconciliation' in which the stories of not only former aircrew but also 'those who suffered as a result of the campaign' will be preserved.[25] The strikingly innocent graphic style adopted for the recently published computer simulation game *Bomber Crew!*, created by the small UK company Rubber Duck, suggests that, at least among a younger set, the air war is an abstraction rather than a matter of moral passion.[26]

At the same time it is hard to ignore the way in which, despite the international success of recent British war pictures dealing with iconic wartime events such as Dunkirk and people such as Churchill apparently spurring a major new Battle of Britain film project, those seeking to project the lives of the bomber boys have run into headwinds. Lack of financial backing seems to have has delayed the completion and sale of a six-episode dramatization by Len Davies of the exploits of airmen from three different Lancaster squadrons as they progress from training to operations that has been in the pipeline for several years.[27] Apparently bereft of serious external funding, Tin Hat Productions had to resort among other things to selling props and models in order to finance its attempt at a retro Lanc crew drama.[28] The subject, after all, does still have the power to generate controversy, what with repeated vandalizing of the Bomber Command memorial in Green

Park and the manner in which some of the remaining bomber boys – including one apparently linked to the IBCC – seeming to correlate the case for leaving the European Union with their wartime struggle against Nazi Germany.[29]

What can be said with certainty is that Harris and his 'old lags', contrary to the post-war rejection narrative,[30] have never been ignored in film and television drama compared to either Fighter Command or their American counterparts in the Eighth Air Force. What has set them apart is not a relative paucity of titles but rather divergence of perspectives.

Though some uncomfortable facts eventually came to light as the Finest Hour receded into history, the Battle of Britain remained a David-versus-Goliath tale that proved comparatively easy to adapt on screen amidst evolving societal tastes and expectations.[31] As for the Eighth Air Force, in spite of the growing recognition in historical circles that mass daylight bombing of German targets from high altitude had in fact been highly inaccurate and killed a great many civilians, the popular perception has remained that the Yanks had been engaged in a comparatively clean and precise campaign: a version of the bombing war both reflected in and perpetuated in a steady succession of mostly successful screen dramas.[32]

The area campaign fought by Bomber Command at night, on the other hand, became controversial both in terms of morality and potency in the decades after the war, which meant that there was less of an uncomplicatedly uplifting master narrative for filmmakers to tap into. The two most common viewpoint adopted in response – concentrating on game-changing one-off attacks and/or the trials and tribulations of the bomber crews and their leaders – often avoided the more awkward issues concerning utility and morality and were largely acceptable to most veterans.[33] What led many former flyers to feel, nonetheless, that the bomber boys and their C-in-C were being sold out on screen was that fact that, unlike their compatriots in Fighter Command or their American cousins of the Mighty Eighth, there were also more disagreeable approaches taken which seemed to question their wartime record. It was disturbing to see Butch Harris vilified as a monster in the manner of *Fireraiser*, upsetting to watch themselves portrayed as terror-struck like Vic Green in *Night Flight*, and doubly distressing to witness both at once in *Death by Moonlight*.[34]

What coming years will hold for perceptions of Bomber Command as the number of still-living bomber boys continues to dip below a thousand remains to be seen.[35] The various film and television dramas discussed herein all have been products of their times, and the future is of course an undiscovered country. The past, though, can always be plundered for present use, and it seems likely that this will continue in dramatic form with reference to the night bombing of Germany – most certainly as long as Brexit sharply divides opinion concerning Britain's relationship with the Continent.[36]

Notes

1 See e.g. Jeremy Black, *Rethinking World War Two: The Conflict and Its Legacy* (London: Bloomsbury, 2015), 160–1.

2 Post-war screen dramas focusing on the Fighter Boys include *Angels One Five* (Templar, 1952), *Malta Story* (Thea, 1953), *Reach for the Sky* (Pinnacle, 1956), *Battle of Britain* (Spitfire, 1969), *Piece of Cake* (Holmes, 1988), *A Perfect Hero* (Havahall, 1991), *Dark Blue World* (Various, 2001), *First Light* (BBC, 2010), *Dunkirk* (Syncopy, 2017) and *Hurricane* (Head Gear, 2018), while post-war screen dramas dealing with Bomber Command – leaving aside various docudramas – include *Appointment in London* (Mayflower, 1953), *The Dam Busters* (ABPC, 1955), *633 Squadron* (Mirisch, 1964), *Mosquito Squadron* (Oakmont, 1969), *Pathfinders* (Warboys, 1972), *Bomber Harris* (BBC, 1989), *Map of the Human Heart* (Working Title, 1993), *Night Flight* (BBC, 2002), *Dresden* (teamWorx, 2006) and *Lancaster Skies* (Tin Hat, 2019). On the British film industry supposedly giving Bomber Command the cold shoulder, see e.g. Angus Calder, *Disasters and Heroes: On War, Memory and Representation* (Cardiff: University of Wales, 2004), 137.

3 On a popular desire to hit back during the Blitz see *Listening to Britain: Home Intelligence Reports on Britain's Finest Hour—May to September 1940*, ed. Paul Addison and Jeremy Crang (London: Bodley Head, 2010), 447, 454, 256, 257. On the very limited scale of wartime protest against RAF bombing, see e.g. Richard Overy, 'Constructing Space for Dissent in War: The Bombing Restriction Committee, 1941–1945', *English Historical Review* 131 (2016), 596–622. On Air Ministry and Ministry of Information shaping of public perceptions of the bombing war see James Chapman, *The British at War: Cinema, State and Propaganda, 1939–1945* (London: I.B. Tauris, 1998); Ian McLaine, *Ministry of Morale: Home Front Morale and the Ministry of Information in World War II* (London: Allen and Unwin, 1979).

4 See Richard Overy, 'Identity, Politics and Technology in the RAF's History', *RUSI Journal* 153, 6 (2008), 77.

5 At the time of writing (December 2018), two leading filmmakers have indicated plans to add to this corpus: a new Battle of Britain film in the case of Ridley Scott and the oft-delayed remake of *The Dam Busters* in the case of Peter Jackson.

6 On the bureaucratic difficulties of filming on active RAF stations during the war see TNA, AIR 41/9, AHB Narrative on Press and Publicity, 2–3.

7 By the 1960s, as noted, there was only a single, intermittently airworthy, Lancaster available, and by the 1970s flyable Mosquitoes has also sunk below acceptable levels for an aerial epic. It might just have been theoretically possible to continue using Fortresses in the manner of *A Family at War* (Granada, 1971) given the number of airworthy examples that could still be assembled for the USAAF-focused *Memphis Belle* (Enigma, 1990); but only one or two squadrons in Bomber Command had ever been equipped with the type.

8 For CGI aerial combat, see e.g. *Fortress* (Bayou, 2012) or *Red Tails* (Lucasfilm, 2012). Working within a microbudget, Tin Hat Productions chose for *Lancaster Skies* (2019) to employ the more traditional scale models: see Tin Hat Productions, untitled model demo, accessed 26 March 2018, https://vimeo.com/179171669.

9 Excerpts from both *Night Bombers* and *Target for Tonight* have been used on multiple occasions over the decades, in the former case as recently as 2006 in *Dresden*.

10 There were no aircraft shots in *Fireraiser*, and *Bomber Harris* used only wartime footage.

11 See e.g. episode 'One Man's Lancaster', tx. 8 November 1972, *Pathfinders* (Toledo, 1972); *Night Flight* (BBC, 2002); *Lancaster Skies* (Tin Hat, 2019). The impossibility of the kind of multi-aircraft aerial and exterior photography possible at the time of *Appointment in London* (Mayflower, 1953), *The Dam Busters* (ABPC, 1955), *633 Squadron* (Mirisch, 1964) and *Mosquito Squadron* (Oakmont, 1969) in the last quarter

of the twentieth century likely was one factor in preventing the oft-anticipated film version of Len Deighton's sprawling, multi-character novel *Bomber* from getting underway. On occasional rumours of such a production in the wind, see e.g. Bomber to finally make it to Celluloid?, The Deighton Dossier, accessed 5 September 2012, http://deightondossier.blogspot.com/search/label/Bomber.

12 Flight Lieutenant Singh (Julian Sherrier), the Sikh character in *633 Squadron* (Mirisch, 1964), for example, was not in the original novel and seems to have been added to help distinguish one masked and goggled face from another in the flying sequences. The few instances where the leading man hails from the Commonwealth or further afield include *Desperate Journey* (Warners, 1942), *633 Squadron* (Mirisch, 1964), *Mosquito Squadron* (Oakmont, 1969), *For the Moment* (Aaron, 1993) and *Map of the Human Heart* (Working Title, 1993), made for a foreign or international audience rather than a primarily for the British market.

13 Exceptions include *Death by Moonlight* (Galafilm, 1992) and *Map of the Human Heart* (Working Title, 1993), where junior Canadian aircrew are depicted as being manipulated by senior British RAF officers. Commonwealth, Empire and other nationals appear as follows. United States: *Desperate Journey* (Warners, 1942), *633 Squadron* (Mirisch, 1964), *Pathfinders* (Toledo, 1972-3); Poland: *Map of the Human Heart* (Working Title, 1993); West Indies: *Appointment in London* (Mayflower, 1953), *Dresden* (teamWorx, 2006); South Africa: *Angel of the Skies* (Welela, 2013); India: *A Matter of Life and Death* (Archers, 1946), *633 Squadron* (Mirisch, 1964); New Zealand: *Target for Tonight* (CFU, 1941), *Map of the Human Heart* (Working Title, 1993); Canada: *Target for Tonight* (CFU, 1941), *One of Our Aircraft Is Missing* (British National, 1942), *Target Berlin* (NFB, 1944), *Maximum Effort* (MoI, 1945), *Journey Together* (RAFFPU, 1946), *Mosquito Squadron* (Oakmont, 1969), *Pathfinders* (Toledo, 1972-3), *Death by Moonlight* (Galafilm, 1992), *For the Moment* (Aaron, 1993), *Map of the Human Heart* (Working Title, 1993), *Night Flight* (BBC, 2002); Australia: *Desperate Journey* (Warners, 1942), *Journey Together* (RAFFPU, 1946), *Appointment in London* (Mayflower, 1953), *The Dam Busters* (ABPC, 1955), *633 Squadron* (Mirisch, 1964), *Pathfinders* (Toledo, 1972-3), *For the Moment* (Aaron, 1993).

14 Northern accents are on display in *Target for Tonight* (CFU, 1941), *One of Our Aircraft Is Missing* (British National, 1942), *A Family at War* (Granada, 1970-2), *Pathfinders* (Toledo, 1972-3) and *Night Flight* (BBC, 2002). Scottish accents are heard in *Target for Tonight* (CFU, 1941), *Journey Together* (RAFFPU, 1946) and *Pathfinders* (Toledo, 1972-3), while Welshmen flyers speak in *One of Our Aircraft Is Missing* (British National, 1942), *Colditz* (BBC, 1972-4) and *Pathfinders* (Toledo, 1972-3), the latter also briefly depicting the single Irish airmen.

15 The three cases where the skipper is depicted as an NCO - albeit of upper-middle-class origin - are *Journey Together* (RAFFPU, 1946), 'One of Ours', *A Family at War* (Granada, 1970-2), tx. 14 July 1970 and *Night Flight* (BBC, 2002).

16 *Night Flight* (BBC, 2002) is a partial exception to the professional unity motif. Working-class British NCO aircrew were common in the wartime films but thereafter appeared only, and in passing, in *Pathfinders* (Warboys, 1972) and, much more substantially, in the character of Vic Green (Edward Woodward/Chris Lennard) in *Night Flight* (BBC, 2002). Exceptions to the rule concerning regional characters being NCOs include second pilot Tom Earnshaw (Eric Portman) in *One of Our Aircraft Is Missing* (British National, 1942) and navigator Hoppy Hopkinson (Angus Lennie) in *633 Squadron* (Mirisch, 1964). Navigator/bomb aimer David Ashton (Colin

Campbell), at least nominally a lower-middle-class Liverpudlian, starts as an NCO but by the latter war years has won a commission.

17 The emotional burdens of squadron command are prominently on display in *Appointment in London* (Mayflower, 1953), *633 Squadron* (Mirisch, 1964) and *Mosquito Squadron* (Oakmont, 1969). Fear and trauma of different kinds feature in various subsequent television plays and series, including 'One of Ours', 'A Hero's Welcome', 'Breaking Point', 'The Lost Ones', *A Family at War* (Granada, 1970–72), tx. 14 July 1970, 30 December 1970, tx. 29 December 1971, tx. 22 December 1971; 'Missing, Presumed Dead', *Colditz* (BBC, 1972–4), tx. 26 October 1972; 'Return Flight', *Dead of Night* (BBC, 1972), tx.12 November 1972; 'Sitting Ducks', 'In the Face of the Enemy', *Pathfinders* (Toledo, 1972), tx. 15 November 1972, 25 January 1973; *Death by Moonlight* (Galafilm, 1992); *Night Flight* (BBC, 2002); *The Haunted Airman* (BBC, 2006).

18 Notable exceptions include *The Haunted Airman* (BBC, 2006), *Map of the Human Heart* (Working Title, 1993), *Death by Moonlight* (Galafilm, 1992) and the *Pathfinders* (Warboys, 1972) episode 'Codename Gomorrah', tx. 13 December 1972.

19 As explained in Chapter 5, the generally sympathetic portrait contained in *Bomber Harris* (BBC, 1989) was screened while the much more damning *Fireraiser* (Barefoot, 1988) was sponsored but never broadcast by Channel 4, the equally venomous version on display in *Death by Moonlight* (Galafilm, 1992) came in for particular criticism when broadcast, and the slightly more nuanced depiction in *Dresden* (teamWorx, 2006), like the film as a whole, pretty much ignored in the Anglosphere beyond commentary on the problems the Germans themselves were having with a love story set amidst the destruction of the city.

20 Prime post-war examples include *The Dam Busters* (ABPC, 1955), *633 Squadron* (Mirisch, 1964) and *Mosquito Squadron* (Oakmont, 1969). Wartime films such as *Target for Tonight* (CFU, 1941), *The Big Blockade* (Ealing, 1942) and *One of Our Aircraft Is Missing* (British National, 1942) had also depicted precision targeting.

21 As literary scholar Petra Rau noted, audiences are 'are not encouraged to think at all of what these men do night after night on their missions, only of how perilous these missions are'. Petra Rau, ' "Knowledge of the Working of Bombs": The Strategic Air Offensive in Rhetoric and Fiction', in *Long Shadows: The Second World War in British Fiction and Film*, ed. Petra Rau (Evanston, IL: Northwestern University Press, 2016), 216.

22 The furore generated by *Death by Moonlight* (Galafilm, 1992) far exceeded what the McKennas had bargained for, while *Pathfinders* was generally dismissed by the critics as unacceptably retrograde in approach.

23 This may explain why, for example, the retrospective public popularity of the straightforward *The Dam Busters* (ABPC, 1955) as against the rather more ambiguous *Appointment in London* (Mayflower, 1953). See Mark Connelly, *Reaching for the Stars: A New History of Bomber Command in World War II* (I.B. Tauris: London, 2001), 144–7.

24 See e.g. Paul Chapman, Fur flies over racist name of Gibson's dog, *Telegraph*, 6 May 2009, accessed 4 April 2018, https://www.telegraph.co.uk/culture/film/5281875/Fur-flies-over-racist-name-of-Dambusters-dog.html; Caroline Bressey, 'It's Only Political Correctness – Race and Racism in British History', in *New Geographies in Race and Racism*, ed. Claire Dwyer and Caroline Bressey (London: Ashgate, 2008), 29–38; James Holland, *Dam Busters* (London: Bantam, 2012), xi. Late in 2018 Peter Jackson

and Christian Rivers were once again promising a remake in the not-to-distant future, possibly in grittier form (see Clarisse Loughrey, Peter Jackson says his *Dam Busters* remake will tell 'the real story', 29 November 2018, *Independent*, accessed 3 March 2019, https://www.independent.co.uk/arts-entertainment/films/news/peter-jackson-dambusters-movie-remake-617-squadron-second-world-war-death-a8657516.html) and possibly in TV miniseries form (see Jack Shepherd, Peter Jackson's *The Dam Busters* remake could be a ten-part series, says director Christian Rivers, 14 December 2018, *Independent*, accessed 3 March 2019, https://www.independent.co.uk/arts-entertainment/tv/news/dambusters-tv-series-remake-peter-jackson-raf-bombing-christian-rivers-second-world-war-a8683316.html). On the aborted *Bomber* film project see Philip Aldrick, Banker Bob Wigley raises funds for film adaptation of Len Deighton's Bomber, 13 April 2010, *Telegraph*, accessed 4 April 2018, https://www.telegraph.co.uk/finance/newsbysector/banksandfinance/7582906/Banker-Bob-Wigley-raises-funds-for-film-adaption-of-Len-Deightons-Bomber.html. As a British historian recently commented, the ABPC film version of the dams raid remains one of those cinematic wartime narratives 'by which we define ourselves'. Charles Foster, *The Complete Dambusters: The 133 Men who Flew on the Dams Raid* (Stroud: History, 2018), 311.

25 About the IBBC, see the IBBC Experience, International Bomber Command Association Centre, accessed 6 April 2018, http://internationalbcc.co.uk/about-ibcc/, http://internationalbcc.co.uk/about-ibcc/the-ibcc-experience/. See also Steve Darlow, Mark Dodds, Dan Ellin, Sean Feast and Robert Owen, *Our Story, Your History: The International Bomber Command Centre* (Hitchin: Fighting High, 2018).

26 See e.g. Charlie Hall, Bomber Crew pits adorable airmen against Nazis, 31 October 2017, Polygon, accessed 6 April 2018, https://www.polygon.com/2017/8/31/16234366/bomber-crew-ftl-nintendo-release-date-platforms. The more conventional card-and-dice board game created by Lee Brimmcombe-Wood, *Bomber Command: The Night Raids 1943–1945*, marketed by GMT Games since 2012, also presents the campaign purely in terms of tactical skill, while Lancaster NX611 appears innocuously in the rather innocent *Doctor Who* Christmas special of 2011, 'The Doctor, the Widow and the Wardrobe'.

27 See Bomber Command, International Movie Database, accessed 6 April 2018, http://www.imdb.com. *Darkest Hour* (Perfect World/Working Title, 2017) and *Dunkirk* (Syncopy, 2017) were each a big success and seem to have prompted veteran British director Ridley Scott to announce a new film project backed by Twentieth Century-Fox on the Battle of Britain (see *Guardian*, 5 April 2017).

28 The budget of Tin Hat's *Lancaster Skies* (2019) was a miniscule £80,000. Lancaster Skies, accessed 7 August 2018, https://www.lancasterskies.com/. On selling costumes and props see Indiegogo, Our Shining Sword – Props and Costumes, Our Shining Sword Lancaster Models, accessed 6 April 2018, https://www.indiegogo.com/projects/our-shining-sword-props-and-costumes-film-war#/, https://www.indiegogo.com/projects/our-shining-sword-lancaster-models#. The end result was described in the *Guardian* as 'doggedly uncinematic and thinly stretched'. Cathy Clarke, Lancaster Skies review, 22 February 2019, accessed 3 March 2019, https://www.theguardian.com/film/2019/feb/22/lancaster-skies-review-callum-burn.

29 James Slack, Jason Groves, James Tapsfield, Matt Dathan and Boris Johnson ridicule David Cameron's claim that Brexit could trigger war in Europe, 10 May 2016, Daily Mail.com, accessed 4 April 2018, https://www.dailymail.co.uk/news/article-3580485/David-Cameron-ramps-EU-referendum-struggle-warning-Brexit-lead-WAR-

continent.html. The original core of the United Kingdom Independence Party, as Nigel Farage recalled, was made up in part of Bomber Command types. See e.g. Decca Aitkenhead, Nigel Farage interview, 7 January 2013, *Guardian*, accessed 6 April 2018, https://www.theguardian.com/politics/2013/jan/07/nigel-farage-party-eccentrics-ukip. On the vandalizing of the Green Park memorial, see e.g. Bomber Command Memorial vandalism – update, 27 February 2017, Royal Air Force Benevolent Fund, accessed 7 April 2018, https://www.rafbf.org/news-and-blogs/bomber-command-memorial-vandalism---update. While the Second World War has been a setting for a number of television dramas in Britain and the Commonwealth over the past decade or so – see e.g. *The Halcyon* (Left Bank, 2017), *My Mother and Other Strangers* (BBC, 2016), *Home Fires* (ITV, 2015–16), *X Company* (Temple Street/Pioneer Stillking, 2015–17), *Bomb Girls* (Muse/Back Alley, 2012–13), *Land Girls* (BBC, 2009–11), *Foyle's War* (ITV, 2002–10) – it is striking that there have been no ongoing or new war-years productions at all in 2018. Even development of the widely anticipated HBO miniseries production *The Mighty Eighth* may have stalled. See Jeff Dinsmore, Is the Mighty Eighth Still a Mighty Go?, HBO Watch, accessed 6 April 2018, https://hbowatch.com/is-the-mighty-eighth-still-a-mighty-go/.

30 See e.g. Christopher Jory, *Lost in the Flames* (Carmarthen: McNidder and Grace, 2015), vi.
31 See S. P. MacKenzie, *The Battle of Britain on Screen: 'The Few' in British Film and Television Drama*, 2nd ed. (London: Bloomsbury, 2016).
32 See e.g. *Command Decision* (MGM, 1948), *Twelve O'Clock High* (Twentieth Century-Fox, 1949), *Bomber's Moon* (Playhouse 90 CBS, 1958), *The War Lover* (Columbia, 1962), *Twelve O'Clock High* (Twentieth Century-Fox Television/Quinn Martin, 1964–7), *The Thousand Plane Raid* (Oakmont, 1969), *Memphis Belle* (Enigma, 1990). UK television series featuring Eighth Air Force bomber crews in a domestic setting such as *Yanks Go Home* (Granada, 1976–77), *We'll Meet Again* (LWT, 1982), *Over Here* (BBC, 1996) and *My Mother and Other Strangers* (BBC, 2016) understandably have little to say about bombing accuracy. On the less than totally discriminate nature of the actual bombing campaign of the Eighth Air Force, see e.g. Ronald Schaffer, *Wings of Judgment: American Bombing in World War II* (New York: Oxford University Press, 1985), 60–106.
33 See e.g. Editorial No. 79662688, London, England, 18 May 1968, Actor Richard Todd meets with the real Dam Busters at a reunion held in the Warners Theatre where there was a special showing of *The Dam Busters* film in which Todd stars as Wing Commander Guy Gibson, VC, Getty Images, accessed 24 January 2018, https://www.gettyimages.ae/license/79662688; Peter Tomlinson remarks on John Thaw in *Bomber Harris* (BBC, 1989) in Henry Probert, *Bomber Harris: His Life and Times* (London: Greenhill, 2001), 151.
34 See e.g. Bomber Harris Trust, *A Battle for Truth: Canadian Aircrews Sue the CBC over Death by Moonlight: Bomber Command* (Agincourt, ON: Ramsay, 1994); *Bomber Command Association Newsletter*, 6 (1988), 1 and April 2002, 2.
35 On the number of veterans dwindling into the hundreds, see e.g. Robert Hardman, A fitting tribute, 17 January 2018, Daily Mail.com, accessed 7 April 2018, https://www.dailymail.co.uk/news/article-5281481/ROBERT-HARDMAN-joins-veterans-Bomber-Command-Centre.html. The prevalence of area bombing, and indeed the relative importance of Bomber Command during the war itself, has been either stoutly defended – see e.g. James Holland, *RAF 100: The Official Story* (London: Andre Deutsch, 2018) – or downplayed – see e.g. Michael Napier, *The Royal Air Force: A*

Centenary of Operations (Oxford: Osprey, 2018) – in books celebrating the one hundredth anniversary of the founding of the Royal Air Force.

36   It seems unlikely that the special showing of a newly restored version of the 1955 feature *The Dam Busters* – complete with a new poster prominently featuring a Union Jack – in the spring of 2018 in the Albert Hall and a hundred cinemas was not just a matter of marking the seventy-fifth anniversary of the raid. See THE DAM BUSTERS – newly restored in 4K, trailer, accessed 7 April 2018, YouTube, https://www.youtube.com; Paul Whitelam, Newly restored film *The Dam Busters* set for world premiere right here in Lincolnshire, 10 March 2018, Lincolnshire Live, accessed 7 April 2018, https://www.lincolnshirelive.co.uk/whats-on/film/newly-restored-film-dam-busters-1314610; Royal Albert Hall Hosts 75th Anniversary of Dams Raid, Channel 5, 5 News report, 27 February 2018, YouTube, accessed 7 April 2018, https://www.youtube.com. See also Daniel Todman, Drunk on Dunkirk spirit, the Brexiters are setting sail for a dangerous future, *Guardian*, 3 June 2017, accessed 26 September 2018, https://www.theguardian.com/commentisfree/2017/jun/03/dunkirk-spirit-brexiters-uk-britain-europe.

BIBLIOGRAPHY

BBC Written Archives Centre
R9/8/2, T6/293-294, T6/301, T6/310

CBC Archives

Canada at War; Production: Canada at War

Imperial War Museum

B6/1, History of the Royal Air Force Film Production Unit

Mass-Observation Archive

FR 15, 57

The National Archives

AIR 2, 14, 19, 20, 28, 29, 32, 41; CAB 102; FO 371; INF 1, 5, 6; T 162

Senate of Canada

Standing Committee on Social Affairs, Science and Technology, Proceedings of the Subcommittee on Veterans Affairs, 1992

Pressbooks (BFI Library)

Appointment in London; The Big Blockade; Bomber Command: Reaping the Whirlwind; Cage of Gold; The Dam Busters; Dambusters; Jericho (Behind These Walls); Journey Together; Mosquito Squadron; One of Our Aircraft Is Missing; Operation Chastise: The Dams Raid Relived; Pathfinders; The Purple Twilight; School for Secrets; 633 Squadron; Target for Tonight; The Valour and the Horror: Death by Moonlight; War in the Air

Taped Interviews

Michael Anderson (BFI); Paul Brickhill (IWM); George Brown (IWM); Douglas Fry (IWM); Joseph Aaron Friedman (TMP); Ernie Lummis (IWM); Robert L. Masters (UVic); Michael Powell (BFI); Richard Todd (IWM); Peter Ustinov (BFI); Harry Watt (BFI, IWM); Frederick Winterbotham (IWM)

Unpublished Personal Papers

John Alfred Chamberlain (RAFM); Arthur Harris (RAFM); Howard Hawks (BYU); Oliver Lyttelton (CAC); Brian McKenna (CUA); J. V. Hopgood (IWM); R. C. Sherriff (SHC); Barnes Wallis (SM)

Newspapers and Periodicals

The Aeroplane; *The Age* [Melbourne]; *Air Mail*; *Alberta Report*; *The Argus* [Melbourne]; *Auckland Star*; *Australian Women's Weekly*; *Bay of Plenty Beacon*; *Birmingham Evening Mail*; *Bomber Command Association Newsletter*; *Broadcast*; *Bradford Target*; *Calgary Herald*; *Campaign*; *Canadian Defence Quarterly*; *Canberra Herald*; *Canberra Times*; *Chicago Tribune*; *Christian Science Monitor*; *Chronicle Herald* [Halifax, NS]; *Commando*; *Daily Express*; *Daily Herald*; *Daily Mail*; *Daily Mirror*; *Daily News* [Perth, WA]; *Daily Post*; *Daily Sketch*; *Daily Telegraph*; *Daily Worker*; *Edmonton Journal*; *Evening News*; *Evening Post* [Wellington, NZ]; *Evening Standard*; *Films and Filming*; *Financial Times*; *Flarepath: Bomber Harris Trust*; *Gazette* [Montreal]; *Glasgow Herald*; *Globe and Mail*; *Hamilton Spectator*; *Irish Times*; *Illustrated London News*; *The Independent*; *Independent on Sunday*; *Index on Censorship*; *Irish Times*; *Jewish Chronicle*; *Kinematograph Weekly*; *Legion*; *Lincolnshire Echo*; *The Listener*; *London Magazine*; *London Review of Books*; *Los Angeles Times*; *MacLean's*; *Mail on Sunday*; *[Manchester] Guardian*; *Metro*; *Monthly Film Bulletin*; *More*; *Morning Star*; *Motion Picture Herald*; *National Post*; *Military Affairs*; *New Society*; *New Statesman*; *New York Times*; *News Chronicle*; *New Zealand Bomber Command Association Newsletter*; *New Zealand Herald*; *News* [Adelaide, SA]; *Northern Champion* [Taree, NSW]; *Observer*; *Ottawa Citizen*; *Peace Magazine*; *Picturegoer*; *Plays and Players*; *Press* [Christchurch, NZ]; *Punch*; *Quill & Quire*; *Radio Times*; *RAF Review*; *Royal Air Forces Quarterly*; *Reynolds News*; *RUSI Journal*; *Scotland on Sunday*; *The Sentinel* [Stoke-on-Trent]; *Sight and Sound*; *Sitrep: Newsmagazine of the Royal Canadian Military Institute*; *Spectator*; *South China Morning Post*; *The Stage*; *The Star*; *The Sun*; *Sun* [Sydney]; *Sunday Dispatch*; *Sunday Express*; *Sunday Graphic*; *Sunday Pictorial*; *Sunday Sun*; *Sunday Telegraph*; *Sunday Times*; *Sydney Morning Herald*; *Telegraph*; *The Times*; *Today*; *Today's Cinema*; *Toronto Star*; *Tribune*; *TV Times*; *West London Observer*; *Vancouver Sun*; *Venue* [Bristol]; *Washington Post*; *Western Mail* [Cardiff]; *Western Mail* [Perth, WA]; *Willesden Chronicle*; *Windsor Star*; *Winnipeg Free Press*; *Variety*; *What's On* [London]; *Yorkshire Post*.

Unpublished Theses

Assersohn, Fiona Jane. 'Propaganda and Policy: The Presentation of the Strategic Air Offensive in the British Mass Media 1939–45'. MA diss., University of Leeds, 1989.
Guy, Stephen. 'After Victory: Projections of the Second World War and Its Aftermath in British Films, 1946–1950'. PhD diss., University of London, 2002.
MacDonald, Monica. 'Producing the Public Past: Canadian History on CBC Television, 1952–2002'. PhD diss., York University, 2007.
O'Neill, Esther Margaret. 'British World War Two Films 1945–65: Catharsis or National Regeneration?' PhD diss., University of Central Lancashire, 2006.

Published Books

Abbott, John. *Cool TV of the 1960s: Three Shows That Changed the World*. Bloomington, IN: CreateSpace, 2015.

Addison, Paul and Jeremy Crang, eds. *Firestorm: The Bombing of Dresden, 1945.* London: Pimlico, 2006.
Addison, Paul and Jeremy Crang, eds. *Listening to Britain: Home Intelligence Reports on Britain's Finest Hour – May to September 1940.* London: Bodley Head, 2010.
Air Ministry. *Bomber Command: The Air Ministry Account of Bomber Command's Offensive against the Axis, September, 1939–July, 1941.* London: HMSO, 1941.
Air Ministry. *Bomber Command Continues: The Air Ministry Account of the Rising Offensive against Germany, July 1941–June 1942.* London: HMSO, 1942.
Aircrew Association, Vancouver Island Branch. *Aircrew Memories.* Victoria, BC: Victoria Publishing, 1999.
Aitkin, Ian. *Alberto Cavalcanti: Realism, Surrealism, and National Cinemas.* Trowbridge: Flicks, 2000.
Aldgate, Anthony and Jeffrey Richards. *Britain Can Take It: The British Cinema in the Second World War.* London: I.B. Tauris, 2007.
Allen, H. R. *The Legacy of Lord Trenchard.* London: Cassell, 1972.
Annakin, Ken. *So You Wanna Be a Director?* Sheffield: Tomahawk, 2001.
Archer, Henry and Edward Pine. *To Perish Never.* London: Cassell, 1954.
Armes, Roy. *A Critical History of the British Cinema.* London: Secker and Warburg, 1978.
Arnold-Foster, Mark. *The World at War.* London: Thames Methuen, 1981.
Ashley, Mark. *Flying Film Stars: The Directory of Aircraft in British World War Two Films.* Walton-on-Thames: Red Kite, 2014.
Attenborough, Richard and Diana Hawkins. *Entirely Up to You, Darling.* London: Hutchinson, 2008.
Babington, Bruce. *Launder and Gilliat.* Manchester: Manchester University Press, 2002.
Bailer, Uri. *The Shadow of the Bomber: The Fear of Air Attack and British Politics, 1932–1939.* London: Royal Historical Society, 1980.
Baker, Kathleen. *A Family at War.* St. Albans: Mayflower, 1970.
Baker, Phil. *The Devil Is a Gentleman: The Life and Times of Dennis Wheatley.* Sawtry: Dedalus, 2009.
Balcon, Michael. *Michael Balcon Presents . . . A Lifetime in Films.* London: Hutchinson, 1969.
Bangert, Alex. *The Nazi Past in Contemporary German Film: Viewing Experiences of Intimacy and Immersion.* Rochester, NY: Camden, 2014.
Barber, Sian. *The British Film Industry in the 1970s: Capital, Culture and Creativity.* Basingstoke: Palgrave, 2013.
Barr, Charles. *Ealing Studios*, 3rd edn. Berkeley: University of California Press, 1998.
Barris, Ted. *Behind the Glory.* Toronto: Macmillan, 1992.
Barris, Ted. *Dam Busters: Canadian Airmen and the Secret Raid against Nazi Germany.* Toronto: HarperCollins, 2018.
Bashow, David L. *No Prouder Place: Canadians and the Bomber Command Experience 1939–1945.* St. Catherines: Vanwell, 2006.
Bashow, David L. *Soldiers Blue: How Bomber Command and Area Bombing Helped Win the Second World War.* Kingston: Canadian Defence Academy Press, 2011.
Bates, H. E. *The World in Ripeness: An Autobiography, Volume Three.* London: Michael Joseph, 1972.
Beaton, Cecil. *Winged Squadrons.* London: Hutchinson, 1942.
Beck, Simon D. *The Aircraft-Spotter's Film and Television Companion.* Jefferson, NC: McFarland, 2016.

Beckett, Andy. *When the Lights Went Out: Britain in the Seventies*. London: Faber, 2009.
Benda-Beckman, Bas von. *German Historians and the Bombing of German Cities: The Contested Air War*. Amsterdam: Amsterdam University Press, 2015.
Bennett, Alan, Peter Cook, Jonathan Miller and Dudley Moore. *Beyond the Fringe*. New York: Random House, 1963.
Bennett, D. C. T. *Pathfinder: A War Autobiography*. London: Muller, 1958.
Bennet, Jill. *Godfrey: A Special Time Remembered*. London: Hodder and Stoughton, 1983.
Bennett, M. Todd. *One World, Big Screen: Hollywood, the Allies, and World War II*. Chapel Hill: University of North Carolina Press, 2012.
Bennett, Ralph. *Behind the Battle: Intelligence in the War with Germany, 1939–1945*. London: Pimlico, 1999.
Bercuson, David J. and S. F. Wise, eds. *The Valour and the Horror Revisited*. Montreal, QB-Kingston: McGill-Queen's University Press, 1994.
Biddle, Tami Davis. *Rhetoric and Reality in Air Warfare: The Evolution of British and American Ideas about Strategic Bombing, 1914–1945*. Princeton, NJ: Princeton University Press, 2002.
Bishop, Patrick. *Bomber Boys: Fighting Back 1940–1945*. London: Harper, 2007.
Black, Jeremy. *Rethinking World War II: The Conflict and Its Legacy*. London: Bloomsbury, 2015.
Bliss, Michael. *Writing History: A Professor's Life*. Toronto: Dundurn, 2011.
Bogarde, Dirk. *Snakes and Ladders*. London: Chatto and Windus, 1978.
Bomber Harris Trust. *A Battle for Truth: Canadian Aircrews Sue the CBC over Death by Moonlight: Bomber Command*. Agincourt: Ramsey, 1994.
Bond, Brian. *Britain's Two World Wars against Germany: Myth, Memory and the Distortions of Hindsight*. Cambridge: Cambridge University Press, 2014.
Bose, Mihir. *Michael Grade: Screening the Image*. London: Virgin, 1992.
Bourne, George. *I Flew with Braddock*. London: D. C. Thomson, 1959.
Bowman, Martin. *RAF Bomber Command: Reflections of War*, 5 vols. Barnsley: Pen and Sword Aviation, 2011–14.
Bowman, Martin W. *Scramble: Memories of the RAF in the Second World War*. Stroud: Tempus, 2006.
Bowyer, Chaz. *Bomber Barons*. London: Kimber, 1983.
Boyne, Walter J. *Clash of Wings: Air Power in World War II*. New York: Simon and Schuster, 1994.
Braine, John. *Room at the Top*. London: Eyre and Spottiswoode, 1957.
Brickhill, Paul. *The Dam Busters*. London: Evans, 1951.
British Bombing Survey Unit. *The Strategic Air War against Germany, 1939–1945*. London: Frank Cass, 1998.
Brooker, Will. *Star Wars*. London: BFI, 2009.
Brown, Maggie. *A Licence to Be Different: The Story of Channel 4*. London: BFI, 2007.
Bruhl, Marshall De. *Firestorm: Allied Airpower and the Destruction of Dresden*. New York: Random House, 2006.
Brunel, Adrian. *Nice Work: The Story of Thirty Years in British Film Production*. London: Forbes Robertson, 1949.
Buchanan, William [William Ray Buck]. *Pathfinder Squadron*. London: Sphere, 1972.
Buckley, John. *Air Power in the Age of Total War*. London: UCL Press, 1999.
Burgess, Anthony. *99 Novels: The Best in English since 1939: A Personal Choice*. New York: Summit, 1984.
Burleigh, Michael. *Moral Combat: A History of World War II*. London: Harper, 2010.

Butler, Margaret. *Film and Community in Britain and France: From* La Règle du Jeu *to* Room at the Top. London: I.B. Tauris, 2004.
Calder, Angus. *Disasters and Heroes: On War, Memory and Representation*. Cardiff: University of Wales Press, 2004.
Call, Steve. *Selling Air Power: Military Aviation and American Popular Culture after World War II*. College Station: Texas A&M University Press, 2009.
Callaghan, Richard. *Assigned! The Unofficial and Unauthorised Guide to* Sapphire & Steel. Prestatyn: Telos, 2009.
Campbell, James. *Maximum Effort*. London: Alison and Busby, 1975.
Campbell, James. *The Bombing of Nuremberg*. London: Alison and Busby, 1973.
Campbell, Ralph. *We Flew by Moonlight*. Orillia: Kerry Hill, 1995.
Campion, Garry. *The Battle of Britain, 1945–1965: The Air Ministry and the Few*. Basingstoke: Palgrave, 2015.
Campion, Garry. *The Good Fight: Battle of Britain Propaganda and the Few*. Basingstoke: Palgrave, 2009.
Carpenter, Humphrey. *That Was Satire That Was*. London: Gollancz, 2000.
Chadderton, H. Clifford. *The Morality of Bomber Command in World War II*. Ottawa: War Amps, 1992.
Challis, Christopher. *Are They Really So Awful? A Cameraman's Chronicles*. London: Janus, 1995.
Chapman, James. *The British at War: Cinema, State and Propaganda, 1939–1945*. London: I.B. Tauris, 1998.
Chapman, James. *British Comics: A Cultural History*. London: Reaktion, 2011.
Chapman, James. *A New History of British Documentary*. Basingstoke: Palgrave, 2015.
Chapman, James. *Past and Present: National Identity and the British Historical Film*. London: I.B. Tauris, 2005.
Chapman, James. *War and Film*. London: Reaktion, 2008.
Chapman, James and Nicholas J. Cull. *Projecting Tomorrow: Science Fiction and Popular Cinema*. London: I.B. Tauris, 2013.
Charlwood, Don. *No Moon Tonight*. Manchester: Crécy, 2000.
Christie, Ian. *Arrows of Desire: The Films of Michael Powell and Emeric Pressburger*. London: Waterstone, 1985.
Christie, Ian. *A Matter of Life and Death*. London: BFI, 2000.
Christie, Ian, ed. *Powell, Pressburger and Others*. London: BFI, 1978.
Clarke, James. *War Films*. London: Virgin, 2006.
Clarke, Peter. *The Cripps Version: The Life of Sir Stafford Cripps, 1889–1952*. London: Allen Lane, 2002.
Cole, George with Brian Hawkins. *The World Was My Lobster: My Autobiography*. London: John Blake, 2013.
Collins, L. John. *Faith under Fire*. London: Leslie Frewin, 1966.
Connelly, Mark. *Reaching for the Stars: A History of Bomber Command*. London: I.B. Tauris, 2014.
Connelly, Mark. *Reaching for the Stars: A New History of Bomber Command in World War II*. London: I.B. Tauris, 2001.
Connelly, Mark. *We Can Take It! Britain and the Memory of the Second World War*. Harlow: Pearson Longman, 2004.
Cook, Tim. *Clios's Warriors: Canadian Historians and the Writing of the World Wars*. Vancouver: UBC Press, 2006.
Cooke, Lez. *British Television Drama: A History*, 2nd edn. London: Palgrave, 2015.

Cooke, Paul and Marc Silberman, eds. *Screening War: Perspective on German Suffering*. Rochester, NY: Camden, 2010.

Copp, Terry with Richard Nielsen. *No Price Too High: Canadians and the Second World War*. Toronto: McGraw-Hill Ryerson, 1996.

Cotter, Jarrod. *The Battle of Britain Memorial Flight: 50 Years of Flying*. Barnsley: Pen and Sword Aviation, 2007.

Coultass, Clive. *Images for Battle: British Film and the Second World War, 1939–1945*. Newark, NJ: University of Delaware Press, 1989.

Crawford, Keith A. and Stuart J. Foster. *War, Nation, Memory: International Perspectives on World War in School History Textbooks*. Charlotte, NC: Information Age, 2008.

Crew, David F. *Bodies and Ruins: Imagining the Bombing of Germany, 1945 to the Present*. Ann Arbor: University of Michigan Press, 2017.

Cripps, Stafford. *Towards Christian Democracy*. New York: Philosophical Library, 1946.

Cull, Nicholas John. *Selling War: The British Propaganda Campaign against American 'Neutrality' in World War II*. New York: Oxford University Press, 1995.

Currie, Jack. *Lancaster Target: The Story of a Crew Who Flew from Wickenby*. London: Goodhall, 1981.

Curtis, Des. *A Most Secret Squadron: The First Full Story of 618 Squadron*. London: Grub Street, 2009.

Custen, George F. *Twentieth Century's Fox: Darryl F. Zanuck and the Culture of Hollywood*. New York: Basic Books, 1997.

Cutter, Jarrod. *The Battle of Britain Memorial Flight: 50 Years of Flying*. Barnsley: Pen and Sword Aviation, 2007.

Dando-Collins, Stephen. *The Hero Maker: A Biography of Paul Brickhill*. North Sydney, NSW: Vintage, 2016.

Danson, Barney with Curtis Fahey. *Not Bad for a Sergeant: The Memoirs of Barney Danson*. Toronto: Dundurn, 2002.

Darlow, Steve, Mark Dodds, Sean Feast and Robert Owen. *Our Story, Your History: The International Bomber Command Centre*. Hitchin: Fighting High, 2018.

Dean, Maurice. *The Royal Air Force in Two World Wars*. London: Cassell, 1979.

Dear, Patrick. *Culture in Camouflage: War, Empire, and Modern British Literature*. Oxford: Oxford University Press, 2009.

Deighton, Len. *Bomber*. London: Jonathan Cape, 1970.

Delderfield, R. F. *For My Own Amusement*. New York: Simon and Schuster, 1972.

Delderfield, R. F. *Stop at a Winner*. London: Hodder and Stoughton, 1961.

Delderfield, R. F. *Worm's Eye View*. London: Samuel French, 1948.

Derry, Martin and Neil Robinson. *Avro Lancaster 1945–1965: In Military Service*. Barnsley: Pen and Sword Aviation, 2014.

Dickens, Gerald. *Bombing and Strategy: The Fallacy of Total War*. London: Sampson Low, Marston, 1947.

Divine, David. *The Blunted Sword*. London: Hutchinson, 1964.

Docherty, Thomas G. *No. 7 Bomber Squadron in World War II*. Barnsley: Pen and Sword Aviation, 2007.

Downing, Taylor. *The World at War*. London: BFI Palgrave, 2012.

Duffin, Allan T. and Paul Matheis. *The 12 O'Clock High Logbook: The Unofficial History of the Novel, Motion Picture, and TV Series*. Boalsburg, PA: BearManor, 2005.

Dunmore, Spencer. *Bomb Run*. London: Davies, 1971.

Dunmore, Spencer and William Carter. *Reap the Whirlwind: The Untold Story of 6 Group, Canada's Bomber Force of World War II*. Toronto: McClelland and Stewart, 1991.

Edwards, Ralph. *In the Thick of It: The Autobiography of a Bomber Pilot.* Upton: Images, 1994.
Evans, Richard J. *Lying about Hitler: History, Holocaust, and the David Irving Trial.* New York: Basic, 2001.
Falconer, Jonathan. *The Bomber Command Handbook.* Stroud: Sutton, 1998.
Falconer, Jonathan. *Filming the Dam Busters.* Stroud: Sutton, 2005.
Falconer, Jonathan. *RAF Bomber Command in Fact, Film and Fiction.* Stroud: Sutton, 1996.
Farmer, James H. *Celluloid Wings: The Impact of Movies on Aviation.* Blue Ridge Summit, PA: Tab, 1984.
Feast, Sean. *Thunder Bird in Bomber Command: The Wartime Letters and Story of Lionel Anderson, the Man Who Inspired a Legend.* Hitchin: Fighting High, 2015.
Fetter, Jonathan. *Quinn Martin, Producer: A Behind-the-Scenes History of QM Productions and Its Founder.* Jefferson, NC: McFarland, 2003.
Finch, John, ed. *Granada Television: The First Generation.* Manchester: Manchester University Press, 2003.
Fishman, Jack. *And the Walls Came Tumbling Down.* London: Macmillan, 1983.
Fopp, Michael, ed. *High Flyers: 30 Reminiscences to Celebrate the 75th Anniversary of the Royal Air Force.* London: Greenhill/RAF Museum, 1993.
Forman, Denis. *Persona Granada: Some Memories of Sidney Bernstein and the Early Days of Independent Television.* London: Deutsch, 1997.
Foster, Charles. *The Complete Dambusters: The 133 Men who Flew on the Dams Raid.* Stroud: History, 2018.
Fox, Jo. *Film Propaganda in Britain and Nazi Germany: World War II Cinema.* Oxford: Berg, 2007.
Francis, Martin. *The Flyer: British Culture and the Royal Air Force 1939–1945.* Oxford: Oxford University Press, 2008.
Frankland, Noble. *Bomber Offensive: The Devastation of Europe.* New York: Ballantine, 1969/London: Macdonald, 1970.
Frankland, Noble. *History at War: The Campaigns of an Historian.* London: DLM, 1998.
Frayling, Christopher. *Things to Come.* London: BFI, 1995.
Freeman, Roger. *The British Airman.* London: Arms and Armour, 1989.
Freeze, Di. *In the Cockpit with Cliff Robertson.* Denver, CO: Freeze Time Media, 2013.
French, John. *Robert Shaw: The Price of Success.* London: Nick Hern, 1993.
Friedrich, Jörg. *The Fire: The Bombing of Germany, 1940–1945.* Translated by Allison Brown. New York: Columbia University Press, 2006.
Frost, David. *An Autobiography.* London: HarperCollins, 1993.
Fry, Stephen. *The Fry Chronicles.* London: Michael Joseph, 2010.
Garrett, Stephen A. *Ethics and Airpower in World War II.* New York: St. Martin's, 1993.
Geraghty, Christine. *British Cinema in the Fifties: Gender, Genre, and the 'New Look'.* London: Routledge, 2000.
Gibb, Robin, Jim Dooley, Gordon Rayner, Steve Darlow and Sean Feast. *The Bomber Command Memorial: We Will Remember Them.* Hitchin: Fighting High, 2012.
Gibson, Guy. *Enemy Coast Ahead.* London: Michael Joseph, 1946.
Gillmor, Don, Achille Michaud and Pierre Sturgeon. *Canada: A People's History: Volume Two.* Toronto: McClelland and Stewart, 2001.
Glancy, Mark. *Hollywood and the Americanization of Britain: From the 1920s to the Present.* London: I.B. Tauris, 2014.
Glancy, Mark. *When Hollywood Loved Britain: The Hollywood 'British' Film, 1939–45.* Manchester: Manchester University Press, 1999.

Gollancz, Victor. *In Darkest Germany*. London: Gollancz, 1947.
Gough-Yates, Kevin. *Michael Powell in Collaboration with Emeric Pressburger*. London: Faber and Faber, 1971.
Grade, Michael. *It Seemed Like a Good Idea at the Time*. London: Macmillan, 1999.
Granatstein, J. L. *Who Killed Canadian History?* Revised and expanded edn. Toronto: Harper Perennial, 2007.
Gray, Peter. *The Leadership, Direction and Legitimacy of the RAF Bomber Offensive from Inception to 1945*. London: Continuum, 2012.
Grayling, A. C. *Among the Dead Cities: Was the Allied Bombing of Civilians in WWII a Necessity or a Crime?* London: Bloomsbury, 2006.
Greene Bennett, Linda. *My Father's Voice: The Biography of Lorne Greene*. New York: iUniverse, 2004.
Greenhous, Brereton, Stephen J. Harris, William C. Johnston and William G. P. Rawling. *The Crucible of War, 1939–1945: The Official History of the Royal Canadian Air Force, Volume III*. Toronto: University of Toronto Press, 1994.
Grierson, Bill. *We Band of Brothers*. Hailsham: J&KH, 1997.
Groot, Jerome de. *Consuming History: Historians and Heritage in Contemporary Popular Culture*. London: Routledge, 2009.
Haapamaki, Michele. *The Coming of the Aerial War: Culture and the Fear of Airborne Attack in Inter-War Britain*. London: I.B. Tauris, 2014.
Halliwell, Leslie. *Seats in All Parts: Half a Lifetime at the Movies*. London: Granada, 1985.
Hampton, James. *Selected for Aircrew: Bomber Command and the Second World War*. Walton-on-Thames: Air Research, 1993.
Hansen, Randall. *Fire and Fury: The Allied Bombing of Germany, 1942–45*. Toronto: Doubleday, 2008.
Hanson, Stuart. *From Silent Screen to Multi-Screen: A History of Cinema Exhibition in Britain since 1896*. Manchester: Manchester University Press, 2007.
Harder, Kenneth A. *The Key to Survival: Bomber Command in World War II*. Maidstone: Mann, 2006.
Harding, John. *The Dancin' Navigator*. Guelph: Asterisk, 1988.
Harris, Arthur. *Bomber Offensive*. London: Collins, 1947.
Hastings, Max. *Bomber Command*. London: Michael Joseph, 1979.
Havardi, Jeremy. *Projecting Britain at War: The National Character in British World War II Films*. Jefferson, NC: McFarland, 2014.
Hennessy, Peter. *Having It So Good: Britain in the Fifties*. London: Allen Lane, 2006.
Hennessy, Peter. *Never Again: Britain, 1945–51*. London: Cape, 1992.
Hetherington, William. *Swimming against the Tide: The Peace Pledge Union Story, 1934–2009*. London: Peace Pledge Union, 2009.
Hewer, Howard. *In for a Penny, In for a Pound: The Adventures and Misadventures of a Wireless Operator in Bomber Command*. Toronto: Stoddart, 2000.
Higson, Andrew. *Waving the Flag: Constructing a National Cinema in Britain*. Oxford: Clarendon, 1995.
Hildred, Stafford and Tim Ewbank. *John Thaw: The Biography*. London: Deutsch, 1998.
Hobson, Dorothy. *Channel 4: The Early Years and the Jeremy Isaacs Legacy*. London: I.B. Tauris, 2008.
Hochhuth, Rolf. *Soldiers: An Obituary for Geneva*. Translated by Robert David MacDonald. London: Andre Deutsch, 1968.
Hodgson, David. *Letters from a Bomber Pilot*. London: Times Metheun, 1985.

Holland, James. *Dam Busters: The Race to Smash the German Dams, 1943*. London: Bantam, 2012.
Holland, James. *RAF 100: The Official Story, 1918–2018*. London: Deutsch, 2018.
Holman, Brett. *The Next War in the Air: Britain's Fear of the Bomber, 1908–1941*. Farnham: Ashgate, 2014.
Holt, Paul. *Target for Tonight: The Book of the Famous Film Target for Tonight: The Record in Text and Pictures of a Bombing Raid on Germany*. London: Hutchinson, 1941.
Hudson, Kate. *CND – Now More Than Ever: The Story of a Peace Movement*. London: Vision, 2005.
Hunt, Albert. *Hopes for Great Happenings: Alternatives in Education and Theatre*. London: Eyre Methuen, 1976.
Irving, David. *The Destruction of Dresden*. London: Kimber, 1963.
Isaacs, Jeremy. *Look Me in the Eye: A Life in Television*. London: Little, Brown, 2006.
Isaacs, Jeremy. *Storm over 4: A Personal Account*. London: Weidenfeld and Nicolson, 1989.
Iveson, Tony and Brian Milton. *Lancaster: The Biography*. London: Deutsch, 2009.
Jackson, Bill. *Three Stripes and Four Brownings*. North Battleford, SK: Turner-Warwick, 1990.
Jacobs, Peter. *Stay the Distance: The Life and Times of Marshal of the Royal Air Force Sir Michael Beetham*. London: Frontline, 2011.
Jeffreys, Kevin. *Retreat from the New Jerusalem: British Politics, 1951–64*. New York: St. Martin's, 1997.
Joel, Tony. *The Dresden Firebombing: Memory and the Politics of Commemorative Destruction*. London: I.B. Tauris, 2013.
Johnson, Brian and H. I. Cozens. *Bombers: The Weapon of Total War*. London: Thames Methuen, 1984.
Johnson, George 'Johnny'. *The Last British Dambuster*. London: Ebury, 2014.
Johnson, Peter. *The Withered Garland: Reflections and Doubts of a Bomber*. London: New European, 1995.
Johnston, John and Nick Carter. *Strong by Night, 'Fortis Nocte': History and Memories of No. 149 (East India) Squadron, 1918/19–1937/56*. Tunbridge Wells: Air-Britain, 2002.
Jones, W. E. *Bomber Intelligence*. Leicester: Midland Counties, 1983.
Jory, Christopher. *Lost in the Flames: A World War II RAF Bomber Command Novel*. Carmathan: McNidder and Grace, 2015.
Kennedy, A. L. *Day*. London: Cape, 2007.
Kennett, Lee. *A History of Strategic Bombing*. New York: Scribner's, 1982.
Kent, Arthur. *Risk and Redemption: Surviving the Network News Wars*. Toronto: Viking, 1996.
Kitcher, Peter W. *The Valour and the Horror: The True Story*. Belleville: Epic, 2005.
Knell, Hermann. *To Destroy a City: Strategic Bombing and Its Human Consequences in World War II*. Cambridge, MA: Da Capo, 2003.
Kynaston, David. *Austerity Britain, 1945–51*. London: Bloomsbury, 2007.
Kynaston, David. *Family Britain, 1951–1957*. New York: Walker, 2009.
Lambert, Max. *Night after Night: New Zealanders in Bomber Command*. Auckland: HarperCollins, 2005.
Langley, Roger. *Patrick McGoohan: Danger Man or Prisoner?* Sheffield: Tomahawk, 2007.
Lanzon, Rémi Fournier. *French Comedy on Screen: A Cinematic History*. Basingstoke: Palgrave, 2014.

Largent, Will. *Wings over Florida: Memories of World War II British Air Cadets*. West Lafayette, IN: Purdue University Press, 2000.
Lejeune, C. A. *Chestnuts in Her Lap, 1936-1946*. London: Phoenix, 1947.
Levine, Alan J. *The Strategic Bombing of Germany, 1940-1945*. Westport, CT: Praeger, 1992.
Liddell Hart, Basil. *History of the Second World War*. London: Cassell, 1970.
Lindqvist, Sven. *A History of Bombing*. London: Granta, 2001.
Longmate, Norman. *The Bombers: The RAF Offensive against Germany, 1939-1945*. London: Hutchinson, 1983.
Lowe, Keith. *Inferno: The Devastation of Hamburg, 1943*. London: Viking, 2007.
Macdonald, Kevin. *Emeric Pressburger: The Life and Death of a Screenwriter*. London: Faber and Faber, 1994.
Mahaddie, T. G. *Hamish: The Memoirs of Group Captain T. G. Mahaddie*. London: Ian Allan, 1989.
Margerison, Russell. *Boys at War*. Bolton: Ross Anderson, 1986.
Markusen, Eric and David Kopf. *The Holocaust and Strategic Bombing: Genocide and Total War in the Twentieth Century*. Boulder: Westview, 1995.
Martin, B. W. *War Memoirs of an Engineer Officer in Bomber Command*. Hailsham: J&KH, 1998.
Matthews, Rupert. *RAF Bomber Command at War*. London: Hale, 2009.
Mayhill, Ron. *Bombs on Target: A Compelling Eye-Witness Account of Bomber Command Operations*. Sparkford: Patrick Stephens, 1991.
McCaffery, Dan. *Battlefields in the Air: Canadians in the Allied Bomber Command*. Toronto: James Lorimer, 1995.
McFarlane, Brian. *An Autobiography of British Cinema*. London: Methuen, 1997.
McLaine, Ian. *Ministry of Morale: Home Front Morale and the Ministry of Information*. London: Allen and Unwin, 1979.
Mendlicott, William Norton. *The Economic Blockade*, Vol. 2. London: HMSO, 1959.
Messenger, Charles. *Bomber Harris and the Strategic Bombing Offensive*. London: Arms and Armour, 1984.
Middlebrook, Martin. *The Battle of Hamburg: Allied Bomber Forces against a German City in 1943*. London: Allen Lane, 1980.
Middlebrook, Martin. *The Berlin Raids: R.A.F. Bomber Command Winter 1943-44*. London: Viking, 1988.
Middlebrook, Martin. *The Nuremberg Raid*. London: Allen Lane, 1973.
Millar, Ronald. *Frieda: A New Play in Three Acts*. London: English Theatre Guild, 1947.
Mills, John. *Up in the Clouds, Gentlemen Please*. New Haven, CT: Ticknor and Fields, 1981.
Mirisch, Walter. *I Thought We Were Making Movies, Not History*. Madison: University of Wisconsin Press, 2008.
Mitchell, John. *Flickering Shadows: A Lifetime in Film*. Malvern Wells: Martin and Redman, 1997.
Moore, Andrew. *Powell & Pressburger: A Cinema of Magic Spaces*. London: I.B. Tauris, 2005.
Moore, Clayton. *Lancaster Valour: The Valour and the Truth*. Warrington: Compaid, 1995.
Moran, Joe. *Armchair Nation: An Intimate History of Britain in Front of the TV*. London: Profile, 2013.

Morgan, Guy. *Red Roses Every Night: An Account of London's Cinemas under Fire.* London: Quality, 1948.
Morgan, Janet. *The Backbench Diaries of Richard Crossman.* London: Hamish Hamilton and Jonathan Cape, 1985.
Morris, Richard. *Cheshire: The Biography of Leonard Cheshire.* London: Viking, 2000.
Morris, Richard. *Guy Gibson.* London: Viking, 1994.
Morse, Barry with Robert E. Wood and Anthony Wynn. *Pulling Faces, Making Noise: A Life on Stage, Screen & Radio.* Bloomington, IN: iUniverse, 2004.
Morton, Desmond. *A Military History of Canada.* Edmonton: Hurtig, 1985.
Mosley, Leonard. *The Battle of Britain: The Making of a Film.* London: Weidenfeld and Nicolson, 1969.
Muirhead, Campbell. *Diary of a Bomb Aimer: Training in America and Flying with 12 Squadron in WWII*, Philip Swan, ed. Barnsley: Pen and Sword Aviation, 2009.
Murphy, Robert. *British Cinema and the Second World War.* London: Continuum, 2000.
Murray, Williamson. *War in the Air, 1914–45.* London: Cassell, 1999.
Musgrove, Gordon. *Operation Gomorrah: The Hamburg Firestorm Raids.* London: Jane's, 1981.
Napier, Michael. *The Royal Air Force: A Centenary of Operations.* Oxford: Osprey, 2018.
Nash, Knowlton. *The Microphone Wars: A History of Triumph and Betrayal at the CBC.* Toronto: McClelland and Stewart, 1994.
Neillands, Robin. *The Bomber War: Arthur Harris and the Allied Bomber Offensive, 1939–1945.* London: John Murray, 2001.
Nelson, Hank. *Chased by the Sun: Courageous Australians in Bomber Command in World War II.* Sydney: ABC, 2002.
Nichol, John. *After the Flood: What the Dambusters Did Next.* London: Collins, 2015.
Nowra, Louis. *Shooting the Moon: A Memoir.* Sydney: Picador, 2004.
Oakley, C. A. *Where We Came In: Seventy Years of the British Film Industry.* London: Allen and Unwin, 1964.
O'Brien, Margaret and Alen Eyles, eds. *Enter the Dream-House: Memories of Cinemas in South London from the Twenties to the Sixties.* London: MOMI, 1993.
Ollis, Ray. *101 Nights.* London: Cassell, 1957.
Ottaway, Susan. *Guy Gibson VC: The Glorious Dambuster.* Hampshire: Speedman, 1994.
Overy, R. J. *The Air War 1939–1945.* London: Europa, 1980.
Overy, R. J. *Bomber Command, 1939–45.* London: HarperCollins, 1997.
Overy, Richard. *The Bombing War: Europe 1939–1945.* London: Allen Lane, 2013.
Page, Bette, ed. *Mynarski's Lanc: The Story of Two Famous Canadian Lancaster Bombers KB726 & FM213.* Erin: Boston Mills, 1989.
Paris, Michael. *From the Wright Brothers to Top Gun: Aviation, Nationalism, and Popular Cinema.* Manchester: Manchester University Press, 1995.
Paris, Michael, ed. *Repicturing the Second World War: Representations in Film and Television.* Basingstoke: Palgrave, 2007.
Paris, Michael. *Warrior Nation: Images of War in British Popular Culture, 1850–2000.* London: Reaktion, 2000.
Parker, R. A. C. *The Second World War: A Short History.* Oxford: Oxford University Press, 1997.
Parkinson, David, ed. *The Graham Greene Film Reader: Mornings in the Dark.* Manchester: Carcanet, 1993.
Parry, Simon W. *Spitfire Hunters.* Walton-on-Thames: Red Kite, 2010.
Peden, Murray. *A Thousand Shall Fall: A Pilot for 214.* Stittsville: Canada's Wings, 1979.

Pelly-Fry, James. *Heavenly Days: Recollections of a Contented Airman.* Manchester: Crécy, 1994.
Pendo, Stephen. *Aviation in the Cinema.* Metuchen, NJ: Scarecrow, 1985.
Phillips, Humphrey with Sean Feast. *A Thousand and One: A Flight Engineer Leader's War from the Thousand Bomber Raids to the Battle of Berlin.* Leeds: Bomber Command Books, 2017.
Porter, Bob. *The Long Return.* Burnaby, BC: Porter, 1997.
Powell, Jonathan. *A Family at War: To the Turn of the Tide.* St. Albans: Mayflower, 1971.
Powell, Michael. *A Life in Movies: An Autobiography.* London: Heinemann, 1986.
Powell, Michael. *One of Our Aircraft Is Missing.* London: HMSO, 1942.
Primoratz, Igor, ed. *Terror from the Sky: The Bombing of German Cities in World War II.* Oxford: Berghahn, 2010.
Probert, Henry. *Bomber Harris: His Life and Times: The Biography of Marshal of the Royal Air Force Sir Arthur Harris, Wartime Chief of Bomber Command.* Toronto: Stoddart, 2001.
Quinlan, Thomas G. *Corkscrew to Safety: A Tail-Gunner's Tour with 103 Squadron RAF, 1944/5.* Bognor Regis: Woodfield, 2011.
Ramsden, John. *The Age of Churchill and Eden, 1940–1957.* London: Longman, 1995.
Ramsden, John. *The Dam Busters.* London: I.B. Tauris, 2003.
Rattigan, Neil. *This Is England: British Film and the People's War, 1939–1945.* Madison, NJ: Farleigh Dickinson University Press, 2001.
Read, Simon. *The Killing Skies: RAF Bomber Command at War.* Stroud: Spellmount, 2006.
Redgrave, Corin. *Michael Redgrave: My Father.* London: Richard Cohen, 1995.
Redgrave, Michael. *In My Mind's Eye: An Autobiography.* London: Weidenfeld and Nicolson, 1983.
Rees, Peter. *Lancaster Men: Aussie Heroes in Bomber Command.* Crows Nest, NSW: Allen and Unwin, 2013.
Reynolds, David. *In Command of History: Churchill Fighting and Writing the Second World War.* London: Allen Lane, 2004.
Reynolds, Quentin. *By Quentin Reynolds.* London: McGraw-Hill, 1963.
Rice, Christina. *Ann Dvorak: Hollywood's Forgotten Rebel.* Lexington: University of Kentucky Press, 2013.
Richards, Denis. *The Hardest Victory: RAF Bomber Command in the Second World War.* London: Hodder and Stoughton, 1995.
Richards, Denis. *It Might Have Been Worse: Recollections, 1941–1996.* London: Smithson Albright, 1998.
Richards, Denis and Hilary St. George Saunders. *Royal Air Force, 1939–1945*, 3 vols. London: HMSO, 1953–4.
Richards, Jeffrey. *Films and British National Identity: From Dickens to Dad's Army.* Manchester: Manchester University Press, 1997.
Richards, Jeffrey and Dorothy Sheridan. *Mass-Observation at the Movies.* London: Routledge and Kegan Paul, 1987.
Richardson, Tony. *The Long-Distance Runner: An Autobiography.* New York: Morrow, 1993.
Rix, Brian. *My Farce from My Elbow: An Autobiography.* London: Secker and Warburg, 1975.
Robinson, Derek. *Damned Good Show.* London: Cassell, 2002.
Robinson, Mark. *100 Greatest TV Ads.* London: HarperCollins, 2000.
Rodgers, C. Wade. *There's No Future in It.* Orford, TAS: Rodgers, 1988.

Russell, Peter. *Flying in Defiance of the Reich: A Lancaster Pilot's Rites of Passage*. Barnsley: Pen and Sword Aviation, 2007.
Russell, Ken. *A British Picture: An Autobiography*. London: Southbank, 2008.
Russell, Ken. *Directing Film: From Pitch to Première*. London: Batsford, 2000.
Russell, Roy. *A Family at War: Towards Victory*. London: Severn House, 1976.
Sandbrook, Dominic. *Seasons in the Sun: The Battle for Britain, 1974–1979*. London: Allen Lane, 2012.
Sandbrook, Dominic. *State of Emergency: The Way We Were: Britain, 1970–1974*. London: Allen Lane, 2010.
Sanders, Bruce. *Bombers Fly East*. London: Herbert Jenkins, 1943.
Saundby, Robert. *Air Bombardment: The Story of Its Development*. London: Chatto and Windus, 1961.
Saward, Dudley. *'Bomber' Harris*. London: Cassell, 1984.
Sawyer, Tom. *Only Owls and Bloody Fools Fly at Night*. London: Kimber, 1982.
Schaffer, Ronald. *Wings of Judgment: American Bombing in World War II*. New York: Oxford University Press, 1985.
Schmitz, Helmut, ed. *A Nation of Victims? Representations of German Wartime Suffering from 1945 to the Present*. Amsterdam: Rodopi, 2008.
Sebald, W. G. *On the Natural History of Destruction*. Translated by Anthea Bell. London: Hamish Hamilton, 2003.
Sellers, Robert. *The Secret Life of Ealing Studios: Britain's Favourite Film Studio*. London: Aurum, 2015.
Shellard, Dominic. *Kenneth Tynan: A Life*. New Haven, CT: Yale University Press, 2003.
Sherriff, R. C. *No Leading Lady: An Autobiography*. London: Gollancz, 1968.
Short, K. R. M. *Screening the Propaganda of British Air Power: From R.A.F. (1935) to The Lion Has Wings (1939)*. Trowbridge: Flicks, 1997.
Shute, Nevil. *Landfall: A Channel Story*. London: Heinemann, 1940.
Simms, Eric. *Birds of the Air: An Autobiography of a Naturalist and Broadcaster*. London: Hutchinson. 1976.
Simpson, Andrew R. B. *'Ops': Victory at All Costs: On Operations over Hitler's Reich with the Crews of Bomber Command: Their War – Their Words*. Pulborough: Tattered Flag, 2012.
Singer, Jack. *Grandpa's War in Bomber Command*. Ottawa: War Amps, 2012.
Sinyard, Neil. *Jack Clayton*. Manchester: Manchester University Press, 2000.
Skeene, Wayne. *Fade to Black: A Requiem for the CBC*. Vancouver: Douglas and McIntyre, 1993.
Skutch, Ira, ed. *Five Directors: The Golden Years of Radio*. Lanham, MD: Scarecrow, 1998.
Smith, Frederick E. *A Youthful Absurdity: An Autobiography, Volume 1*. Bicester: Emissary, 2010.
Smith, Frederick E. *An Author's Absurdities: An Autobiography, Volume 2*. Bicester: Emissary, 2012.
Smith, Frederick E. *The Final Absurdities: An Autobiography, Volume 3*. Bicester: Emissary, 2012.
Spicer, Andrew. *Typical Men: The Representation of Masculinity in Popular British Cinema*. London: I.B. Tauris, 2001.
Starowicz, Mark. *Making History: The Remarkable Story behind* Canada: A People's History. Toronto: McClelland and Stewart, 2003.
Stoker, Brian. *If the Flak Doesn't Get You the Fighters Will*. Hailsham: J&KH, 1995.

Sturrock, Donald. *Storyteller: The Authorized Biography of Roald Dahl*. New York: Simon and Schuster, 2010.
Suid, Lawrence H. *Guts & Glory: The Making of the American Military Image on Film*. Revised and expanded edn. Lexington: University Press of Kentucky, 2002.
Sussex, Elizabeth. *The Rise and Fall of British Documentary: The Story of the Film Movement Founded by John Grierson*. Berkeley: University of California Press, 1975.
Sutherland, John. *Bestsellers: Popular Fiction of the 1970s*. London: Routledge and Kegan Paul, 1981.
Sweetman, John. *Bomber Crew: Taking on the Reich*. London: Little, Brown, 2004.
Sweetman, John. *The Dambusters Raid*. London: Cassell, 2002.
Sweetman, John. *The Official Dambusters Experience*. London: Carlton, 2013.
Sweetman, John. *Operation Chastise: The Dams Raid: Epic or Myth*. London: Jane's, 1982.
Tabori, Paul. *Alexander Korda*. London: Oldbourne, 1959.
Tanaka, Yuki and Marilyn B. Young, eds. *Bombing Civilians: A Twentieth-Century History*. New York: New Press, 2009.
Taylor, James and Martin Davidson. *Bomber Crew*. London: Hodder and Stoughton, 2004.
Taylor, Mark. *Dresden: Tuesday 13 February 1945*. London: Bloomsbury, 2004.
Taylor, Philip M. *British Propaganda in the 20th Century*. Edinburgh: Edinburgh University Press, 1999.
Terraine, John. *The Right of the Line: The RAF in the European War, 1939–1945*. London: Hodder and Stoughton, 1985/London: Sphere, 1988.
Theatre Workshop. *Oh, What a Lovely War*. London: Bloomsbury Methuen Drama, 2014.
Thomas, David Wayne. *Target for Tonight: Wargaming Lancaster Bomber Raids against Germany 1942–1944*. Edited by Jack Curry. Bloomington, IN: lulu.com, 2018.
Thompson, Carlos. *The Assassination of Winston Churchill*. Gerrards Cross: Colin Smythe, 1969.
Thompson, Walter. *Lancaster to Berlin*. London: Goodall, 1985.
Todd, Richard. *In Camera*. London: Hutchinson, 1989.
Tomlinson, David. *Luckier Than Most*. London: John Curtis, 1990.
Tooze, Adam. *The Wages of Destruction: The Making and Breaking of the Nazi Economy*. London: Allen Lane, 2006.
Tripp, Miles. *Faith Is a Windsock*. London: Peter Davies, 1952.
Tripp, Miles. *The Eighth Passenger: A Flight of Recollection and Discovery*. London: Macmillan, 1969.
Tynan, Kenneth. *Kenneth Tynan: Letters*. Edited by Kathleen Tynan. New York: Random House, 1998.
Ustinov, Peter. *Dear Me*. Boston, MA: Little Brown, 1977.
Vansant, Wayne. *Bombing Nazi Germany: The Graphic History of the Allied Air Campaign That Defeated Hitler in World War II*. Minneapolis, MN: Zenith, 2013.
Verrier, Anthony. *The Bomber Offensive*. London: Batsford, 1968/ New York: Macmillan, 1969.
Vonnegut, Kurt, Jr. *Slaughter-House Five; or, the Children's Crusade: A Duty-Dance with Death*. London: Cape, 1970.
Waddington, Patrick S. *Patrick – or, That Awful Warning*. York: Waddington, 1986.
Wakelam, Randall T. *The Science of Bombing: Operational Research in RAF Bomber Command*. Toronto: University of Toronto Press, 2009.
Wales, Roland. *From Journey's End to the Dam Busters: The Life of R. C. Sherriff, Playwright of the Trenches*. Barnsley: Pen and Sword Military, 2016.

Wall, Max, with Peter Ford. *The Fool on the Hill*. London: Quartet, 1975.
Wansell, Geoffrey. *Terence Rattigan*. London: Fourth Estate, 1997.
Ware, John. *The Lion Has Wings*. London: Collins, 1940.
Warman, Eric. *A Matter of Life and Death: The Book of the Film*. London: World Film, 1946.
Watson, John. *Johnny Kinsman*. London: Cassell, 1955.
Watt, Harry. *Don't Look at the Camera!* London: Elek, 1974.
Webster, Charles and Noble Frankland. *The Strategic Air Offensive against Germany*, 4 vols. London: HMSO, 1961.
Weinberg, Gerhard L. *A World at Arms: A Global History of World War Two*. New York: Cambridge University Press, 1994.
Weisbord, Merrily and Merilyn Simonds Mohr. *The Valour and the Horror: The Untold Story of Canadians in the Second World War*. Toronto: HarperCollins, 1991.
Wheatley, Dennis. *The Haunting of Toby Jugg*. London: Hutchinson, 1948.
White, Arthur. *Bread and Butter Bomber Boys*. Upton-on-Severn: Square One, 1995.
Williams, Jack. *Entertaining the Nation: A Social History of British Television*. Stroud: Sutton, 2004.
Wilms, Wilfried and William Rasch, eds. *Bombs Away! Representing the Air War over Europe and Japan*. Amsterdam: Rodopi, 2006.
Wilson, Kevin. *Bomber Boys: The RAF Offensive of 1943*. London: Weidenfeld and Nicolson, 2005.
Wilson, Kevin. *Journey's End: Bomber Command's Battle from Arnhem to Dresden and Beyond*. London: Weidenfeld and Nicolson, 2010.
Wilson, Kevin. *Men of the Air: Doomed Youth of Bomber Command, 1944*. London: Weidenfeld and Nicolson, 2007.
Wingham, Tom. *Halifax Down! On the Run from the Gestapo, 1944*. London: Grub Street, 2009.
Wohl, Robert. *The Spectacle of Flight: Aviation and the Western Imagination, 1920-1950*. New Haven, CT: Yale University Press, 2005.
Wooldridge, John de Lacy. *Low Level Attack: The Story of Royal Air Force Squadrons from May, 1940 to May, 1943*. London: Sampson, Low, Marston, 1944.
Yates, Harry. *Luck and a Lancaster: Chance and Survival in World War II*. Shrewsbury: Airlife, 1999.
Yule, Royan. *On a Wing and a Prayer*. Derby: Derby Books, 2012.

Articles and Chapters

Anon. 'Mosquito Film Stars', *After the Battle* 18 (1978): 19-21.
Barker, Clive. 'Rampant Pacifism: The Work of the Bradford College of Art Group, 1967-1973'. In *Acts of War: The Representation of Military Conflict on the British State and Television since 1945*, edited by Tony Howard and John Stokes, 98-109. Aldershot: Scolar, 1996.
Barr, Charles. '"Much Pleasure and Relaxation in These Hard Times": Churchill and Cinema in the Second World War'. *Historical Journal of Film, Radio and Television* 31 (2001): 561-8.
Bashow, David L. 'The Balance Sheet: The Costs and Gains of the Bombing Campaign'. *Canadian Military History* 15, 3&4 (2006): 43-70.

Bercuson, David J. 'The Canadian War Museum and Bomber Command'. *Canadian Military History* 20 (2011): 55-62.
Biddle, Tami Davis. 'Air Power'. In *The Laws of War: Constraints on Warfare in the Western World*, edited by Michael Howard, George J. Andreopoulos and Mark R. Schulman, 140-59. New Haven, CT: Yale University Press, 1994.
Biddle, Tami Davis. 'Dresden 1945: Reality, History, and Memory'. *Journal of Military History* 72 (2008): 413-49.
Bloxham, Donald. 'Dresden as a War Crime'. In *Firestorm: The Bombing of Dresden 1945*, edited by Paul Addison and Jeremy Crang, 180-208. London: Pimlico, 2006.
Bothwell, Robert, Randall Hansen and Margaret MacMillan. 'Controversy, Commemoration, and Capitulation: The Canadian War Museum and Bomber Command'. *Queen's Quarterly* 115 (2008): 367-87.
Bressey, Caroline, 'Its Only Political Correctness – Race and Racism in British History'. In *New Geographies in Race and Racism*, edited by Claire Dwyer and Caroline Bressey, 29-40. Aldershot: Ashgate, 2008.
Buckman, Keith. 'The Royal Air Force Film Production Unit'. *Historical Journal of Film, Radio and Television* 17 (1997): 219-44.
Burrows, Kerry Ann. 'Night Flight'. *Eyepiece* 22, no. 5 (2001): 15-16.
Cameron, Neil. 'The Bombing of Brian McKenna'. *Discourse: The Journal of the St. Lawrence Institute for the Advancement of Learning* 12 (Summer 1993), http://www.stlawrenceinstitute.org/Disc12.html (accessed 22 September 2012).
Carr, Graham. 'Rules of Engagement: Public History and the Drama of Legitimation'. *Canadian Historical Review* 86 (2005): 317-54.
Carr, Graham. 'War, History, and the Education of (Canadian) Memory'. In *Memory, History, Nation: Contested Pasts*, edited by Katherine Hodgkin and Susannah Radstone, 57-78. London: Routledge, 2005.
Chapman, James. 'Television and History: *The World at War*'. *Historical Journal of Film, Radio and Television* 31 (2011): 247-75.
Collins, Anne. 'The Battle over "The Valour and the Horror"'. *Saturday Night* 108, no. 4 (May 1993): 44-9, 72-6.
Connelly, Mark. 'The British People, the Press, and the Strategic Air Campaign against Germany, 1939-45'. *Contemporary British History* 16, no. 2 (2002): 39-58.
Connelly, Mark. '*Bomber Harris*: Raking Through the Ashes of the Strategic Air Campaign'. In *Repicturing the Second World War: Representations in Film and Television*, edited by Michael Paris, 162-76. Basingstoke: Palgrave, 2007.
Connelly, Mark. '"We Can Take It!": Britain and the Memory of the Home Front'. In *Experience and Memory: The Second World War in Europe*, edited by Jörge Echternkamp and Stefan Martens, 54-69. Oxford: Berghahn, 2010.
Cooke, Paul. '*Dresden* (2006), TeamWorx and *Titanic* (1997): German Wartime Suffering as Hollywood Disaster Movie'. *German Life and Letters* 61 (2008): 279-94.
Cox, Sebastian. 'Setting the Historical Agenda: Webster and Frankland and the Debate over the Strategic Bombing Offensive against Germany, 1939-1945'. *Contributions to the Study of World History* 106 (2003): 147-74.
Crew, David F. 'Sleeping with the Enemy? A Fiction Film for German Television about the Bombing of Dresden'. *Central European History* 40 (2007): 117-32.
Dalrymple, Ian. 'The Crown Film Unit, 1940-43'. In *Propaganda, Politics and Film, 1918-45*, edited by Nicholas Pronay and D. W. Spring, 202-20. London: Macmillan, 1982.

Dean, David. 'Museums as Conflict Zones: The Canadian War Museum and Bomber Command'. *Museum and Society* 71 (2009): 1–15.
Dick, Ernest J. 'History on Television: A Critical Examination of "*The Valour and the Horror*"'. *Archivaria* 34 (1992): 199–216.
Dick, Ernest J. '"*The Valour and the Horror*" Continued: Do We Still Want Our History on Television?" *Archivaria* 35 (1993): 253–69.
Downie, John. 'Seeing Is Not Believing'. *Illusions* (1 July 1993): 4–6.
Drazin, Charles. 'The Distribution of Powell and Pressburger's Films in the United States'. *Historical Journal of Film, Radio and Television* 33 (2013): 55–76.
Ehland, Christoph. 'London Remembers: The Bomber Command Memorial and Recent Memories of War in the British Capital'. In *London Post-2010 in British Literature and Culture*, edited by Oliver von Knebel Doeberitz and Ralf Schneider, 138–59. Leiden: Brill Rodopi, 2017.
Ely, Geoff. 'Finding the People's War: Film, Collective Memory, and World War II'. *American Historical Review* 106 (2001): 818–38.
Farmer, Richard. '"The Dominions Will Love It": *The Lion Has Wings* (1939) and British Film Propaganda in Wartime Australia'. *Studies in Australasian Cinema* 7, no. 1 (2013): 35–47.
Finney, Patrick. 'Isaac Fadoyebo's Journey: Remembering the British Empire's Second World War'. In *Remembering the Second World War*, edited by Patrick Finney, 71–88. London: Routledge, 2018.
Flanagan, Kevin M. 'Ken Russell's Wartime Imagery'. *Journal of British Cinema and Television* 12 (2015): 539–55.
Francis, Martin. 'Men of the Royal Air Force, the Cultural Memory of the Second World War and the Twilight of the British Empire'. In *Gender, Labour, War and Empire: Essays on Modern Britain*, edited by Philippa Levine and Susan R. Grayzel, 179–96. Basingstoke: Palgrave, 2009.
Geraghty, Christine. 'Masculinity'. In *National Fictions: World War Two in British Film and Television*, edited by Geoff Hurd, 63–7. London: BFI, 1984.
Gillett, John. 'Westfront 1957'. *Sight and Sound* 27 (1957/8): 123–7.
Glancy, Mark. '*Picturegoer*: The Fan Magazine and Popular Film in Britain during the Second World War'. *Historical Journal of Film, Radio and Television* 31 (2011): 453–78.
Goulter, J. M. Christina, 'British Official Histories of the Air War'. In *The Last Word: Essays on Official History in the United States and the British Commonwealth*, edited by Jeffrey Grey, 133–46. London: Praeger, 2003.
Grant, Mariel. 'Towards a Central Office of Information: Continuity and Change in British Government Information Policy, 1939–51'. *Journal of Contemporary History* 34 (1999): 49–63.
Gray, Peter. 'A Culture of Official Squeamishness? Britain's Air Ministry and the Strategic Air Offensive against Germany'. *Journal of Military History* 77 (2013): 1349–77.
Gray, Peter. 'The Gloves Will Have to Come Off: A Reappraisal of the Legitimacy of the RAF Bomber Offensive against Germany'. *RAF Air Power Review* 13, 3 (2010): 9–40.
Haggith, Toby. 'Journey Together'. In *The Family Way: The Boulting Brothers British Film*, edited by T. O'Sullivan and P. Wells, 109–58. Trowbridge: Flicks, 2000.
Harper, Sue and Vincent Porter. 'Cinema Audience Tastes in 1950s Britain'. *Journal of Popular British Cinema* 2 (1999): 66–82.
Harrisson, Tom. 'Films and the Home Front: The Evaluation of Their Effectiveness by "Mass-Observation"'. In *Propaganda, Politics and Film, 1918–45*, edited by Nicholas Pronay and D. W. Spring, 234–45. London: Macmillan, 1982.

Hastings, Max. 'The Controversy over Bombers & Bombing'. *Encounter* 59, 2 (1982): 62–6.
Hastings, Max. 'The Lonely Passion of Bomber Harris'. *MHQ: Quarterly Journal of Military History* 6, no. 2 (1994): 58–69.
Hodgson, Guy. 'All in This Together? Manchester and the Newspapers in the Aftermath of the Christmas Blitz 1940'. In *World War II & the Media: A Collection of Essays*, edited by Christopher Hart, Guy Hodgson and Simon Gwyn Roberts, 95–118. Chester: University of Chester, 2014.
Houghton, Francis. 'The "Missing Chapter": Bomber Command Aircrew in the 1990s and 2000s'. In *British Cultural Memory and the Second World War*, edited by Lucy Noakes and Juliette Pattinson, 155–74. London: Bloomsbury, 2014.
Iacobelli, Teresa. ' "A Participant's History?" The Canadian Broadcasting Corporation and the Manipulation of Oral History'. *Oral History Review* 38, no. 2 (2011): 331–48.
Inglis, Fred. 'National Snapshots: Fixing the Past in English War Films'. In *British Cinema of the 1950s: A Celebration*, edited by Ian MacKillop and Neil Sinyard, 35–50. Manchester: Manchester University Press, 2003.
Jaeger, Stephan. 'Visualizations of the Bombing of Dresden: The Efforts of German Television to Capture History'. *Seminar: A Journal of Germanic Studies* 45 (2009): 407–20.
Kelebay, Yarema Gregory. 'The Valour and the Horror: A Perspective from Quebec'. *Canadian Social Studies* 28, no. 2 (1994): 55–6.
Kingsepp, Eva. 'Experiencing and Performing Memory: Second World War Videogames as a Practice of Remembrance'. In *Remembering the Second World War*, edited by Patrick Finney, 217–33. London: Routledge, 2018.
Kirsch, Griseldis. 'Memory and Myth: The Bombing of Dresden and Hiroshima in German and Japanese Film Drama'. *Contemporary Japan* 24 (2012): 51–70.
Knapp, Andrew, 'The Horror and the Glory: Bomber Command in British Memories since 1945', SciencesPo article, 5 December 2016, http://www.sciencespo.fr (accessed 3 February 2017).
Knapp, Andrew. 'The Allied Bombing Offensive in the British Media, 1942–45'. In *Liberal Democracies at War: Conflict and Representation*, edited by Andrew Knapp and Hilary Footitt, 39–66. London: Bloomsbury, 2013.
Lovell, Terry. 'Frieda'. In *National Fictions: World War Two in British Films and Television*, edited by Geoff Hurd, 30–4. London: BFI, 1984.
McCabe, Jane and Kin Akass. 'It's Not TV, It's HBO's Original Programming'. In *It's Not TV: Watching HBO in the Post-Television Era*, edited by Marc Leverette, Brian L. Ott and Cara Louise Buckley, 83–93. London: Routledge, 2008.
McDonald, Ken. 'Justice Denied: The Bomber Harris Trust Story'. *Airforce*, 75th Anniversary Issue, 22, no. 3 (Fall 1998): 84–5.
McKenna, A. T. 'Joseph E. Levine and *A Bridge Too Far* (1977): A Producer's Labour of Love'. *Historical Journal of Film, Radio and Television* 31 (2011): 211–27.
Medhurst, Andy, '1950s War Films'. In *National Fictions: World War Two in British Film and Television*, edited by Geoff Hurd, 35–8. London: BFI, 1984.
Nowra, Louis. 'The Fever: The Making of *Map of the Human Heart*'. *Australian-Canadian Studies* 11, nos. 1–2 (1993): 113–38.
O'Hara, Bob. '633 Squadron'. In *The Making of the Great Aviation Films, Vol. 2*, edited by Edwin Schnepf, 85–7. Chatsworth, CA: Challenge, 1989.
Overy, Richard. 'Identity, Politics and Technology in the RAF's History'. *RUSI Journal* 153, no. 6 (2008): 74–7.

Overy, Richard. 'Constructing Space for Dissent in War: The Bombing Restriction Committee, 1941-1945'. *English Historical Review* 131 (2016): 596-622.

Paris, Michael. 'The RAF on Screen 1940-42'. *History Today* 40, no. 8 (1990): 39-46.

Peloquin, Laurie. 'A Conspiracy of Silence? The Popular Press and the Strategic Bombing Campaign in Europe'. *Canadian Military History* 3, no. 2 (1994): 22-30.

Poole, Julian. 'British Cinema Attendance in Wartime: Audience Preference at the Majestic, Macclesfield, 1939-1946'. *Historical Journal of Film, Radio and Television* 7 (1987): 15-35.

Popple, Trevor. 'Appointment in London'. *After the Battle* 106 (2000): 42-4.

Porter, Vincent. 'Outsiders in England: The Films of the Associated British Picture Corporation, 1949-1958'. In *British Cinema, Past and Present*, edited by Justine Ashby and Andrew Higson, 152-65. London: Routledge, 2000.

Porter, Vincent. 'The Robert Clark Account: Films Released in Britain by Associated British Pictures, British Lion, MGM, and Warner Bros., 1946-1957'. *Historical Journal of Film, Radio and Television* 20 (2000): 469-511.

Pronay, Nicholas. 'The British Post-Bellum Cinema: A Survey of the Films Related to World War II Made in Britain between 1945 and 1960'. *Historical Journal of Film, Radio and Television* 8 (1988): 39-54.

Rains, Stephanie. 'Making Strange: Journeys through the Unfamiliar in the Films of Vincent Ward'. In *New Zealand Filmmakers*, edited by Ian Conrich and Stuart Murray, 273-88. Detroit: Wayne State University Press, 2007.

Ramsden, John. 'Refocusing "The People's War": British War Films of the 1950s'. *Journal of Contemporary History* 33 (1998): 35-63.

Rattigan, Neil. 'The Last Gasp of the British Middle Class: British War Films of the 1950s'. In *Re-Viewing British Cinema, 1900-1992*, edited by Wheeler Winston Dixon, 143-53. Albany: State University of New York Press, 1994.

Rau, Petra. '"Knowledge of the Working of Bombs": The Strategic Air Offensive in Rhetoric and Fiction'. In *Long Shadows: The Second World War in British Fiction and Film*, edited by Petra Rau, 197-220. Evanston, IL: Northwestern University Press, 2016.

Robertson, Linda. '*Dresden* (2006): Marketing the Bombing of Dresden in Germany, Great Britain, and the United States'. In *A Companion to the War Film*, edited by Douglas A. Cunningham and John C. Nelson, 234-52. Oxford: Wiley-Blackwell, 2016.

Robertson, Scot. 'In the Shadow of Death by Moonlight'. In *The Valour and the Horror Revisited*, edited by David J. Bercuson and S. F. Wise, 154-79. Montreal, QB; Kingston: McGill-Queen's University Press, 1994.

Roy, R. H. 'Bulletproof History'. *Canadian Social Studies* 28, no. 2 (1994): 59-61.

Sabin, Philip. 'Airpower in British Popular Culture'. *RUSI Journal* 163, no. 3 (2018): 22-7.

Schnepf, Ed. '633 Squadron'. *Air Classics* 2 (1964): 44.

Scutts, J. C. 'The Dam Busters'. *After the Battle* 10 (1975): 46-8.

Short, K. R. M. 'RAF Bomber Command's "Target for Tonight" (1941)'. *Historical Journal of Film, Radio and Television* 17 (1997): 181-218.

Sloniowski, Jeanette. 'Popularizing History: *The Valour and the Horror*'. In *Slippery Pastimes: Reading the Popular in Canadian Culture*, edited by Joan Nicks and Jeannette Sloniowski, 159-74. Waterloo: Wilfrid Laurier University Press, 2002.

Smith, Justin. 'Glam, Spam and Uncle Sam: Funding Diversity in 1970s British Film Production'. In *Seventies British Cinema*, edited by Robert Shail, 67-80. Basingstoke: Palgrave, 2008.

Smith, Melden E., Jr. 'The Strategic Bombing Debate: The Second World War and Vietnam'. *Journal of Contemporary History* 12 (1977): 175–91.

Stubbs, Jonathan. 'The Eady Levy: A Runaway Bribe? Hollywood Production and British Subsidy in the Early 1960s'. *Journal of British Cinema and Television* 6 (2009): 1–20.

Summerfield, Penny. 'Film and Popular Memory of the Second World War in Britain, 1950–1959'. In *Gender, Labour, War and Empire: Essays on Modern Britain*, edited by Philippa Levine and Susan R. Grayzel, 157–75. Basingstoke: Palgrave, 2009.

Süss, Dietmar. 'The Air War, the Public, and Cycles of Memory'. In *Experience and Memory: The Second World War in Europe*, edited by Jörge Echternkamp and Stefan Martens, 181–96. Oxford: Berghahn, 2010.

Taras, David. 'The Struggle over *The Valour and the Horror*: Media Power and the Portrayal of War'. *Canadian Journal of Political Science* 28 (1995): 725–48.

Taylor, Hugh. 'Counterpoint: "The Valour and the Horror": Hypertext as History?'. *Archivaria* 36 (1993): 189–93.

Taylor, Philip M. 'Film as a Weapon during the Second World War'. In *Statecraft and Diplomacy in the Twentieth Century*, edited by David Dutton, 135–54. Liverpool: Liverpool University Press, 1995.

Wainwright, J. A. 'Australia North: The Gaze from Above / Down Under in *Map of the Human Heart*'. *Australian-Canadian Studies* 12, no. 2 (1994): 29–38.

Warkentin, Erwin. '*Death by Moonlight*: A Canadian Debate over Guilt, Grief and Remembering the Hamburg Raids'. In *Bombs Away! Representing the Air War over Europe and Japan*, edited by Wilfried Wilms and William Rosch, 249–63. Amsterdam: Rodopi, 2006.

Wilms, Wilfried. '*Dresden*: The Return of History as Soap'. In *Collapse of the Conventional: German Film and Politics at the Turn of the Twenty-First Century*, edited by Jaimey Fisher and Brad Prager, 136–56. Detroit: Wayne State University Press, 2010.

INDEX

Note: The letter 'n' following locations refers to notes.

Aachen 48
Above Us the Waves (film) 81 n.23
Addinsell, Richard 8
Admiralty 15
Air Historical Branch 46
Air Ministry 5, 10–12, 14–15, 17, 20–1, 24, 27–8, 30 n.25, 32 n.49, 43, 46, 47, 49–50, 57, 61 n.48, 66 n.103, 70–1, 82 n.30, 113, 126
Airline (TV series) 107
Albert Hall 168 n.36
Alkin, John 91–2
Allen, H. R. 105 n.78
Amiens 78
Anderson, Michael 50, 55
Anderson, Willian Edwin 39 n.161
Andrew, Nigel 146
Andrews, Harry 75, 83 n.45, 83 n.51
Angels One Five (film) 163 n.2
Anka, Paul 82 n.42
Ann-Margret 100 n.12
Anson (aircraft) 78, 125
Anstey, Edgar 13, 16–17
ANZAC (TV documentary) 71
Appointment in London (film) 43–6, 49–51, 54–6, 62 n.59, 72, 163 n.2, 165 n.17, 165 n.23
Archer, Barbara 75
Archer, Henry 66 n.98
Artransa Park Television 71
Ascherson, Neal 97
Asquith, Anthony 21
Associated British Picture Corporation (ABPC) 43, 49–50, 57, 62 n.60
Associated British Film Corporation (ABPC) 48–9, 58
Associated British Film Distributors 13
Association of Cinematography, Television and Allied Technologies 112
Athenia (ship) 6
Attack on the Iron Coast (film) 84 n.64
Attenborough, Richard vi, 4, 25, 27, 40 n.171, 41 n.179, 41 n.183
Attlee, Clement 148, 155 n.38
Auckland Memorial Museum 157 n.53
Australia 24, 26, 54, 70, 74, 103 n.46, 108, 125, 138 n.37, 160, 164 n.13

Australian Broadcasting Corporation (ABC) 108
Australian War Memorial 157 n.53

B-17 (aircraft) 19, 20, 45, 91–2, 102 n.31, 163 n.7
B-25 (aircraft) 75
Baker, George 51–2
Baker, Tom 125
Balcon, Michael 15, 34 n.85
Baldwin, J. A. 11
Banks-Smith, Nancy 95, 128–9
Barefoot Video 110
Baring, Aubrey 43, 48
Baron, Alexander 92
Bates, Bert 75
Bates, H. E. 21
Battle (aircraft) 30 n.24
Battle of Britain 9, 161–2, 163 n.2
Battle of Britain Memorial Flight 108, 126, 146, 157 n.48
Battle of Britain (film) 78, 85 n.86, 89, 93
Battle of the Bombers (TV documentary) 124
Battle of the V-1 (film) 57
Battlefields (TV series) 144
Bazely, Sally 94
Bean, Adrian 124–5
Beddington, Jack 10, 11
Beetham, Alex 124, 132–3
Beetham, Michael 132
Bell, George 76
Bennett, Alan 69
Bennett, Don 65–6 n.98, 102 n.41, 108
Bercuson, David 135 n.37
Bergin, Patrick 126
Berlin 18, 19, 23, 24, 26, 28, 48, 71, 95, 96, 113–14, 133
Bernstein, Sidney 10
Berton, Pierre 137 n.35
Best, Richard 62 n.60
Bettinson, Helen 124
Beyond the Fringe (stage revue) 69–70
The Big Blockade (film) 15–17, 58 n.4, 165 n.20
The Big Sleep (film) 49
Billings, Josh 46

Billion Dollar Brain (film) 99 n.4
Billson, Anne 126
The Biter Bit (film) 21
Black, Peter 95
Blackpool 92
Blenheim (aircraft) 39 n.156
Bliss, Michael 138 n.35
The Blitz 10, 14, 21, 133, 144
Board of Trade 15
Bogarde, Dirk 44
Bomb Girls (TV series) 167 n.29
Bomb Run (book) 100 n.14, 134 n.10
Bomber (book) 89, 90, 99 n.3, 102 n.33, 117 n.2, 119 n.22, 124, 161, 164 n.11
Bomber (documentary) 144
Bomber (film) 152 n.5
Bomber (radio play) 99 n.7, 119 n.22, 124–5
Bomber (TV documentary) 108
Bomber Boys (TV documentary) 150
Bomber Boys: The Fighting Lancaster (TV programme) 144
Bomber Boys Revealed (TV documentary) 150
Bomber Command (book) 97
Bomber Command (TV documentary) 150–1
Bomber Command Association 110, 123, 128, 132, 140 n.67, 146, 150
Bomber Command monument (Green Park) 150–1, 158 n.59, 161–2
Bomber Command Museum of Canada 135 n.15, 157 n.53
Bomber Command, 1939–1945 (book) 133
Bomber Command: Reaping the Whirlwind (documentary) 132–3
Bomber Crew! (game) 161
Bomber Harris (TV play) vi, 106, 112–17, 163 n.2, 165 n.19
Bomber Harris Trust 128
Bomber's Moon (stage play) 156 n.47
Bomber's Moon (TV play) 167 n.32
The Bombers (radio documentary) 97
Bombing Germany (TV documentary) 143
The Bombing of Nuremburg (book) 97
Bonney, John 74
Boston (aircraft) 39 n.156, 82 n.39
Boulting, John 35
Bovingdon 75, 85 n.86, 93
The Boys of Kelvin High (documentary) 153 n.14
Braden, Su 110
Bradley, Mike 146
Bradley-Smith, Douglas 28
Brain, John 66 n.98
Braithwaite, Derek 124
Bray Studios 146

Bremen 24
Brexit 162
Brickhill, Paul 49, 55, 57, 63 n.71
A Bridge Too Far (film) 90
Brief Encounter (film) 79
British Board of Film Censors 11
British Bombing Survey 130
British Broadcasting Corporation (BBC) 47, 53–4, 56, 77, 90–2, 95, 97–8, 99 n.7, 103 n.62, 106, 108, 110–12, 116, 118 n.12, 124–5, 143–4, 146, 148–50
British Film Production Fund 73
British Lion 46
British National Films 17
Brittain, Donald 71
Brooke, Alan 149
Brooks, Ray 94, 103 n.48
Brown, George 25, 27
Brown, Gerald 92–3, 95
Brown, Ken 127
Brunswig, Hans 96
The Brylcreem Boys (TV play) 98
Buck, David 77, 85 n.76
Buck, William Ray 104 n.64
Buckley, John 139 n.55, 141 n.75
Building the Bouncing Bomb (TV documentary) 150
Bulletproof? You Be the Judge! (documentary) 131
Burden, Hugh 18
Burgess, Mark 129
Burton, Richard 83 n.51
Bushell, Anthony 6–9, 29 n.16, 30 n.23
Byrnes, Ed 103 n.46

Cage of Gold (film) 41 n.186, 56, 64 n.84
Cagney, Jimmy 38 n.146
Cambridge 25
Campbell, Colin 91–2, 103 n.51, 164–5 n.16
Campbell, Graham 129
Campbell, James 97, 100 n.14
Campbell, Patrick 95
Campbell, William Bryce 39 n.161
Canada 11–12, 17, 23, 25, 26, 37 n.140, 38 n.146, 71–2, 79, 82 n.34, 84 n.67, 103 n.46, 108, 125–34, 144–5, 160, 164 n.13
Canada at War (TV documentary) 71–2, 135 n.26
Canadian Broadcasting Corporation (CBC) 71, 127–8, 132, 144
Canadian National Film Board (NFB) 71
Canadian Radio-television and Telecommunications Commission (CRTC) 128

Canadian War Museum 144
Canadian Warplane Heritage Museum 126, 134, 157 n.38
Cann, David 98
Captains of the Clouds (film) 38 n.146
Carson, Charles 54
Carter, William 130
Casablanca 132
Cashin, Fergus 86 n.96
Cathcart-Jones, O. 37 n.140
Central Television 124
Chakiris, George 74, 76, 82 n.42
Chamberlain, Neville 6
Channel 4 (UK) 108, 110–12, 124, 128–9, 133, 144, 147–8, 150
Channel 5 (UK) 143, 150
Channel 7 (Australia) 71
Channel 9 (Australia) 104 n.64
Channel Television 104 n.63
Chapman, James vii
Charters, Anderson 131
Chatterton, Cliff 131
Cherwell, Lord. *See* Lindemann, Frederick
Cheshire, Leonard 61 n.48
Childs, Ted 96
Christie, Ian 79
Churchill, Winston 5, 14, 21, 31 n.28, 36 n.125, 43, 70, 76, 106, 111, 113–15, 132–3, 148–9, 155 nn.37–8, 156 n.39, 161
Cinecam Productions 132
Clark, Ernest 51
Clark, Robert 48–51, 54, 57
Clavell, James 73–4, 83 n.45, 83 n.50, 84 n.51
Coates, Eric 51
Cochrane, Ralph 50–2
Colditz (TV series) 91, 100 n.16
Cole, George 26
College of Aeronautics 72
Collins, Brian 124
Collins, John 114, 116
Collins, Joseph William 39 n.161
Cologne 20, 21, 47, 114, 147
Command Decision (film) 167 n.32
The Commanders (TV documentary) 104 n.62
Commando Comics. *See* war comics
Common as Muck (TV series) 145
Commonwealth Air Training Plan Museum 125
Connelly, Mark 57, 115
Cook, Judith 98
Cook, Peter 69
Copp, Terry 131, 137 n.35
Coren, Alan 116
Coventry 21, 80 n.18

Cozens, Henry Iliffe 118 n.6, 144, 148, 155 n.34, 159
Cranham, Kenneth 145
Creil 92
Crichton, Charles 15
Cripps, Stafford 114
Crowe, Russell 125
Crown Film Unit (CFU) 10
Crowther, Bosley 37 n.141
The Crucible (TV documentary series episode) 144
Crucible of War (book) 130
Currie, Jack 107–8

D-day 71, 132–3
Dahl, Roald 49
Dakota (aircraft) 107
Dale, Robert 129
Dalrymple, Ian 5, 30 n.25
The Dam Busters (book) 49, 57
The Dam Busters (film) 42–57, 58 n. 5, 61 n.42, 64 n.84, 69, 72–5, 82–3 n.44, 83 n.45, 93, 108, 163 n.2, 165 n.20, 165 n.23, 168 n.36
The Dam Busters (film remake) 149, 161, 166 n.24
The Dam Busters (radio play) 49
dams raid 48–54, 70, 82 n.30, 82–3 n.44, 96, 127
Dambusters! (TV documentary) 124
Dambusters Declassified (TV documentary) 150
The Dambusters Raid (TV documentary) 124
Danger U.X.B. (TV series) 100 n.16
Danson, Barney 131
Dark Blue World (film) 163 n.2
Darlow, Michael 115–16
Darren, James 82 n.43
Davies, Bernard 95
Davies, Len 161
Davies, Trudi 110
Davis, Carl 96
Davis, David 85 n.83
Davis, Phil 146
Day (book) 154 n.28
Day-Lewis, Sean 109, 138 n.41
Dead of Night (TV series) 91
Death by Moonlight: Bomber Command (TV documentary series episode) 127–31, 133, 136 n.27, 144, 162, 165 nn.18–19, 165 n.22
Deighton, Len 89, 90, 99 n.3–4, 102 n.33, 119 n.22, 124
Delderfield, R. F. 64 n.84
Denham Studios 6, 8, 11, 17, 25
Desbarats, Peter 131
Desperate Journey (film) 20–1

Dimbleby, Jonathan 124
Dorté, Philip 47
Douglas, Colin 91
Douglas, Donald 94
Douglas, Robert 7
Dowding, Hugh 123, 155 n.35
Dresden 70–1, 80 n.18, 81 n.19, 90, 97, 107, 111–12, 114, 124–6, 132–3, 143, 147–50
Dresden (TV film) 145, 147–8, 163 n.2, 165 n.20
Dresden: Forgotten Anniversary (TV documentary) 108
The Destruction of Dresden (stage piece) 110
Dresden 1945: The Devil's Tinderbox (book) 107
Duering, Carl 45
Dugdale, John 147
Dunkirk 10, 41 n.186, 132, 161
Dunkirk (film) 163 n.2, 166 n.47
Dunlop, Joe 124
Dunmore, Spencer 100 n.14, 130, 134 n.10
Durlacher, Chris 146
Durrant, Peter 98
Dusseldorf 21
Dvorak, Ann 22
Dyson, Freeman 129

Eady Levy 73
Eagle Squadron (film) 37 n.127
Eaker, Ira 113
Ealing Studios 15, 17, 49
East Kirby 146
Eden, Anthony 111
Eighth Air Force (USAAF) 1, 57, 113, 162
Eisenhower, Dwight D. 133
Elstree Studios 12, 51, 93
Emmett, E. V. H. 6–8
Enemy at the Door (TV series) 100 n.16
Enemy Coast Ahead (book) 49
Enemy Coast Ahead (radio play) 49
Essen 21
Ethics and Airpower in World War II (book) 130
Evans, David 15
Ezard, Alex 71

Falcon Field 21
A Family at War (TV series) 91–2, 100 n.16, 103 n.51, 163 n.7, 165 n.17
Farage, Nigel 167 n.29
Farmer, Suzan 49
Farr, Derek 52
Farrar, David 28
Fenton, Leslie 21
Fifty Years of the R.A.F. (documentary) 77
Fighter Command 159
Film Aviation Services 75

Finch, John 91–2
Finch, Peter 59 n.15
Finch, Scott 83 n.49
50 Squadron 15, 156 n.47
Fireraiser (TV documentary) 110–12, 162, 165 n.19
First Light (TV film) 163 n.2
Fitzgerald, Walter 44
Flare Path (stage play) 22–3, 156 n.47
Fleming, Marvin 129
Flying Fortress (film) 19–20
The Flying Schoolboys and the Wild Sow (TV documentary) 123–4
Flying Training Command 25
Flynn, Barbara 145
Flynn, Errol 20
Fogerty, F. J. 11
For the Moment (film) 125
Forbes, Bryan 44, 59 n.11
Ford, Cecil 75
Forde, Walter 19
The Forsythe Saga (TV series) 85 n.76
Fortress (aircraft). *See* B-17
Fortress (film) 163 n.8
49th Parallel (film) 15, 20
Foster, Preston 21
463 Squadron 24
Foyle's War (TV series) 167 n.29
Frankland, Noble 70–1, 76, 104 n.69, 108–9
Franklyn, William 98
Fraser, John 51–2
Frees, Wolf 45
Frend, Charles 15
Frieda (film) 41 n.186
Friston 25
Fry, Stephen 149–50
Funeral in Berlin (film) 99 n.4

Gainsborough Pictures 21
Galafilm 136 n.27
Garrett, Stephen A. 130
games 108–9, 144, 161
The Gathering Storm (TV film) 155 n.37
Geldorf, Bob 65 n.95
Get Some In! (TV series) 105 n.85
Gibbs, Patrick 83 n.45
Gibson, Eve 56
Gibson, Guy 49–56, 61 n.48, 63 n.71, 63 n.75, 64 n.84, 109, 149, 161
Gibson, Mel 149
Gilliat, Sidney 21
Gillies, Andrew 129
Giudice, Fillipo Del 27
Glanville, William 50

Godfrey, Brian 91
Golombeck, David 108
Goodliffe, Michael 75, 83 n.45, 84 n.51
Goodwin, Harold 55
Goodwin, Ron 75
Grade, Michael 111–12
Graham, Denys 53
Granada Television 91, 116
Granatstein, Jack 130, 136 n.35
La grande vadrouille (film) 102 n.31
Grantham 52–3, 63 n.71
Grauman, Walter 75
Gray, Charles 78
Greeff, Peter De 15
Greene, Grahame 9
Greene, Lorne 23
Greene, Richard 19, 37 n.130
Greenhous, Brereton 140 n.57
The Great Escape (film) 72, 84 n.51
Gretton, Lee 151
Griffen, Gordon 91
Gunn, Reg 39 n.161
The Guns of Navarone (film) 81 n.27, 82 n.42
Guy, Alan 91

Haig, Douglas 109
The Halcyon (TV series) 167 n.29
Halifax (aircraft) 133, 141 n.72, 144
Halton 146
Hamburg 20, 24, 28, 48, 71, 80 n.18, 94, 96–7, 113–14, 127, 130, 132
Hammond, P. J. 98
Hampden (aircraft) 15–16
Hankinson, Michael 23
Hannover 15
Harbord, Jane 119 n.26
Harbour, Michael 91
The Hardest Victory (book) 130, 139 n.55
Hardy, Robert vi, 106, 115
HarperCollins (publisher) 133
Harris, Arthur 20, 21, 23, 26, 28, 38 n.148, 46, 48, 50–1, 63 n.54, 70–1, 76, 96–17, 123, 128–30, 132, 140 n.57, 143, 147–9, 155 n.38, 156 n.39, 159–60, 162, 165 n.19
Harris statue 123
Harrison, Rex 41 n.179
Harrisson, Tom 30 n.23, 31 n.39
Harvey, Doug 127
Harvey, Laurence 66n. 98
Hastings, Max 97, 109, 116, 131, 137 n.35
The Haunted Airman (TV film) 146–7
The Haunting of Toby Jugg (book) 146
Le Havre 118 n.12
Hawks, Howard 49

Haws, Chris 124
Heath, Sophie 148
Hemswell 118 n.6, 144
Henry V (film) 121 n.60
Herbert, Hugh 124
The Heroes of Telemark (film) 81 n.27, 82 n.40
Hitler, Adolf 24, 72, 111
Hochhuth, Rolf 76
Hodgson, Bob 109
Hodgson, David 109
Hoggart, Paul 146
Holder, Roy 103 n.51
Holmes, Robert 91
The Holocaust and Strategic Bombing (book) 130
Holt, Paul 13
Home, Charles Douglas 96
Home Box Office (HBO) 148
Home Fires (TV series) 167 n.29
Hood, Stuart 97
Hopgood, J. V. 52
Hopkins, Anthony 116
Houston, Donald 75, 83 n.51
How I Won the War (film) 83 n.50
Howard, Tom 75
Howard, Trevor 23
Howell, John 25
Hoyle, Martin 125
Huculak, Maggie 144
Hudson (aircraft) 37 n.140
Hughes, J. B. 103 n.48
Hunt, Albert 110–11, 123–4
Hunt, Claire 110
Hunter, Ian 44, 59 n.18
Huntley, Raymond 27
Hurricane (film) 163 n.2
Hurst, Desmond 6
Hutchinson (publisher) 13, 73
Hutchinson, Robert 63 n.71

Ice Cold in Alex (film) 83 n.51
Icon Pictures 149
I'll Never Forget What's'isname (film) 79
Ilsa, She Wolf of the SS (film) 82 n.39
Independent Television (ITV) 90–3, 95, 98, 108–9, 115, 124, 150
India. *See* Sikhs
Inspector Morse (TV series) 116
International Bomber Command Centre (IBCC) 161–2
International Squadron (film) 37 n. 127, n.132
Into the Storm (TV film) 145, 148–9
Into the Wind (documentary) 150
Institut Géographique National 92

Index

The Ipcress File (film) 99 n.4
Ireland 94, 103 n.47, 160
Irving, David 71, 80 n.17, 107
Isaacs, Jeremy 96, 110–11
Iveson, Tony 146
Ivory, William 145–6, 156 n.47

Jackson, Gordon 22
Jackson, Peter 149, 165 n.24
Jaffe, Carl 45
James, Clive 95
Jameson, Susan 94
Jeffries, Stuart 133, 150
Jenkins, Simon 151
Jéricho (film) 78, 85 n.82
Johnson, Aaron Kim 125
Jones, Emrys 18
Joubert, Philip 10, 32 n.46, 71
Journey Together (film) vi, 4, 24–8, 45, 55, 93
Journey's End (film) 9
Justin, John 25–6

Kassel 21
Kay, Bernard 115
Keegan, John 107, 137 n.35
Kennedy, A. L. 154 n.28
Kent, Arthur 140 n.65
Kerr, Bill 44, 51
Kiel 5, 9, 48
The Killing Ground (TV documentary) 127
King, Sydney 19
King's College London 133
Kirkness, Geoffrey 149
Kirton-in-Lindsey 63 n.64
Knapp, Bud 71
Knight, Les 53
Koch, Howard 74
Kolditz, Stefan 147
Korda, Alexander 5, 9, 21, 31 n.28
Kraemer, Nikolaus 147
Krefeld 89
Kydd, Sam 45, 60 n.19

Lack of Moral Fibre (LMF) 117
Lancaster (aircraft) 23–5, 39 n.156, 44, 48, 49–50, 57–8, 59 n.9, 62 n.59, 67 n.107, 70, 72, 89–91, 93, 99 n.6, 101 n.29, 124, 126–7, 129, 134, 141 n.72, 143–5, 148, 151, 157 n.48, 159, 163 n.7
Lancaster (short film) 151
Lancaster FM213 126–7, 134, 157 n.48
Lancaster NX611 92, 146, 151
Lancaster PA474 67 n.107, 72, 81 n.26–8, 89, 93, 96, 105 n.86, 108, 127, 146, 150, 157 n.48

Lancaster R5868 98, 105 n.86, 124
Lancaster (scale models) 88, 93
The Lancaster Legend: A Pilot's Story (TV docudrama) 107–9
Lancaster Skies (film) 163 n.2, 163 n.8, 166 n.28
Land Girls (TV series) 167 n.29
Landfall (film) 42 n.186, 43
Lane, Reg 23
Lane, Stuart 109
Last Flight to Berlin (documentary) 144
Last of the Dambusters (TV documentary) 143
Latta, C. J. 57
Lauder, Frank 21
Laurie, Hugh 109
laws of war 30 n.17
Leacock, Philip 44
Lean, David 18
Lee, Jason Scott vi, 122, 125
Leech, Richard 52
The Legacy of Lord Trenchard (book) 105 n.78
Lejeune, C. A. 27
Lennard, Chris 145
Lennie, Angus 75, 83 n.51
Leon, Anne 44
Lester, Richard 83 n.50
Letters from a Bomber Pilot (TV docudrama) 109
Levine, Alan J. 139 n.56
Liddell Hart, Basil 99 n.6
Light, John 147
Lincoln 161
Lincoln (aircraft) 59 n.9
Lincoln Aviation Heritage Centre 146
Lindemann, Frederick 76, 132
Linnell, Lloyd, 133, 144
Linnell, Robert, 133, 144
The Lion Has Wings (film) 5–11, 15
Littlewood, Joan 83 n.50
Llewelyn, Roger 115–16
Lloyd, Innis 112, 116
Lockyer, Malcolm 95
Lodge, David 107
London Can Take It! (film) 10
London Films 5, 7
Longden, John 26
The Longest Day (film) 81 n.25, 82 n.42, 83 n.51
Longinotto, Kim 110, 112
Longmate, Norman 97, 115
Lord of the Rings (film) 149
Love, Bessie 40 n.172
Lowndes Productions 99 n.4
Lloyd, Innes 112
Lubeck 96
Lucas, George 83 n.44

Index

Lucas, Leighton 13
Luftwaffe 10, 21, 47, 54, 108, 123, 133
Lumley, Joanna 98

MacGlachlan, James 82 n.43
Magdeburg 91
Mahaddie, Hamish 75, 92, 96
Maida Vale studios 124
Malcolm, Christian 145
Malleson, Miles 41 n.179
Malta Story (film) 58 n.5, 162 n.2
Maltby, David 52
The Man from U.N.C.L.E. (series) 77
The Man Who Never Was (film) 82 n.30
Manchester 25
Mandel, Ernest 110–11
Manhunt (TV series) 100 n.16
Mannheim 24
Mannock, P. L. 33 n.68
Mantel, Hilary 133
Manville, Roger 18
Map of the Human Heart (film) vi, 122, 125–6, 163 n.2, 165 n.18
Marham 17
Marney, Derrick De 6, 8, 30 n.23
Marsden, Roy 107
Marshal, Glen Osmond 39 n.161
Martin, Dean 73
Martin, Ian Kennedy 91
Martin, H. B. 51–2, 63 n.71
Mass-Observation 30 n.23
Massie, Paul 94
Matheson, Muir 8
A Matter of Life and Death (film) 26, 28
Maudslay, Henry 52
Maximum Effort (book) 100 n.14
Maximum Effort (film) 23–4
May, Jack 102 n.37
Mayflower Films 43, 48, 50
McCalla, Harry 155 n.34
McCallum, David 77–8, 91, 98
McEwan, Hamish 129
McFarlane, Leslie 23
McGoohan, Patrick 51, 64 n.77
McGregor, Colin 150
McGregor, Ewan 150
McKee, Alexander 49, 107
McKenna, Brian 127–31, 138 n.43, 165 n.22
McKenna, Terence 127–31, 165 n.22
McManus, Mark 103 n.46
McPhail, Angus 15
Me-108 (aircraft) 75
Meillon, John 74
Memphis Belle (film) 163 n.7, 167 n.32

Merlin Films 23
Methwold 25
Middlebrook, Martin 97, 107
Midland Montague 93
Mighty Eighth (TV project) 3 n.4, 167 n.29
Mildenhall 5–6, 11
Miles, Bernard 18
Miller, Gavin 115
Miller, Jonathan 69
Millions Like Us (film) 21
Mills, John 15, 16, 23
Milne, Tom 79
Ministry of Aircraft Production 63 n.71
Ministry of Defence 78, 89, 93
Ministry of Economic Warfare 15, 17
Ministry of Information (MoI) 5, 10, 13, 15, 17, 21, 23–4, 34 n.85, 43, 58 n.1
Minley Manor 78
Mirisch Corporation 72–7, 79, 90
Mirisch, Walter 73, 75, 82 n.42
Moore, Dudley 69
Moore, Rowan 151
More, Alexander 11
More, Marilyn Simonds 139 n.53
Morse, Barry 21
Mortil, Janne 129
Morton, Desmond 118–19 n.20, 138 n.35
Mosquito (aircraft) 73, 75, 78, 82 n.33, 85 n.84, 89, 163 n.7
Mosquito Squadron (film) 77–9, 85 n.85, 85 n.86, 89–91, 93, 98, 163 n.2, 165 n.17, 165 n.20
Mueller, Andrew 151
Muldoon, Jeannie 131
Mulheim 21
Murray, Mike 92
Murray, Williamson 141 n.75
My Mother and Other Strangers (TV series) 167 n.29, 167 n.32
Myserscough-Jones, David 115

National Council of Veterans Associations 128
National Film Board of Canada (NFB) 23, 108, 125, 127, 131
Neame, Ronald 18
Netherlands 17
Nettleton, John 115
Neve, Suzanne 77, 85 n.76
New Zealand 11, 23, 37 n.130, 125, 149, 160, 164 n.13
Newman, Alex 145
Nielsen, Richard 131
Night Flight (TV film) vi, 142, 144–6, 162, 163 n.2, 164 n.16

The Night We Dropped a Clanger (film) 64 n.84
90 Squadron 19
Niven, David 26
No Price Too High (book) 132
No Price Too High (documentary) 131–2
Norflicks Productions 131
November, Joe 7
Nunn, Trevor 156 n.47
Nuremberg 71, 97, 107, 127, 129
The Nuremburg Raid (book) 97

Oakamont Productions 77
Oakington 21, 36 n.117
O'Callaghan, Linda 125
O'Connor, D'Arcy 129
Oh, What a Lovely War (stage play) 83 n.50
Olivier, Laurence 96–7
Ollis, Ray 66 n.98
On the Fiddle (film) 64 n.84
On the Wings of Valour: In Defense of Bomber Command (documentary) 131
115 Squadron 17
149 Squadron 5–8, 11, 32 n.49, 36 n.117
One of Our Aircraft Is Missing (film) 17–19, 20, 58 n.4, 164 n.16, 165 n.20
One of Our Bombes Is No Longer Missing (TV documentary) 108
The One That Got Away (film) 84 n.51
106 Squadron 43, 49, 63 n.71
Operation Chastise. *See* dams raid
Operation Chastise: The Dams Raid Relived (TV documentary) 108
Operation Crossbow (film) 76, 81 n.27, 85 n.85
Operation Crucible (book) 85 n.77
Operation Rhine Maiden (book) 85 n.77
Orchard, Julian 102 n.37
Orphüls, Marcel 127
O'Sullivan, Thaddeus 148
Outerbridge, Peter 125
Overy, Richard 133, 149–50, 155 n.32
Owen, Bill 23, 39 n.157
Owen, Frank 15

Palmer, Alex 145
Parillaud, Anne 126
Paterson, Bill 148
Pathfinders (TV series) vi, 88, 90, 92–5, 97–8, 163 n.2, 164 n.16, 165 n.18, 165 n.22
Patterson, Peter 138 n.41, 146
Pattinson, Robert 146
peace movement 134 n.2
Peck, Richard 11
Peenemünde 60 n.21, 72, 76, 132
Pembrey 25

Penfold, Chris 103 n.48
Pennington, Michael 148
A Perfect Hero (TV series) 163 n.2
Perry, Joyce 77
Perschy, Maria 75
Petty, Moira 125
Pforzheim 150
Phoenix Films 24
Pickard, P. C. 11, 78
Piece of Cake (TV series) 163 n.2
Pierse, Richard 11
Pine, Edward 66 n.98
Pinewood Studios 24–5
Plummer, Christopher vi, 142, 145
Poland 160, 164 n.13
Polebrooke 19
Polymath Pictures 151
Portal, Charles 70, 115
Porter, Philip 98
Portman, Eric 18
Potts, Andrew Lee 145
Powell, Dilys 76, 79
Powell, J. A. 11, 17
Powell, Michael 5–6, 17, 20, 26, 36 n.114
Powell, Robert 100 n.12
Power, Vicki 150
Pratt, Mike 94
Prelude to Victory (film) 118 n.6
Pressburger, Emeric 17, 18, 26
Proctor, Kelly 125
Pujji, Mohinder Singh 82 n.43
The Purple Plain (film) 30 n.23, 58 n.5, 82 n.33
The Purple Twilight (TV play) 98
Pye, David 50

Queen Elizabeth II 150
Queen Mother (Elizabeth) 123, 128
Quinn Martin (QM) Productions 93

RAAF Over Europe (film) 24
Race to Smash the German Dams (TV documentary) 150
Rachmil, Lewis 75, 77
Radcliffe, Douglas 150
Radiotelevisione Italiana (RAI) 93
Raegan, Ronald 20
Rank Organization 60 n.20, 64 n.84
Rattigan, Terence 22, 24–5, 38 n.153, 39 n.157, 55
Rau, Petra 165 n.21
Reach for the Sky (film) 58 n.5, 163 n.2
Reap the Whirlwind (book) 130
The Red Beret (film) 83 n.51

Red Dog Pictures 151
Redcap (TV series) 116
Redgrave, Michael 15, 23, 50, 53, 83 n.45
Redifussion Television (RTV) 104 n.64
Reed, Oliver 86 n.94, 100 n.12
Rees, Ken 141 n.72
Regensburg 113
Relyea, Bob 75
Rendel, Robert 6
Rennie, Michael 15
Renton, Nicholas 146
Return to Dresden (TV documentary) 108
Reynolds, Stanley 92
Richards, Denis 46, 130, 139 n.55
Richardson, Ralph 27, 29 n.16
Richter, Roland Suso 147
Riddell, Peter 11
The Right of the Line (book) 109
Right to Reply (TV programme) 129
Ripper, Michael 60 n.19
Rivers, Christian 149, 166 n.24
Rix, Brian 64 n.84
RKO-Radio Pictures 27
Roberts, Andrew 128
Robertson, Cliff 74, 85 n.84
Robinson, Edward G. 25
Roc, Patricia 21
Rodska, Christian 147
Room at the Top (book and film) 66 n.98
Rostock 96
Rotterdam 133
The Royal Air Force, 1939-1945 (book) 46-7
Royal Air Force (RAF) centenary 167-8 n.35
Royal Air Force (RAF) Central Band 13
Royal Air Force (RAF) Film Production Unit 24-8
Royal Air Force (RAF) Museum 98, 124
Royal Aircraft Establishment 78
Royal Australian Air Force (RAAF) 71, 74, 103 n.46
Royal Canadian Air Force (RCAF) 37 n.140, 38 n.146, 39 n.161, 70, 94, 103 n.46, 127, 130, 144
Royal New Zealand Air Force (RNZAF) 39 n.161
Royal Canadian Legion 128, 131
Rubber Duck 161
Ruffle, Jonathan 124-5
Russell, Ken 90, 100 n.12

Sagal, Boris 77, 79
St Clement Danes church 123
Salmon, Hilary 145
Saltzman, Harry 89, 99 n.4
Sandford, Donald 77

Sapper, Alan 112
Sapphire & Steel (TV series) 98
Saundby, Robert 11, 47, 71, 80 n.12, 115, 119 n.22, 147-8
Saunders, Hilary St. John 46
Saward, Dudley 119 n.21
Scaife, Ted 75
Scampton 50-1, 63 n.64
Shackleton (aircraft) 78
Shannon, David 52-3
Shaw, Don 112, 115
Shaw, Robert 51, 62 n.55
School for Secrets (film) 27-8
Schweinfurt 113
Scotland 11, 26, 94-5, 103 n.47, 160, 164 n.13
Scott, Margaretta 59 n.10
Scottish Television 95
The Sea Shall Not Have Them (film) 58 n.5
Secret Army (TV series) 100 n.16
Secret History (TV series) 124
Senate Subcommittee on Veterans Affairs (Canada) 128
Sergeant, John 150
Serling, Rod 73
Setton, Maxwell 43, 48
7 Squadron 22, 36 n.117
75 Squadron 23, 108
Sewell, J. E. 16
Shaw, Don 112, 114
Shaw, Robert 55, 64 n.80
Shepperton Studios 44
Sheridan, Andy 145
Sheridan, Dinah 44
Sherrier, Julian 74, 164 n.12
Sherriff, R. C. 49, 55-6, 63 n.75, 83 n.50
Shute, Nevil 43
Siddons, Harold 51
Sikhs 74, 160, 164 n.12, 164 n.13
Sikorski, Władysław 76
Sim, Alastair 41 n.179
Sim, Sheila 41 n.179
Singer, Campbell 60 n.19
Sink the Bismarck! (film) 72
617 Squadron 48-51, 53-4, 57, 63 n.71, 64 n.80, 72, 78, 81 n.23, 94, 150
618 Squadron 77
633 Squadron (book) 72-3, 82 n.30, 82-3 n.44, 85 n.77
633 Squadron (film) vi, 68, 72-3, 79, 82-3 n.44, 85 n.45, 85 n.78, 99 n.6, 163 n.2, 164 n.16
Skegg, Martin 147
Skellingthorpe 15
Slaughterhouse-Five (book and film) 90, 99-100 n.8

Smith, Douglas B. 108
Smith, Frederick E. 72–4, 77, 82 n.34, 85 n.77, 90
Smith, Martin 97
Soldiers (stage play) 76
The Sorrow and the Pity (documentary) 127
South Africa 103 n.46, 160, 164 n.13
Southern Television 104 n.63
Soviet Union 15, 147
Spaatz, Carl 113
Spitfire (aircraft) 9, 30 n.24
Squire, Ronald 40 n.172
Stalin, Joseph 114, 132
Star Wars (film) 66 n.100, 83 n.44
Steel, Christian 145
Stevens, Philip 151
Stevens, Roy 75
Stevenson, John 91
Stewart, Bruce 103 n.51
Stewart, Donald 19
Stirling (aircraft) 18, 22, 36 n.117, 39 n.156
Stock, Nigel 51
Stokes, Richard 114
Strand Films 21
The Strategic Air Offensive against Germany 1939–1945 (book) 70–1, 76
The Strategic Bombing of Germany, 1940–1945 (book) 139 n.56
Stringer, Michael 75
Sturges, John 73
Stuttgart 18, 48
Submarine X-1 (film) 84 n.64
Summers, Joseph 50
Sutcliffe, Tom 128
Sutton, John 21
The Sweeney (TV series) 116
Sydney, Basil 51
Sylvester, William 44

Target, Berlin (film) 23
Target Germany (film) 24
Target For Tonight (film) 10–14, 15, 17, 23, 24, 26, 28, 46, 47, 72, 78, 91–2, 96, 132, 151 n.1, 165 n.20
Taylor, Rod 49
teamWorx 147
Tearle, Godrey 18
Teddington Studios 19
Telefilm Canada 131
Terraine, John 109
Thames Television 93, 95–6, 109
Thaw, John vi, 106, 116
There's a Future in It (film) 21
They Were Not Divided (film) 58 n.5

Thomas, Clive 115
Thomas, James 95
Thompson-Noel, Michael 116
The Thousand Plane Raid (film) 167 n.32
Thunder Birds: Soldiers of the Air (film) 21
Tierney, Gene 21
Tiger Moth (aircraft) 125
Timewatch (TV series) 124, 143
Tin Hat Productions 161
Tirpitz (battleship) 72, 82 n.30
Titanic (film) 147
Tizard, Henry 27
Thorpe, Richard 52, 92
Threlfall, David 98
To Have and Have Not (film) 49
To Serve Them All My Days (TV series) 121 n.60
Todd, Richard 42, 50, 53, 56, 83 n.45, 108, 167 n.33
Toledo Films 92–3
Tomlinson, David 24–8
Tomlinson, Peter 167 n.33
Tommy (film) 90
Torrens, Pip 147
Tremarcio, Christine 145
Trenchard, Hugh 111
Treves, Frederick 115
A Tribute to Bomber Command (TV programme) 150
Tripp, Miles 66 n.98
Turnbull, John 22
Twelve O'Clock High (film) 45, 58 n. 5, 59 n.12, 167 n.32
Twelve O'Clock High (TV series) 93, 167 n.32
Twentieth Century-Fox 21
Twist, Derek 11
Two Cities Films 21, 27

Ulster Television 104 n.63
United Artists 78
United Kingdom Independence Party (UKIP) 167 n.29
United States 19, 103 n.46, 94, 160, 164 n.13
University of Western Ontario 131
Upwood 44
Urquhart, Robert 93
Ustinov, Peter 27
Uxbridge 12

Valentine, J. B. 103 n.48
The Valour and the Horror (book) 133, 139 n.53
The Valour and the Horror (TV docudrama series). See *Death by Moonlight: Bomber Command*
Varley, Beatrice 22

Index

Varsity (aircraft) 62 n.52
Verrier, Anthony 76
Very Important Person (film) 72
Victory at Sea (TV documentary series) 47
Vietnam 81 n.19
Vonnegut, Kurt 90

Waddington 89, 93
Waddington, Patrick 27
Wales 18, 91, 94, 103 n.47, 160, 164 n.13
Walker, Tim 149
The Wall (film) 65 n. 95
Wall, Max 110, 112, 119 n.26, 119–20 n.31
Wallis, Barnes 50–5, 63 n.71, 64 n.84, 77, 129
Wallis, James 58
Wallis, Molly 50
Walsh, Raoul 20
Walsh, Tom 151
War Amps 131
War at Sea: The Black Pit (documentary) 136 n.27
war comics 64–5 n.85, 72, 77, 81 n.22, 101 n.18, 108, 121 n.68, 141 n.75, 153 n.10
War in the Air, 1914–45 (book) 147 n.75
War in the Air (TV documentary series) 47–8, 71
Warboys 92
Warboys Film Productions 93
Ward, James Allen 37 n.130
Ward, Vincent 125–6
Ware, John 6
Warner Brothers 19, 20, 49, 57
Warriors of the Night (documentary) 133–4
Warsaw 133
Watling, Jack 25, 93
Waterbeach 25
Waterman, Dennis 94, 103 n.48
Watson, John 66 n.98
Watson-Watt, Robert 27
Watt, Harry 10–14, 29 n.16, 159
Waxman, Harry 25
The Way to the Stars (film) 22–3, 24, 38 n.153, 45, 55
Waymark, Patrick 116
Webster, Charles 70–1, 109
Weinberg, Gerhard 39 n.56
Weisbord, Marrily 139 n.53
Weldon, T. D. 114–15
We'll Meet Again (TV series) 167 n.32
Wellman, William A. 21
Wellington (aircraft) 5–8, 11–14, 17, 30 n.17, 37 n.130, 51, 62 n.52, 66 n.98, 91, 101 n.29, 109
West, Sam 125

West Indies 160, 164 n.13
West Malling 93
West Side Story (film) 82 n.42
Westbrook, John 66 n.98
Westerly, Robert 43
What the Dambusters Did Next (TV documentary) 150
Wheatley, Dennis 146
Whispers in the Air (TV documentary) 117
Whitebait, William 13, 16
Whitehead, Philip 97
Whitemore, Hugh 148, 155 n.37
Whitrow, Benjamin 152 n.5
Whitworth, John 50
The Who 90
Wickenby 108
Williams, Bill 10
Williams, Brock 19
Williams, Hugh 18
Wilson, Andrew 109
Wilson, Arnold 18
Wilson, Cecil 86 n.95
Wilson, Ronald 52
Wingate, Orde 112
WingNut Films 149
Wings of the Storm (TV documentary) 108
Winston Churchill: The Wilderness Years (TV series) 115
Wise, Sydney 135 n.37
Witting, Francis 39 n.161
The Wooden Horse (film) 59 n.11
Woodward, Edward vi, 142, 145
Woolatt, Gordon 11
Wooldridge, John 15, 43, 45, 49, 55, 59 n.10, 62 n.48
Woollams, Erika 110, 124
The World at War (TV series) 96–7
Worm's Eye View (film) 64 n.84
Worsley, T. C. 95
Wright, H. M. S. 5
Würzburg 143

X Company (TV series) 167 n.19

A Yank in the R.A.F. (film) 37 n.127
Yanks Go Home (TV series) 167 n.32
Yes, Minister (TV series) 120 n.56
Yes, Prime Minister (TV series) 120 n.56
Yesterday (channel) 150
Yorkshire Television 108
Young, H. M. 52

Zweites Deutsches Fernsehen (ZDF) 147

www.ingramcontent.com/pod-product-compliance
Lightning Source LLC
Chambersburg PA
CBHW052043300426
44117CB00012B/1955